Hannah Arendt and the History of Thought

CONTINENTAL PHILOSOPHY AND THE HISTORY OF THOUGHT

Series Editors: Christian Lotz, Michigan State University, and

Antonio Calcagno, King's University College at Western University

Advisory Board: Smaranda Aldea, Amy Allen, Silvia Benso, Jeffrey Bloechl, Andrew Cutrofello, Marguerite La Caze, Christina M. Gschwandtner, Dermot Moran, Ann Murphy, Michael Naas, Eric Nelson, Marjolein Oele, Mariana Ortega, Elena Pulcini, Alan Schrift, Anthony Steinbock, Brad Stone

The *Continental Philosophy and the History of Thought* series seeks to augment and amplify scholarship in continental philosophy by exploring its rich and complex relationships to figures, schools of thought, and philosophical movements that are crucial for its evolution and development. A historical focus allows potential authors to uncover important but understudied thinkers and ideas that were nonetheless foundational for various continental schools of thought. Furthermore, critical scholarship on the histories of continental philosophy will also help re-position, challenge, and even overturn dominant interpretations of established, well-known philosophical views while refining and reinterpreting them in light of new historical discoveries and textual analyses. The series seeks to publish carefully edited collections and high quality monographs that present the best of scholarship in continental philosophy and its histories.

Titles in series:

Hannah Arendt and the History of Thought, edited by Daniel Brennan and Marguerite La Caze
Rethinking Philosophy with Borges, Zambrano, Paz, and Plato, by Hugo Moreno
The Ontological Roots of Phenomenology: Rethinking the History of Phenomenology and Its Religious Turn, by Anna Jani
Negative Dialectics and Event: Nonidentity, Culture, and the Historical Adequacy of Consciousness, by Vangelis Giannakakis
Marxism and Phenomenology: The Dialectical Horizons of Critique, edited by Bryan Smyth and Richard Westerman
Groundwork of Phenomenological Marxism: Crisis, Body, World, by Ian H. Angus
Max Stirner on the Path of Doubt, by Lawrence S. Stepelevich

Hannah Arendt and the History of Thought

Edited by

Daniel Brennan and Marguerite La Caze

LEXINGTON BOOKS
Lanham • Boulder • New York • London

Published by Lexington Books
An imprint of The Rowman & Littlefield Publishing Group, Inc.
4501 Forbes Boulevard, Suite 200, Lanham, Maryland 20706
www.rowman.com

86-90 Paul Street, London EC2A 4NE

Copyright © 2022 by The Rowman & Littlefield Publishing Group, Inc.

All rights reserved. No part of this book may be reproduced in any form or by any electronic or mechanical means, including information storage and retrieval systems, without written permission from the publisher, except by a reviewer who may quote passages in a review.

British Library Cataloguing in Publication Information Available

Library of Congress Cataloging-in-Publication Data

Names: Brennan, Daniel, 1982- editor. | La Caze, Marguerite, editor.
 Title: Hannah Arendt and the history of thought / edited by Daniel Brennan and Marguerite La Caze.
 Description: Lanham : Lexington Books, [2022] | Series: Continental philosophy and the history of thought | Includes bibliographical references and index. | Summary: "This edited collection enriches scholarship on Arendt by considering her contributions to and reflections on the history of thought. The chapters bring Arendt into new conversations with her contemporaries, as well as examining the themes of Arendt's writing in light of her engagement with philosophical and literary history"-- Provided by publisher.
 Identifiers: LCCN 2022008085 (print) | LCCN 2022008086 (ebook) | ISBN 9781666900859 (cloth) | ISBN 9781666900873 (paperback) | ISBN 9781666900866 (epub)
 Subjects: LCSH: Arendt, Hannah, 1906-1975. | Philosophy, Modern--20th century. | Political science--Philosophy--History--20th century. | Jewish women philosophers--Germany--Biography.
 Classification: LCC B945.A694 H35 2022 (print) | LCC B945.A694 (ebook) | DDC 191--dc23/eng/20220429
 LC record available at https://lccn.loc.gov/2022008085
 LC ebook record available at https://lccn.loc.gov/2022008086

∞™ The paper used in this publication meets the minimum requirements of American National Standard for Information Sciences—Permanence of Paper for Printed Library Materials, ANSI/NISO Z39.48-1992.

Contents

Acknowledgments — vii

Introduction — 1
Daniel Brennan and Marguerite La Caze

PART I: ANTECEDENTS — 19

Chapter One: "The Course of True Love": Arendt's Shakespeare, Love, and the Practice of Storytelling — 21
Paul Dahlgren

Chapter Two: Jaspers, Kant, and the Origins of Hannah Arendt's Theory of Judgment — 39
Matthew Wester

Chapter Three: Hannah Arendt and Early German Romanticism — 55
Kimberly Maslin

Chapter Four: The Gendered Politics of Love: An Arendtian Reading — 77
Maria Tamboukou

PART II: PEERS — 95

Chapter Five: Arendt and Beauvoir on Romantic Love — 97
Liesbeth Schoonheim1

Chapter Six: Arendt and Hans Jonas: Acting and Thinking after Heidegger — 117
Eric Stéphane Pommier

Chapter Seven: Hannah Arendt's Influence on Eastern European Dissidence: The Example of Poland — 135
Katarzyna Stokłosa

PART III: IN PROSPECT 149

Chapter Eight: The Phenomenological Sense of Hannah Arendt:
    Plurality, Modernity, and Political Action 151
Laura McMahon

Chapter Nine: Arendt's Phenomenologically Informed Political
    Thinking: A Proto-Normative Account of Human Worldliness 181
Marieke Borren

Chapter Ten: Denaturalizing Hannah Arendt and Claudia Jones:
    Statelessness, Citizenship, and Racialization 205
Andrew Schaap

Chapter Eleven: The Life of the Unruly in Ada Ushpiz's *Vita
    Activa: The Spirit of Hannah Arendt (2015)* 229
Joel Rosenberg

About the Contributors 265

Acknowledgments

We would like to thank Antonio Calcagno and Christian Lotz for inviting us to edit this volume in the Continental Philosophy and the History of Thought series; it's a wonderful opportunity. We are also grateful to all the authors for their inspiring contributions and to an anonymous reviewer for their insightful reading of the volume. Jana Hodges-Kluck and Sydney Wedbush from Lexington deserve thanks for their encouragement and expertise. The volume is indebted for an author suggestion for one of the chapters from Joanne Faulkner. We also appreciate the great working relationship we have relied on throughout the editing of this collection, as well as our partners for their support.

Introduction

Daniel Brennan and Marguerite La Caze

The breadth and depth of Hannah Arendt's reception in the world of ideas has been growing rapidly in recent decades. Her life and her writing continue to excite scholars, students, social thinkers, political commentators, filmmakers, and general readers alike. Numerous biographies have tried to capture the sense of Arendt's life as a narrative to study, by reading her ideas through the events of her life, and there is already a sizeable body of secondary literature that reads Arendt's thought for whatever specialist issue the volume considers—race, law, literature, politics, feminism (Young-Bruehl, 1982; Ettinger, 1995; Kristeva, 2001; Honig, 1995; Goldini, 2012; Gines, 2014; King 2015; Baehr and Walsh, 2017; Gratton and Sari, 2020).

Young-Bruehl and Kristeva's respective and seminal biographies of Arendt have provided scholars with a picture of Arendt as a life to be studied; however, each provides a different perspective on how that life should be read. On one hand, Young-Bruehl provides insight into Arendt's life to help explain the development of her political theory. Kristeva, on the other hand is not so much interested in how Arendt came to develop certain theories, but rather how the themes of love, and narrative, mostly in her earlier work on love in Augustine, and Arendt's biography of Rahel Varnhagen, with its unique discussion of Jewish identity, offer a complex portrait of humanity that is both in Arendt's writing and in her own life. This volume moves past those important works for understanding Arendt's life in two ways. Firstly, by in a sense combining historical, narrative, and philosophical perspectives the papers of this volume, taken together, offer a complex and nuanced account of the difficulty of unpicking one aspect of Arendt's thought from another. For example, in Laura McMahon's chapter, "The Phenomenological Sense of Hannah Arendt: Plurality, Modernity, and Political Action," the author shows how a consideration of Arendt's phenomenology necessarily leads to her political theory, and her enthusiasm for civil disobedience. Additionally, Paul Dahlgren's chapter "'The Course of True love': Arendt's Shakespeare, Love, and the Practice of Storytelling," looks at Arendt's readings of Shakespeare and other literary texts, while also considering events in Arendt's life and relationships to help enrich the discussion. The second way this volume moves past the older biographies of Arendt and collections of essays on her work is by taking into account the ideas only relatively recently published in Arendt's thought diaries—her *Denktagebuch*.

More recently *The Bloomsbury Companion to Arendt*, a broad-ranging collection of scholarship on Arendt, demonstrated the incredible profundity and range of Arendt's thought, as it contains sixty-seven chapters, each devoted to a theme of Arendt's writing and life, from her key writings, philosophical foundations, politics, and social thought. However, by separating Arendt's themes from her writing, and from her sources, something can be missed, despite the size of the volume. The present volume, rather than asking Arendt's ideas to fit loose categories, considers her contribution to and involvement in the history of ideas. That perspective change allows the authors of this volume to show much more nuance to Arendt's thinking, as they are able to see a bigger picture, or as Arendt might say, an "enlarged" idea, by combining history, thematic focus, philosophical bases, and social and political thought. Hence pausing to consider Arendt as a thinker embedded in the history of ideas, and not as an outlier on the periphery of philosophy, despite her own denials that she is a philosopher or writing philosophy, is timely. This volume adds depth to those debates in which Arendt's ideas are now considered, by increasing our consideration of her role in the history of ideas, both as an inheritor of history and a driver of change.

Arendt was thorough in her engagement with thinkers of the past, from Ancient Greece, early Christianity, Rome, the Enlightenment, Romanticism, and phenomenology. She was equally as thorough and rigorous in her engagement with those contemporaneous to herself. In her editor's introduction to Arendt's *Rahel Varnhagen: The Life of a Jewess*, Liliane Weissberg recounts an anecdote shared by Alfred Kazin. It is worth recounting here:

> I met Hannah Arendt in 1946 at a dinner party given for Rabbi Leo Baeck by Eliot Cohen, the editor of *Commentary*. It was that long ago. She was a handsome, vivacious forty-year-old woman who was to charm me and others, by no means unerotically, because her interest in her new country, and for literature in English, became as much a part of her as her accent and her passion for discussing Plato, Kant, Nietzsche, Kafka, even Duns Scotus, as if they all lived with her and her strenuous husband Heinrich Bluecher in the shabby rooming house on West 95th Street. (Kazin in Weissberg, Arendt, 1997, 3)

Weissberg considers the anecdote, suggesting that Arendt is not described as a philosopher but as a host, "a person who offered room as well as words for others" (1997, 3). The consideration of Arendt as a host for Weissberg leads to a discussion of Varnhagen's salon, and the significance of such places that could create light in dark times—the theme of her later book (1983). But to think this quote differently, to read against its sexism, many decades after its original context, one can also discern, along with the problematic reduction of the woman intellectual to a lively host, a recognition of her incredible knowledge across the history of ideas. Arendt herself invites us to consider the malleability of the roles society places on us. In the prologue to *Responsibility and Judgement*, which is the transcript of a speech delivered by Arendt upon receiving the Danish Sonning Prize, Arendt writes that individuals are recognized by the roles assigned to us through our professions, but within those professional masks there is the potential for natality to transform the meaning of the persona (2003, 13).

> It is through this role, sounding through it, as it were, that something else manifests itself, something entirely idiosyncratic and undefinable and still unmistakably identifiable, so that we are not confused by a sudden change of roles, when for instance… a hostess, whom socially we know as a physician, serves drinks instead of taking care of her patients. In other words, the advantage of adopting the notion of *persona* for my consideration lies in the fact that the masks or roles which the world assigns us, and which we must accept and even acquire if we wish to take part in the world's play at all, are exchangeable. (Arendt 2003, 13)

Arendt is obviously more than mere host. Her knowledge of and engagement with Augustine and Rousseau, for instance, and the philosophical autobiographical tradition, deeply informed her writing of the Varnhagen biography, and as one glances at the sheer breadth of her writing's themes and references, these are more than conversational contributions. Even though the idea of the Berlin salon and the place of a meeting of the intelligentsia were formative spaces for Arendt, her work on historical thinkers and contemporaries lives outside of such rooms and conversations as well.

Her ability to inspire critique and drive public discourse decades after her death means that the time is right to take stock of Arendt's standing in the history of ideas, and to encourage new avenues for scholarship. Rather than acting only as a primer on Arendt's texts and the themes therein, this volume of essays offers a guide to the ideas that drove Arendt's writing by exploring the contexts in which they were written, and the thinkers she worked through. Her readings of canonical figures offered different ways to understand established interpretations, and some of the chapters of this volume explore Arendt's way of reading and interpreting these figures. Essentially, Arendt's defense of the inherent pluralism of the world and concern with the dangers of imposing a certainty upon human affairs was not only a theoretical matter, explained in political writings as a warning against philosophical systems promising truth and fixed certainties, but embedded in her practice of thinking and writing as well.

This volume is strategically divided into three parts, Antecedents, Peers, and Prospects, which each aim to capture the way that Arendt simultaneously mined and undermined the history of ideas, while critically engaging with her contemporaries, and also inspiring future debates by leaving a body of work that can be used to initiate new conversations with those writing today, and also with those writing in her time that she did not explicitly enter into dialogue with, such as Simone de Beauvoir and Claudia Jones.

The volume also treats themes that are pressing and crucial to understanding Arendt's work, such as feminism, questions of ethnicity and race, civil disobedience, phenomenology, and thinking. The rigorous and broad reading Arendt extends through all of her explorations in ideas means that there is a need to expand the frames of reference for Arendt scholarship—this volume does just that. Arendt reads great works of philosophy and literature as multifaceted, pluralistic gems. As the author of the first chapter of this volume, Paul Dahlgren announces, there is also much more to say by reading the writers such as Shakespeare that Arendt quotes, beyond the parts that she quoted. When Arendt writes her biography of Rahel Varnhagen, she is, as Kimberly Maslin notes in her chapter "Hannah Arendt and Early German Romanticism" doing more than exploring questions of Jewish identity, she is also employing the style and form of the disparate traditions of the Enlightenment and Romanticism to say something new.

The chapters of this book hence pay attention to Arendt's unique and varied style, and the processes of crafting her arguments, such as the way she reads Immanuel Kant's aesthetics, or how her relationships and letters can shed light on her thought beyond the semantic content of the writing. Discussions of Arendt's *Denktagebuch* (journal) also enriches the chapters' engagement with her reflections on the themes and philosophers' work (2002; Berkowitz and Storey, 2017). Furthermore, the book looks for the specters of ideas through her thought, which at times emerge explicitly, and other times remain beneath the surface of the text. For example, as a student Arendt's doctoral dissertation, supervised by Karl Jaspers and defended in 1928, reached back to the thought of Saint Augustine of Hippo. As Julia Kristeva notes in her biography of Arendt, years after the thesis was defended Arendt wrote to Jaspers that she was surprised to find traces of herself in the thesis (2001, 31). The thesis explored Augustine's thoughts on love. Arendt was searching for a paradigm of love in Augustine's work, and the resulting, quite secular account, written in a language very much indebted to Arendt's phenomenological education, is far from Augustine's intended theological arguments. Yet this is not to say that Arendt is a mis-reader; rather her reading is infused with a philosophical desire to say something new. While reading Augustine, Arendt is not only asking, "what is he saying?," but also "what does this mean for me?" This kind of reading, that Jaspers noted in his comments on the dissertation as perhaps doing "violence to the text" is arguably a feature of Arendt's engagement with the history of ideas and some of the chapters in this volume, such as Matthew Wester's "Kant, Jaspers, and the Origins of Hannah Arendt's Theory of Judgment" show the productive nuance to Arendt's readings which transform accepted interpretations, revealing new considerations concerning the autonomy of judgment. Furthermore, as Arendt herself notes in her glance back at her early thesis, her reading of the history of ideas leaves traces throughout her oeuvre. These traces, especially on love, are picked up by the contributors to this volume, as Arendt's unique style of reading was employed to make startingly original arguments.

One especially sharp trace in Arendt's work is, as Kazin notes in the previously quoted anecdote, the literature that Arendt read voraciously and referred to throughout her writing. Authors like Karen Blixen, Franz Kafka, and Bertolt Brecht are the subject of essays and lengthy discussion in her work. Yet also throughout her writing are scatterings of references to contemporary authors, who appear fleetingly, yet are appropriately in place in her work. For instance, Patchen Markell has recently explored the references to William Faulkner's novels in Arendt (2015). Markell notes that in her references to Faulkner, Arendt adds nuance to her descriptions of action by including anonymity, whereas usually the activity of the unnamed is found in labor or a depersonalized society (2015, 78). That attention to the literary images and passages that Arendt cites can add to the pluralistic interpretation of concepts usually considered quite settled in the reception of her ideas is important. In her essay "Some Questions of Moral Philosophy," Arendt concludes her discussion by suggesting that the examples found in literature are richer ways to consider one's duties, and that one can even learn to judge through a consideration of the examples of great works of literature (2003, 145). Arendt makes explicit reference to the examples of Shakespeare's tragedies, such as *King Lear*. She is also saying something more than that literature provides mere instruction to follow. If we look at Arendt's response to Eric Vogelin's criticisms of *The Origins of Totalitarianism*, originally published in *The Review of Politics* and now found in the collection *Essays in Understanding*, Arendt discusses her perception of the role of style, the feature most fully embodied in literary truths, which might be empty of objective statements.

> Thus, the question of style is bound up with the problem of understanding, which has plagued the historical sciences almost from their beginnings. I do not wish to go into this matter here, but I may add that I am convinced that understanding is closely related to that faculty of imagination which Kant

called *Einbildungskraft* and which has nothing in common with fictional ability. (Arendt, 1994, 404)

Style does more than evoke images. Style shows things to the imagination which turns the vision of understanding to show a different face to the world. Hence when Arendt evokes the literary examples of *Hamlet* and *King Lear* for instance, she is not simply suggesting that one emulates literature, but that more significantly literature reinforces pluralism, and through the operations of imagination, on which style leaves impressions, increases the effectiveness of judgment.

The first part of the book, "Antecedents," explores in detail Arendt's literary considerations, her style, and her thoughts on the imagination's role in judgment. The chapters in this part open up new directions for research on Arendt by exploring her engagement with canonical figures in the history of ideas, from literature, and philosophy. In the collection's first chapter, "'The course of true love': Arendt's Shakespeare, Love, and the Practice of Storytelling," Paul Dahlgren explores Arendt's privileging of literature in her writing and her relationships with writers (and her influence on them). He has focused on the role of Shakespeare in previous work, an emerging interest in Arendt studies (2006). Dahlgren demonstrates that despite the great deal of scholarship around Arendt and literature, and Arendtian interpretations of literature (especially literary treatments of refugees and human rights) the picture is incomplete and requires further expansion. Dahlgren focuses on Arendt's debt to William Shakespeare, contending that Arendt's style, especially in the later writings, is deeply influenced by Shakespeare's plays. Consider, for instance, the notion of the two-in-one in thinking that is an essential feature of Shakespearean drama. That Arendt's references to Shakespeare are few, and short, is for Dahlgren an opportunity to further flesh out some of her thinking, especially on the theme of love. Through a reading of *A Midsummers Night's Dream*, Dahlgren considers Arendt's fascination with Karen Blixen (Isak Dinesen), her failed marriage to Günther Anders, and her affair with Martin Heidegger. The figure of Titania and her love for Bottom, a comic feature of the play, suggest how Arendt might have considered the flights of love and also hint at the unexplained depth to her conception of the private realm and the desires that dwell therein. For Dahlgren, Arendt's use of Shakespeare, and the play itself when read beyond Arendt's brief mention, give a more vivid understanding of the depths of Arendt's thoughts on love. The chapter suggests that the same expanding of horizons for scholarship on Arendt might be found in her treatment of other authors such as Randall Jarrell and Herman Broch.

For Arendt literature operates on our understanding, not just in the sense of making up fictions, but in showing things to us which might change our minds and aid our judgments. Arendt draws a lot of her ideas about imagination and understanding from the thought of Kant and the Enlightenment. Her relationship to Kant is famously ambivalent; however, even when Arendt is disagreeing with Kant it is not to cast his ideas aside, but rather to work through them. A seemingly trite example will illustrate the point; in her essay on Kafka, Arendt invokes Kant's description of the genius only to disagree (1994, 79). Arendt uses Kant's definition of genius, the innate disposition through which nature gives the rule to art, to offer her own variation where nature is replaced by humanity (1994, 79). On the face of it the disagreement need not have been printed. Why bother to announce an idea only to reject it and propose something else—especially if the rejected idea is not the topic of the essay? Yet there it remains, and in fact operates as a launching pad from which Arendt can present her own ideas—rather than Kant being wrong, he is the starting point from which to twist and turn an idea to reveal its other facets. Kant's philosophy is like a specter through Arendt's writing.

Matthew Wester, in the second chapter of this volume, "Jaspers, Kant, and the Origins of Hannah Arendt's Theory of Judgment," looks past the existing scholarship on Arendt and Kant, to insights found in the yet to be translated into English (although it has been translated into French) *Denktagebuch*, that is her diary of ideas. He has previously published on the relation between Arendt's and Kant's thought (Wester in Gratton and Sari, 2020). Wester focuses on Arendt's reading, and misreading of Kant's *Critique of Judgment*, to show how Arendt developed her ideas, under the influence of her mentor Jaspers and his interpretation of Kant, of judgment in the political sphere. What Wester locates is a strong claim by Arendt to have discovered a political philosophy in Kant's aesthetic theory. Wester points out that for Arendt, Kant was unaware that when he was writing on aesthetic judgments he was also describing a political theory that she claims supports her idea of the pluralism at the heart of judgment. The ability of Arendt to see something that the author did not is for Wester in part due to Jaspers's influence on Arendt. Jaspers, who wrote *The Great Philosophers* (1962), Wester contends, specifically inspired Arendt to read Kant's aesthetic theory to find political insights. Jasper's treatment of reflective judgment in Kant allowed Arendt to read Kant as not abandoning the particularity of phenomena in judgments—significantly, as particularity is so central to Arendt's understanding of politics. As Wester notes, her reading of Kant through Jaspers was happening at the time that she was preparing the final draft of *The Human Condition* (1998). Even if not explicit until later, that reading's presence is still there early on her writing, guiding the direction her thought will take.

Arendt not only engaged with Enlightenment thinkers including Kant but also with Romanticism. Kimberly Maslin, in her chapter, "Hannah Arendt and Early German Romanticism," the third chapter of this volume, shows how the style of Arendt's biography of Rahel Varnhagen marked her break with philosophy, allowing her to make her own mark in the world of ideas. If Kant's philosophy grounded the fact of pluralism for Arendt, Maslin shows that the writing of the Varnhagen biography is Arendt's own attempt at writing to engender pluralism. Maslin appeals to Arendt's use of images of twilight rather than daylight to blur attempts of politics or philosophy to arrive at truth or certainty. For Maslin, Arendt revels in contradictions and the ability of art to shake certainties in a manner consistent with the Romantics. Maslin shows how Arendt employed irony in her biography to place contrasting and incompatible ideas beside each other so meaning can in a sense organically emerge through the activity of considering them, of active reading. For Maslin, the Romantic style, using irony and in fragments, allowed the space for her Jewish writings to consider how to foster a Jewish identity. Maslin contends that the style, developed in the Varnhagen biography, permeates her other Jewish writing—that is, the Romantic experiments with writing, and their focus on the passion gave Arendt a means of recasting Jewish identity as heroic, by using the literariness of the style to rethink history. That rethinking is not to rethink what happened, but the meaning of what happened.

As noted above, another powerful theme in Arendt, developed early in her writing, which is still present even when not explicitly articulated, is love. The ideas from Arendt's thesis on Augustine and love are found throughout her writing, developing, and inflecting her depictions of people acting with and toward each other. Wolfram Elienberger, in *Time of the Magicians*, marks her dissertation as a decisive move from Heidegger, after their relationship, and a response to his philosophy—a filling of gaps that she identified in his work.

> Arendt's philosophizing is distinguished by the ability to trace, illuminate, and elaborate all existential dimensions of the event of "You"—to which Heidegger, in the dwelling of his thought, had to remain blind, (Elienberger, 2020, 192)

For Elienberger, the development of *amor mundi* in Arendt's work is a part of the ennobling of public action, that moves beyond Heidegger's more pessimistic conception of the collective "they." Whereas Heidegger saw us entangled in the world, Arendt's love allows us to make it anew—it fills relations in private spaces, and illuminates action by resisting certainty and embodying spontaneity. Looking at the multiple meanings of love in Arendt's work, apart from *amor mundi*, Maria Tamboukou's chapter 4, "The Gendered Politics of Love: An Arendtian Reading," explores the connection between the myriad kinds of love, gender, and her conception of pluralistic politics. Tamboukou's interest in Arendt relates to narratives and life-writing, and she has previous considered Arendt's thought in relation to Rosa Luxemburg's letters and writings (2014). She focuses on Arendt's *Denktagebuch* to bring out how much more there is to say on the topic of love in Arendt that has not been remarked in scholarship hitherto. By showing how the original notion of the otherworldliness of love—that is, the way love flies away from the world to find its beginning—developed in her thesis on Augustine, to the larger, and at times only implied consideration of love across Arendt's oeuvre and in her diary, Tamboukou demonstrates the richness of Arendt's uses of love by describing it through literary consideration of two examples of epistolary discourse. Through an analysis of the letters of the feminist activist Désirée Véret-Gay, Tamboukou adds layers to our understanding of *amor mundi* as a reconnection, through love, to the network of human relations in our social lives. Similarly, the letters of the activist Emma Goldman, brimful with the oscillations of passion, and exacerbated by the complex political situations Goldman found herself in, for Tamboukou demonstrate the complex way that love, as a destabilizing force, adds to the unpredictability of the human condition, demonstrating the way that plays out in all of the human interactions that Arendt characterizes in her writing.

The second part of the book, "Peers," looks closely at Arendt's relationships with her contemporaries, in her inner circle, and in her reception as she published. In the chapter on Gotthold Lessing in *Men in Dark Times*, Arendt celebrates the ability that the speech and action between friends has to preserve a space of openness and plurality, even under political conditions that threaten such spaces (1983, 30). As a student of Heidegger, Arendt was described by Richard Wolin as one of Heidegger's children (2015). Arendt's philosophical response to Heidegger has already been alluded to; however, in exploring the relationship she had with her contemporaries, it is necessary to search further into that Heideggerian collective, and Arendt's place in phenomenology more generally. In the fourth chapter of this volume, "Arendt and Beauvoir on Romantic Love," Liesbeth Schoonheim uses Arendt's break with Heidegger, especially his understanding of *Mitsein*, to place Arendt into dialogue with Simone de Beauvoir's, philosophy which was similarly indebted to Heidegger's *Mitsein*. Her research investigates themes of freedom and resistance in Arendt, Beauvoir, and Foucault, and she has considered Arendt's phenomenology of love in relation to personhood (2018). In exploring the differing ways that Arendt and Beauvoir responded to the strengths and weaknesses of Heidegger's ideas, Schoonheim is able to position the two thinkers, who had little to say about each other in their lifetimes, into a fruitful exchange that shows further how the concept of love, in the differing kinds of relationships where it can emerge and operate, adds to our understanding of how the personal and political impact on each other. Furthermore Schoonheim, through the conversation she initiates, is able to use Beauvoir's thought to highlight important questions that Arendt considered misplaced, such as the role of embodied romantic love in political situations, further shedding light on the complicated relationship Arendt's ideas have to feminism.

Another of Arendt's peers with a shared Heideggerian departure point is Hans Jonas. Jonas, another of "Heidegger's children," who delivered the eulogy at Arendt's funeral, is placed into contrast with Arendt in the sixth chapter of this volume, Eric Stephane Pommier's "Arendt and Hans Jonas: Acting and Thinking After Heidegger." Pommier has published a significant body of work on Hans Jonas, bringing Jonas's thought into conversation with major figures in phenomenology such as Maurice Merleau-Ponty, Martin Heidegger, and Hannah Arendt. With Arendt, he has already provided an important comparison with Jonas, looking at their respective moral and political ideas (2013). Pommier has more recently focused on the biological philosophy of Jonas and in this volume the insights from that research enable a more thorough and updated comparison and contrast between Arendt and Jonas (2017).

While the philosophical positions of Arendt and Jonas are quite distinct, Pommier traces their origins to certain disagreements with how to move past Heidegger, especially from a humanist standpoint. Pommier considers the relationship between thinking and acting in both scholars, showing that whereas for Arendt they are distinct, although thought can lead back to action, for Jonas, thought can *be* action. The differences, in Pommier's account, provide a fruitful way to approach the complexities of questions of science and technology, especially in developing the environmentally responsible actions required of us today. Rather than simply placing Arendt and Jonas into contrast, Pommier uses the opportunity to compare their thought to highlight gaps in both Arendt and Jonas, and to use the thought of the other to fill those gaps with a meaningful response.

The rich knowledge found by placing Arendt in dialogue with her peers is continued in a slightly different vein in Kataryzna Stokłosa's paper, the seventh chapter of this volume, "Hannah Arendt's Influence on Eastern European Dissidence: The Example of Poland." Stokłosa has previously published on Arendt's influence in Polish intellectual circles, and her large scholarship on Eastern bloc social and political crises, historical and current, are at the forefront in this revitalized look at how Arendt's ideas were received and circulated in Poland (2008). An emergent theme found across the chapters of this volume is the changing shape and terms of debates that have been conducted through Arendt's ideas. For instance, a number of the chapters have pointed out that the relatively recent publication of Arendt's thought diaries has revealed new avenues for scholarship and thinking that recast seemingly settled debates. What Stokłosa demonstrates is that in Eastern Europe, where significant dissidents were influenced by Arendt, such as Jan Patočka and Adam Michnik, the staggered publications of Arendt's work, and the manner in which her ideas could be debated publicly, as well as the drastic and rapid social and political changes, mean that it is impossible to speak of a unitary influence on Eastern European thought. That is, Stokłosa's chapter charts the historical reception of Arendt over time, noting its change as political events force a different perspective to be taken.

Focusing on the shifts in debate and focus on Arendt in Poland, Stokłosa looks at the Polish reception of Arendt's ideas, from her thoughts on the 1956 revolution in Hungary, through to the reception of her writing today, asking the question, "Why read Arendt in Poland any more?" It is accurate to say that Arendt's reception in Polish ideas was and remains turbulent. Arendt's thought has helped political theorists in Poland to frame discussions, from the teaching of Arendt's *The Origins of Totalitarianism* clandestinely, in unofficial and private seminars, in the 1970s, to the publication of her major works in the late 1980s and early 1990s, where major differences between Eastern and Western European political theory became blurred as Eastern thinkers quickly adopted many Western ideas as the iron curtain fell. Many Polish political thinkers, in the 1970s, used the ideas of Arendt they had access to and debated them in ways that were permitted in public discourse, or smaller audiences discussed them in secret. Even then, when limited numbers of people engaged in debate, Stokłosa demonstrates that the conversation was far from surface level. For instance, Polish political thinkers were pointing out that her definitions of totalitarianism, and the inherent use of violence in such systems did not quite capture their own experience of living under totalitarianism. Ultimately Stokłosa shows how Arendt was both a figure of freedom and a philosophical source—that is. she inspired action, but also was rigorously thought through—and even though the totalitarian system failed, Stokłosa details how Arendt's reception continues as issues of freedom and equality still pervade Polish political life, as they do elsewhere.

The final part of this volume, "Prospects," looks to explore the conversations Arendt might not have had and consider new directions in her research. The eighth chapter, Laura McMahon's "The Phenomenological Sense of Hannah Arendt: Plurality, Modernity, and Political Action," rather than looking at Arendt's reception over a period of political upheaval, instead takes a fresh look at Arendt's phenomenological perspective to revitalize Arendt's political thought. McMahon in her previous research has placed Arendt's ideas, such as natality and temporality, into conversation with those of major phenomenologists such as Merleau-Ponty, to add to our understanding of those concepts (2019). There has been much made of whether Arendt supplies a sufficiently systematic phenomenology to be considered a phenomenologist, and McMahon joins the debate by demonstrating not only the cohesion of Arendt's phenomenological account of the world in which we each share, but also the distinct place Arendt has alongside her peers and forebears in phenomenology. She does this by showing the consistency with which Arendt reflects the ideas and foci of major phenomenological writings. Beginning with Arendt's phenomenological account of pluralism, and situating it alongside the thought of Edmund Husserl, Maurice Merleau-Ponty, and Martin Heidegger, McMahon explores the problematic nature of modern bureaucratic logics that dehumanize and resist pluralism. In McMahon's account, when considering Arendt's critique of science, it has to be through Husserl's late works on the crisis of the sciences, as well as, more obviously, Heidegger's critique of technology, and Erich Fromm and Merleau-Ponty's work. By linking the phenomenology of pluralism to modernity's attempt to preclude plurality from our understanding of appearances, McMahon uses the phenomenology of Arendt to shine light on her political ideas. However, the effect is larger than simply declaring Arendt to be a phenomenologist, as McMahon demonstrates the essential connection between the phenomenological account of the world, and Arendt's politics. Also, importantly, her account of the political reinforces the significance of the phenomenology to her work, and, vice versa, the focus on the phenomenology also reinforces the strength of the political ideals.

The chapter addresses the complex question of the relationship between phenomenological thought and politics, as in Schoonheim's paper on Arendt and Beauvoir. McMahon weaves the phenomenological perspective of Arendt's ideas concerning political action through a discussion of the disability activists, who in 1977, organized by Judith Heumann, took part in a twenty-five-day sit-in protest to petition for disability rights to accessibility to become written into law. McMahon considers the protest, and uses both Arendt's phenomenology and politics to unpack the powerful significance of this protest, and the years leading up to it (now publicized in the documentary *Crip Camp* [2020]*).*

Arendt has become a major touchpoint for thinking about human rights, the meaning of experiences of statelessness, and the crimes committed against those whose rights are withheld from them. In part this is due not only to the writing she produced on the topic, but also to the seeming absence of a normative account of human rights. Critics of Arendt have sought in many different ways to ground a theory of human rights in Arendt's work, and all take different departure locations in her style and writings to do so. For instance, in *Hannah Arendt and Human Rights*, Peg Birmingham examined Arendt's work, especially that on literature, to ground a theory of rights based in a shared humanity (2006). More critically than Birmingham, Seyla Benhabib explored Arendt's thoughts on communication in the public sphere as the starting point for a discourse on rights, arguing that the thought of other thinkers, such as Jürgen Habermas, is needed to fill in gaps in thinking that Benhabib identifies (2007). Taking stock of the many approaches to Arendt's thoughts on rights, Marieke Borren's "Arendt's Phenomenological Political Thinking: A Proto-Normative Account," the ninth chapter of this volume, observes that thus far no major consideration of Arendt's thoughts on rights and stateless has started from her phenomenological perspective. Borren specializes in Arendt's work, political philosophy, and philosophical anthropology, and has published influential work on Arendt and statelessness and refugees (2008). Again, the importance of using Arendt's phenomenology to show the relationship of phenomenological modes of thinking to politics highlights not only the uniqueness of Arendt's phenomenology, but also the depth of her political thinking.

Borren notes that a feature of Arendt's distinctive phenomenology is not a shared humanness, but worldliness. As in McMahon's earlier chapter, Borren, by turning close attention to the phenomenological description of worldliness in Arendt, especially in *The Human Condition* (1958), discusses the political solutions offered by Arendt as being grounded in her phenomenology. Borren considers how throughout Arendt's writing on rights and statelessness, her concern is always a loss of a world, a place and that consequently human dignity is tied to worldliness rather than a human essence. Borren hence demonstrates that the criticisms of Arendt for not offering a normative account of rights miss the point that deeply embedded in her phenomenological account of human action is a proto-normative notion of human dignity. Again, it is the theme of *amor mundi*, which appears in a number of the contributions to this volume, that shows this dignity as worldliness.

Further exploring Arendt's thoughts on the stateless, the condition of statelessness and her related ideas on the "right to have rights," Andrew Schaap, in chapter ten of this volume, places Arendt into conversation with her contemporary Claudia Jones. There is a clear gulf between the two political thinkers that stems from their respective views on the American Republic and its promise of beginning anew. On one hand, Richard King, in *Arendt and America*, describes Arendt's fascination with the American Republic as leading to the development of the idea of natality (2015, 2). For Arendt, America's promise to overturn corrupt practices, and begin things anew, was a counterpoint to the totalitarianism she witnessed and analyzed in Europe. She was, according to King, thus working to advance those aspects of republicanism in America that allowed new political beginnings and working to identify and resist the tendencies in the same system that could lead to a nation of thoughtless consumption and bureaucracy (King, 2015, 3). Claudia Jones, on the other hand, had a vastly more pessimistic view of the promise to empower new beginnings for immigrants and refugees due to her experience of racism, exclusion, and eventual deportation from America.

Arendt and Jones never met, nor referred to each other, and they are distanced by many other factors than their perception of the American republic, including Arendt's critique of socialism and Jones's support for it, Jones's preclusion from the European canon of political ideas and their never having discussed each other's work; however, Schaap demonstrates the timely necessity of bringing these thinkers into conversation. What Schaap brings out is that Arendt and Jones in fact shared many similar experiences, such as statelessness, McCarthyist politics, and the postwar anti-communist fervor of the United States, and that these shared experiences were central to the ideas of these respective writers. Hence it is very interesting that their ideas are so different. Schaap has previously written on Arendt's political ideas in relation to democracy and struggles for emancipation and inclusion (2020). In this chapter he breaks new ground by overcoming the neglect of Jones's important thought and bringing it to bear on Arendt's established ideas which are starting to gain the recognition they deserve (Dunstan and Owens, 2021). Rather than forcing a philosophical framework on them both and claiming that it is shared, Schaap treats their respective thought in its difference, using the historical events and experiences they shared to open the comparison. The chapter forges new paths in considering the importance and limitations of Arendt's understanding of race in her political theory, and also in showing the strength and nuance to Jones's thoughts, as well as where she diverges from more mainstream political thought.

Schaap uses the concepts of citizenship and statelessness—issues central to the lived experience of Arendt and Jones, and to their writing, to show how these concepts impact racialization and violent totalitarian responses to immigrants and refugees. Schaap shows how a racial understanding of citizenship, something Arendt failed to adequately recognize, and the operations of politics that make people stateless, mutually reinforce each other in the maintenance of political structures. Arendt has already been criticized for her lack of understanding of the way that political racialization affected people of color in the United States (Gines, 2014). Schaap, by approaching this issue through the experiences and ideas of Jones, points to new directions in research, which are not simply a furthering of Arendt criticism, but an insightful look at how racialization impacts the creation of stateless people—for instance he considers the recent treatment of Windrush migrants in Britain who were denied their rights through politically and racially motivated processes. By expanding the canon and removing postcolonial prejudices that preclude Jones from canonical political debate, Schaap shows how that when we think with Arendt on issues of citizenship and rights, we must keep the very real and concrete processes of racialization and racially charged criminalization in the forefront of our minds as well, something that the European influenced lens of Arendt's analytical eye was not able to always focus on.

The final chapter of this volume takes stock of the ways that engagement with Arendt's ideas have moved from written arguments to filmic depictions.

Its aim is to show how Arendt studies is moving into this new field of philosophy and film and the way the medium of film can expand our understanding of Arendt's thought. Focusing on Ada Ushpiz's (2015) documentary film *Vita Activa: The Spirit of Hannah Arendt*, but also drawing from Margarethe von Trotta's earlier fictionalized film *Hannah Arendt* (2012), which he has published work on previously (2014), Joel Rosenburg creates a tripartite dialogue between the depiction of Arendt's ideas on film, her written ideas, and the events of her time. Rosenberg considers how Arendt's thoughts on statelessness, between the world wars and after, is understood as it appears in selected shots, with the voices of actors softening or punctuating what usually is read on text. Arendt's ideas, as fragments in a documentary, for Rosenburg engage with themes through that layering of visual imagery. According to him, the film, even though it is made for a general audience, and focuses on Arendt's more generally popular works, is also an opportunity to return to her writing and see it with a fresh perspective enabled by having seen the ideas presented through the imaginative devices of film. Presented through a voice-over in the film, her words make her a kind of narrator and storyteller of the documentary. Like a number of other chapters, this chapter focuses on the role of love, conceived as unruly by Rosenberg, in Arendt's life and thought, which she felt affirms us and creates a home in the midst of the world. This experience of love, for Arendt, can act as a kind of counter to the experience of rightlessness.

Cumulatively these chapters, by focusing on Arendt and her role and place in the history of ideas, has done much more than catalog and reinforce a canon. While Arendt's commitment to pluralism is at the heart of her project, these chapters demonstrate that the attempt to look at the historical Arendt and her ideas in fact opens new roads for scholarship. The papers reconsider Arendt's writing as a whole, reading the ghosts in her texts, and the themes that travel across her writing. Love is clearly a central concern, not only in her doctoral theses, but through her phenomenological analysis of the social world, through to her diaries and personal private experiences, and her thoughts on action and her public activities. The link between her phenomenology and politics is another example, as the contributions of this volume show that when reading her politics one should always keep her phenomenological approach in mind as well. The world, which for Arendt is a human concept, discovered through phenomenological deliberations, is shown in these chapters as another of these ghosts throughout Arendt's writing, and visible as *amor mundi*—a concept linking love, phenomenology, politics, thought, and action. Arendt's work has also been placed into conversation with thinkers of her time, such as Beauvoir, of whose work she wrote little, despite their shared interests. Those conversations have shown promising ways to critique, and move with and past Arendt, in debates ranging from love, to race, literature, rights, disability, identity, gender, the world and the environment. The consideration of Arendt and her relation to the history of the philosophical tradition is enriched and broadened, and new paths of inquiry are indicated.

BIBLIOGRAPHY

Arendt, Hannah. 1976 [1951]. *The Origins of Totalitarianism*. San Diego: Harcourt Brace.
Arendt, Hannah. 1983. *Men in Dark Times*. San Diego: Harcourt Brace.
Arendt, Hannah. 1997. *Rahel Varnhagen: The Life of a Jewess*, edited by Liliane Weissberg, Trans. Richard and Clara Winston, Baltimore: The John Hopkins University Press.
Arendt, Hannah. 1998 [1958]. *The Human Condition*. 2nd ed. Chicago: University of Chicago Press.
Arendt, Hannah. 2002. *Denktagebuch. 1950 bis 1973*, edited by Ursula Ludz and Ingeborg Nordmann Munich: Piper.
Arendt, Hannah. 2003. *Responsibility and Judgement*. New York: Schocken.
Baehr, Peter, and Walsh, Philip, ed. *The Anthem Companion to Hannah Arendt*. London: Anthem Press.
Benhabib, Seyla. 2007. *Situating the Self: Gender, Community and Postmodernism in Contemporary Ethics*. Malden, MA: Polity Press.
Berkowitz, Roger, and Storey, Ian, ed. 2017. *Artifacts of Thinking: Reading Arendt's Denktagebuch*. New York: Fordham University Press.
Birmingham, Peg. 2006. *Hannah Arendt and Human Rights*; The Predicament of Common Responsibility. Indiana: Indiana University Press. JCRT 7(2): 34–46.
Borren, Marieke. 2008. "Towards an Arendtian Politics of In/Visibility: On Stateless Refugees and Undocumented Aliens." *Ethical Perspectives* 15, 2: 213–37.
Crip Camp. 2020. Dir. James Lebrecht and Nicole Newnham. USA: Higher Ground Productions.
Dahlgren, Paul. 2006. "Reflections on a Small Island: Hannah Arendt, Shakespeare's *The Tempest*, and the Politics of Childhood." *Journal of Religious and Cultural Theory*, no/2: 34–46.
Dunstan, Sarah, and Patricia Owens. 2021. "Claudia Jones, International Thinker." *Modern Intellectual History*, 1–24. doi:10.1017/S1479244321000093.
Elienberger, Wolfram. 2020. *Time of the Magicians*. City of Westminster: Penguin Random House.
Ettinger, Elżbieta. 1995. *Hannah Arendt/Martin Heidegger*. New Haven: Yale University Press.
Gines, Kathryn T. 2014. *Hannah Arendt and the Negro Question*. Indiana: Indiana University Press.
Goldini, Marco. Ed. 2012. *Hannah Arendt and the Law*. London: Bloomsbury.

Gratton, Peter, and Sari, Yasemin, ed. 2020. *Bloomsbury Companion to Hannah Arendt*. London: Bloomsbury.
Hannah Arendt. 2012. Dir. Ada Ushpiz. Margarethe von Trotta. Germany: Heimatfilm.
Honig, Bonnie, ed. 1995. *Feminist Interpretations of Hannah Arendt*. University Park, PA: Pennsylvania State University Press.
Jaspers, Karl. 1962. *The Great Philosophers: Volume 1*. San Diego, CA: Harcourt Publishing.
Kant, Immanuel. 2007. *Critique of Judgment*. Translated by Nicholas Walker. Oxford: Oxford University Press.
King, Richard. H. 2015. *Arendt and America*. Chicago: Chicago University Press.
Kristeva, Julia. 2001. *Hannah Arendt: Life is Narrative*. Trans. Frank Collins. New York: Columbia University Press.
Markell, Patchen. 2015 "Anonymous Glory." In *European Journal of Political Theory*. 16, 1: 77–99. doi:10.1177/1474885114567344.
McMahon, Laura. 2019. "Freedom as Expression: Natality and the Temporality of Action in Merleau-Ponty and Arendt." In *Southern Journal of Philosophy* 57, 1: 56–79.
Pommier, Eric. 2013. "Ética y política en Hans Jonas y Hannah Arendt." *Revue de Métaphysique et Morale* 2, 78: 271–86.
———. 2017. "Hans Jonas's Biological Philosophy: Metaphysics or Phenomenology?" *International Philosophical Quarterly* 1 no. 4: 453–69 DOI: https://doi.org/10.5840/ipq201791894.
Rosenberg, Joel. 2014. "Into the Woods: Eichmann, Heidegger, and Margarethe von Trotta's *Hannah Arendt*." *Jewish Film and New Media*, 2 no.2 Article 5. https://digitalcommons.wayne.edu/jewishfilm/vol2/iss2/5/.
Schaap, Andrew. 2020. "Radical Democracy within Limits." In *The Bloomsbury Companion to Arendt*, edited by Peter Gratton and Yasemin Sari, 481–91. London: Bloomsbury Academic.
Schoonheim, Liesbeth. 2018. "Among Lovers: Politics and Personhood in Hannah Arendt," *Arendt Studies* 1 no.2: 99–124.
Stokłosa, Kataryzna. 2008. "Democratizing Poland with Hannah Arendt" *Topos* 19: 137–43.
Tamboukou, Maria. 2014. "Imagining and Living the Revolution: An Arendtian Reading of Rosa Luxemburg's Letters and Writings." *Feminist Review* 106, 24–42.
Vita Activa: The Spirit of Hannah Arendt. 2015. Dir. Ada Ushpiz. Israel: Fernesbüro.
Wolin, Richard. 2015. *Heidegger's Children: Hannah Arendt, Karl Löwith, Hans Jonas, and Herbert Marcuse*. Princeton: Princeton University Press.
Young-Bruehl, Elisabeth. 1982. *Hannah Arendt: For Love of the World*, New Haven: Yale University Press.

PART I
Antecedents

Chapter One

"The Course of True Love"

Arendt's Shakespeare, Love, and the Practice of Storytelling

Paul Dahlgren

> The performing arts, on the contrary, have indeed a strong affinity with politics. Performing artists—dancers, play-actors, musicians, and the like—need an audience to show their virtuosity, just as acting men need the presence of others before whom they can appear, both need a publicly organized space for their "work," and both depend upon others for the performance itself. Such a space of appearances is not to be taken for granted whenever men live together in a community. The Greek polis once was precisely that "form of government" which provided men with a space of appearances where they could act, with a kind of theater where freedom could appear. (Arendt 1977, 135)

In passages like the one above, Arendt spends considerable energy untangling the relationship between politics and the arts. Art is not freedom but a product of freedom, nor does it belong to the realm of action but is a product of work. However, art, especially the performing arts and especially drama and theater, work in a manner parallel to Arendt's vision of politics. They happen in a "space of appearances" with an audience and demonstrate a kind of virtuosity of either the political or dramatic actors. Thus politics is a form of display, identification, performance, and revelation—including self-revelation. That is not to say that to study art is to study politics but it means studying a parallel system in the public realm that relates very closely to the political. Indeed, Arendt's peculiar mode of doing political theory requires us to engage both as readers of political philosophy and poetry simultaneously, and she frequently draws from both domains.

This chapter uses a literary source to understand a central idea in Arendt's philosophical work: the concept of love and how it interacts with other elements of her philosophy. In short, I argue that love was a topic Arendt explored off and on for much of her lifetime, but one whose definition never gets fully fixed or fully explored. I further contend that this lack of fixity is a product of the phenomenal quality of love, an idea Arendt explores most clearly in *The Human Condition*. However, if we think with Arendt and explore some of her literary sources, like Shakespeare, we gain a more vivid understanding of why and how love works the way it does. Furthermore, this may in turn help us interpret Shakespeare and other literary sources in novel ways. And, indeed, we may have a fuller sense of the rich and strange ideas that love and natality might bring to any number of conversations. This chapter, in other words, serves as a thought experiment in much the same way Arendt conducted such thought experiments with literature in her own writing.

At first glance, the use of Shakespeare, or any literary work, in this process may seem somewhat arbitrary. However, scholars working on Arendt have long noted the importance of literature to her thinking. As Richard King explains, "Arendt found in literature a fertile source of thought experiments, exemplary figures and world-historical events that helped her illuminate the 'dark times' of modernity" (King 2017, 106). Her relationships with contemporaries like Mary McCarthy and Philip Roth are well-documented, and a number of studies examine the influence other figures like W. H. Auden, Herman Broch, Ralph Ellison, and Herman Melville had on her and in some cases how these individuals were influenced by her.[1] Given her humanistic education in the *Bildung* tradition, which put a premium on literature, especially Greek and Roman classics, this is not at all surprising. Furthermore, although she never published them, Arendt wrote at least seventy-four poems in German which were clearly quite meaningful for her. As Samantha Rose eloquently puts it: "Arendt was a poetic thinker without being a poet . . . Poems for Arendt were a way of thinking that resisted the crystallizing effect prose can sometimes have. There is no end in thinking, and poetic form allows for a kind of openness and play that defined Arendt's work" (Holmes 2021). Hill rightly emphasizes the open-ended quality to Arendt's work, which seemingly begs the reader to draw out her framework into new contexts much in the way literary texts demand interpretation. Literary scholars, especially those interested in refugee crises, Jewish thought, and political theology, have not hesitated to use Arendt's thinking for their own ends both to interpret individual works from an Arendtian framework or to develop an Arendtian frame for literary theory.[2]

The importance of Shakespeare for Arendt is a more complex problem. Arendt certainly references his work often enough, as I document below, but certainly Shakespeare is not as visible as many of Arendt's other literary sources. And yet they share many of the same intellectual sources and preoccupations. Both Arendt and Shakespeare turned to Greek tragedy, Italian republican theory, and their respective contemporary political situations as ways of understanding both political life and the complexity of the human experience. Especially important to both is the poet of change, Ovid. Shakespeare takes narratives from *Metamorphosis* and creates them into new forms art, oftentimes interleaving Ovid's stories with his own. Arendt makes change and transformation a central part of her philosophy. What we know as natality is a kind metamorphosis, one that is often best described in the metaphoric language of poetry.

But much work remains to be done in studying Arendt's relationship to literature. She often gives short interpretations of stories, poems, and drama that are counterintuitive and ripe for development. Expanding on these readings can shed light on her own philosophical system and help us see its limitations. In this chapter I argue that the open-ended quality of Arendt's writing on literary texts is purposeful and directly related to the condition of natality. As a storyteller, she drew methodologically from Walter Benjamin's essay on Leskov as well as from the work of Karen Blixen, thus using brevity as a tool to make her own ideas memorable and also to provoke her readers into more extensive meditations on those ideas.[3] Her writing on love provides us with an opportunity to understand this process better. We will explore this poetic term by drawing on and drawing out her thoughts on literary texts that explore this term, especially Shakespeare's *A Midsummer's Night Dream*.[4] In so doing I will demonstrate a dramaturgical element of element of Arendt's philosophy, one that is indebted to Shakespeare and other playwrights and is similar and related to midcentury, philosophically informed, sociology.[5] Although she references Shakespeare sparingly, Arendt's dramaturgy, particularly in her late writings, is specifically indebted to him as it includes the two-in-one of thinking that is fundamental to Shakespearean drama as well as meta-theatrical play, and many key themes including the idea of *theatrum mundi*, the nature of tyranny, the power of tradition and authority, and perhaps most important for our purposes, the complexity of love.

Of course, for the scholar interested in Arendt's use and understanding of Shakespeare, there are several challenges. She discusses Shakespeare in a number of moments in some of her most important works, but she rarely develops these readings and it is not always clear if she means to simply quote him or if she is instead taking a few isolated lines and using them for her own poetic-philosophical ends. Furthermore, we do not know which performances she may have attended and how these might have influenced her. Influence her, Shakespeare most certainly did. *The Life of the Mind* contains a relatively extended reading of Ariel's song in *The Tempest* (Arendt 1978, 212), as does her famous essay on Walter Benjamin (Arendt 1968, 193); *Richard III* tantalizingly appears in several discussions about the nature of evil (Arendt 2003, 187–189; *The Promise of Politics* and other unpublished works briefly explore *Hamlet*; and Shakespeare is often mentioned in passing across almost all of her works (Arendt 2005, 203 and Arendt 2018, 130, 565, and 583). The choice of plays she mentions may itself be telling, however. Both Benjamin and Carl Schmitt discuss *Hamlet* and Arendt's citation of that play may indicate an effort to reframe questions of sovereignty. In *Origin of the German Trauerspiel* (2019), Benjamin describes *Hamlet* as an exemplary version of *Trauerspiel*, a genre he understood as being primarily about sovereignty and violence. In the process of making this argument, Benjamin subtly transforms Schmitt's concept of the sovereign in the context of baroque drama. Whereas Schmitt famously sees the sovereign as "he who decides the state of exception" (Schmitt 1985, 5), Benjamin argues that, at least in the baroque period, avoiding such a crisis is the primary function of the prince (Benjamin 2019, 49). Decades later, in response to Benjamin's reading of *Hamlet*, Schmitt developed a very different interpretation in *Hamlet or Hecuba: The Intrusion of the Time into the Play*, which sought to bolster his conception of sovereignty. Arendt's brief citation of *Hamlet* does not clearly situate her reading in one camp or the other, but instead relates the play to her own understanding of time in the public realm. Unpacking and developing what her reading of this play might be is beyond the scope of this chapter, but how Arendt's *Hamlet* might relate to these and other philosophical readings of the play is certainly a worthwhile endeavor.

Furthermore, Arendt's attention to comedy, especially problem comedies, over tragedy suggests just how much natality impacted Arendt's approach to drama. Comedies, after all, with endings that focus on marriage and plots that require forced serendipity, stress the horizons of newness. But this is all speculation. Arendt's references to Shakespeare, while telling, are also short, generally restricted to a handful of lines with the expectation that her readers will fill in the gaps of her discussion.

Indeed, we might see Arendt's gnomic readings as a missed opportunity. A deeper engagement with Shakespeare's drama and poetry might have illuminated some of her less developed ideas. However, we might see these brief readings as an intellectual opportunity. As the historian of rhetoric David Marshall cogently argues in a chapter on Arendt, "the historian of thought qua thinker has something like a duty to continue the line of inquiry that could have been but was not" (Marshall 2020, 130). In this chapter I travel a path Arendt never went down but do so following her line of inquiry. In so doing, I demonstrate the value of developing Arendt's ideas about literary texts with reference to her philosophical system. Specifically, I look at her comments on *A Midsummer's Night Dream* in an essay about the author Karen Blixen (Isak Dinesen) and develop a reading which demonstrates the significance of Arendt's unfinished conception of love for her political writings and the potential troubles we run into if we do not think carefully about love. With the collection of many of Arendt's previously unpublished works as well as the digitalization of many of her works by the Library of Congress, the significance of the various conceptions of love Arendt explored in her work has become more clearly important, but some philosophical problems remain. Arendt does not clearly define love in her work, if such a thing is possible, and seems to refer to potentially different conceptions of love in different places. This chapter will not resolve these ambiguities but will only demonstrate what is at stake in them, which is related to the constitution of the public realm itself. Love, importantly, floats between the private and the public and thus can never fully be defined because it is what we might today call an affect. That is, love is an emotional resonance that is imbricated in complex ways in subject formation, the environment, and intersubjectivity.

ARENDT AND LOVE

Although less studied than many other key concepts, scholars have long noted the importance of love to Arendt's work.[6] Indeed, a quick perusal of biographies on Arendt give a sense of how important some conception of love might be to her work. These include Elisabeth Young-Bruehl's *For Love of the World* (1982), Antonia Grunenberg's *Hannah Arendt and Martin Heidegger: History of a Love* (2017) and most recently, Ann Heberlein's *On Love and Tyranny: The Life and Politics of Hannah* Arendt (2020). Both of Arendt's earliest books *Love and St. Augustine* (1996) and *Rahel Varnhagen* (1997) deal with both the philosophical and practical conceptions of love. *Love and St. Augustine*, Arendt's doctoral thesis, explores the centrality of love in Augustine's philosophical and theological writings. Briefly put, Arendt explores three major concepts: love as craving, love between man and creator, and neighborly love. Although she did not use the word "natality" in the original version of this document Arendt scholars generally acknowledge that she was developing this concept. *Rahel Varnhagen* was Arendt's *Habilitationsschrift*, and is a biography of a nineteenth-century Jewish socialite who frequently reflected on love and was involved in a number of love affairs. Both of these works were not published in Arendt's lifetime and it is difficult to say the full extent to which they reflected her later thinking, especially since both were originally written before Arendt fled Nazi-occupied Europe. In terms of works written after that period, love slips to the background in *The Origins of Totalitarianism* (1973), is briefly discussed in *The Human Condition* (1958) and is almost never mentioned in subsequent works. This is not to say that the concept is unimportant. Indeed, it arguably has a unique role in Arendt's thinking, but in a way that does not lend it to systematization. It is, in other words, a poetic term, and for reasons related to Arendt's phenomenology, remains indistinct. As she explains in *The Human Condition*, "Love, by its very nature, is unworldly, and it is for this reason rather than its rarity that it is not only apolitical but antipolitical, perhaps the most powerful of all antipolitical human forces" (Arendt 1958, 242). The antipolitical quality of love should attract our attention. Love, alongside the rise of the social and the emergence of totalitarianism, is one of the few distinctive forces that specifically disturbs the public realm and is also one of the few that has primarily positive value. In a famous short passage from her thought diary (*Denktagebuch*), Arendt remarks: "*Amor mundi—warum ist es so schwer, die Welt zu lieben?*" [Love of the world—why is it so difficult to love the world?] (Arendt 2002, 522). We might answer this question any number of ways but observe that if we take this phrase alongside Arendt's comments in *The Human Condition*, we realize that our love of the world may create a powerful antipolitical force, and furthermore a force that may indeed be necessary as it constitutes a place in the world for the public realm itself. We must accept the world, and all of its flaws, to change it or to allow for the forces that can cause change to emerge. Perhaps. Or perhaps we are talking about two distinct forms of love. The context of these two documents is so far apart that it is difficult to know.

When we examine what Arendt would surely consider her private documents such as her letters and *Denktagebuch*, we see that she never fully gave up thinking and experiencing love and we may gain some insights into what role this conception might play in her philosophical system. There are no easy answers here: Arendt never fully develops her ideas about love. Tatjana Noemi Tömmel has been especially useful in charting new distinctions in Arendt's work (Tömmel 2017). She charts at least four distinct understandings of love in the *Denktagebuch*: love as worldless passion from *The Human Condition*, love as desire from Plato, *Amor Mundi* or love of the world, and an Augustine notion of love as unconditional affirmation or "*volo ut sis*" (Tömmel 2017, 109). She argues that these definitions cannot be subsumed into "a single, consistent concept of love" and the complications and contradictions that arises as a result of these different definitions were a result of Arendt's unique form of dialectic thinking. She says: "we should keep the diversity of her concepts and the liveliness of her thinking. It is the variety of forms of love, which must not be given up in favor for a logical system, because it corresponds to the different modes of human existing" (Tömmel 2017, 119). I propose a slightly different answer: love, no matter which of Arendt's definitions we work with, sits on the border between the public and private realms and is thus never fully present in the public. This makes the term only partially legible, which is to say that we never fully know what love is, what it means to a person who declares their love, and what the significance of that love might be. Indeed, it seems that even the person who declares their love or experiences love may not fully be aware of the significance of their declaration or their experience. Love does not always work out. But it often does, and we may have the ability to negotiate that meaning for ourselves even as our understanding of it changes. We are likely to do this on a minute-by-minute basis, and *A Midsummer Night's Dream*, as well as Arendt's writing on that play, can help us understand how that might happen.

LOVE IN DARK TIMES

While discussions of love outside of Arendt's early work are rare, they do happen, and they happen in significant places. She returns to the topic of desire as love in *The Life of the Mind*, but perhaps surprisingly some of her longest reflections on the topic come from her essay "Isak Dinesen 1885–1963" in *Men in Dark Times*. Here too are some of Arendt's longest reflections on Shakespeare, specifically *A Midsummer Night's Dream* as well as a passing reference to *As You Like It*. The essay is a strange one in a strange book, but one that scholars are finding critical for understanding Arendt. Both Julia Kristeva and Adrianna Cavarero reference it specifically, and it is generally considered critical to understand Arendt's narrative rhetoric (Kristeva 2001; Cavarero 1997; and Benhabib 2003) Originally a review of Parmenia Migel's *Titania: The Biography of Isak Dinesen* (1967), it is one of Arendt's most acidic works with a biting tone directed squarely at Migel who Arendt believes has done a deep disservice to a favored writer, Karen Blixen, who, at the time, was better known as Isak Dinesen.

It is hard not to see Arendt's essay on Blixen as unnecessarily overprotective and fraught with identification. We know Arendt admired Dinesen from at least 1958 (Arendt and Jaspers 1992, 359) and she referred to Blixen's work elsewhere. Furthermore, near the end of her life, she referred to herself neither as a philosopher, the field she was trained in, nor a political theorist, her adopted field in the United States, but rather as a "storyteller," a title she arrived at likely through her readings of both Blixen and Benjamin. Furthermore, Arendt's explication of Blixen's nickname "Titania" could apply equally well to herself. In her criticism of the biography, Arendt remarks:

> Parmenia Migel has chosen the name [Titania] as title for her biography and it wouldn't have been a bad title if she had remembered that the name implies more than the Queen of the fairies and her "magic." The two lovers between whom the name first fell, forever quoting Shakespeare to each other, knew of course better; they knew that the Queen of the fairies was quite capable of

falling in love with Bottom and that she had a rather unrealistic estimate of her own magical powers. (Arendt 1968, 102–3)

Without going too deep into her biography, Arendt had her share of failed loves when she wrote these lines, including her first marriage to Günther Anders and her notorious affair with Martin Heidegger. Now married to Blücher for over twenty years, we might imagine she would look back at these relationships with some ironic distance. Her estimation of Heidegger was considerably less than it was when she was young.[7] In other words, Heidegger was Arendt's Bottom. That is to say, a figure she was once enchanted with, but who, in the light of experience, does not appear nearly so enchanting. I do not mean to trivialize their intellectual relationship; it seems that by the time she wrote on Karen Blixen her romantic feelings for him had long passed and she might feel a tinge of distant regret about having those feelings in the first place. I bring this up, not only to laugh at Heidegger's expense, but as a demonstration about how over time one's emotions and one's understanding of those emotions change. This point will be critical for understanding love in *A Midsummer Night's Dream*: love is always an interpretation of an affect by the lover, the beloved, and the public. As many of us know all too well, a couple of decades can provide perspective and reveal more about younger selves than we want to know, but sometimes this happens much more quickly, as in the play itself.

Later in her life, Arendt embraced both Blixen and Shakespeare more fully. Although she never adopted a nickname like Titania, when she explicated her method as a storyteller she drew, not on the essay by Benjamin on this topic, but on Ariel's song in *The Tempest*. The choice, which I have written about elsewhere, is not simply whimsical, but demonstrates how historical work might create the conditions of natality: that is, it might bring something new into the world.[8] At the end of the first volume of *The Life of the Mind*, Arendt explains that the past, in the form of tradition, has been broken and that what is left is a fragmented past which, if we are to use, we must transform. This process is not a form of reconstructing the past, which may well be impossible, but is transforming it into something different in the present. I would argue that this is the same kind of thing we do with literary works and other works of art. As we encounter them we cannot help but reshape them to fit our own understanding; at the same time they reshape us. We see something like this happen in Arendt's use of literature. She cites a particular work, implying a particular interpretation, some of which are not readily apparent or which seem to distort the literary work. However, if we are willing to entertain the interpretations she implies are there, we often find a very different and interesting work as a result. Not only do we get a novel interpretation, but oftentimes the literary work allows us to see some of Arendt's ideas in a different light. In my own experience, this is especially true of Shakespeare's plays, which resonate deeply with Arendt's ideas. Curiously, *A Midsummer Night's Dream*, with its exploration of love and the seemingly invisible forces around it, is an especially useful work to study since it speaks to an idea that is clearly central to Arendt's thinking, but which goes underexplored.

A MIDSUMMER NIGHT'S DREAM

Arendt's discussion of Titania's love of Bottom is as good a place as any to begin my discussion of Shakespeare. There is something odd about Arendt's description of Titania in that she states that Titania was "capable of falling in love" with Bottom and this is not exactly what actually happens in the play. Puck gives her the juice of the flower "love-in-idleness" to make her fall in love with the rude mechanical Bottom, a move that eliminates any agency Titania might have had in this affair. Before we accuse Puck of attempted rape, it helps to understand what this flower is in the context of the play. We are told that this flower is where "a bolt of Cupid fell" and thus should be understood as erotic desire, which is not a thing one generally has agency over in the first place (2.1.165). The fairies in this play, invisible to almost all human characters, represent the shadowy, chaotic, and incomprehensible nature of Arendt's private realm, which includes irrational desire.

This claim requires some unpacking. Let us begin with a few observations that will be familiar to most Arendt scholars. Arendt defines the public realm phenomenologically, stating: "For us, appearance—something that is being seen and heard by others as well as by ourselves—constitutes reality" (Arendt 1958, 50). It is easy to underestimate how important appearance really is in Arendtian thought and to understand what happens when something cannot be fully visible. Just a little later, we read: "Indeed, the most intense feeling we know of, intense to the point of blotting out all other experiences, namely the experience of great bodily pain, is at the same time the most private and least communicable of all" (Arendt 1958, 50–51). Pain, as well as many other sensations, emotions, and affects, lies in the border space between the public and private world. Love, as I have argued, does so as well but with added complexity. All of these emotions are also communication problems; in other words, you can explain to someone that you feel an emotion you both have some understanding of but can never fully explain the sensation. I suspect, in part, this is because the person experiencing the emotion does not ever have full access to the experience of the emotion itself. It appears within them as a force whose origins are often unclear. The less describable a feeling is, the less worldly it appears. Love, as Arendt explains, is decidedly unworldly.

This observation about love can bring us to a number of other curious ideas about the nature of emotions in Arendt. She tells us: "[L]ove, in distinction from friendship, is killed, or rather extinguished, the moment it is displayed in public ('Never seek to tell thy love/ Love that never told can be.') Because of its inherent worldlessness, love can only become false and perverted when it is used for political purposes such as change or salvation of the world" (Arendt 1958, 51–52). The passage flirts with several different notions of love. It begins coquettishly with a description of love that feels like love as a kind of desire which once fulfilled will vanish. Then, Arendt's invocation of William Blake suggests a romantic notion of love, but the subsequent sentence suggest something different, love as a political force. Especially with the mentioning of this idea it is hard to know what exactly Arendt is referring to. She may mean that marriages made for political purposes are rarely about love or she may be remembering the perverse love of country she witnessed back in Germany as the Nazis rose to power. These are both perversions of love for similar reasons, but they seem far afield from expressions of romantic love between individuals. Indeed, on some level, we must believe that love requires a space of appearance to fully exist. Love is itself a problem of representation. It not only signifies many things, but its meaning is always private and thus epistemologically suspect. We can never really know if someone loves us. Worse, in many circumstances, it can even be difficult to know if we really love someone else. In the Renaissance and the modern world, a series of public conventions and social expectations were developed to deal with these problems but, at best, they only defer them.

Much like pain, we struggle to articulate love and, as both Arendt and Shakespeare tell us, the very act of articulating it seems to trivialize the feeling. But it is not just articulation that troubles us. We struggle to understand it and to manage it and ourselves when we are under its thrall, particularly when we are young. We see these struggles with our young Athenian lovers. Helena, seemingly speaking for everyone, notes:

> Love can transpose to form and dignity.
> Love looks not with the eyes, but with the mind.
> And therefore is winged Cupid painted blind.
> Not hath Love's mind of any judgement taste;
> Wings and no eyes figure unheedy haste,
> And therefore is Love said to be a child,
> Because in choice he is so oft beguiled.
> As waggish boys in games themselves forswear,
> So the boy Love is perjured everywhere (1.1.233–41)

In other words, love is a force that no one, especially no young person, can hope to understand; it is fickle, unpredictable, and not really accountable for its actions. If it was only confined to the private realm, this would not be an issue. However, the trouble with love is that it cannot be confined either to the public space of appearances or to the wholly private realm. Indeed, it is needed to constitute the public realm itself but can never fully enter it. *Amor Mundi* requires us to embrace the world as it is, in all of its complexity, and to love it. It is a public form of love, one that allows us to create the space between men that allows for the public to emerge. However, as I explained earlier, love cannot manifest in the public realm until it is transformed into art and that art has some distance from how the emotion is experienced. Love is thus a philosophical and rhetorical aporia which cannot be resolved. Shakespeare's most popular comedy follows four Athenians as they get lost in the woods while fleeing the manipulations of the state and their parents who want them to marry those that they do not love. Seemingly leaving the ancient Peloponnese and arriving in the shadowy domain of English folklore, their affections are manipulated by local spirits' magics and things go to pot until those magics are reversed. Our Athenians, almost all of whom seek a visible form of love in the experience of marriage, represent the public realm. The fairies in the play whose actions and magic are inscrutable to the Athenians represent an experience of the private realm. Of course, neither of these realms is wholly independent of the other and we might quickly observe that the private realm seemingly mirrors the public. This is appropriate because Arendt explains that the only way the private realm becomes visible to us is through being made into the stuff of the public in the form of a story. Similarly, this play, which verges on the nonsensical as is, would be wholly incomprehensible without Oberon, Puck, Titania, and their retinue. They make the play into a workable comedy. Yet, despite the play's classification as a comedy and the many weddings it ends with, it is surprisingly grim. The seriousness is in part due to the toying with conceptions of love that float between public and private and thus threaten to destabilize the political realm.

We get a sense of this trouble very early on in the play. There, Theseus tells his soon-to-be wife: "Hippolyta I wooed thee with my sword,/ And won thy love doing thee injuries./ But I will wed thee in another key:/ With pomp, with triumph and with revelling" (1.1.16–19). The relationship between these two is not the subject of the play, and we know precious little about their relationship. Theseus's words suggest both literal and sexual conquest but not consent and it is unclear if his pomp and reveling are meant to address what he understands as a deficiency or if he is instead going through the motions of making a public show of this relationship. We get no sense about her feelings as she simply does not have much to say in the scenes where she is present. Titania seemingly alludes to a relationship between her and Oberon later in the play, but it is impossible to make any definitive statement with her comments. Instead, we are faced with one of the challenges love brings us. Hippolyta's feelings are her own and cannot be made fully public, especially by someone who is not her. For his own political purposes, Theseus needs such a public declaration or, at least, the contract implied in marriage, which would legitimate his conquest. While he gets his contract off stage, something about this relationship casts a shadow over much of the rest of the play. We must ask ourselves whether any of the lovers have or can create a space where their private feelings are truly manifest in an appropriate public forum.

The marriage that frames the play is not the one that augurs poorly. Egeus's wish for his daughter to marry Demetrius against the will of Hermia, who prefers Lysander, is troubling and speaks to a similar issue of the public life of love. Per the ancient "privilege of Athens," Egeus has the absolute right to marry his daughter to whomever he wishes and to have her executed for disobedience. While this particular instance of *patria potestas* is more easily traced to Roman law than Athenian, marriage in Athens was considered a matter of public concern and responsibility. We are not made aware of Egeus's objections to Lysander, which are immaterial to the exercise of his rights.[9] However, we are given the sense that Egeus does not trust him as he claims that he "bewitched the bosom of my child/ . . . given her rhymes/ And interchanged love tokens with my child/ Thou has by moonlight at her window sung/ With feigning voice verses of feigning love / And stol'n the impression of her fantasy" (1.1.28–31). These public signs of love are discounted by Egeus who, either because he is an overprotective father or because it interferes with his political designs, does not trust Lysander's actions.

But as anyone who has seen this play knows, no one can trust anyone when it comes to love. Lysander and Demetrius nearly engage in a fatal duel; Helena and Hermia exchange cruel enough words that their lifelong friendship is nearly destroyed; and there is more than enough poor treatment to go around. The conventions of comedy, which demand reasonable marriages at the end, may indeed be the thing that saves everyone. In fact, there is something that allows us to have a modicum of confidence about the various pairings that appear at the end of the play. That is love itself, which, again by its nature, is unknowable and thus can be reinterpreted as needed. Titania provides the most vivid example of how this might work. When she is first enchanted and encounters Bottom, she is positively besotted, stating to the ass-headed object of her affection: "My ear is much enamored of thy note;/ So is mine eye enthrallèd to thy shape,/ And thy fair virtue's force, perforce, doth move me/ On the first view to say, to swear, I do love thee" (3.1.120–4). These words suggest pure animalistic desire just as much as Bottom's new head reflects Renaissance ideas about sexuality Kott (1975, 213). But her tune changes almost comically quickly when, in response to his words she says, "Thou art as wise as thou art beautiful" (3.1.130). Although this line is used for comic effect, the shift from Bottom's physical features to his mind demonstrates a shifting form of love from erotic desire to something more like *Volo ut sis*, the absolute affirmation of an individual as they are. This same shift happens in other places in the play as well, when the Athenian lovers sort themselves out romantically in Act IV. Helena again, perhaps rationalizing her own feelings, articulates this sense most clearly when she exclaims: "And I have found Demetrius like a jewel,/ Mine own, and not mine own" (4.2.187–88). Demetrius, her new lover, might rightly be claimed like a missing jewel by its rightful owner, but Helena knows this will not happen. He is her jewel now and she will be able to keep him. Many critics, most notably Jan Kott, have noted just how dark this play really is, despite its classification as comedy (Kott 1974, 213–20). It centers around an unnecessary clash between longtime friends. The comedic effect of these struggles is enhanced by what we know of Hermia and Helena, which is to say: very little. The only difference mentioned in the text is their height, and the similarity in names suggests they are practically interchangeable. It turns out after a strange night in the woods they actually are.

Titania and our Athenian lovers are allowed to shrug off this strange night in the woods as if nothing serious happened. It is only to be laughed at and perhaps that is appropriate. What happens in the woods, stays in the woods? In a sense, yes, as this shadowy realm represents that which is private and, in effect, what happens here never really happens. But that is not fully true. When Oberon wakes her, Titania looks at the face of her would-be paramour and is merely confused. She asks: "How come these things to pass!" and follows up with "O, how mine eyes do loath his visage now!" (4.1.75–76). The morning light conquers the forest shadow, and Titania is momentarily confronted with this deed. The private actions are momentarily public. But there is no way to make them permanently so, as Titania, Oberon, and company cannot be made visible to the Athenians except through the mythological stories they represent. Their actions can thus have no consequences; they exist merely as narrative. In this particular sense, the fairies represent the darkest element of the play and that is simply the chaos and unknowability of love.

META-THEATER

In contrast to the relatively gloomy narratives with our Athenian lovers and the court of the fairies is the love story told by the rude mechanicals. While ostensibly a tragedy, "Pyramus and Thisbe" reads like a comedy because it is executed so unsuccessfully. However, because of its emphasis on its own artifice, the play-within-a-play foregrounds the process in which narratives are made, which both reinforces the impact of Shakespeare's primary narrative and helps us understand the process in which emotions in the private realm are transformed into narratives for the public realm. In a comparison between the private and public realms, Arendt explains that

> [c]ompared with the reality which comes from being seen and heard, even the greatest forces of intimate life—the passions of the heart, the thoughts of the mind, the delights of the senses—lead an uncertain, shadowy kind of existence unless and until they are transformed, deprivatized and deindividualized, as it were into a shape to fit them for public appearance. The most current of such transformations occurs in storytelling and generally in artistic transposition of individual experience. (Arendt 1958, 50)

Arendt further clarifies that artistic production generally falls into the category of work and is the province of *homo faber* even if the stories themselves end up being part of the public realm. The performers of "Pyramus and Thisbe," artisans all, most clearly belong and are at home in, the world of fabrication, although not the forms of fabrication we typically associate with theatre. Their lack of practiced artistry dramatizes the importance of work to the process of making the raw stuff of narrative and poetry into a coherent production for the public. Critics have long suggested that the play they perform may in fact be a parody of one Shakespeare's most famous works, *Romeo and Juliet*, which may have been written at the same time (Dickenson 2016, 305). And yet, despite the lack of artistry, their play is actually moving. Pyramus's line "O grim-looked night, O night with hue so black,/ O night which ever art when day is not,/ O night, O night, alack, alack, alack" (5.1.168–71) sounds much like a line from Helena earlier in the play "O weary night, O long and tedious night" (3.3.19) and the mechanicals, who clearly have no sense of what they are doing, gain even some of their aristocratic audience's approval.[10] Despite its flaws and perhaps even because of them the play works, albeit not exactly in the way the mechanicals imagine. In short, it works in much the same way as Arendt describes natality: unpredictably, and out of the control of the individual actors. Hyppolita's description of the play as "strange and admirable" is actually key. Arendt's discussions of Shakespeare invoke these terms frequently when discussing storytelling, and it is quite fitting for the condition of natality. The product of natality is not the product of specific intentions; its appearance in the world is completely inexplicable. This truism is what makes it so profound, and why the mechanicals' performance represents a powerful statement about natality itself.

Yet there is more. In terms of *Midsummer Night*, when compared to the Athenian nobility and Arcadian fairies, the mechanicals are the most realistic and likeable of the characters as if to say that performance of "Pyramus and

Thisbe" is itself an act of realism. This performance dramatizes the process of making private experience into a public performance, albeit poorly. But even the most artful performances are indeed poorly executed and cannot fully reflect the private experiences that they bring into the world. Arendt alludes to this point at various times in her writing, but perhaps best in her discussion of poetry in *The Human Condition* where she says: "Poetry, whose material is language, is perhaps the most human and least worldly of the arts, the one in which the end product remains closest to the thoughts that inspired it" (Arendt 1958, 169). The term "closest" is key. A poem or any work of art goes through a process of transformation, one that is never really described in Arendt's work except metaphorically, as it moves from thought to work. If the artist is lucky and practiced, that transformation enhances the experience of thought but no individual is fully in control of what art becomes.

This notion of art as acting beyond the intentions of its artist is neither unique to Shakespeare nor to Arendt, although it is crucial to the way both think about their work. In other words, Shakespearean drama and Arendtian political philosophy are only made real in action and interpretation. Both must be performed, and only in performance do they press us to think and act in the world differently. Having made this point, it seems worthwhile to state that despite the vast array of scholarship on Arendt, we have only barely scratched the surface of the literary Arendt. Work remains to be done on Arendt's many literary influences including Randall Jarrell, Herman Broch, William Faulkner, Bertolt Brecht, and William Blake, as well as the many artists and thinkers who have since been influenced by Arendt. Poetry, in particular, looks like an especially promising avenue of research because of Arendt's many references to poets and her own poetry. What paths this work will take us toward we thankfully cannot predict, but that is why work on Arendt is so rewarding.

BIBLIOGRAPHY

Arendt, Hannah. 1958. *The Human Condition.* Chicago: University of Chicago Press.
———. 1968. *Men in Dark Times.* New York: Harcourt Brace & Company.
———. 1973. *The Origins of Totalitarianism.* New Ed. New York: Harcourt Brace & Company.
———. 1977. *Between Past and Future: Eight Exercises in Political Thought.* New York: Penguin Books.
———. 1978. *The Life of the Mind.* One Vol Ed. New York: Harcourt Brace Jovanovich.

———. 1994. "Heidegger the Fox." *Essays in Understanding 1930–1954: Formation, Exile, and Totalitarianism*, edited by Jerome Kohn, 361–62. New York: Schocken Books, 1994.

———. 1996. *Love and St. Augustine*. Edited by Joanna Vecchiarelli Scott and Judith Chelius Stark. Chicago: University of Chicago Press

———. 1997. *Rahel Varnhagen: The Life of a Jewess*. Translated by Richard Winston, and Clara Richard. Edited by Liliane Weissberg. Baltimore: John Hopkins University Press.

———. 2002. *Denktagebuch 1950–1973*, edited by Ursula Ludz and Ingrid Nordmann, Munich: Piper.

———. 2003. *Responsibility and Judgement*, edited by Jerome Kohn. New York: Schocken Books.

———. 2005. *The Promise of Politics*, edited by Jerome Kohn. New York: Schocken Books.

———. 2018. *The Modern Challenge to Tradition: Fragmente eines Buchs.* Göttingen: Wallstein Verlag.

Arendt, Hannah, Karl Jaspers, Lotte Köhler, and Hans Saner. 1992. *Hannah Arendt/ Karl Jaspers correspondence, 1926–1969*. New York: Harcourt Brace Jovanovich.

Arnett, Ronald. 2013. *Communication Ethics in Dark Times: Hannah Arendt's Rhetoric of Warning and Hope*. Carbondale: Southern Illinois University Press.

Benhabib, Seyla. 2003. *The Reluctant Modernism of Hannah Arendt*. Lanham: Rowman & Littlefield Publishers.

Benjamin, Walter. 1968. "The Storyteller: Reflections on the Work of Nikolai Leskov." *Illuminations: Essays and Reflections*, edited by Hannah Arendt, 83–109. New York: Harcourt Brace Jovanovich.

———. 2019. *Origin of the German Trauerspiel*. Cambridge, MA: Harvard University Press.

Bhaumik, Munia. 2015. "Literary Arendt: The Right to Political Allegory" *The Yearbook of Comparative Literature* 5, no. 61: 11–34.

Cavarero, Adriana. 1997. *Relating Narratives: Storytelling and Selfhood*. Translated by Paul Kottman New York: Routledge.

Dahlgren, Paul. 2006. "Reflections on a Small Island: Hannah Arendt, Shakespeare's *The Tempest*, and the Politics of Childhood." *Journal of Religious and Cultural Theory* 7, no. 2: 34–46.

Gottlieb, Susannah Young-ah. 2003. *Regions of Sorrow: Anxiety and Messianism in Hannah Arendt and W. H. Auden*. Palo Alto: Stanford University Press.

Grunenberg, Antonia. 2017. *Hannah Arendt and Martin Heidegger: History of a Love*. Translated by Peg Birmingham, Kristina Lebedeva, and Elizabeth von Witzke Birmingham. Bloomington: Indiana University Press.

Hadfield, Andrew. 2005. *Shakespeare and Republicanism*. Cambridge: Cambridge University Press.

Halpern, Richard. 2011. "Theater and Democratic Thought: Arendt to Rancière." *Critical Inquiry* 37, no. 3 (Spring): 545–72.

Heberlein, Ann. 2020. *On Love and Tyranny: The Life and Politics of Hannah Arendt*. Trans. Alice Menzies. Toronto: Anansi International.

Holmes, Anne. 2021. "The Poetic Hannah Arendt: A Conversation with Arendt Researcher Samantha Rose Hill." Library of Congress. June 14, 2021. https://blogs.loc.gov/catbird/2021/06/the-poetic-hannah-arendt-a-conversation-with-arendt-researcher-samantha-rose-hill/.

Hutchison, Anthony. 2006. "Freedom, Necessity, Judgement Trilling, Arendt and '9/11 Liberalism,'" *Comparative American Studies: An International Journal* 4, no. 1: 67–84.

King, Richard. 2017. "Hannah Arendt and the Uses of Literature" *Raritan* 36, no. 4 (Spring), 106–24.

Kott, Jan. 1974. *Shakespeare Our Contemporary.* Translated by Boleslaw Taborski. New York: W. W. Norton & Co.

Kottman, Paul. 2007. *A Politics of the Scene.* Palo Alto: Stanford University Press.

Kristeva, Julia. 2001. *Hannah Arendt: Life is a Narrative.* Toronto: University of Toronto Press.

Lupton, Julia. 2005. *Citizen-Saints: Shakespeare and Political Theology.* Chicago: University of Chicago Press.

———. 2011. *Thinking with Shakespeare: Essays on Politics and Life.* Chicago: University of Chicago Press.

Marshall, David. 2020. *The Weimar Origins of Rhetorical Inquiry.* Chicago: University of Chicago Press.

Migel, Parmenia. 1967. *Titania: The Biography of Isak Dinesen.* New York: Random House.

Miller, Nichole. 2014. *Violence and Grace: Exceptional Life Between Shakespeare and Modernity.* Evanston: Northwestern University Press.

O'Gorman, Ned. 2020. *Politics for Everybody: Reading Hannah Arendt in Uncertain Times.* Chicago: University of Chicago Press.

Pirro, Robert. 2001. *Hannah Arendt and the Politics of Tragedy.* DeKalb: Northern Illinois Press.

Rust, Jennifer. 2013. *The Body in Mystery: The Political Theology of the Corpus Mysticum in the Literature of Reformation England.* Evanston: Northwestern University Press, 2013.

Schmitt, Carl. 2005. *Political Theology: Four Chapters on the Concept of Sovereignty.* Translated by George Schwab. Chicago: University of Chicago Press.

———. 2009. *Hamlet or Hecuba: The Intrusion of Time into the Play.* Translated by David Pan and Jennifer Rust. New York: Telos Press.

Shakespeare, William. 2018. *A Midsummer Night's Dream.* Edited by Grace Ioppolo. New York: W.W. Norton and Company.

Sjöholm, Cecilia. 2015. *Doing Aesthetics with Arendt: How to See Things.* New York: Columbia University Press.

Tömmel, Tatjana Noemi. 2017. "Vita Passiva: Love in Arendt's Denktagebuch." In *Artifacts of Thinking: Reading Hannah Arendt's Denktagebuch,* edited by Roger Berkowitz and Ian Storey, 106–23. New York. Fordham University Press.

Young-Bruehl, Elisabeth. 1982. *Hannah Arendt: For Love of the World.* New Haven: Yale University Press.

NOTES

1. See Gottlieb (2003), Hutchison (2006), and Bhaumik (2015) for excellent examples of this work.
2. In Shakespeare studies, scholars working in political theology and related fields have made especially notable contributions. In addition to others mentioned in this chapter, these include Kottman (2007), Lupton (2011), Lupton (2005), Miller (2014), and Rust (2013). Stonebridge (2018) is an excellent example of a literary scholar using Arendt to discuss refugees.
3. Benjamin (1968).
4. All citations for *A Midsummer Night's Dream* come from the Norton Critical Edition (2018).
5. Goffman (1959) and Burke (1969) are both important examples of this work.
6. See Hayden (2014). Tömmel, Scott, and Stark give the most comprehensive discussions of love in Arendt's work and its importance.
7. See "Heidegger the Fox" in Arendt (1994).
8. See Dahlgren (2006).
9. Thesius states "in his kind, wanting your father's voice,/ the other must be held the worthier" (1.1.56–57).
10. Hippolyta says that their play "grows to something of great constancy;/ But howsoever, strange and admirable" (5.1.26–27).

Chapter Two

Jaspers, Kant, and the Origins of Hannah Arendt's Theory of Judgment

Matthew Wester

One of the most confounding aspects of Hannah Arendt's writings is her treatment of Kant's *Critique of Judgment*. Arendt was obviously not concerned with accurately representing Kant's thought when she claimed that his third *Critique* contained an unwritten political philosophy. Indeed, Arendt built this claim on a wholesale dismissal of his actual political philosophy. In *Lectures on Kant's Political Philosophy*, she stated that Kant's political works such as "Toward Perpetual Peace" and the *Metaphysics of Morals* were of such a quality that "it is difficult not to agree with Schopenhauer, who said about it: 'It is as if it were not the work of this great man'" (Arendt, 1989, 8). For Arendt, Kant's political insights are not to be found in his political writings, but in his aesthetics. More specifically, one must turn to the portion of the *Critique of Judgment* entitled the "Critique of the Aesthetic Power of Judgment" in order to appreciate the political dimensions of Kant's transcendental idealism.

To make interpretive matters more difficult, Arendt's texts about Kant's political philosophy are either incomplete or in service of another thesis. Texts that she actually dedicated to outlining her interpretation of Kant's *Critique of Judgment* she did not live to finish (*Lectures on Kant's Political Philosophy*) or did not intend to publish (*Denktagebuch*). Although directed specifically at expounding her claims about Kant's political philosophy, these works are fragmentary and incomplete. Completed works such as "The Crisis in Culture" and "Truth and Politics" include interpretation of the *Critique of Judgment*, but are not dedicated to that theme and her treatment of Kant's aesthetics is unfortunately brief. Thus, one of the chief characteristics of these writings—complete and incomplete—is their relative inconsistency with one another. It is not clear how (if at all) Arendt intended her earlier texts such as "The Crisis in Culture" and "Truth and Politics" to complement later texts such as *Lectures on Kant's Political Philosophy*. As a result, much of the scholarly commentary on these texts has focused on trying to figure out how they relate to one another.[1]

In this chapter, I shall take another approach. In my view, a better starting point for appreciating Arendt's writings on political judgment is to think about how and why Arendt concluded that one ought to disregard Kant's political writings in favor of his aesthetics. Doing so allows us to situate Arendt in the history of ideas and to appreciate her unique reasons for (mis)reading Kant in the way that she chose to do. Accordingly, in this chapter I will focus on two such reasons, neither of which have figured prominently in the secondary literature: (i) the work of her mentor, Karl Jaspers, and (ii) the fact that Kant's commitment to the autonomy of the faculty of judgment in relation to the other faculties of cognition resonated with Arendt's commitment toward the political sphere as an autonomous realm of human life.

KARL JASPERS AND *THE CRITIQUE OF JUDGMENT*

In this section I shall argue that, in large part, Arendt's unique reading of Kant's aesthetic theory was done under the influence of her mentor, Karl Jaspers. Before I discuss how Jaspers inspired Arendt to read the *Critique of Judgment* in the way that she did, it is important to note that neither the *Critique of Judgment* nor Kant's political writings were unknown to Arendt. In fact, she was familiar with these texts long before she concluded that Kant's aesthetics contain disguised political insights. Jaspers inspired Arendt to *return* to works with which she was already familiar. Jaspers appears to have been responsible for inspiring Arendt to develop a new interpretive lens with which to reexamine the *Critique of Judgment*.

Arendt gave a seminar on Kant's political philosophy at the University of California at Berkeley in 1955, but the *Critique of Judgment* was not a part of that lecture course.[2] We have no reason to believe that Arendt saw the third *Critique* as related to Kant's political philosophy prior to late 1957. In the Berkeley lecture course, Arendt's judgment of Kant's political philosophy was negative—a consistent theme in her published and unpublished writings. In discussing the content of this lecture course David C. Marshall notes that, "Her verdict on Kantian political thought is damning. [Kant's] account of political community begins with what Arendt terms 'worldlessness.' All of Kant's intellectual energy, according to Arendt, is invested in examining the moral relationship of individuals to themselves [and not] how it is that connections *between* human beings are forged" (Marshall 2010, 368). To put this in a different light, Arendt based her negative assessment of Kant's stated philosophy on the simple fact that Kant's political philosophy was an application of his moral philosophy. That is, Kant's political philosophy was not rooted in the realities of human social and political life; instead, it was based on a philosophical framework that would only be explanatory if "there were only one or two men or only identical men," as she put it in "Introduction into Politics" (Arendt 2007, 93).

The available evidence shows that Arendt did not conclude that the *Critique of Judgment* contained political insights until August 1957. In the following section, I will discuss her likely motivations for doing so; here, I want to focus on the circumstances and influences that caused her changed orientation toward Kant's third *Critique.* Any accurate understanding of Arendt's account of political judgment must be grounded in an appreciation for the decisive impact of her mentor, Karl Jaspers. Indeed, it appears that it was Jaspers's 1957 text *Die Grossen Philosophen* that inspired Arendt to return to the *Critique of Judgment* with a newfound interest in gleaning concealed political insights from it.

In the early 1960s, Arendt served as editor for the English translation of *The Great Philosophers.* Several years prior to her involvement in bringing this text to English readers, the Arendt-Jaspers correspondence shows that Arendt was profoundly influenced by Jaspers's treatment of Kant in the German edition of that text. In a letter dated August 29, 1957, Arendt wrote to Jaspers that she had read the first volume of this work, which contained chapters on Socrates, Buddha, Confucius, Jesus, Plato, Augustine, and Kant. The majority of the philosophical content of this letter is devoted to Jaspers's treatment of Kant. Arendt referred to Jaspers's treatment of Kant as "the real center [of your book]" and as its "high point" along with his chapter on Augustine. (Arendt and Jaspers 1993, 317) Arendt wrote,

> At the moment I'm reading the *Kritik der Urteilskraft* with increasing fascination. There, and not in the *Kritik der Praktischen Vernunft,* is where Kant's real political philosophy is hidden. His praise for "common sense," which is so often scorned; the phenomenon of taste taken seriously as the basic phenomenon of judgment—which it probably is in all aristocracies—; the "expanded mode of thought" that is part and parcel of judgment, so that one can think from someone else's point of view. The demand for communicativeness. These incorporate the experiences young Kant had in society, and then the old man made them come to life again. I've always loved this book most of Kant's critiques, but it has never before spoken to me as powerfully as it does now that I have read your Kant chapter. (Arendt and Jaspers 1993, 318)

In my opinion this passage is of decisive importance for understanding the circumstances in which Arendt began to read the third *Critique* as a political text. The *Critique of Judgment* was not new to Arendt. She had read it before—indeed, she preferred it to the *Critique of Pure Reason* and the *Critique of Practical Reason*—but she had not interpreted it as containing a "hidden political philosophy." Jaspers's text appears to have led Arendt to revisit Kant's aesthetic theory with the explicit intention of excavating social and political insights from it. The high praise that she reserved for Jaspers's work in the letter cited above is proof that, upon reading it, she decided to reread the *Critique of Judgment*. Further, she explicitly suggests that it is thanks to Jaspers that Kant's text spoke to her with a newfound sense of urgency. Finally, it is worth noting that Jaspers's treatment of Kant in *The Great Philosophers* appears to have inspired Arendt to read Kant's *Critique of Judgment* in a very specific way. Arendt states in the letter that her newfound interpretive framework for reading the *Critique of Judgment* was to translate *social* insights into *political* ones. Thus, according to Arendt, Kant was a powerful observer of human social life (elsewhere in her writings she calls this "worldliness"), but was unable to realize the inherently political nature of the model of judgment he offered in the third *Critique*.

The *Denktagebuch*[3] contains the notes she took on Kant's *Critique of Judgment* around the same time as her letter to Jaspers. From these notes (*Denktagebuch* XXII) it is clear that Arendt changed her mind about Kant and his political philosophy. While she did not change her negative assessment of Kant's actual political philosophy, she did conclude that his *Critique of Judgment* contained political insights that were far more valuable than any of his stated views about the political realm in his practical philosophy. She wrote that, "It will always remain memorable that Kant exemplifies the tremendous phenomenon of the power of judgment in taste. However much this speaks to his worldliness, it remains characteristic of political cluelessness."[4] After rereading the third *Critique*, Arendt no longer thought Kant "worldless" in his understanding of human life; instead, she concluded that Kant's account of reflective judgment contained substantial political insights. However, Arendt believed that these insights needed to be excavated from Kant's third *Critique* because Kant believed that these insights were merely social. Thus, the problem with Kant's political philosophy—according to Arendt—is not that he lacked one, but that he did not really understand what politics was in the first place. He was, in her words, politically clueless. This meant that his actual political writings could not be trusted to say anything meaningful about politics. Further, had he not been so clueless, he would not have limited his notion of reflective judgment to the social realm (viz., judgments of *taste* that we make about works of natural and artificial beauty). A little over ten years later, in *Lectures on Kant's Political Philosophy*, Arendt had not changed her basic assessment of Kant's third *Critique*. In Arendt's view, Kant framed political insights as social ones because of his lack of political experience. She emphasized that "In [. . .] a country under the rule of an absolute monarch, advised by a rather enlightened bureaucracy of civil servants, who, like the monarch were completely separated from 'the subjects'—there could be no truly public realm other than this reading and writing public" (Arendt 1989, 60). Clearly, Arendt believed that Kant was unable to recognize the inherently political nature of his theory of reflective judgment because he did not have any experience with a truly public realm where individuals could appear before one another in speech and action to deliberate about how best to preserve the common world.

All of this background raises an important question: what was it that Arendt saw in Jaspers's analysis of Kant's philosophy that led her to return to the *Critique of Judgment* and to discover a hidden political philosophy? In the remainder of this section, I will sketch an answer to this question. The true extent of Jaspers's influence on Arendt's reading of Kant's third *Critique* is a matter of speculation. The unfortunate fact is that Arendt is not more specific in her letter to Jaspers concerning what about his treatment of Kant inspired her to revisit the third *Critique*. However, there are broad characteristics of Jaspers's analysis of Kant that clearly appealed to well-known assumptions that Arendt had about politics.

In *The Great Philosophers*, Jaspers insisted that the issue at stake in reflective judgment was "always holding to the particular, never slipping into the abyss of the insensible and unintelligible" (Jaspers 1962, 289). According to Jaspers's gloss of Kant's aesthetic theory, determinative judgment stripped away the particularity of a given object by subsuming it under a universal category. Reflective judgment, however, was different. Reflective judgment did not strip away the particularity of an appearance. Instead, according to Jaspers, reflective judgment united an object with a universal while retaining its particularity.

Jaspers's emphasis on particularity and reflective judgment would have resonated strongly with Arendt. Her published writings reflect a suspicion of the tendency of philosophers to pollute political philosophy with notions of philosophical universality. In writings such as *The Human Condition* and *Between Past and Future*, Arendt argued that human speech and action disclosed actors in their uniqueness (viz., their particularity). While she was reading Jaspers's work, she was also in the process of finishing *The Human Condition*, which argued that human speech and action inevitably carried a degree of particularity and spontaneity that transcended universal notions of truth and goodness. She was also convinced that politics ought not be reduced to a subspecies of epistemology (the search for truth) or morality (the pursuit of goodness). While she believed that epistemological and moral categories were not irrelevant to politics, she also believed that politics was an *autonomous* realm of human experience that should not be reduced to others. I will return to this theme in depth in the following section. For now, we should keep in mind that she found Jaspers's emphasis on particularity attractive because she believed that politics was about the particular, and not about the universal.

Thus, an important reason for Arendt's turn to Kant's *Critique of Judgment* was done under Jaspers's influence. Jaspers's exegesis likely acted as a sort of road map for Arendt. She recognized and appreciated Jaspers's emphasis on particularity against philosophical universality. More specifically, Arendt was drawn to the first part of the *Critique of Judgment*—the "Critique of Aesthetic Judgment"—because she recognized that it was there that Kant's commitment to particularity was at its strongest. There is a good deal of evidence in support of this claim in *Denktagebuch* XXII. The very first fragment references Jaspers's reading of Kant explicitly and begins with, "Judgment: Kant: the impossibility of subsuming the particular."[5] In the same fragment Arendt wrote that, "in determining judgment I start from the experience of the 'I think' and thus from self-given (a priori) principles, in reflective judgment from the experience of the world in its particularity."[6]

To be sure, this wholesale emphasis on particularity that Arendt and Jaspers emphasized was not the most accurate reading of Kant. In the *Critique of Judgment*, Kant did eschew cognitive/moral universality, but this did not imply a wholesale embracing of particularity per se. For now, however, I merely wish to underscore the importance of particularity to Jaspers's and Arendt's readings of Kant's third *Critique*. Of course, Arendt's appreciation for Kant's commitment to particularity is not the only reason why she turned to it to develop an account of political judgment. As we shall see in the next section, Arendt recognized that Kant's *Critique of Judgment* did not actually make a firm commitment to particularity. Much of her subsequent writings on judgment, in my view, were her attempts to use the resources that she found in the third *Critique* in order to assemble an account of political judgment that emphasized particularity in the way she believed Kant's text ought to have done. In the following section, I will emphasize some of Arendt's reasons for developing her heterodox interpretation of Kant's *Critique of Judgment* that were her own, and were not found in Jaspers's work.

ARENDT, KANT, AND THE AUTONOMY OF JUDGMENT

Thus far, I have surveyed the degree to which the work of Karl Jaspers influenced Hannah Arendt's thinking on Kant's *Critique of Judgment.* In doing so, my purpose is not to reduce Arendt's thinking to that of Jaspers. Jaspers's reading of Kant's third *Critique* as eschewing philosophical universality in favor of particularity might have suggested to Arendt that there was more to Kant's text than she had previously thought, but it certainly did no more than that. Arendt herself made the connection between a purported valorization of the particular and political speech and action. She was the one who developed the claim that the merely social model of judgment developed by Kant was actually political. The details of Arendt's reading of the *Critique of Judgment* are strikingly original; so much so that much of the secondary literature has been devoted to pointing out that Arendt's reading is, for lack of a better term, simply incorrect.[7] Other commentators remain perplexed as to *why* one might read Kant's aesthetic theory in such a way that is clearly not in line with Kant's stated intentions for the completion of his critical philosophy. Elsewhere, I have argued that in reading Kant the way that she did, Arendt was consciously engaged in reading Kant against his own stated intentions. There is substantial textual evidence that Arendt believed she located methodological errors in Kant's approach and that much of her own reading of him was an attempt to correct these errors, offering the account of judgment that Kant could not have offered, but should have (in Arendt's view).[8]

In this section, I will focus on another important reason for Arendt's original take on the *Critique of Judgment*—the concept of "worldliness." In the first section of this chapter, I showed how Karl Jaspers's *The Great Philosophers* led Arendt to change her mind about Kant. She came to realize that his political writings were worldless, but his political philosophy was not. She came to this curious conclusion because she became convinced that his political philosophy and his political writings were two separate things. If one wanted to know what Kant thought about politics, then one ought to read his writings on history and politics; but if one wanted to know about his political insights, then one ought to read his aesthetics. In the remainder of this chapter, I wish to explore Arendt's association between reflective judgment and "worldliness" in greater detail by connecting it to definite aspects of Kant's philosophy.

When reading Arendt's writings on judgment, it is important to keep in mind that she was developing these writings at the same time as she was preparing to publish *The Human Condition.* Thus, it is probable that when she reread Kant's *Critique of Judgment* under the influence of Jaspers's newly published *Die Grossen Philosophen*, she reread it with the same concerns with which she composed *The Human Condition*. In *The Human Condition*, Arendt sought to catalog and articulate what she called the "Vita Activa." By this term she meant "three fundamental activities: labor, work, and action. They are fundamental because each corresponds to one of the basic conditions under which life on earth has been given to man" (Arendt 2018, 7). "Labor" corresponded to those activities that we must undertake in order to preserve the physical aspect of our existence (viz., the meeting of basic biological needs). "Work" corresponded to those activities that we must undertake in order to transform the *earth* into a *human world*. Through working, we construct a human artifice in which alone a distinctly human life is both possible and meaningful. "Action" corresponded to those activities that we undertake in order to decide how to preserve the human world. To Arendt's mind, *politics* was the activity that corresponded to human action. It is no exaggeration to say that at its most general, *The Human Condition* is simply about what Arendt called human "worldliness."

Notably, she excluded the "Vita Contemplativa" from consideration because she considered traditional philosophical speculation to be at odds with human worldliness. In her view, the philosopher neglected the world in order to discover eternal truths. She would not return to the "Vita Contemplativa" until the end of her life, with *The Life of the Mind*. There, we also find Arendt critical of Kant, claiming that his distinction between thinking and knowledge was not fully thought through. Like much of her claims about Kant's theory of judgment, Arendt believed that many of Kant's most important insights into the process of thinking were ultimately betrayed by his own systematicity.[9] Previously, I emphasized that Jaspers's work allowed Arendt to associate Kant's *Critique of Judgment* with worldliness. She was able to make this connection because Jaspers's writing made her aware of the degree to which particularity was emphasized in the last of Kant's *Critiques*. From there, she reread the *Critique of Judgment*, seeing a powerful model of political judgment that was capable of explaining what we do when we do politics and how we ought to evaluate the substance of politics (human speech and action). What Arendt recognized in Kant's account of judgments of taste was that these judgments had a certain sort of validity that was not derived from their truth-value or their moral content. In the *Critique of Judgment* Kant called this "subjective universal validity" (*subjektiv allgemeine gültigkeit*). In other words, Arendt was struck by the fact that Kant had discovered that we take certain judgments to be non-relative, but also not by virtue of their being true or by their being morally right. Instead, these judgments are taken to be non-relative because we *expect* others to agree with us because we take the source of the judgment to be something that would be common to any disinterested observer of the same object. From this point, Arendt easily made the connection between this "subjective universal" mode of validity and the way the inherently intersubjective way that political speech and action ought to be evaluated.

My purpose in this section is to discuss the reasons why Arendt made this connection. These reasons go deeper to the core of Kant's critical idealism than the secondary literature tends to recognize. Whereas much of the secondary literature tends (in my opinion) to become bogged down in questions about whether or not her reading of Kant was accurate or whether or not she offered one or two models of judgment, the more productive question is to figure out what, exactly, drew Arendt to the *Critique of Judgment*. Perhaps the single most important element of Kant's critical philosophy that Arendt found attractive is best found in Kant's introduction to the *Critique of Judgment*. There, we find Kant's commitment to the *autonomy* of judgment in relation to the other faculties of cognition.

Arendt viewed politics as an autonomous realm of human life. Furthermore, she concluded that Kant's *Critique of Judgment* contained a hidden political philosophy. Given these facts, it was natural for her to find Kant's commitment to the autonomy of the faculty of judgment to be a muddled and unclear commitment to the autonomy of the political. In large part, I believe that her skepticism about and dissatisfaction with the Western philosophical tradition led her to read the *Critique of Judgment* in this way. Arendt's skepticism was twofold: she believed that the traditional yardsticks by which Western philosophers evaluated politics were those of "truth" and "moral goodness." To be sure, Arendt believed that epistemological and moral resources were obviously of value in assessing political speech and action. However, she did not believe that political speech and action should be reduced to its truth-content or moral value. Unfortunately, she did not live to develop her account of why moral goodness was insufficient. However, her reasons on why we should not reduce political speech and action to its truth-value are found in her essay "Truth and Politics."[10, 11]

In arguing that political speech and action should not be reduced to its truth-content, Arendt was partially allying herself with a larger strain of Western political thought, best represented by thinkers such as Machiavelli, Nietzsche, and Marx (among others)—all of whom insisted (albeit in very different ways) that the end of political life had little (if anything) to do with the search for truth or the pursuit of moral goodness. Like Machiavelli, Nietzsche, and Marx, Arendt believed that it was a mistake to think that politics was merely morality writ large. In what follows, we shall see that Arendt believed that certain truths were indispensable to politics; however, in Arendt's view political speech did not primarily seek truth (or falsehood).

Arendt was suspicious of the traditional philosophical claim that political speech and action ought to be evaluated primarily by way of its truth-content. However, Arendt's wariness of truth and the end of political life does not mean that she believed that truth and politics were unrelated or that certain truths were not indispensable to political life. Indeed, there is one important difference between Arendt's position that differentiates her from other thinkers who share her reluctance to align truth and politics. Throughout all of her writings on political judgment, Arendt insisted that political speech and action were simultaneously not about transmitting "truth" *and* were not equivalent to rhetorical manipulation. Thinkers such as Nietzsche, Machiavelli, or Marx were not concerned to save political discourse from simply being rhetorical manipulation toward some desirable state of affairs. In composing "The Crisis in Culture" and "Truth and Politics," Arendt was concerned with developing an account of an *extra-epistemological* source of validity. Insofar as she could locate this extra-epistemological validity within the framework of aesthetic judgment, Arendt could claim that politics should not be understood in terms of its truth-value *and* that political discourse was characterized by a measure of objectivity that saved it from being mere sophistry and manipulation.

In "Truth and Politics," Arendt argued that "factual truths" are part and parcel of politics because "facts and [political] opinions, though they must be kept apart, are not antagonistic to each other; they belong to the same realm [. . .] In other words, factual truth informs political thought just as rational truth informs philosophical speculation" (Arendt 2006, 234). Arendt maintained that political discourse must be oriented by factual reality while nevertheless not being characterized by the sort of epistemological finality found in factual truth(s). She had several reasons for this position.

First, Arendt thought that if there could ever be a "final say" in political discourse, then political discourse could be "finished" once and for all. Given her primarily dialogical understanding of the political process, it is highly unlikely that she thought that political discourse could (or should) ever come to an end. Arendt based her political theory on the Greek political experience because it was, in Dana Villa's words, "a politics of talk and opinion, one which gave a central place to human plurality and the equality of citizens (for the Greeks, the adult male heads of households)" (Villa 2000, 9). Insofar as the search for truth terminates in the discovery of what is true, Arendt believed that relegating politics to a subspecies of the search for truth was to instrumentalize it. Second, and much more important to my purposes, is Arendt's claim that truth—whether rational or factual—is coercive and therefore, at best, pre-political. Epistemological objectivity, Arendt argued, precluded the proliferation of discourse and, as such, could not be political in any direct sense of the word for the simple reason that it did not foster dialogue.

In the words of Maurizio Passerin D'Entrèves, "Set against the plurality of opinions, truth has a despotic character: it compels universal assent, leaves the mind little freedom of movement, eliminates the diversity of views and reduces the richness of human discourse. In this respect, truth is anti-political, since by eliminating debate and diversity it eliminates the very principles of political life" (Passerin D'Entrèves 1994, 124). Arendt believed that politics was about opinion and judgment, and that truth was about something else entirely. While Arendt believed that good opinions and sound judgments are always rooted in and guided by the facts, Arendt believed it was a mistake to consider political speech as being something more than opinion.

Hence, Arendt's account of political thinking (and judgment) emphasized opinion, rather than truth. "Opinion," she wrote, "and not truth, belongs among the indispensable prerequisites of all power" (Arendt 2006, 229). In Arendt's view, politics was not primarily concerned with discovering truth because politics was primarily concerned with the world and how to change it. This, of course, did not mean that politics had nothing to do with truth. Maurizio Passerin D'Entrèves has warned against a simplistic reading of Arendt on truth, writing that, "we must be careful not to impute to Arendt the view that truth has no legitimate role to play in politics or in the sphere of human affairs" (Passerin D'Entrèves 1994, 128). Because human action was by definition concerned with changing the world (and hence going beyond what *is*), it must also by definition be grounded in a correct understanding of the facts that were part and parcel of the common world. But truths about the world are only the starting point for discourse about how to change it and why; these truths cannot be mistaken for the raison d'etre of politics.

Although she did not develop her reservations about thinking of politics as morality writ large in any of her published or unpublished writings, an important passage from "The Crisis in Culture" allows us to surmise what these reservations were. There, she claimed (briefly, and without much argument) that ethics and logic both proceed a relation that one has to oneself (Arendt 2006, 216–17). In order to understand what she meant, the best place to turn is her gloss on Kant's *Critique of Judgment* from her notebooks. There, Arendt repeats this claim and, surprisingly, states that Kant moves beyond it. In the *Critique of Judgment*, Kant offered the three maxims of "common human understanding" (*der gemeine Menschenverstand*) (Kant 2002, 173–76). In Kant's mind, each maxim corresponded to one of the faculties of rational cognition. Maxim one ("to think for oneself") corresponded to the faculty of concepts, the understanding. Maxim two ("to think from the standpoint of everyone else") corresponded to the faculty of judgment. The third maxim ("to think always consistently") corresponded to the faculty of reason. According to her, maxims one and three—the maxims corresponding to human thought as it was oriented toward the search for truth and the pursuit of goodness—articulated a relationship to the self, and not to others. Western logic, Arendt believed, was based in the principle of noncontradiction and Western ethics was based in the principle that one must remain in agreement with one's own conscience. The second maxim, however, described a relationship to others.

In *Denktagebuch* XXII, but not in any of her published writings, we find this claim multiple times. "In determining judgment (cognitive or moral judgment)," she wrote, "I start from the experience of the 'I think' and thus from self-given (a priori) principles."[12] Arendt understood that in Kant's system both practical and cognitive judgment was always judgment in its determining function. Likewise, in the same fragment, Arendt explicitly stated that moral judgment is not a suitable model of a theory of political judgment because it is not based on the presence of others. Speaking again in Kantian terms, she wrote that, "because legislating reason" proceeds from the noncontradictory self, it excludes others. That is its flaw."[13] This passage concerns only judgment in its practical capacity and is the perfect complement to "Truth and Politics" because it demonstrates Arendt's clear rejection of truth and goodness as sufficient evaluative criteria for political action and speech. Arendt rejected moral goodness for the same reason she rejects truth: it did not require others.

With the above in mind, let's consider some important passages from Kant's introduction to the *Critique of Judgment*. In his introduction, Kant argued that each faculty of cognition (reason, the understanding, and judgment) had its own a priori principle. He wrote that "all of the soul's powers or capacities can be reduced to three that cannot be further derived from a common basis: the *cognitive power*, the *feeling of pleasure and displeasure*, and the *power of desire*" (Kant 2002, 64–65). In other words epistemological judgments were made by way of the cognitive power (viz., the understanding), reflective judgments were made by way of the feeling of pleasure and displeasure (viz., the power of judgment), and moral judgments by way of the power of desire (viz., the faculty of reason). In the passage cited above, Kant clearly states that each of these is not reducible to any of the others in that they do not share a "common ground." While Kant believed that judgment was often used in the service of the search for truth (cognition) or the pursuit of goodness (moral life), he also believed that the faculty of judgment had an autonomous function, in which it did not act in the service of another faculty of cognition.

The faculty of judgment in its autonomy was the topic of the *Critique of Judgment*. Having introduced Arendt's skepticism concerning truth and moral goodness as adequate standards by which to understand politics as a realm of human life, we are in optimal position to appreciate why Arendt believed that Kant's aesthetics were actually political. Arendt did not think it was a mere coincidence that's Kant's account of judgment in all its "worldliness" was also Kant's account of judgment in its autonomy. We have already seen that Arendt believed that politics was a realm of human life that was not reducible to other realms of human life. In other words, Arendt believed that in order to understand politics and political things, an *internal standard* needed to be applied and not an external one derived from other areas of human experience. We have also already seen that Arendt was suspicious of the Western philosophical tradition when it came to talking about politics. Arendt took issue with its tendency to reduce politics to being a function of the search for truth or the pursuit of goodness just as much as she took issue with the claim that politics was simply disguised rhetoric and domination.

It seems clear, I think, that Arendt's turn to Kant's *Critique of Judgment* was motivated in large part by the fact that she was attracted to the part of Kant's work wherein he committed himself to the claim that judgment can function apart from reason and the understanding. Furthermore, following Jaspers, she saw an autonomous faculty of judgment as dealing primarily with particulars without subsuming them under universal concepts. She also believed that the predominantly social model of judgment that Kant produced in his *Critique of Judgment* was "worldly" to such a degree that it contained substantial political insights that Kant was unable to appreciate.

So far so good, it would seem. We have reconstructed some plausible reasons why Arendt might offer such a surprising interpretation of Kant. However, in order to complete our account, we need to answer one important question that the above considerations have raised. I have emphasized Arendt's belief that politics was its own realm of human experience and that, in order to properly understand it, an internal standard needed to be developed. However, an "internal standard" would need to be a standard that was inherently political. How, in other words, was Arendt applying an internal standard by turning to a work in aesthetics? We must discover how it was that, in turning to Kant's aesthetics, Arendt believed she had located an internal standard by which political action and speech could be understood adequately. Fortunately, we have all of the resources that we need in order to answer this question. In doing so, I shall reference some key features of Arendt's reading of Kant's notion of reflective judgment.

We have seen that Arendt was suspicious of Kant's claim that aesthetic judgments of taste were a purely social phenomenon. While she did not take issue with the fact that these judgments could appear in the social realm in the form of judgments of beauty, she also clearly believed that their hidden political dimension was far more important. In order to see *why* she came to believe that Kant had discovered the standard according to which political judgment took place, we must return to Kant's maxims of common human understanding; more specifically, we need to consider the second maxim.

The second maxim corresponded to the faculty of judgment in its autonomy and reads: "to think from the standpoint of everyone else" (Kant 2002, 174). Unlike the other two maxims, which only referred to the self, the second maxim referred to the presence of others.

Insofar as reflective judgment made necessary reference to others, it is not surprising that Arendt concluded that it was the inherently political element in human cognition. In her more well-known writings, Arendt stated that politics "deals with the coexistence and association of different men" (Arendt 2007, 93). Arendt defined politics as something that goes on in between individuals and groups and not something that proceeds from, say, self-evident moral axioms. Thus, when Arendt returned to the *Critique of Judgment* in the late 1950s, she believed she had discovered a "hidden political philosophy" in Kant's notion of reflective judgment. All of the aspects of Kant's theory that Arendt appropriated—terms such as common sense, reflection, disinterestedness, enlarged mentality, and so on—were elements that necessarily referred to other individuals, or so Arendt thought. To put it another way, Arendt believed that she had located an element of human cognition that corresponded to what she called "the fact of human plurality" (Arendt 2007, 93). In other words, against Kant's transcendental model of reflection, Arendt posited a thoroughly empirical model of political judgment whereby in one's reflection one necessarily stood in relation to actual other viewpoints.

CONCLUDING REMARKS

In this chapter, I have tried to situate Arendt's engagement with Kant's *Critique of Judgment* in the history of ideas. I have emphasized her debt to her onetime teacher, Karl Jaspers. Were it not for Jaspers's work *The Great Philosophers*, we might not have Arendt's theory of political judgment, incomplete as it is. Jaspers's emphasis on particularity as opposed to universality in Kant's *Critique of Judgment* allowed Arendt to translate many central aspects of her political theory into a unique and striking reading of Kant as a philosopher who did not know he was writing a political philosophy when he wrote his aesthetic theory.

I have also tried to show that in reading Kant in the way that Arendt did, she was struggling with and against the Western philosophical tradition when it came to thinking about politics. Arendt's commitment to Kant's third *Critique* was motivated in large part by her commitment to the autonomy and dignity of the political as a distinct realm of human experience. In reading him the way she did, she was trying to develop an *internal* standard by which to understand what we do when we engage in political speech and action.

BIBLIOGRAPHY

Arendt, Hannah. 1978. *The Life of the Mind*. San Diego: Harcourt Brace.
Arendt, Hannah. 1989. *Lectures on Kant's Political Philosophy*, edited by Ronald Beiner. Chicago: The University of Chicago Press.
Arendt, Hannah. 2006. *Between Past and Future*. New York: Schocken Press.
Arendt, Hannah. 2007. *The Promise of Politics*. New York: Schocken Press.
Arendt, Hannah. 2018. *The Human Condition*. Chicago: The University of Chicago Press.
Arendt, Hannah. 2020. *Denktagebuch: 1950–1973*. Münich: Piper Verlag GmbH.
Arendt, Hannah, and Jaspers, Karl. 1993. *Correspondence 1926–1969*, edited by Lotte Kohler and Hans Saner. New York: Harcourt Brace Jovanovich, Publishers.
Beiner, Ronald. 2008. "Rereading 'Truth and Politics,'" *Philosophy & Social Criticism*, 34, 1–2: 123–36.
Benhabib, Seyla. 2003. *The Reluctant Modernism of Hannah Arendt*. New York: Rowman & Littlefield.
Bernstein, Richard J. 2002. *Radical Evil: A Philosophical Interrogation*. Cambridge: Polity Press.
Canovan, Margaret. 1974. *The Political Thought of Hannah Arendt*. London: J.M. Dent & Sons, Ltd.
D'Entrèves, Maurizio Passerin. 1994. *The Political Philosophy of Hannah Arendt*. London: Routledge Press.
Gottsegen, Michael G. 1994. *The Political Thought of Hannah Arendt*. Albany: SUNY Press.
Jaspers, Karl. 1962. *The Great Philosophers: The Foundations*, edited by Hannah Arendt. New York: Harcourt Brace & World.
Kant, Immanuel. 2002. *Critique of the Power of Judgment*, edited by Paul Guyer and Allen W. Wood. Cambridge: Cambridge University Press.
Kateb, George. 1984. *Hannah Arendt: Politics, Philosophy, Evil*. Totowa: Rowman & Allanheld.
Marshall, David C. 2010. "The Origin and Character of Hannah Arendt's Theory of Judgment." *Political Theory* 38, no. 3: 367–93.
McGowan, John. 1998. *Hannah Arendt: An Introduction*. Minneapolis: University of Minneapolis Press.
Pashkova, Valeria, and Pashkov, Mikhail. 2018. 'Truth and Truthfulness in Politics: Rereading Hannah Arendt's Essay "Socrates." *Philosophy Today*, 62 no. 2: 447–70.
Passerin D'Entrèves, Maurizio. 1994. *The Political Philosophy of Hannah Arendt*. New York: Routledge Press.
Villa, Dana. 1999. "Thinking and Judging," in *Politics, Philosophy Terror: Essays on the Thought of Hannah Arendt*. Princeton: Princeton University Press, 87–106.
Villa, Dana. 2000. "Introduction: The Development of Arendt's Political Thought." In *The Cambridge Companion to Arendt*. Cambridge: Cambridge University Press.
Weidenfeld, Matthew C. 2012. "Visions of Judgment: Arendt, Kant, and the Misreading of Judgment." *Political Research Quarterly* 66, no. 2: 254–66. htpps://doi.org/10.1177/1065912912446228.

Wester, Matthew. 2018. "Reading Kant Against Himself: Arendt and the Appropriation of Enlarged Mentality." *Arendt Studies* 2:193–214.

NOTES

1. For the argument that Arendt presents us with *two* distinct accounts of political judgment in her writings, see D'Entrèves (1994, 101–38). Dana Villa, on the other hand, has argued that Arendt's writings on political judgment are not in tension with one another and that they represent a unified, coherent account of political judgment. See Villa (1999, 87–106). Besides the studies of Dana Villa and Maurizio Passerin D'Entrèves referenced above, other book-length studies of Arendt's writings that include segments dedicated to Arendt's writings on judgment are those of McGowan (1998, 120–37); Gottsegen (1994, 171–95); Canovan (1974, 111–13, 116); Benhabib (2003, 173–99); Bernstein (2002, 205–20); and Kateb (1984).

2. For a helpful summary of the contents of this lecture and of the drastic shift that Arendt's thinking on Kant's political philosophy underwent in her later years see Marshall (2010, 367–93).

3. There is no English translation of this text. Therefore, all translations are mine. The corresponding German text may be found in footnotes.

4. D, XXII [27]; "Es wird immer denkwürdig bleiben, dass Kant das ungeheure Phänomen der Urteilskraft gerade am Geschmack exemplifiziert. Wie sehr dies auch für seinen Weltsinn spricht, so bleibt es doch auch charakteristisch für die politische Ahnungslosigkeit."

5. D, XXII [19]; "Urteilen: Kant: die Unmöglichkeit, das Individuelle zu subsumieren."

6. D, XXII [19]; "In der bestimmenden Urteilskraft gehe ich von der Erfahrung des "Ich denke" und der also im Selbst gegebenen (apriorischen) Prinzipien, in der reflektierenden Urteilskraft von der Erfahrung der Welt in ihrer Besonderheit aus."

7. See, for instance, Weidenfeld (2012, 254–66).

8. See Wester (2018).

9. See Arendt 1978, 64. I am grateful to Daniel Brennan for bringing this to my attention.

10. I wish to note that Arendt's claims about truth in "Truth and Politics" are somewhat controversial. Arendt's notion of truth is remarkably narrow—perhaps unreasonably so. Some commentators have argued that there are serious flaws in Arendt's argumentation because of her narrow definition of truth. For an in-depth and insightful discussion of the limitations of Arendt's notion of truth in 'Truth and Politics,' see Beiner (2008, 130).

11. It is also worth noting that some commentators have argued that the notion of truth is integral to Arendt's account of politics. See Pashkova and Pashkov (2018, 447–70).

12. D, XXII[19]: "Denn die "gesetzgebende Vernunft" geht nur von dem sich nicht widersprechenden Selbst aus, lässt also die Anderen aus. Das ist ihr Fehler."

13. Ibid.

Chapter Three

Hannah Arendt and Early German Romanticism

Kimberly Maslin

Hannah Arendt never intended "to write a book *about* Rahel; about her personality . . . nor about her position in Romanticism . . . nor about the significance of her salon." Her sole objective was "to narrate the story of Rahel's life as she herself might have told it" (Arendt 1997, 81). The aspiration to narrate Rahel's story "as she herself might have" is certainly a bold one. It is usually interpreted as a claim regarding the similarity of their stories and Arendt's intimate understanding of Rahel's emotional turmoil.[1] In addition to shared emotional upheaval, Arendt discovered Rahel while preparing a "monograph on German Romanticism" (Young-Bruehl 1982, 56).[2] Moreover, she wrote her "peculiar biography" while preparing two more traditional manuscripts on this general topic "The Enlightenment and the Jewish Question," as well as "Original Assimilation" (Cutting-Gray 1991, 229). Among the questions that were clearly on her mind at the time, the construction of Judaism in a modern world figured prominently. Additionally, many of the arguments that Arendt develops in *Rahel Varnhagen: The Life of a Jewess*, regarding assimilation and Judaism more generally, are also made elsewhere.[3] What distinguishes *Rahel Varnhagen* within the Arendt canon is less the content than the form. In short, Arendt never abandoned her monograph; she simply changed its form. She adopted the Romantic aesthetic philosophy that content should dictate form. She took on the philosophical questions regarding Judaism that connected her unique historical moment with Rahel's. How can a traditional way of life, like Judaism, survive in a modern, secular world? If Jewishness has already become less of a religion, and more of an identity, can it be constructed as an identity, as a culture?[4] If Rahel was going to tackle these questions, she would have done so within the *Frühromantik* aesthetic. She would do it with drama, irony and by allowing her dreams to speak.

In this chapter, I examine Arendt's claim to "to narrate the story of Rahel's life as she herself might have told it," (Arendt 1997, 81) as a matter of form. Arendt tells Rahel's story by stepping into Romanticism as an aesthetic approach to the philosophical problem of community-building: how can an old, religious tradition combine with modern philosophical developments to reconstitute itself as a secular identity and a political culture? Moreover, Arendt sought, as she told Jaspers, to "argue further with her [Rahel] . . . the way she argued with herself . . . within the categories that were available to her."[5] In other words, Arendt adopted the "categories that were available" to Rahel as the method of telling her story. She adopted the Romantic aesthetic philosophy that content should dictate form. In the spirit of criticism, she created *Frühromantik* biography as a form, employed irony and fragments, as a community building exercise. Thus, the oft-misunderstood claim to tell Rahel's story "as she herself might have told it" refers to the construction of an entirely new *genre*, employing romantic techniques. Moreover, her desire to argue further with Rahel "the way she argued with herself" refers to Arendt's aim of entering into a critical dialogue with Rahel regarding reason, as an epistemology. In short, Hannah Arendt created *Frühromantik* biography as the most fitting form in which to share Rahel's life story and to create a fragment of Jewish history on which to build a modern, Jewish culture.

RAHEL VARNHAGEN: A GERMAN-JEWISH INTELLECTUAL OF THE ROMANTIC ERA

Rahel Varnhagen, virtually unknown in the United States, was born Rahel Levin in Berlin in 1771, the eldest of five children. Her father, a Jewish diamond merchant, was a wealthy man who did not educate his daughters and left all his money to his sons. He died young, and Rahel subsequently took responsibility for educating her younger siblings. After her mother died, Levin found herself financially dependent upon her brothers. She grew up in Berlin in the late 1700s during a time when the spirit of the French Revolution and the ideals of the Enlightenment, held out the brief, if fleeting, hope "that one could—out of the materials of one's own particular mind and soul—literally create one's own life" (Gornick 1975, 33). Traditional constraints of class, wealth, and education gave way to originality and personality. In this atmosphere, intellectuals (Hegel, Goethe, Schlegel, and Humboldt) and noblemen flocked to Jewish salons, although the invitation to social gatherings was not reciprocal. Not formally educated, Levin read widely. She was bright but not trained, insightful yet not predictable. She "never had a memorized formula ready . . . lived in no particular order of the world . . . her wit could unite the most incongruous things, in the most intimately unified things it could discern incongruities" (Arendt 1933, 25). Her first salon (1799–1806) was notable for more than just her wit and creativity. Rahel's salon was known as more of a philosophical gathering than a literary one (although her appreciation for and interpretation of Goethe's early work remains legendary). It operated on the principle that Schleiermacher would come to call *enlightened sociability*.

Rahel viewed socializing not only as an innately human activity, "[w]ithout companions, without comrades during this earthly existence, we would ourselves not be persons, and any ethical action, law or thought [would be] impossible" but also as part and parcel of the creative endeavor, "with each particular relationship something new is created." For that reason, creativity itself is "predicated on treating each person as unique, equal and an end in itself" (Tewarson 1998, 43). Her emphasis on sociability and her keen intellect, as well as her skill at engaging each guest, distinguished her salon as the most intellectual of the Berlin salons. Arendt's text not only explores Rahel's life but uses Romantic methods to do so. Before turning to the text, we will briefly explore Arendt's critique of the Enlightenment, because in many ways Varnhagen is a product of the Enlightenment.

HANNAH ARENDT AND THE ENLIGHTENMENT

Although the relationship of Romanticism to the Enlightenment remains a matter of some debate (Beiser 2003, 43–53), with respect to Rahel Varnhagen, one thing is clear: the opportunities that appear during the Romantic Era simply would not be possible without the liberalization of the Enlightenment. The manner in which that liberalization occurred, however, left an ambiguous legacy for German Jews. While writing her "hopelessly abstract" biography of Rahel Varnhagen (Bedford 1958, 23), Arendt was also developing a more conventional argument about the major intellectual developments, entitled "The Enlightenment and the Jewish Question." Arendt examines the way in which reason, humanism and religious tolerance shaped the Jewish response to their social exclusion. Arendt alerts us to the purpose of her examination of Judaism in the first two sentences of the essay. The Jewish question, she argues, derives from the Enlightenment; it was the "non-Jewish world that posed it. Its formulation and its answer have defined the behavior and assimilation of Jews" (Arendt 1932, 3). In this essay, Arendt aspires to an unconcealment of the ways in which Jewish existence has been shaped and defined by the non-Jewish world. To speak of *the* Jewish question is already to invite contestation since there is no consensus as to what *the Jewish question* is. To the degree that a single Jewish question exists, it is likely to be—what is to be done about the Jews? This question is posed by "the non-Jewish world" as it positions the Jews as a problem to be remedied, rather than conceptualizing anti-Semitism as the problem to be remedied. The Jewish question emerged during the Enlightenment as ideals such as natural rights, tolerance and improvement prompted questions about the responsibility of the state regarding social, political and religious differences. In Germany in particular, these ideals included *Bildung* or self-formation. The implicit goal of Arendt's text is for Jews themselves to take a more active and critical role in shaping both the questions and the answers.

Many non-Jews, such as Gotthold Lessing, created bold, courageous "answers." For Arendt the paradox is simply this—despite his friendship with Moses Mendelssohn and his advocacy of the Jewish cause in a variety of different forms, Lessing's impact on the structures that pressed upon Jews is not unambiguous, owing principally to the role of reason. Among the chief characteristics of the context in which the Jewish question emerges is the quasi-hegemonic status afforded the role of reason. Arendt draws our attention to the importance of reason as a path to Jewish emancipation, as well as the ways in which reason, as a path to truth, negates both religion and history. In short, the concept of reason that emerges during the Enlightenment emphasizes humanity and tolerance; these values clearly pave the way for Jewish emancipation. Yet the reliance on reason as the universal path to truth also "removes the seeker of truth from history" (Arendt 1932, 8). In other words, if reason yields a universal truth then the experiences, uniqueness (language, history, religion) and perspective of the truth-seeker are irrelevant in the quest for truth. Thus, the prioritization afforded to reason during the Enlightenment, under the guise of humaneness and tolerance, had the unintended effect of removing the Jews from their religion and their history, in other words, most of the things that gave them a sense of belonging. Moreover, in minimizing the importance of history and religion, Jewishness, as an identity, was reduced to mere antisemitic stereotypes. In short, Lessing embodies the mixed blessing of the Enlightenment for the Jewish community. One finds in his work an attempt to discredit an antisemitic stereotype (in *The Jews*), as well as a justification of religious tolerance (in *Nathan the Wise*), but also a philosophical approach to the truth that, in its universality, negates the uniqueness of Judaism. As we shall soon see, it is another non-Jew (Johann Herder) who identifies the Jews not only as a people, but as a foreign people; thus, the unifying features of Jewishness became not religion nor history, but personal traits, characteristics, and otherness. In other words, Arendt argues that once you remove religion and history from Jewishness, you are left with stereotypes and a vague notion of foreignness.

Johann Herder is another figure widely regarded as a "friend" of the Jews. He advocated religious tolerance, viewed the attempt to assimilate the Jews through conversion as entirely unrealistic and attributed many "innate" characteristics to the difficulty of living with no homeland, in the midst of hostility. Yet Herder is also a critic of the Enlightenment and, arguably, an advocate of nationalism, who views language as well as cultural and historical context as formative. In this vein, he asserts that the "consequences of historical events give rise to differences among men and peoples" (Arendt 1932, 12). As such Herder provides a rationale for recognizing the Jews as a people, a nation within a nation, as Arendt will later say, which also simultaneously labels them foreigners, a significant shift away from Lessing's focus on "their sameness with other peoples" (Arendt 1932, 13). Arendt's point vis-à-vis Herder is that despite the fact that Herder was in many ways an advocate of humanism and a friend to the Jews, he also inadvertently laid the groundwork for anti-Semitism to emerge as a national principle. His ambition became for the Jews to "regain their self-respect, their honor, their own true national character" (Barnard 1959, 534). Thus, one of the foremost advocates of humanism and religious tolerance ends up laying the groundwork for the stereotype of Jews as foreign invaders.[6]

Moreover, he serves as a prime example of the way in which the Jewish question was defined, hence Jewish behavior was proscribed for Jews by non-Jews. In short, the Enlightenment elevates the Jews to the status of fully human, and simultaneously leaves them vulnerable, as their full participation in society hinges on the goodwill of others. Lessing provides a rationale for emphasizing universal humanism, whereas Herder laid out the logic for maintaining a sense of Jewish uniqueness. In short, Lessing hands to the Jews, a rationale for assimilation; Herder provides the logic of Jewish nationalism. Thus, the Jews' understanding of their own past, as well as the potential paths forward, are handed to them by non-Jews, secularized for them by non-Jews and they are forced to make their way in a "European secularized world" they are forced to adapt, "to form themselves" (Arendt 1932, 16). But both the process and the content of that formation is dictated by the non-Jewish world. In the concluding paragraph of this essay, Arendt lays out her epistemological purpose: "if the present is to be understood at all, then the past must be explicitly seized anew" (Arendt 1932, 16). This sentence, in part, explains the diverse forms and topics of Arendt's Jewish writings. Understanding the present requires an ongoing reappraisal of the past, not because the past will have changed, but the meaning of the past may be understood in new and different ways as the present unfolds. Simply put, in examining the Enlightenment, Arendt aspires, as a Jew, to a reinterpretation of Jewish history, one that invites the Jewish people to become cocreators not only in a reappraisal of the past, but in forming an identity and a culture.

Chapter Three

EARLY GERMAN ROMANTICISM

The term "early German romanticism" (or *Frühromantik*) refers to a group of artists and philosophers who lived and worked in Jena (1798–1804) and published in the *Athenaeum*, a journal founded by Friedrich Schlegel. In addition to Schlegel, the group included his brother, August Wilhelm Schlegel, Friedrich Schleiermacher, Georg Philipp von Hardenberg (also known as Novalis), Johann Fichte and Friedrich Schelling. They often met and developed their ideas in salons hosted by Jewish women, most notably Rahel Varnhagen and Henriette Herz. At its core, early German Romanticism endorsed, at least as a theoretical matter, the egalitarian impulse at work in the French and American revolutions. Isaiah Berlin finds self-creation or self-authorship to be central to Romanticism: "[Y]our universe is as you choose to make it" (1999, 138). "The universe must not be conceived of as a set of facts, as a pattern of events, as a collection of lumps in space, three dimensional entities bound together by certain unbreakable relations" but is rather "perpetual self-creation" (1999, 139). Frederick Beiser argues that although Romanticism is primarily an aesthetic movement, it is also a political movement in the sense that the aesthetic impulse serves a political purpose. Contra the self-sufficient, atomized individualism found in social contract theory, the Romantics foster community by collaboratively supporting the slumbering artists in us all, thus constituting the community as a work of art. In other words, the Romantics sought holism through art. In order to appreciate what the Romantics attempted, we have to understand it as an epistemological undertaking. They reject cause and effect in favor of an organic theory in which "a force . . . becomes what it is . . . through its actualization, realization or manifestation" (Beiser 2003, 85). Moreover, the Romantics approached this epistemological challenge in the wake of Immanuel Kant.

Generally speaking, philosophers sought to establish a mode of inquiry that could discern truth with a mathematical precision. In this endeavor Kant offers us the phenomenal-noumenal dichotomy, in which the phenomenal is observable and the noumenal consists of truths that we can never access. The unity of the phenomenal with the noumenal is often referred to as the Absolute. The challenge that Kant bequeaths to later generations (including Fichte, Novalis and Schlegel) is nothing less than the challenge of identifying a first principle or an absolute starting point from which truth could be derived with mathematical precision.

One way of making sense of Early German Romanticism is that the Romantics abandoned the search for a first principle, in a move Elizabeth Millán-Zaibert describes as "epistemological humility" (2007, 39). They also reject the notion of absolute truth in favor of a mosaic approach wherein the closest thing we have to truth derives from bringing multiple perspectives to bear. Each tile within the mosaic represents an experience or a perspective on truth. In keeping with this approach, a painting or a poem may come closer to conveying the truth about the human experience than any system of thought. In short, although the Absolute may be unattainable, it is the "aesthetic experience [which] allows us to approximate the Absolute" (Millán-Zaibert 2007, 39). In other words, it is through the experience of creating a sculpture or a novel that we can approach transcendence. In this context, the Romantics sought to undermine disciplinary boundaries of all kinds. Philosophy, politics, and aesthetics could not and should not be disparate modes of inquiry. They also discarded classical forms and embraced the possibility of revealing some unique truth about the human experience in letters or through a dialogue just as well as in a philosophical treatise. The form of expression thus depended upon the content, rather than the other way around. Finally, they sought to deconstruct the boundary between art and life. One could create the beauty or the drama in one's own life, just as one's life could become an aesthetic undertaking. In this context, Rahel's letters attain an artistic status that letters have not enjoyed before or since.

Ontologically, the Romantics viewed human nature as the embodiment of contradictions, oscillating between the infinite and the finite, comprehension and incomprehensibility. Thus, part of the philosophical challenge faced by the Romantics is that of identifying an artistic form that will allow for an accurate depiction of the contradictions inherent in human nature. Irony and fragments, thus, become preferred forms of expression, reflecting the "authentic contradiction of our I," the "inwardly split and divided, full of contradictions, and incomprehensibilities, in short as a patchwork, rather opposed to unity" (Schlegel, quoted in Frank 2004, 218). Schlegel describes irony as the "continual self-creating interchange of two conflicting thoughts" that is partially instinctive and partially intentional (Schlegel 1971, 176). "If it is simply instinctive, then it's childlike, childish or silly; if it's merely intentional, then it gives rise to affectation. The beautiful, poetical, ideal naïve must combine intention and instinct" (Schlegel 1971, 167). Romantic irony, thus, refers to an aesthetic process of presenting two incompatible ideas to provoke the audience to grapple with both ideas simultaneously, without an expectation of synthesis, since the resolution of our inherently contradictory nature is impossible.

ARENDT AND IRONY

Irony may be the Romantic methodology with which Arendt enjoys the most ambivalent relationship. She disparagingly calls attention to the way that dramatic irony allows the audience to impose its own interpretation and it is her use of irony in *Eichmann in Jerusalem* that earns her the wrath of the Jewish community (Arendt 1958, 335; Arendt 1963, 468). At its core, irony involves holding two contradictory ideas simultaneously. In *Rahel Varnhagen*, Arendt uses irony, in the Romantic sense to provoke the reader to think through the Jewish question, gender constraints, and the nature of truth. Friedrich Schlegel views human nature as aspiring to unity and wholeness, even with incongruous things. In this "instinct for unity" there is a temptation to aspire to "a kind of completion" by uniting things that "simply can't be made whole" (Schlegel 1971, 155). Schlegel, thus, views irony as an invaluable technique, as it "contains and arouses a feeling of indissoluble antagonism between the absolute and the relative, between the impossibility and necessity of complete communication" (Schlegel 1971, 156). In so doing, it provokes the reader to grapple with the incongruity. The other key aspect of irony for Schlegel is that the author must resist the temptation to move toward synthesis. Irony not only reveals inherent contradictions; the feature of not moving toward synthesis preserves a pivotal role for the reader. Irony in Schlegel, in particular, and irony, in general, places a great deal of responsibility on the reader. "The critic," he argues, "is a reader who ruminates. Therefore, he ought to have more than one stomach" (Schlegel 1971, 145). The notion of more than one stomach illustrates the expectation of turning the text over and over, in the attempt to extract meaning, as cows extract nutrients from grass. Although he speaks of the critic, it is certainly fair to say that Schlegel also expects his reader to ruminate.

Irony also plays a role in *Bildung*, since "[g]racefulness is life lived correctly, is sensuality contemplating and shaping itself" (Schlegel 1971, 145) In short, the well-lived life requires contemplation, and as such, is self-constituting. The notion of shaping one's Self is another key component of Romanticism. While Arendt rejects some applications of self-shaping, she certainly takes contemplation seriously, as well as its potential to be constitutive not only of the individual, but also the community. Romanticism does not aim for a text's meaning to be superficially apparent or resolve itself into a clear message. Rather, the process of deliberately working one's way through an ironic text creates not only better readers, but the kind of thoughtfulness upon which enlightenment depends. According to Schlegel "[a] classical text must never be entirely comprehensible. But those who are cultivated and who cultivate themselves must always want to learn more from it" (Schlegel 1971, 144–45). In short, for Schlegel and the Romantics, the goal of irony is to provoke others to think through an apparent paradox, and thus to invite others to become the cocreators of meaning in a self-critical way. The juxtaposition of two contradictory ideas involves the creation of distance between the two ideas, as well as between the author and her text. Marie Luise Knott argues that this detachment is Arendt's way of "holding experience at arm's length in order to think it through" (Knott 2011, 9–10). It is in this sense that Arendt uses irony in *Rahel Varnhagen* to invite the reader to become cocreator in extracting meaning from the life of one of Romanticism's most original thinkers. In particular, she uses Romantic irony to lure the reader into contemplating the impact of Jewishness, gender and a particular epistemological perspective on Rahel's life.

In the attempt to provoke the audience to think through Rahel's Jewish identity, Arendt writes, "The Old Testament was an element of culture, perhaps 'one of the oldest documents of the human race' (Herder) but the Jews were merely members of an oppressed, uncultured, backward people who must be brought into the fold of humanity. What was wanted was to make human beings out of the Jews. Of course it was unfortunate that Jews existed at all; but since they did there was nothing for it but to make a people out of them" (Arendt 1997, 89). This excerpt juxtaposes different aspects of common rhetoric about the Jews or the Jewish question. The Jews are simultaneously contributors to culturally significant achievements and a backward people. They are identified as a group with a shared history and characteristics, yet it is necessary to *make* human beings out of them. How can both things be true? If they are responsible for monumental cultural achievements, how can they be *un*cultured? The reader is left to ponder—is one's humanity contingent on membership in an identifiable group? Why is it necessary to bring anyone into the "fold of humanity" and how is one "brought" into it? Who has the agency to bring an individual or a group into the "fold of humanity"?

One of the things that makes this text perplexing is that Arendt does not resolve this tension for her reader. Thus, she appears to be describing the Jews as a backward and uncultured people; she appears to be characterizing Jewish existence as "unfortunate." In keeping with Romantic irony, she simply allows two incompatible ideas to sit side by side. She does not move toward synthesis nor does she even draw attention to the incongruity. In this case, the technique of juxtaposing the two incompatible claims renders one untenable. Moreover, the unresolved nature of the text leaves the reader in the position of striving for meaning. The unresolved incongruity invites the reader to ruminate, to inquire whether *bringing* a group into the "fold of humanity" (which seemingly places the agency elsewhere) necessarily requires the recognition and affirmation of the dominant, cultural group. The lack of synthesis also contributes to the complexity of the text and leads Deborah Hertz to find in Arendt's text an empathetic portrait while Julia Kristeva argues that Arendt seems to approach Varnhagen as if she were "settling a score with . . . an alter ego" (Hertz 1984; 77; Kristeva 2001, 49). In short, reading *Rahel Varnhagen* with romantic irony in mind renders Arendt's text more complex, but in some ways less opaque.

In addition to Jewishness, gender features prominently in Arendt's text even though she is sometimes accused of understating the importance of gender in Rahel's life (Hertz 1984; Tewarson 1998). While Arendt clearly devotes more time to an explicit discussion of Rahel's Jewish identity, gender is far from neglected.[7] In the treatment of romance throughout the text and in particular in her ironic references to Dorothea Schlegel, Arendt invites the reader to contemplate the question of gender in conjunction with Jewishness. She claims, for example,

> [a]s the youngest daughter of Moses Mendelssohn, [Dorothea Schlegel] could with some justice and without too great malice be considered the perfect product of her father's naively ambiguous orthodoxy. For he allowed her the advantages of a modern European education—then married her off in good old Jewish fashion, without her having a word to say in the matter . . . The result: she ran off from her husband and two children, ran to Friedrich Schlegel like a moth to a candle . . . she succeeded in freeing herself, in attaching herself to a man and being drawn by him through the world . . . Dorothea Schlegel encountered life just once, when she met Schlegel and he loved her. But she abandoned life again by immortalizing this one moment . . . She simply threw her life away upon a moment. (Arendt 1997, 107–8)

Arendt's discussion of Dorothea Schlegel appears in the same chapter in which she discusses the beginning of Rahel's relationship with Finckenstein. As such the chapter contains several ironic juxtapositions.

Generally speaking, Arendt contrasts Rahel with Dorothea. Dorothea had all the "advantages of a modern European education"; as for Rahel "[a]ll her life she remained 'the greatest ignoramus'" (Arendt 1997, 87). She juxtaposes an enlightened Jewish father and a wealthy one. Dorothea's father was supposedly enlightened; he provided her with an education and then married her off, without consulting her. In this excerpt, Arendt highlights the paradox that Mendelssohn could be considered *enlightened* while holding archaic views of women and handing over his favorite child like a piece of luggage. What good does enlightenment actually do if one retains the standard, demeaning views of women? She juxtaposes an educated and non-educated Jewish woman. What good was Dorothea's education, if she had to free herself *and* freeing herself meant "being drawn by [a man] through the world"? Perhaps the most interesting line in Arendt's account is that "Dorothea Schlegel encountered life just once." Arendt does not miss, downplay, nor understate the importance of gender. She presents the reader with a paradox and does not resolve it. The quintessential representative of the Enlightenment and Jewish emancipation treats his own daughter like chattel. Despite the advantages of her modern education, Dorothea does not find any alternatives to "being drawn by [a man] through the world." What does Arendt mean when she says that Dorothea "abandoned life" in marrying Friedrich Schlegel? Dorothea chose a marriage based on love, rather than an arranged and loveless marriage. Herein lies the reader's opportunity to strive for meaning, to become cocreator in extracting meaning from Rahel's life. Why does Arendt accuse Dorothea of throwing "her life away upon a moment"? What exactly did she abandon, in opting for a marriage based on love? Did she abandon her own independent intellectual pursuits, the struggle for a Jewish identity? Rahel, in contrast, walks away from her relationship with Finckenstein, opting instead to move through the world on her own and forging an independent identity as a Jewish intellectual.

Among the other issues that Arendt drew attention to in her discussions of the Enlightenment was the epistemological developments. What is reality? What is truth and how do we identify it? In *Rahel Varnhagen*, she uses irony to draw attention to these conundrums, which she explores more conventionally in "The Enlightenment and the Jewish Question." Rational knowledge is one legacy of the Enlightenment that Rahel embraces and Arendt regards dubiously. "Perhaps reality consists only in the agreement of everybody, is perhaps only a social phenomenon, would perhaps collapse as soon as someone had the courage forthrightly to deny its existence. Every event passes—who may claim to know tomorrow whether it really took place? Whatever is not proved by thinking is not provable—therefore, make your denials, falsify by lies, make use of your freedom to change and render reality ineffective at will. Only truths discovered by reason are irrefutable, only these can always be made plain to everyone" (Arendt 1997, 92). In this excerpt Arendt presents Varnhagen's preference for rational knowledge. Given that this is a text that draws on historical texts to tell Rahel's life story, Arendt is implicitly contrasting historical and rational knowledge. Events pass, rendering verification of historical *facts* an issue, but is rational knowledge a firmer ground? Does truth depend on something as flimsy as the "agreement of everybody"? What is the consequence of the failure to agree? Can reality itself collapse? From the perspective of an underrepresented group the ability to deny reality could be as beneficial as it is problematic, as we see in Rahel's life. As a woman, she can escape from her Jewishness through marriage, changing her name or moving to a new location, although the milieu of her salon collapses just as quickly. Arendt "argues further" with Rahel by devoting most of her effort to an interrogation of rational knowledge. In this exploration of the life of a woman who intended her letters be left to posterity, historical facts remain the implied contrast. The epistemological irony of Rahel is that she devotes herself to leaving historical evidence while simultaneously claiming that only the rational truth is reliable. Given Rahel's epistemological stance, the ironic Arendt thus opens the door for a ruminating reader to question Varnhagen's existence.

DREAMS ARE FRAGMENTS

The most perplexing chapter in *Rahel Varnhagen* is "Day and Night" in which Arendt takes the reader through four of the dreams that appear in Rahel's papers, as well as Rahel's interpretations of these dreams. Rahel wrote a detailed description of five recurring dreams in a diary entitled "The Dreams." She also recounts individual dreams in letters to Marwitz, Varnhagen and the Schleiermachers. According to Heidi Tewarson, "It was obviously another form of self-presentation; only this time it wasn't she who spoke but rather the dream and it carried its own kind of truth and objectivity" (Tewarson 1998, 116). Tewarson also observes that "Rahel's dreams were invariably much more pessimistic and somber than her letters. In them anxieties surfaced with an acuteness and clarity that Rahel clearly fought against in her waking hours. The letters may be replete with lamentations, but in the dreams her situation appears desperate, even helpless" (Tewarson 1998, 121). It is this disconnect between the experiences that Rahel consciously shares in her waking hours and her suppressed feelings of hopelessness intruding into her dreams that Arendt explores in her ongoing epistemological debate with Varnhagen.

That the fragment is a quintessentially Romantic form as well as a core component of the aesthetic theory at work in early German Romanticism are not contested: the purpose that the fragment, as a form, serves within the Romantic tradition, however, is the subject of some dispute. Beiser views fragments as projects in a state of incompletion (Beiser 2002, 467). Phillipe Lacoue-Labarthe and Jean-Luc Nancy find in this form the "most distinctive mark of [Romanticism's] originality" and a "sign of its radical modernity" (1988, 40). Millàn-Zaibert argues that fragments represent an epistemological perspective that is not only quintessentially Romantic, but fragments are the form that most closely approximates the view of truth embraced by the Romantics. Since philosophy is an endless search for truth, an "infinite process of becoming," (2007, 47) a form that perfectly captures a single moment or insight while simultaneously awaiting completion reflects the provisional nature of each work and of truth itself. In short, the fragment is not only a form, part and parcel of an aesthetic theory; it is also an epistemological answer to a philosophical problem. Rahel's dreams are themselves fragments: incomplete, opaque, yet whole, in and of themselves, perfectly capturing a moment, a mood, representing one aspect of her experience as a German Jewess of the Romantic period.[8] Tewarson notes that Rahel recounts the dreams as a source of objective truth and Arendt speaks about the dreams as if they have agency, juxtaposing Rahel's dreams with her will. "Night and dream confirmed and reproduced what day glossed over or hid. The dream stopped at nothing, exposed the naked phenomena and did not mind their incomprehensibility. With ease it conquered the will which was reluctant to accept what it could not understand or could not change" (Arendt 1997, 193).[9] Both Tewarson's observation and Arendt's characterization draw attention to two things. First, Rahel conceptualizes her dreams as fragments since "[w]ithout an objective and without an author" fragments "strive to be absolutely self-posited" (Lacoue-Labarthe and Nancy 1988, 40–41). As with fragments themselves, Rahel's dreams have epistemological significance. Second, Rahel's dreams highlight the philosophical debate underlying much of early German Romanticism insofar as they alert us to the implications of Kant's phenomena–noumena dichotomy.

At the onset of the chapter, Arendt cites Rahel as recognizing that "[h]er senses . . . had grown disloyal, betrayed her and her understanding." (Arendt 1997, 185). This observation alerts us to the epistemological issue at stake, by alluding to Kant's transcendental idealism. If, as Kant suggests, we can only *know* that which we perceive with our senses, through our subjective position, how does one arrive at truth if sense perception is not reliable? Rahel's response is to impose rational knowledge instead. "She must be certain that her senses behaved rationally" (Arendt 1997, 185). She simply wills her senses to get on board, setting reason and sense perception on a collision course, while Arendt observes, "[i]f she did not want to lose her dominance over her daily life, she must deceive that daily life, deceive the others, deceive herself" (Arendt 1997, 185). The radical assertion of reason, thus, requires deception of both Self and others. If reason is the universal path to truth, rational knowledge dominates over historical knowledge, as well as knowledge based on emotion or sense perception. In accepting rational truth, one denies any of her own experiences that deviate from the universal. Moreover, as Rahel soon discovers, the assertion of day over night, reason over emotion fails to remedy the epistemological problem as she grapples with the intrusion of her suppressed feelings into her dreams.

Rahel's struggle takes place in the philosophical context of an emerging debate between Fichte and Novalis regarding Kant's transcendental idealism. Kant leaves German philosophy grappling with the question—if phenomena is the observable world or things as they appear in the world and noumena consists of things as they really are, inaccessible to mere mortals—how can we ever approach absolute truth? What is the task of the philosopher? Is it to study phenomena, things as they appear in the world? Or is it to study noumena, things as they actually are, given that we may never have access to things as they really are? Romantics take up this challenge. In the "Day and Night" chapter, Arendt steps into this debate and offers an alternative that is in many ways in step with Romanticism: philosophy can ill afford to choose either phenomena or noumena. In this chapter or in this period of Rahel's life, the day represents what she chooses to show the world or things as they appear (phenomena) and night represents things as they really are (noumema), the unspeakable, her suppressed feelings of despair and exclusion. Throughout most of Romantic poetry, the night signifies despair of a personal or spiritual nature and is usually linked to modernity. For Novalis, on the other hand, the night represents mystery, the unknown or the unknowable; it is in the night that he reconciles himself to Sophie's death and finds transcendence from despair. Rahel's dreams have elements of both transcendence and despair. It is in this context that Arendt begins to speak about twilight, the time between day and night, as well as the philosophical importance of ambiguity.

In this sense, Arendt "argue[s] further with [Rahel], the way she argued with herself . . . within the categories that were available to her" (Arendt to Jaspers September 7, 1952). In arguing with Rahel further, Arendt rejects the possibility of a philosophical system based on a first principle. Of Rahel's attempt to assert her will, Arendt concludes, "[s]he could no longer trust her opinions because she had lost herself. But whether lies or truth, whatever she said determined her daily life, forced it into a specific pattern of unanimity and unambiguity in its living continuance" (Arendt 1997, 185). The attempt to impose one's ego or assert a reality necessarily fails. In Rahel's case, her suppressed feelings and experiences reemerge in the dreams that keep returning. By suppressing her feelings of despair and denying her lived experiences, Rahel is engaged in self-denial. Arendt's characterization is also a precursor to the notion of loneliness which she will fully develop in her later work.

Loneliness is at its most profound, Arendt proffers, "when all by myself, I am deserted by my own self." Thinking, for Arendt, is an iterative experience of recalling experiences and making sense of them in the two-in-one, which is to say with one's inner partner, the "only one you are forced to live together with when you have left company behind" (Arendt 1978, 188). Over time the inability to connect with one's inner partner renders thought and the validation of one's experiences (and therefore understanding) utterly impossible. In short, the self-denial or loss of the two-in-one results in the subsequent loss of thought, experience and judgment; it is an ontological condition. In other words, "[t]his is the thinking of loneliness where I preserve a hollow identity through avoiding contradictions and remain in contact with others only because all others are like me literally" (Arendt 1953, 10). Rahel's attempt to posit the I, to impose her egoistic Self or silence her inner partner ultimately renders understanding impossible and judgment unreliable because one's inner partner is necessary for thought and the validation of one's experiences. On one hand, Arendt's notions of thinking, judgment and common sense are, thus, the basis of her anti-foundationalism. Rahel, on the other hand, talks about remaining in the day. "The shame which was ashamed to name the ultimate misfortune must not be breached; it was the sole protection her life had. Others, and Rahel herself, had no business being concerned with anything but the events of the day" (Arendt 1997, 185). The shame, the ultimate misfortune that "must not be breached" is, of course her Jewishness. At this point, for Rahel, remaining in the day refers to denying her Jewishness and the feelings of despair associated with her exclusion from society. Moreover, if the day represents phenomena or things as they appear, Rahel is actively engaged in suppressing the night, the unknown, the part of herself that she would prefer to deny. It is precisely this self-denial that Arendt argues leads to loneliness as an ontological condition, an inability to trust in one's senses, one's judgment.

In the first dream, Rahel finds herself wandering around the grounds, gardens, and forest of a stately home. She could talk to the servants, but she could never reach the party, despite trying. Her companion on this journey was an animal, described as part goat, part sheep, from whom she felt unconditional love. In the final version of the dream, the animal is revealed to be nothing but a pelt. Rahel's interpretation is that the animal represents the commitment or loyalty of two of her lovers: Finckenstein and Urquijo: "The dream stopped at nothing, exposed the naked phenomena . . . It dragged all hidden things into the light" (Arendt 1997, 193). Arendt's cautionary note, however, is that noumena's challenge to phenomena marks only the beginning, "the continuity of the day was constantly challenged by the night . . . Thus it came about that everything subsequently took on the color of ambiguity" (Arendt 1997, 193). One does not simply replace deference to phenomena with noumena, simply adopt an interpretation of the dream. The grappling with things as they appear and as they really are is never straightforward. Thus, Arendt proposes a way forward, a way of overcoming Kant's transcendental idealism:

> Once consciousness is clouded, once it is no longer certain that one single world accompanies and surrounds us from birth to death, ambiguity enters of its own accord, like twilight in the interval between day and night. The disgrace which no man and no God can remove is by day an obsessional idea. Moving on, assimilation, learning history, are at night a comically hopeless game. When such a gulf yawns, only ambiguity points a permanent way out, by taking neither extreme seriously and engendering, in the twilight in which both extremes are mixed, resignation and new strength. (Arendt 1997, 193)

Thus, Arendt concludes the chapter by taking aim at the goals of unity, continuity, and wholeness. She offers no easy or straightforward answers instead, but the opportunity to grapple with truth and strive for meaning in an ambiguous world. In lieu of day or night, she proposes twilight, a time between day and night in which visibility is still possible and ambiguity is undeniable. Twilight requires philosophy to give up on the goal of an absolute and discover itself anew in the context of ambiguity. She relinquishes hope that a first principle of philosophy, a grand system or absolute truth is possible. Instead, like the Romantics, she accepts the essential nature of contradictions and the possibility that the arts can facilitate both understanding and the human quest for a place in the world. Arendt comes to appreciate *sensus communis*,[10] thinking in the two-in-one and she stakes out judgment as a philosophical concept. Judgment does not derive from a ready-made formula or grand system and it can neither overcome the contradictions inherent in human life nor arrive at truth with mathematical precision. It is, instead, an invitation to continually search for meaning and understanding amidst uncertainty.

REMNANTS OF ROMANTICISM IN ARENDT'S LATER JEWISH WORK

Although Arendt claimed not to be a Zionist, she also viewed the development of a Jewish homeland as an important development in the recognition and "integration of the Jewish people into the future community of European peoples" (Arendt 1944a, 201). She consistently refers to the Jews as a "people like all others" by which she means "a people [that] . . . have special interests and demands that we must represent one way or another" (Arendt 1944b, 357; Arendt 1945, 238). She firmly roots her political agenda in an understanding of Jewish history, and she attempts to reconstruct historical fragments for the Jewish people by telling the stories of resistance. She tells, for example, the story of the Warsaw ghetto uprising (Arendt 1944c, 214–17). But Arendt does not simply tell the story, she reinterprets the story. Instead of using it to illustrate the futility of resistance, she demonstrates the value of a heroic death. She casts it as a new beginning, in which the resistance fighters decided, "if they themselves could not be saved . . . to salvage 'the honor and glory of the Jewish people'" (Arendt 1944a, 199). She reinterprets Jewish history and hands back to her fellow Jews an alternative to the victim role. She draws on fragments of the past to create the possibility of a new self-interpretation. At the same time, she offers an alternative narrative to the antisemitic narrative of a calculating people aspiring to world domination, suggesting instead a people seeking acceptance, survival, and in some cases, even honor, in other words, "a people like all others."

The fragments that she offers are not only historical; they may also be philosophical or literary. In "Creating a Cultural Atmosphere" Arendt offers some suggestions for reclaiming "a remarkably great number of authentic Jewish writers, artists and thinkers" (Arendt 1947, 300). These efforts should in her view focus on two crucial pieces. The first is a question, perhaps philosophical, of how a traditional way of life makes room for or adapts itself to the new. She hopes that Jewish scholarship could offer "the first models for that new amalgamation of older traditions with new impulses and awareness" (Arendt 1947, 301). Second, she aspires to "rescue . . . the Yiddish writers of Eastern Europe" (Arendt 1947, 301). The reason for her optimism regarding a new Jewish culture is political, and Palestine lies at the heart of it. Palestine can provide Jewish writers and artists with an audience but also allow artists the opportunity to practice their craft—as Jews. In other words, the emergence of a Jewish culture would provide Jews with the opportunity to learn and grow from the experiences of others; it also provides Jewish artists with the opportunity to achieve transcendence. In this way Arendt shows that historical, literary, and even philosophical fragments can be collected and interpreted anew as part of the process of creating a Jewish identity, as well as a political culture.

CONCLUSION

The Romantics gathered in salons, hosted mostly by Jewish women, in the effort to cocreate philosophy, poetry and even themselves. They explored passion as well as despair, constructed an aesthetic theory that incorporated nature as well as art. They experimented with form and genre and tore down disciplinary boundaries. Fragments, irony, and criticism are part their legacy. *Rahel Varnhagen* is the text in which Arendt makes her break with philosophy and begins to experiment with her own methodological approach. In lieu of philosophy, she adopts a fragmentary approach to history since "even in the darkest of times we have the right to expect some illumination, and that illumination may well come less from theories and concepts than from the uncertain, flickering and often weak light that some men and women in their lives and their work, will kindle" (Arendt 1968, ix). Thus, if the Romantic fragment is literary for Lacoue-Labarthe and Nancy, for Arendt, it is primarily historical. The truthfulness of these fragments has no bearing on their epistemological value since as Jerome Kohn recounts, "[w]hat is crucial for Arendt is that the specific meaning of an event that happened in the past remains potentially alive" so that its meaning can be discussed, debated and contested (Kohn 2005, xxi). Her approach to history is, following Walter Benjamin, "radically fragmented,"[11] at times ironic, hence *provisional*. That the meaning of these fragments continues to be contested is essential, injecting into the examination of history an "infinite reflexivity" (Lacoue-Labarthe and Nancy 1988, 86). Thus, Arendt uses fragments not only to reassert the epistemological value of history vis-à-vis reason, but to offer an alternative to Kant's ideology of progress. These fragments are the legacy of the past, a way of understanding both what remains, as well as inviting others to become cocreators in our quest to derive meaning from the past, such that we may collectively forge a future. In that way, she hopes that the collective may reconcile itself to events and take from them a guide to the future, even if that guide is more of a sporadic insight than a first principle or grand philosophical system.

BIBLIOGRAPHY

Arendt, Hannah. 1997. *Rahel Varnhagen: The Life of a Jewess,* edited by Liliane Weissberg. Baltimore: John Hopkins University Press.
Arendt, Hannah. 1958. *The Origins of Totalitarianism.* 2nd ed. New York: Harcourt Brace.
Arendt, Hannah. 1968. *Men in Dark Times.* New York: Harcourt Brace.
Arendt, Hannah. 1978. *Life of the Mind: Thinking.* New York: Harcourt Brace.
Arendt, Hannah. 1992. *Lectures on Kant's Political Philosophy*, edited and with an interpretive essay by Ronald Beiner. Chicago: The University of Chicago Press.
Arendt, Hannah. 1932 [2007]. "The Enlightenment and the Jewish Question." In *The Jewish Writings* edited by Jerome Kohn and Ron H. Feldman, 3–18. New York: Schocken Books.
Arendt, Hannah. 1933 [2007]. "Original Assimilation: An Epilogue to the One Hundredth Anniversary of Rahel Varnhagen's Death." In *The Jewish Writings*, eds. Jerome Kohn and Ron H. Feldman, 22–28. New York: Schocken Books.
Arendt, Hannah. 1938 [2007]. "Antisemitism." In *The Jewish Writings* edited by Jerome Kohn and Ron H. Feldman, 46–121. New York: Schocken Books.
Arendt, Hannah. 1943. "We Refugees." *The Menorah Journal* 31: 69–77.
Arendt, Hannah. 1944a [2007]. "For the Honor and Glory of the Jewish People." In *The Jewish Writings* edited by Jerome Kohn and Ron H. Feldman, 199–201. New York: Schocken Books.
Arendt, Hannah. 1944b [2007]. "Zionism Reconsidered." In *The Jewish Writings* edited by Jerome Kohn and Ron H. Feldman, 343–74. New York: Schocken Books.
Arendt, Hannah. 1944c [2007]. "Days of Change." In *The Jewish Writings* edited by Jerome Kohn and Ron H. Feldman, 214–17. New York: Schocken Books.
Arendt, Hannah. 1945 [2007]. "Jewish Chances: Sparse Prospects, Divided Representation." In *The Jewish Writings* edited by Jerome Kohn and Ron H. Feldman, 238–40. New York: Schocken Books.
Arendt, Hannah. 1947 [2007]. "Creating a Cultural Atmosphere." In *The Jewish Writings* edited by Jerome Kohn and Ron H. Feldman, 298–302. New York: Schocken Books.
Arendt, Hannah. 1953. "The Great Tradition and the Nature of Totalitarianism." Lecture presented at the New School for Social Research, New York. Hannah Arendt Papers, Manuscript Division, Library of Congress, Container # 74.
Arendt, Hannah. 1963 [2007]. "A Letter to Gershom Scholem." In *The Jewish Writings* edited by Jerome Kohn and Ron H. Feldman, 465–71. New York: Schocken Books.

Barnard, F. M. 1959. "The Hebrews and Herder's Political Creed." *Modern Language Review* 54: 533–46.
Bedford, Sybille. 1958. "Emancipation and Destiny." *Reconstructionist*, December 12.
Beiner, Ronald. 1984. "Walter Benjamin's Philosophy of History." *Political Theory* 12: 423–34.
Beiser, Frederick C. 2002. *German Idealism: The Struggle against Subjectivism, 1781–1801*. Cambridge, MA: Harvard University Press.
Beiser, Frederick C. 2003. *The Romantic Imperative: The Concept of Early German Romanticism*. Cambridge, MA: Harvard University Press.
Benhabib, Seyla. 1995. "The Pariah and Her Shadow: Hannah Arendt's Biography of Rahel Varnhagen." *Political Theory* 23: 5–24.
Benjamin, Walter. 1969. *Illuminations*. Edited by Hannah Arendt. New York: Schocken Books.
Berlin, Isaiah, and Henry Hardy. 1999. *The Roots of Romanticism*. Princeton, N.J.: Princeton University Press.
Cutting-Gray, Joanne. 1991. "Hannah Arendt's *Rahel Varnhagen*." *Philosophy and Literature* 15: 229–45.
Degryse, Annelies. 2011. "*Sensus Communis* as a Foundation for Men as Political Beings: Arendt's Reading of Kant's Critique of Judgment." *Philosophy and Social Criticism* 37: 345–58.
Frank, Manfred. 2004. *The Philosophical Foundations of Early German Romanticism*. Translated by Elizabeth Millán-Zaibert. Albany: State University of New York Press.
Gornick, Vivian. 1975. "Outsideness Personified," *The Village Voice*, January 6.
Hertz, Deborah. 1984. "Hannah Arendt's Rahel Varnhagen." In *German Women in the Nineteenth Century: A Social History*, edited by J. C. Fout, 73–87. New York: Holmes & Meier.
Knott, Marie Luise. 2011. *Unlearning with Hannah Arendt*. New York: Other Press.
Kohler, Lotte, and Hans Saner, eds. *Hannah Arendt—Karl Jaspers Correspondence, 1926–1969*. New York: Harcourt, 1992.
Kohn, Jerome. 2005. "Introduction." In *The Promise of Politics* by Hannah Arendt, vii-xxxiii. New York: Schocken Books.
Kristeva, Julia. 2001. *Hannah Arendt*. New York: Colombia University Press.
Lacoue-Labarthe, Phillipe and Jean-Luc Nancy. 1988. *The Literary Absolute: The Theory of Literature in German Romanticism*. Translated by Philip Barnard and Cheryl Lester. Albany: State University of New York Press.
Lessing, Gotthold. 2002. *Two Jewish Plays: The Jews / Nathan the Wise*. Translated by Noel Clark. London: Oberon Books.
Millán-Zaibert, Elizabeth. 2007. *Friedrich Schlegel and the Emergence of Romantic Philosophy*. Albany: State University of New York Press.
Sandford, Stella. 2016. "The Dream is a Fragment: Freud, Transdisciplinarity and Early German Romanticism." *Radical Philosophy* 198: 25–34.
Schlegel, Friedrich. 1971. *Friedrich Schlegel's Lucinde and the Fragments*. Translated by Peter Firchow. Minneapolis: University of Minnesota Press.

Tewarson, Heidi Thomann. 1998. *Rahel Levin Varnhagen: The Life and Work of a German Jewish Intellectual*. Lincoln: University of Nebraska Press.
Weissberg, Liliane. 1997. "Hannah Arendt, Rahel Varnhagen and Writing of (Auto) biography." In *Rahel Varnhagen: The Life of a Jewess*, edited by Liliane Weissberg, 3–69. Baltimore: John Hopkins University Press.
Young-Bruehl, Elisabeth. 1982. *Hannah Arendt: For Love of the World*. New Haven: Yale University Press.

NOTES

1. Kristeva refers to Rahel as Arendt's alter ego, "a being held dear, an alter ego that Hannah herself could never be although it threatened her, an alter ego that she dislodged of any compassionate depth with a relentless severity that was as ruthless as it was insightful" (2001, 49). Seyla Benhabib talks about the *mirror effect*. "In telling Rahel's story, Hannah Arendt was bearing testimony to a political and spiritual transformation that she herself was undergoing. There is thus a mirror effect in the narrative. The one narrated about becomes the mirror in which the narrator also portrays herself" (Benhabib 1995, 11). See also Young-Bruehl 1982, 56–59 and Weissberg 1997, 17.

2. It is also worth noting that the German title is *Rahel Varnhagen: Lebensgeschichte einer deutschen Jüdin aus der Romantik* (*Rahel Varnhagen*: Life story of a German Jew from the Romantic period). The English title, *Rahel Varnhagen: The Life of a Jewess*, de-emphasizes romanticism, though romanticism remains a key theme in the text, as we shall see.

3. Arendt (1943) deals with cultural assimilation, for example, in "We Refugees." She discusses Jewish assimilation and the salons in "Original Assimilation" and her "Antisemitism" essay. She tackles the impact of Mendelssohn, Lessing and Herder in "The Enlightenment and the Jewish Question" as well as "Antisemitism."

4. These are among the questions that Arendt poses in "Creating a Cultural Atmosphere" (1947).

5. Arendt to Jaspers September 7, 1952 in *Hannah Arendt-Karl Jaspers Correspondence,* 200; Hannah Arendt, *Rahel Varnhagen: The Life of a Jewess*, ed. Liliane Weissberg (Baltimore: John Hopkins University Press, 1997), 81.

6. Although the issue of Herder's thoughts about and legacy regarding the Jewish question is still very much a contentious issue, according to Barnard, "[i]t must be admitted that a number of Herder's statements on the Jews admirably lend themselves, when taken out of their context, to anti-Semitic perversions. For this Herder cannot be held entirely blameless. Yet no one with even the slightest familiarity with Herder's *Weltanschauung* could doubt for a moment that he would have recoiled at the mere suggestion. Nothing was more abhorrent to his very being than persecution of any kind" (Barnard 1959, 536).

7. Part of the reason Arendt focuses on Rahel's Jewish identity is that she views Karl Varnhagen as having deliberately obscured Rahel's Jewishness, a claim that Tewarson (1999) disputes (Arendt to Jaspers, September 7, 1952).

8. Stella Sandford explores the dream as fragment in Freud's The Interpretation of Dreams. She observes that he added a footnote in 1919 in which he describes the relationship of the dream to a larger and unknowable whole as "a fragment [Stückchen] of that background, an allusion [Anspielung] to it . . . made quite incomprehensible by being isolated" (2016, 31).

9. The use of the term incomprehensibility is a clear reference to Schlegel's "OnIncomprehensibility" (Schlegel 1971, 257–71).

10. On Arendt's interpretation and use of *sensus communis*, see in particular Arendt (1992, 70–77) and Degryse (2011).

11. In this characterization, Beiner (1984, 424) refers to Benjamin's "Theses on the Philosophy of History" (Benjamin 1969, 253–64). Beiner briefly examines the connection between Benjamin's approach to history and Arendt's judgment in footnote #12.

Chapter Four

The Gendered Politics of Love
An Arendtian Reading

Maria Tamboukou

Hannah Arendt's philosophical approach to love is a rather neglected area in the rich corpus of scholarship around her work. This is perhaps because her doctoral thesis on *Love and St Augustine* (Arendt 1996) was her last book-length manuscript to be published in English, twenty-one years after her death. Moreover, her philosophical diary, her *Denktagebuch*, which is the richest source of Arendt's multilevel approaches and reflections on love (see Tömmel, 2017) has yet to be translated into English in its entirety, with the exception of a critical volume as a response to it, *Artifacts of Thinking: Reading Hannah Arendt's Denktagebuch* (Berkowitz and Storey, 2017). This gap has greatly shaped the ways Arendtian notions have been read, operationalized, defended, or disputed in political theory in general and its feminist strands in particular. This chapter is thus situated in a field of scholarship that has followed the publication of Arendt's Augustinian thesis (see, among others, Hammer, 2000; Kampowski, 2009; Kristeva, 2001; Scott and Stark, 1996; Tamboukou, 2013, Tömmel, 2017), as well as the German publication of her *Denktagebuch* (Arendt 2002). It has to be noted, however, that this field has become controversial, and, as Joanna Scott and Judith Stark, the editors of *Love and St Augustine*, have noted, the field will continue to evolve until the whole corpus of Arendt's work is translated and evaluated. It is this important gap in the Arendtian scholarship that this chapter will be filling from the particular angle of the tripartite connection between love, gender and agonistic politics.

    The chapter unfolds in four sections. After this introduction, I make connections between the diverse, multilevel, and entangled ways that Arendt thought and wrote about love. I then consider the importance of analysing epistolary narratives as archives of experiences and knowledges, particularly considering the possibilities and limitations of working with letters as fragmented and ephemeral expressions of the self. In the third and fourth sections I interweave Arendt's insights with epistolary lines erupting from the correspondence of two revolutionary women and activists in the long durée of the nineteenth and twentieth centuries in Europe and the United States: Désirée Véret-Gay and Emma Goldman. What I finally suggest in the concluding section is that Arendt's philosophy of love can throw light on dangerous liaisons between love, gender and agonistic politics.

LOVE AND NARRATIVES IN ARENDT'S THOUGHT

In the *Human Condition,* Arendt argued that "Love, by its very nature, is unworldly, and it is for this reason rather than its rarity that it is not only apolitical but antipolitical, perhaps the most powerful of all antipolitical forces" (1998, 242). She has further pointed out that "love in distinction from friendship, is killed or rather extinguished, the moment it is displayed in public" (1998, 51), also adding that "love can only become false and perverted when it is used for political purposes such as the change or salvation of the world" (1998, 52). But the question arises as to how a political theorist who has written about the antipolitical nature of love has also raised the question of "why it is so difficult to love the world?"[1] thus coining the notion of "amor mundi," love for the world.

Love in Arendt's work has thus become a complex entanglement, and this is because there are many "loves" in her thinking and writing, as Tatjana Noemi Tömmel has pointed out (2017). In reading closely Arendt's philosophical notebooks, her *Denktagebuch,* Tömmel has argued that one can discern multiple levels in Arendt's conceptualization of love—some of which, but not all, found a place in her published works. (2017, 106) Being at the heart of Arendt's philosophical thought, love is intertwined with the crucial concept of plurality in her unique take on politics: "In this realm of plurality, which is the political realm, one has to ask the old questions—what is love, what is friendship, what is solitude, what is acting, thinking, etc., but not the one question of philosophy: Who is Man?" Arendt wrote in an entry in the *Denktagebuch* (D XIII.2.295).

There are thus four modalities of love in Tömmel's reading of Arendt's *Denktagebuch*: love as "a worldless passion"; love as "eros [. . .] a desire of what is not"; love as "amor mundi" and finally love as "unconditional affirmation" (2017, 109). Looking particularly into the affinities of "passion" and "affirmation," Tömmel argues that love is not as unworldly as Arendt proclaims it to be in the *Human Condition.* Taken as a "creative force," love may become "politically destructive," but it is "nevertheless generative of human plurality" (1998, 109). In exposing Arendt's ambivalence toward the unworldliness of love, Tömmel draws on the philosopher's correspondence with Martin Heidegger, the much discussed love relation in the background of Arendt's take of love as a "worldless passion": "I would lose my right to live if I lost my love for you, but I would lose this love and its *reality* if I shirked the responsibility it forces on me" Arendt wrote to Heidegger on April 22, 1928, from Heidelberg, while working on her doctoral thesis.[2]

What I therefore want to add to Tömmel's pithy analysis, is that Arendt's powerful epistolary ending to Heidegger above fleshes out the twofold configuration of love in her work: a) love as a memory journey that connects us with our emergence in the world and b) love as a *fort-da* movement, a force of radical futurity, that brings us back into the web of human relations, the sphere of politics par excellence in Arendt's political thought (see Tamboukou 2013). How does this double configuration of love work? When in love, we fly away from the world, in search of past time, the memory of our beginning: this is the Augustinian memory journey that underpins Arendt's thesis on the unworldliness of love. But once we have sensed the strength of our beginning, we are ready to return to the world with all its disillusions and horrors. We need to love the world as it is, reconcile with its tragedies and this is "only possible on the foundation of gratitude for what has been given," Arendt wrote in her *Denktagebuch* (D I.1.4). Reconciliation is the precondition of political judgment, but also the only way to go on living, hoping dreaming and acting: "Who has never endured this power, does not live, does not belong to the living" Arendt wrote (D XVI.3.373). Love can therefore be an "antipolitical" force, but while it detaches us from the world, it also creates conditions of possibility for our ultimate immersion in the web of human relations, the necessary condition for the constitution of the political. In this sense love is "a conditio sine qua non," but not "the conditio per quam" of the political (Tamboukou 2013, 44).

But while love is a multifaceted, complex and often elusive concept in Arendt's work, her take on narratives is a well-established area that has become catalytic in the way we read, understand and analyze political narratives in general and auto/biographical stories in particular. It is through stories that we enter the web of human relations, Arendt (1998) has argued, and it is through narration that not only do we create meaning in our lives but also understand the world we emerge from, and by sharing meaning we act in concert, in-the-world-with-others. As Julia Kristeva has beautifully put it about Arendt's understanding of narratives within the political: "only action as narration and narration as action can fulfill life in terms of what is 'specifically human' about it" (2001, 8).

It is this idea of a life lived as action that can be narrativized and shared by others, who did not necessarily participate in the narrated action, that makes the Arendtian conceptualization of narratives so compelling and so relevant to her overall work as a political philosopher. In Arendt's thought, actors make history only if their action is recorded and becomes memorable: this memorialization is the role of narratives. But how is this memory constituted? As Kristeva has succinctly commented, "it is spectators who complete the story in question, and they do so through thought, thought that follows upon the act. This is a completion that takes place through evoked memory, without which there is nothing to tell" (2001, 16). Crucial as it is in memory work, narrative meaning however is never fixed, but always negotiated by its audience, the political community of remembrance that stories are addressed to.

In thus following Arendt's (1960) argument that narratives ground theoretical abstractions, flesh out ideas and create real and imaginary connections in the web of human relations, in this chapter I follow lines of love letters written by two revolutionary women: the romantic socialist Désirée Véret-Gay and the anarchist Emma Goldman. What I argue is that, seen through Arendtian lenses, their epistolary narratives create an archive of memory for feminist political histories in the making. But in making this argument, I also need to clear the epistemological grounds of what it is that we can know from analysing letters and correspondences.

EPISTOLARY NARRATIVES AS EPHEMERAL TRACES OF THE SELF

Letters are important "documents of life" (Plummer 2001) in revealing meaning about sociohistorical practices and there is an interesting body of literature about their use in auto/biographical research in the humanities and the social sciences, as well as different trends and evaluations within this literature (see Stanley 2015, Jolly 2008). Keith Plummer (2001) has maintained however, that the overwhelming, fragmentary, unfocused and idiosyncratic nature of letters cannot provide useful sources for sociological analyses in life history research. Liz Stanley (2015) has taken issue with Plummer's (2001) reluctance to recognize letters as useful "documents of life," arguing instead that letters and particularly correspondences can create rich fields of auto/biographical insights in sociological research and chart innovative methodological approaches in biographical research and the sociological imagination.

But how much can letters "reveal" about their sender? Letters are only fragments of lived experiences: they cannot be brought together by any Aristotelian coherence of beginning, middle and end and they absolutely lack the closure of canonical narratives. Indeed, letters "reveal" as much as they conceal: they leave traces of ideas, discourses and action, but they can never encompass any "truth" about who their sender or addressee, "really were" or how they felt.

While Stanley (2015) has urged for a robust analytical approach to the use of letters in research in the social sciences, Elizabeth MacArthur (1990) has turned her attention to the analysis of the dynamics of the epistolary form in revealing meaning about subjects and their entanglement in the web of human relations, as well as in the sphere of action. While written to the moment and of the moment, letters "privilege the energy that propels them" (1990, 25) and create meaning by narrating the present without knowing what the future of this narrated present will be, how it will ultimately become past. However, as MacArthur notes, a present that unfolds is narrated differently than a present that has already "chosen its course" (1990, 8). Rather than imposing an overarching meaning derived from a central character, letters open up a diversity of perspectives and reveal multiple layers of meaning in the form of epistolary stories that are ephemeral, incomplete, irresolute or broken. Yet when brought together, these fragmented stories create a milieu of communication where the silenced, the secret and the unsaid release forces that remind us of the limits of human communication, the inability of language and representation to express the world (see Tamboukou 2013).

It goes without saying that working with letters as "documents of life" (Plummer 2001) raises a quite complex spectrum of questions around representation, context, truth, power, desire, identity, subjectivity, memory and ethics, questions that are now well identified and richly explored in the field of life narratives (see Smith and Watson, 2001). However, epistolary narratives have their own take on these questions and indeed demand ways of analysis that are particularly oriented to the specificities of their ontological and epistemological nature. It is, I suggest, by working within specific contexts that methodological problems in analyzing epistolary narratives can best be addressed, as I will show in the next sections.

IN ACTION AND IN LOVE

"I was born on April 4, 1810."[3] Désirée Véret-Gay wrote to the old friend and lover of her youth Victor Considerant,[4] on June 21, 1890, from Place St Gudule in Brussels. Her twelve letters to Considerant, sent between 1890 and 1891 are "among the most beautiful and moving documents in the whole Considerant archive," historian Jonathan Beecher has noted (2001, 441) in his extended studies of the Fourierist social movement, wherein Considerant was a leading figure.[5] Désirée was born and grew up in turbulent times marked by fierce political uprisings, constitutional changes, radical economic development, and intense labor activism. As a young proletarian girl working in the Parisian garment industry, she was among those workers who were involved in the European romantic socialist movements: Saint-Simonianism and Fourierism in France and Owenism in Britain. Désirée threw herself into the revolutionary uprisings that marked the *July Monarchy*[6] from its very beginning. But she soon became disillusioned by the way the Saint Simonian hierarchy marginalized women, despite the egalitarian principles of their doctrine, and this is why she took the decision to detach herself from the movement. In August 1832 she founded *La Femme Libre*, the first autonomous feminist newspaper, and three months later she officially withdrew from the Saint-Simonian circles and turned to Fourierism.

Désirée was indeed courageous enough not only to initiate a feminist newspaper, but also to break her bonds with the Saint-Simonian movement. But apart from being a feisty proletarian feminist, she was also a woman in love with the leader of the movement she was withdrawing from. Before breaking the ties with the Saint-Simonian circles, she sent a letter to Enfantin explaining the reasons for her detachment: "I am of the people, as I always communicate with them when I see them gather in public squares"[7] she wrote. But despite her love for the people, which was immense and made her eyes "fill with tears,"[8] she could also understand that not all Saint-Simonian men were embracing the idea of women's equal participation in the movement. It thus fell on women to organize for a better future: "for us women, our work starts, to us women the duty is to search for social love."[9] It is this idea of "social love" that I have found intriguing, particularly so within the Arendtian framework of my analysis. Taken as a creative force, an "unconditional affirmation" in Tömmel's (2017) analysis, love has inspired revolutionary eruptions that have marked discontinuities in the course of history, even if such events have only momentarily enlightened dark times. As Arendt has put it, "love dedicates itself to the darkness of the heart, which lights up and illuminates itself . . . for moments only" (D VI.3.127).

It was thus in the event of being in love that Désirée dared write to Enfantin about the need for women's autonomous organization. In making this bold move she was open and frank about the emotional difficulties of her decision to withdraw. And yet her letter to the Saint-Simonian leader was a definitive adieu in the same line as Arendt's adieu to Heidegger in her 1928 letter from Heidelberg:

> It is something stronger than my will that makes me write to you [. . .] yet you are the only one with whom I can be free [. . .] I am strong enough to endure your frankness and your advice and I am not afraid any more of the influence that can interfere with my work [. . .] Farewell, I embrace you and all humanity![10]

Désirée's love for Enfantin was thus an inspiration for her political will to change the world and women's lives within it, but she would not "use it" as a tool for her politics; quite the opposite: she loved Enfantin despite her feminist politics. As I have already noted above, love can inspire revolutions, but it cannot be used to justify or ground them; it certainly "paves the way for a conceptualization of life as mobility, alterity and alteration," Julia Kristeva has aptly commented (2001, 34). In this light Arendt's conception of "amor mundi" has more to do with understanding and critical thinking than with sentiment or affect, Samantha Rose Hill has argued in an article in *Open Democracy* (2017). Arendt's "amor mundi," which I have traced in Désirée's letters, was indeed about reconciling the young passionate seamstress with the world, as it was: harsh, exploitative, patriarchal.

In the spring of 1833 Désirée decided to move to London, where she worked as a seamstress for almost two years and got involved in the Owenite circles. Her letters to Charles Fourier from Manchester Square in London, paint a grim image of a proletarian woman's life in the early phases of the industrial revolution. Not only was the young seamstress disillusioned and frustrated by capitalist exploitation, but she had also come to interrogate some of Fourier's ideas about the power of love:

> You expect, my dear M. Fourier, that love will come along to distract me, the love of an Englishman, isn't this what you are thinking? In this they are the same as they are in mechanics. They can only handle the material side or a fanciful love that exists only in the imagination. I have had lovers here, I can confide this to you, but they have only given me sensual pleasures. The English are cold, egotistical, even in their pleasures, in making love, in dining. Everyone thinks only of himself. Never shall I have the sort of love I properly need. I have made my decision about it and have settled for pleasure.[11]

Désirée's sincere and lively letter to Fourier forcefully throws us into a material and grounded understanding of the affective forces that traversed her constitution as a subject. It was love as *Eros*, passion and desire, a force for life, a mutual recognition, a movement toward the other that Désirée was missing. According to Tömmel's reading of Arendt's *Denktagebuch*, *Eros* is one of the four modes of love that perhaps never found an outlet in the philosopher's published works. But what also emerges from Désirée's discourse around desire, love and pleasure is that pleasure was for her a notion heavily invested and indeed constrained by the segmentarities of capitalism and patriarchy. It was only by following forces of passion and desire that she could envision a radical future. Her letters to Fourier thus opened up different spaces in the misery of her life in England and powerfully show that it was despite and not because of pleasure that she went on working, writing, fighting, and dreaming:

> My dear Mr. Fourier, if you were not a great genius, I would never dare write such silly things to you. I leave my pen roam free, certain that nothing can be lost with you and that, amid the complaints of this poor civilized creature, you will find a few seeds that will create a happy harmony between the pivot of my thoughts and your theory. This will be the only thing that will draw me out of my apathy and I always think about it in happiness; but a dry theory is only good for the spirit, I am therefore impatient to grow old, so that I can see the dawn of its materialization.[12]

Désirée did indeed grow old to see the dawn of a different world for workers, but not so much for women. Writing to Considerant from Brussels she remembered Fourier's love as reciprocal recognition, as well as the soothing impact that their correspondence had upon her life as a struggling young seamstress, who was still dreaming of happiness:

> It is today the anniversary of the death of Charles Fourier in 1837. I have no doubt that you are also thinking of him, like me. What a genius man, both simple and great, full of ideas and of intelligence.
>
> On the occasion of every anniversary of those who have gone, I need to remember them, be reflective. Fourier was the console of pains; for me as for the others he loved. My youth, my social enthusiasm, my inexperience of life, inspired him to put reasoning into theory and track the reason of my sadness. "You have so many dominant passions", he wrote to me and would urge me to believe in civilizations.[13]

On returning to France in 1834, Désirée worked in Dieppe first in the women's clothing industry and then in Paris again, while remaining active in the Fourierist and Owenite circles. It was during this time that she had a brief affair with Considerant:

> I guessed from the beginning your defects and your qualities and in spite of myself I loved everything about you. Nothing has escaped my memory: from your arrival in Paris in 1832 and your visit with Fugère up until the last time I saw you in 1837 at Robert Owen's rooms in the Hôtel de l'Angleterre.[14]

Throughout her life Désirée let her passions dominate her; perhaps this is why she kept her revolutionary spirit high even when she got married and had two children. "We cannot die without finishing the work that has been at the heart of our whole existence"[15] she wrote to Enfantin on February 8, 1848, shortly before she joined the demonstrations and street fighting. The February revolution initiated processes for the creation of a new body politic and it was in the revolutionary spirit of the days that Désirée took to the streets demanding that women workers should be part of the struggle for democracy; in linking the right to work with the right to vote she worked simultaneously for both. During the time of the February revolution Désirée wrote fiery articles in *La Voix des Femmes* first and then in *La Politique des Femmes*. But at the end of 1849 she had retreated from public life and she was eventually forced to take the route of voluntary exile, following her husband Jules Gay, whose editorial activities had been censored in France.

In one of her last letters to Considerant she wrote about her life in dark times: "I didn't use to like either Belgium, or the Belgians. I moved here against my will [. . .] And, well, now that I am as free as I have never been, I live here voluntarily and I feel more and more attached to them, having learnt to know them."[16] Having written profoundly and tenderly about her life in exile Désirée would also give away the mystery of her passionate involvement, but also of her recurrent disappearances from the editorial and activists' groups as well as the workers' associations she had so tirelessly worked to put together: "After the struggle I used to fly off into the clouds of reverie, where I fashioned an ideal world for myself. Real, earthly life has always been painful for me,"[17] she wrote to Considerant in July 1891, shortly before she died.

Désirée's epistolary discourse is a beautiful exemplar of the Arendtian love for the world, an expression of her need to remember her immanence in the web of human relations and reconnect with it through the bond of social love, a concept that was at the heart of the Saint-Simonian movement. Social love seemed to surpass bourgeois moral constraints, opening up paths to existential freedom, also powerfully expressed in the love letters of her old age:

> I dreamed of free love and I knew that your feelings were engaged and that the line of your destiny had been traced. But I loved your apostolic soul and I united my soul with yours in the social love that has been the dominant passion of my life, just as it is still the dominant passion of my impotent but fervent old age.[18]

By the time she wrote the letter above to Considerant, Désirée was old enough to have realised that free love was and had remained a dream only. Social love however was still a possibility, "the dominant passion" of her life, but also a central concept of the romantic socialist movements she had emerged from. Despite its heteronormative nature, the Saint-Simonian take on love irrevocably troubled and shattered the waters of their community, particularly since it was linked to sexual equality, the harmonization of sexual differences, and women's emancipation. Love erupted as a force that took their lives by storm and was differently and unpredictably unfolded in their ideas, actions, and memories, as I will further discuss in the next section.

86   *Chapter Four*

GOOD NIGHT AND GOOD BYE: SPACE/ TIME ENTANGLEMENTS IN LOVE

> I have tried so hard and so very hard to sleep, to forget that awful scene at the Restaurant, but I can not [sic], I can not! My head feels, as if fire had been set to it, and my heart, my heart is convulsed in agony over the abyss between our lives [. . .] I shall never be able to tell you how much, how very much you have grown to mean to me, how much I appreciated the love and devotion you showed me [. . .] But all the love in the world could not induce me to deny my principles, my work, my self-respect—Believe me it is best for you to keep away from my World of war, bitter relentless war, everlasting strife and battle until death. Thank you dear for your great devotion and esteem. For your courage and assistance. It has meant so much, so very very much to me to have met you to have been taken by you in a land of dreams, of flowers and beauty, but in the world of my brave comrades in Paris that I have quoted "I have no little business there."
>
> GOOD NIGHT, GOOD BY [sic][19]

The above extract from an agonizing letter that Emma Goldman sent to Ben Reitman after realizing that he was on friendly terms with police officers in Chicago sets the scene of a stormy love relationship that went on for more than ten years, which were also amongst the most energetic and productive in Goldman's life as an agitator and activist in the US political scene. Apart from being a big love in her life, Reitman was also Goldman's very effective manager. He organized her lecture tours across the country and oversaw the publication and selling of anarchist literature that supported and sustained Goldman's political activities. And yet the Goldman-Reitman amorous relationship was bursting with eruptions and tensions, high and low points, continually interchanging as the following extract from a letter written on the day after the "Good night, Good by" letter above forcefully shows:

> Ben dear, I know my letter of last night has caused you great pain. I cannot tell you how terrible I feel that I had to write in such a tune, but frankness and honesty have been the guiding stars on my stormy path. If not for their light I should have stumbled never to rise up again. I know you love me dear with a great and pure love and though I fear I do not regret to have awakened such a love [. . .] I therefore welcome your past, it has cleared you from greed and [. . .] You mean very much to me, more than I care to express in paper and possibly can express in words. But [. . .] my principles will never permit me to do anything [. . .] I only want you to know my attitude [. . .] As a man you will not want me to say pretty things if I do not mean them [. . .] write me and tell me of yourself, all you want me to know, I wish I could write you all I feel but I cannot and must

not. I must remain strange [. . .] for I would rather never, never see you again, than to go through last night's experience once more. I know if you were here and could look into my eyes, you would understand [. . .]

Good bye dear, your friend, E.[20]

Just a day after her harsh letter of rejection, Goldman would reconsider her attitude and would write in a more conciliatory tone to express her sorrow and understanding, offering friendship while still being determined to stay apart from Reitman. This is a letter written on the move, while she was traveling to Milwaukee for a lecture. Indeed, as the correspondence of this very first month unfolds, it seems that space/time distances would create a milieu wherein Goldman's love and passion for Reitman would rise from "the abyss"[21] of the differences that initially seemed to keep them apart:

Ben, my dear. It is foolish of me to expect a letter from you, after I sent you such a one from Milwaukee, is it not? I respect your silence, it only shows that you do have a deep sense of honour, though you denied it. This only makes you dearer to me. Though I waited consciously and so anxiously for a line from you, I understand that you could not write. [. . .] I want to hear from you so very, very much yet, I do not wish you to write unless you feel like it [. . .]

May life bring you joy, great joy. Your, E[22]

Goldman's letter above fills gaps of silence in communication. The initially disgraced beloved has been transposed to a man of honor, whose feelings have been hurt and thus his silence is both understood and accepted as a latent mode of apology. Goldman's change of mood is vividly expressed not only in the tone and discourse of her letters but also in the changing form of her salutations: the cold "Goodbye and Goodnight" of the first letter (24/3/1908) has been transformed into "your friend E." on March 25, to finally become "Your E." on the 26th, just in the course of two days being away from the beloved. Epistolary salutations emit signs of emotional and psychological states, but in the case of a revolutionary woman like Goldman, epistolary salutations should also be read as active technologies directing and shaping the relationship of the two parts of the correspondence. By the end of the month the tone of the correspondence had reached emotional heights again. Love had taken over and Goldman had let herself in its whirl:

Ben, my Ben, my beautifully tender and brutal sweetheart. With your own often repeated wound what shall I do? Where shall I go? My God, I love you so so much I can exclaim. Where shall I find peace? How can I continue my work with peace and calm and concentration? [. . .] I simply can not [sic] gather my thoughts to write, you are before me dear, so beautiful and kind. You thrill me so and my soul is full of my intense longing. I feel so very, very lonely without you dear.

Affectionately, Your E.[23]

When Goldman finally arrived at Winnipeg on March 31, 1908, the experience of being away from the beloved had become unbearable and it would continue to be so for the next ten years of their life together: "Ben my dear. I wrote to you en route and mailed it this morning on my arrival. I have nothing new to tell you except that I long for you very, very much. [. . .] I shall be very anxious until tomorrow, when I hope to hear from you. It's almost unbearable to be torn away from you so suddenly and then to wait for a line from you."[24]

A week is clearly a very short time span for a revolutionary woman like Goldman to experience and express acute emotional upheavals for a man she had just met, or was it? What is important to consider in the seriality of the letters above is not just time, but also space, and movement between places and spaces. In the course of a week Goldman had moved from Chicago to Minneapolis and back and had ended up in Winnipeg, Canada, where the last letter of the month was written from. It is therefore not just time or space that is crucial in understanding Goldman's swift emotional changes, but actually space/time entanglements within which a revolutionary woman falls in and out of love.

As I was following Goldman's change of moods and rhythms from day to night and from city to city my reading was becoming more and more focused on the Arendtian themes that were running like red threads throughout her amorous correspondence: Goldman's agonistic relation to issues of solitude, comradeship, and love; the importance of work and action, the tensions of inhabiting multiple and uneven power positions vis-à-vis the beloved, contradictions between revolutionary ideals and uncontrollable passions, the struggle with the asocial and anti-political aspects of love. Short and fragmented as they are, the extracts from Goldman's letters above allow glimpses into the harshness of gender restrictions that have been historically imposed upon women's experiences of love.

As I have discussed at length elsewhere (Tamboukou, 2013), love and Eros have been thematic recurrences in women's auto/biographical narratives. There is a lot of work involved for "the *Scene of the Two,* which is love" to be more than a miraculous event and exist in duration, Alain Badiou has argued: "it has to be on the breach, it has to be watched out; it has to meet up with the other; it has to think, act, transform" (2009, 70). Love for Badiou is an essential condition of any philosophical project: "Philosophy requires its practitioners of either gender to assume the roles of savant, artist, activist and lover. I have called them the four conditions of philosophy" (2009). Here he concurs with Arendt's interest in the Augustinian philosophy of love, the topic of her doctorate as we have already seen. For both philosophers then, love is an existential project, entangled in the experience of being-in-the-world with others. But although politics and love are contested areas in Arendt's thought, as already discussed above, love for Badiou has firm and strong connections to politics, unfolding counter positions to capitalism's insistence on uniformity and the tyranny of sameness: "The identity cult of repetition must be challenged by love of what is different, is unique, is unrepeatable, unstable and foreign" (98). In discussing the complexity of love, Badiou acknowledges however, like Arendt, the dangerous liaisons between love and politics: "I don't think you can mix up love and politics" (2009, 56).

Goldman's love letters to Reitman burst with signs of a lot of hard work on love. Her passion for Reitman was indeed the "asocial" kind of love that both Arendt (1998) and Badiou (2009) have configured: love opposing social contracts and normative regulations, staging little wars and micro-revolutions in the order of things they were surrounded by. Goldman was thirty-nine years old, and Reitman was ten years younger when they met. She was a leading figure in the anarchist movement of her era, and he was a wandering figure, the "hobo-doctor" of the Chicago underworld, a rough apolitical womanizer her anarchist friends never really welcomed (see Falk, 1984). Indeed, Goldman's love letters to Reitman leave textual traces of the unworldly and anti-political nature of love that Arendt has suggested in the *Human Condition* (1998, 242). Love is a struggle against the necessity of the law, and lovers always stage a struggle against the law of the family "supported by the Church and the State," Badiou has further argued (2009, 75–76). But how more difficult is this struggle of love when the conflict is not with the family, the state, or the church, but with their very opponents, the anarchist movement in Goldman's case?

Despite being fully aware of all the differences that were tearing them apart from the very beginning, Goldman nevertheless immersed herself in the play of forces that love was energizing around her: as a revolutionary spirit she was more than willing to submit to the whirl of these forces, no matter how destructive they could actually become. Goldman's amorous epistolary narratives seem to reinforce Badiou's endorsement of the Portuguese poet's Fernando Pessoa's enunciation that "love is a thought" (2009, 74). Love as a thinking process here is not disembodied or idealistic; it is taken as a force intervening in the regulatory violence of life's common sense: to think [and therefore to love] is to experiment with life's possibilities, with "good" and "bad" encounters between bodies and minds. Love for Badiou is also "a procedure of truth," that is, an experience within which a certain type of truth is being constructed (2009, 39) and in this sense it has to be declared:

"To declare love, is to pass from the event-encounter to the beginning of a construction of truth. It is to fix the contingency of the encounter in the form of a beginning" (2009, 42). Goldman's letters to Reitman forcefully unfold this "procedure of truth," written as they are on the move, in strange hotel rooms or on train compartments as she was traveling from one city to another: "'write me and tell me of yourself, all you want me to know'" she was writing, en route to Milwaukee.[25] Apart from shedding light on the dark paths of women's troubled relationships with love, Goldman's love letters to Reitman have also created a plane of consistency for the framework of this chapter: complex interrelations between love, gender and agonistic politics.

LOVE IN POLITICS, POLITICS IN LOVE

Reading lines of two revolutionary women's epistolary narratives, what I have suggested in this chapter is that their letters create an interesting archive wherein the epistolary form dramatizes and gives specificity to the relationship between politics and love. Revolutionary women's love letters have thus been read as Arendtian stories: tangible traces of the contingency of action and the unpredictability of the human condition, constitutive of politics and of the discourse of history. In acting and speaking together, human beings expose themselves to each other, reveal the uniqueness of *who* they are and, through taking the risk of disclosure, they connect with others. In this light, narration creates conditions of possibility for uniqueness, plurality and communication to be enacted within the Arendtian configuration of love in its entanglement with agonistic politics. Love as an effect of the journey of memory and as a force of life is crucial here: through love we reconnect with the moment of our beginning, thus becoming existentially aware of freedom as an inherent possibility of the human condition, a principle "created when man was created but not before" (Arendt, 1998, 177).

Arendt's correspondence with Martin Heidegger (2004) and Heinrich Blücher (2000), her multiple entries on love in her philosophical diary (see Tömmel, 2017), as well as her constant references to love in her major published works carry tracks and traces of her lifelong preoccupation with love as a complex entanglement of existential forces, passions, feelings, world standpoints and views, and subject positions within human relations. Love in Arendt's work has thus created a conceptual archive that needs to be excavated more (see Tamboukou, forthcoming). The translation of her philosophical diary into English is a much-anticipated event that will throw new light in the existing body of Arendtian scholarship on love. What I therefore envisage in the future is further explorations in the concept of love in Arendt's corpus that will bring together and in dialogue her political work, her philosophical diary, her unpublished notes on her lectures in different universities in the United States and Europe, her newspaper articles, and her own correspondence with her lovers, friends, and intellectual collaborators.

BIBLIOGRAPHY

Arendt, Hannah. 1996. *Love and St Augustine*, edited by Joanna V. Scott and Judith C. Stark. Chicago: University of Chicago Press.

Arendt, Hannah. 1998. [1958]. *The Human Condition*. Chicago: University of Chicago Press.

Arendt, Hannah. 2002. *Denktagebuch. Bd. 1: 1950–1973. Bd 2: 1973–1975*, edited by Ursula Ludz and Ingrid Nordmann. München and Zürich: Piper.

Arendt, Hannah, and Heinrich Blücher. 2000. *Within Four Walls: The Correspondence Between Hannah Arendt and Heinrich Blucher, 1936–1968*. New York: Harcourt.

Arendt, Hannah, and Martin Heidegger. 2004. *Letters, 1925–1975*, edited by Ursula Ludz. Translated by Andrew Shields. New York: Harcourt.

Arendt, Hannah, and Karl Jaspers. 1993. *Correspondence, 1926–1969*, edited by L. Köhler and H. Saner. Translated by Robert and Rita Kimber. New York: Harcourt.

Badiou, Alain. 2009. *Eloge de l'amour*. Paris: Flammarion.

Beecher, Jonathan. 2001. *Victor Considerant and the Rise and Fall of French Romantic Socialism*. Berkeley: University of California Press.

Berkowitz, Roger, and Ian Storey, eds. 2017. *Artifacts of Thinking: Reading Hannah Arendt's Denktagebuch*, New York: Fordham University Press.

Falk, Candace. 1984. *Love, Anarchy and Emma Goldman*. New York: Holt, Rinehart and Winston.

Hammer, David. 2000. "Freedom and Fatefulness: Augustine, Arendt and the Journey of Memory," *Theory, Culture & Society* 17, no. 2: 83–104.

Hill, Samantha, R. 2017. "What does it Mean to Love the World?" *Open Democracy*, https://www.opendemocracy.net/transformation/samantha-rose-hill/what-does-it-mean-to-love-world-hannah-arendt-and-amor-mundi [Accessed December 10, 2017].

Jolly, Margareta. 2008. *In Love and Struggle: Letters in Contemporary Feminism*. New York: Columbia University Press.

Kampowski, Stephan. 2009. *Arendt, Augustine, and the New Beginning: The Action Theory and Moral Thought of Hannah Arendt in the Light of Her Dissertation on St. Augustine*. Grand Rapids, MI: William B. Eerdmans Publishing.

Kristeva, Julia. 2001. *Hannah Arendt*. Translated by Ross Guberman, New York: Columbia University Press.

MacArthur, Elizabeth. 1990. *Extravagant Narratives: Closure and Dynamics in the Epistolary Form*. Princeton: Princeton University Press.

Plummer, Ken. 2001. *Documents of Life 2*. London: Sage.

Popkin, Jeremy, D. 2010. *Press, Revolution and Social Identities in France, 1830–1835*. Philadelphia: Pennsylvania University Press.

Scott, Joanna, V. and Judith, C. Stark. 1996. "Preface: Rediscovering Love and St Augustine." In: Arendt H., *Love and St Augustine*, edited by Joanna V. Scott and Judith C. Stark, vii-xvii. Chicago: University of Chicago Press.

Smith, Sidonie. and Watson, Julia. 2001. *Reading Autobiography: A Guide for Interpreting Life Narratives.* Minneapolis: University of Minnesota Press.

Stanley Liz. 2015. "The Death of the Letter? Epistolary Intent, Letterness and the Many Ends of Letter-writing," *Cultural Sociology* 9 (2): 240–55.

Stanley Liz, Helen Dampier, and Andrea Salter. 2012. "The Epistolary Pact, Letterness and the Schreiner Epistolarium," *a/b: Auto/Biographical Studies*, 27, 262–93.

Tamboukou, Maria. 2013. "Love, Narratives, Politics: Encounters between Hannah Arendt and Rosa Luxemburg," *Theory, Culture and Society* 30 (1): 35–56.

Tamboukou, Maria. 2023. *Epistolary Narratives of Love, Gender and Agonistic Politics: An Arendtian approach.* London: Routledge. (forthcoming)

Tömmel, Tatjana, N. 2017. "Vita Passiva: Love in Arendt's Denktagebuch," in *Artifacts of Thinking: Reading Hannah Arendt's Denktagebuch*, edited by Roger Berkowitz and Ian Storey, 106–123. New York: Fordham University Press.

NOTES

1. This question is included in Arendt's (2002) intellectual diary, *Denktagebuch*: "warum ist es so schwer, die Welt zu lieben?" (*D* XXI.21.522).

2. Arendt to Heidegger, letter dated April 22, 1928. In Arendt-Heidegger, 2004, 50.

3. Désirée Véret, veuve Gay to Victor Considerant, letter dated, 21 June, 1890. Archives Nationales Archives Nationales de France, Fonds Fourier et Considérant, Correspondance des membres, Dossier 8, Lettres de Désirée Véret, veuve Gay (AnF/10AS42/8/DVG/59/2.).

4. Victor Considerant (1808–1893) was a follower of Charles Fourier's ideas and a significant historical figure in the movement of French Romantic Socialism. See Beecher 2001, for a rich intellectual biography.

5. See Beecher, 2001.

6. Also known as the "bourgeois monarchy," this is the period of the reign of Louis-Philippe (1830–1848) who was brought to the throne after the 1830 July revolution that led to the abdication of Charles X and the fall of the Bourbon monarchy. For historical studies about the *July Monarchy* 1830–1848, see Popkin 2010.

7. Désirée to Enfantin, letter dated, October 20, 1832, BnF/BdA/FE/Ms7608/CdG(D)/DJ/43, p. 1.

8. Ibid.

9. Ibid., p. 2.

10. Désirée to Enfantin, Désirée to Enfantin, letter dated, October 20, 1832, BnF/BdA/FE/Ms7608/CdG(D)/DJ/43, pp. 3–4.

11. Ibid., 7.

12. Ibid., 8.

13. Désirée to Considerant, letter dated, October 9, 1890 (AnF/10AS42/8/DVG/66/1).

14. Désirée to Considerant, letter dated, October 2, 1890 (AnF/10AS42/8/DVG/64/2).

15. Désirée to Enfantin, letter dated February 8, 1848. (BnF/BdA/FE/CD).

16. Désirée to Considerant, letter dated, September 1, 1890 (AnF/10AS42/8/DVG/61/1–3).

17. Désirée to Considerant, letter dated, July 6, 1891. (AnF/10AS42/8/DVG/68/3).

18. Véret-Gay to Considerant, letter dated, June 21, 1890 (AnF/10AS42/8/DVG/59/1).

19. Emma Goldman to Ben Reitman, March 24, 1908, from Minneapolis, Emma Goldman Papers, UC Berkeley Libraries (EGP/UCBL).

20. Goldman to Reitman, March 25, 1908, en route to Milwaukee (EGP/UCBL).

21. This is a phrase that Goldman repetitively used in her correspondence to describe the huge differences between her and Reitman.

22. Goldman to Reitman, letter dated March 26, 1908, from Minneapolis (EGP/UCBL).

23. Goldman to Reitman, letter dated March 30, 1908, en route to Winnipeg (EGP/UCBL).

24. Goldman to Reitman, letter dated March 31, 1908, from Winnipeg (EGP/UCBL).

25. Goldman to Reitman, March 25, 1908, en route to Milwaukee (EGP/UCBL).

PART II

Peers

Chapter Five

Arendt and Beauvoir on Romantic Love

Liesbeth Schoonheim[1]

Recently, Hannah Arendt has been situated in the phenomenological and hermeneutical debates of the mid-twentieth century (Loidolt 2017; Vasterling 2011; Borren 2013). This chapter contributes to this scholarship by juxtaposing Arendt's writings of the forties and fifties with French existentialism.[2] In particular, I compare her conception of romantic love with that of Simone de Beauvoir, with whom she shares a relational conception of the self.

This comparison underscores the structural (dis-)similarities between their accounts. Despite the striking similarities between their ideas, they did not directly influence each other. In the highly polarized postwar period, they were associated with opposing camps: hence, Arendt and Beauvoir were familiar with each other's work, but they did not systematically engage with it. Beauvoir approvingly refers to Arendt's thesis on the banality of evil, but she does so only once and very late in her life (Beauvoir 1977, 189)—which is not surprising because of Arendt's sympathy with Albert Camus, with whom Beauvoir disagreed about politics, and because her work was introduced to France by Raymond Aron, with whom Beauvoir had likewise fallen out. Arendt, in her turn, only commented in private on Beauvoir's writings and did so disparagingly, taking issue with Beauvoir's complacency before and during the war.[3]

Ideological divides made a dialogue between Arendt and Beauvoir difficult during their lifetime. As these oppositions abate, we can better appreciate the more profound intersections of their thought. For all their differences, they started from a shared philosophical tradition, a tradition, moreover, from which they intentionally distanced themselves, branching off into disciplines such as political theory (Arendt) and literature (Beauvoir). Unsurprisingly, they incorporate elements from that other critic of metaphysics, Martin Heidegger. In particular, they politicize his critique of Cartesianism, stressing that the presence of others is a requirement for freedom and individual uniqueness. Arendt and Beauvoir break with the typically modern solipsism to show that our relations to others precede any understanding we can have of ourselves and the world. From this relational self, they conclude how institutions and social dynamics should be organized—thus giving their analysis a political and even emancipatory impulse that is lacking in Heidegger.

This relational dimension pertains to the most personal and intimate bonds as well as our participation in bigger social collectives. Reading Arendt and Beauvoir side by side, we can ask how the former links to the latter—we can ask, in other words, the perennial feminist question concerning how the personal relates to the political. That question is of course much indebted to Beauvoir who, more than Arendt, pays attention to love's potential to turn into manipulation and control, and is highly critical of romantic mystifications due to their function in women's oppression and complicity. Beyond her feminist critique of romantic love, she also positively appreciates it when it consists in reciprocal recognition. Arendt, who refrains from systematically thinking through the links between gender, oppression and affection, develops a similar account of love albeit in the distinctively un-Hegelian terminology of self-disclosure. However, in contradistinction from Beauvoir, who considers our affective bonds a crucial site for overcoming oppression, Arendt places these affiliations squarely out of the political sphere. Rather than asking where that leaves us when we wish to recuperate Arendt for a feminist agenda (Dietz 1995), I explain this difference by their diverging appropriations of Heidegger, and in particular of the notion of *Mitsein*. I will start this chapter with a reconstruction of Arendt's account of romantic love on the basis of her notes and comments that are scattered through her writings.[4] The next section focuses on Beauvoir and Arendt's appropriation of Heidegger's *Mitsein*, showing how Arendt and Beauvoir disagree on the productive logic implicit in this being-with. I will conclude with a reflection on ambiguity, a key term in Beauvoir's ethics, to argue that she could respond to the Arendtian objection that her concept of romantic love is too instrumental.

Before we start, it is good to be reminded that the texts of the forties and fifties, on which this chapter draws, move within a heterosexual framework. Assuming that romantic love pertains to a relationship between a man and a woman, Beauvoir and Arendt reflect extensively on the issue of sexual reproduction. A reconstruction of their account is hence limited in relevance for contemporary social and political issues. Although I believe parts of their analyses can be recuperated for thinking through current struggles, the aim of this paper is more modest. It sets up a dialogue between two authors whose philosophical merits have often been reduced to the influence of their more famous male counterparts. By staging this conversation, I also hope to consolidate their status as pioneers in what is now called critical phenomenology (Salamon 2018). Their thought is critical in the sense that it exposes social and political injustices,[5] and in their emphasis on the contingent historical conditions under which subjectivity emerges.

ARENDT ON ROMANTIC LOVE

Arendt is usually not read as a philosopher of love.[6] If anything, she presents herself as a theorist of political action, which she claims relies on publicity—and publicity, she argues, is opposed to love because it requires privacy. However, she also stresses the relational dimension of the self. Our relationships to others are prior to those with ourselves, and insofar as these relationships form a site of self-disclosure, they consist of an encounter with the other as an unfathomably unique individual. Arendt flips the notion of the self inside out: she rejects a deep notion of the self that supposedly precedes its expression through which it loses its authenticity, and substitutes it for a uniqueness that emerges in our appearance to others and that evades our own grasp.

This relational dimension is a crucial aspect of her notion of political praxis, but additionally, I argue, of her notion of love. Thinking about love allows her to refine relationality in the typically Arendtian fashion of drawing distinctions: the classical distinction between *agape*, *philia*, and *eros*, which she rearticulates with reference to worldliness (Arendt 2003a, 548ff) and with regard to the tripartite structure of the *vita activa*, as well as the faculties of willing and thinking. Of the various oppositions that she draws, the one with action is the most pronounced. To reconstruct her account of love thus involves venturing into her reflections on the private sphere where it is granted "darkness and protection against the light of the public" (Arendt 1984, 96). Methodologically, it is hence not surprising that we find most of her writings on romantic love in her posthumously published *Denktagebuch* as well as in her correspondences (Schoonheim 2018, 102). And yet, as we will see, Arendt's definition of love proceeds not only by demarcating its proper sphere, but also by the tensions that arise from in between the public and private space. We see references to romantic love pop up in the very places where we would have least expected them, such as at the heart of her exposition on political action in *The Human Condition* (Arendt 2013, 242).

What is love then, according to Arendt? In keeping with her inversion of the classic concept of the self, love is not an emotion (Arendt 2003a, 51, 83). It is experienced as a force that comes from elsewhere and that eludes our control; indeed, any attempt to reduce it to a feeling testifies to a late-modern self that in vain asserts its sovereignty (Arendt 2003a, 83). Furthermore, it is a force that brings together two people: while action brings together a crowd, love concerns only two (Arendt 2003a, 372; 2013, 242). Rather than a normative comment that sanctions monogamy, we should read this remark in the light of her phenomenology of plurality, where the structures of our perception depend on our modes of being-together. Arendt's point is that what is disclosed in a love relationship appears solely to two people. In this sense, it is distinct from action, where each participant contributes to the reality of phenomena by naming and describing them from their own perspective. The quantitative difference between love and action also implies a qualitative difference. When we are in love, we perceive the beloved's unicity in what is given about them: their looks, the sound of their voice, the touch of their skin (Arendt 2013, 242; 2003a, 126). The facticity of their existence (to use Beauvoir's terminology) is affirmed in love, at the expense of those activities through which the beloved transcends whatever they happen to be (Arendt 2013, 242). Importantly, facticity is mostly theorized by Arendt as the passive, contingent but unique determinations of an individual which are transcended in action:

> In acting and speaking, men show who they are, reveal actively their unique personal identities and thus make their appearance in the human world, while their physical identities appear without any activity of their own in the unique shape of the body and sound of the voice. (Arendt 2013, 179)

Arendt's appreciation of facticity is not consistent, equating it at times with our "whatness" that reduces each one of us to a set of traits shared with many others, and then with a primordial difference between bodies that is actualized in action. Either way, in action it constitutes the "dark background of mere givenness" that defies change and control (Arendt 1966, 301). Love, however, foregrounds this facticity. The claim that love disregards action is elaborated on in *Vita Activa*, the German edition of *The Human Condition*:

> Das heißt aber, daß der Scharfblick der Liebe gegen all die Aspekte und Qualitäten abblendet, denen wir unsere Stellung und unseren Stand in der Welt verdanken, daß sie das, was sonst nur mitgesehen wird, in einer aus allen weltlichen Bezügen herausgelösten Reinheit erblickt. (Arendt 2002, 309)[7]

As we will see, this element of Arendt's conception of love allows for a perceptual break between different modes of being-together while Beauvoir conceives love on a continuum of relating to others in their ambiguity, that is, their simultaneously embodied and transcending existence.

To summarize: Arendt understands romantic love as an involuntary force that opens up a space of appearance of just two people, who perceive and affirm each other regardless of their public standing. This account elicits an objection that is quite similar to the one often raised against her concept of politics: how does this description relate to those relationships and instances that we commonly refer to as love—isn't her account too far removed from everyday life and hence too idealized and too demanding? Arendt's own response would probably be that real love is indeed a rare occurrence, and one that hardly lasts for long stretches of time. This rareness however is inversely proportional to its formative influence, and despite its brevity it permanently reconfigures our attitude toward others and the world (Arendt 2003a, 470). Echoing her celebration of rupture with regard to revolutionary politics, Arendt describes love as a "flash" that disrupts the normal, linearly unfolding current of affairs and alienates us from what is evident. In this sense, love is not different from these few authentic moments of action-in-concert that still inform and inspire politics today. Could we say that in politics as in love, Arendt romanticizes these moments of authentic being-together by disregarding the power inequalities that underpin it? For sure, her project is not one of debunking the past (whether collective or personal) but of keeping open the spaces of appearance that emerge in these moments.

A more damning criticism can be leveled against Arendt's assertion of love's *worldlessness*. The neglect for the common, enduring world is the most distinctive feature of love and renders it apolitical or even anti-political. "Die Liebe verbrennt, durchschlägt wie der Blitz das Zwischen, d.h. den Welt-Raum zwischen den Menschen" (Arendt 2003a, 372).[8] For Arendt, the in-between or inter-esse refers to those shared conditions that are disclosed through speech and action; political action is ideally driven by *amor mundi*, the love for the world and the establishment of a durable institutional home for those activities that render human life meaningful (Arendt 2005, 202). The suggestion seems to be that love eliminates the mediation by a common world. In other words, the lovers do not share a common perspective or commitment to the worldly conditions under which they live. It is hard not to think of her love relationship with Heidegger when Arendt writes "Liebe ohne Kinder oder ohne neue Welt ist immer zerstörisch (anti-politisch!); aber sie bringt gerade dann das eigentlich Menschliche in Reinheit hervor" (Arendt 2003a, 374).[9] In contradistinction from her marriage to Heinrich Blücher, with whom she created a "tiny microworld where you can always escape from the world" (Arendt and Heidegger 2004, 173, letter 127), and with whom she was in a close dialogue on current affairs, her relationship with Heidegger centered on their discussion on philosophy (mostly his and not hers [Arendt and Jaspers 1993, 457, letter 297]) and their fondness of being together. Love is hence antithetical to solidarity, if we understand both these terms in the way Arendt does: the latter unites a group of people in a shared effort to improve the worldly conditions under which plurality can take place, and where the participants disregard each other's motives or pre-given markers (Arendt 1984, 89); the former forges a highly personal bond between two people who in exclusively attending to each other in their givenness disdain the world in which they life. Too much love, in other words, smothers one's sense of responsibility for the world.

The tension is not restricted to the opposition between love and politics, or the private and the public space; it also reverberates within the private space. Worldlessness does not imply that love does not require any concrete conditions: the lovers are still situated in the world. The resemblances to philosophy are instructive here. Like the philosopher who takes flight into abstractions, the lovers escape into the sensuous presence of the beloved (Arendt 2003a, 464). Both cases involve turning away from the public dialogue with others who dare to disagree with the philosopher's speculations and with the adulation of the beloved (Arendt 1990, 90–94). Furthermore, worldlessness indicates that loving (just like thinking) is not determined by the historical, institutional context in which it takes place. In the most positive sense, love has the capacity to bring about bonds that defy the institutional and social segregation of society—something that must have appealed to Arendt, as her two great loves belonged to different classes and racialized groups than she did. At its very best, love has a potential for social and political transformation by forging bonds that overcome differences—a potential that Arendt (1968a) occasionally alludes to but simultaneously qualifies as a very minor political and social force of change.[10]

At the same time, this worldlessness is not absolute: the lovers are still living in a specific moment furnished by particular political events and legal institutions. Historically, Arendt suggests (without elaborating) that the private sphere as a space of intimacy did not exist in Greek antiquity.[11] The private sphere as a space to connect with friends and lovers, with whom we choose to be with because of their "unlikeness to all other people we know" (Arendt 2003b, 208) is a recent phenomenon, one that only emerged during industrialization in response to a public space marked by growing anonymity and social competition (Arendt 2013, 38). Normatively, she asserts the right to a private space, and especially the right to marry whom one wants. Staunchly opposing Jim Crow anti-miscegenation laws, she argues that — "[t]he right to marry whoever one wishes is an elementary right" to which — "[e]ven political rights, like the right to vote (. . .) are secondary" (Arendt 2003b, 202–3).[12] If anything, her opposition illustrates her appreciation of the private sphere as a space of plurality. Yet, what both the historical transformations of the private sphere and the political contestation of civil law indicates, is that romantic love cannot create the institutional conditions under which it can develop into a long-lasting relationship. In Arendtian terms, these institutions (and she thinks primarily of marriage) provide a "house" that shelters that mode of being-together, while these institutions themselves are the result of political action-in-concert (Arendt 2003a, 49ff). In contradistinction from political action, which can establish its own institutional conditions of possibility (Arendt 2013, 199), love cannot.

The problem with Arendt's framing of romantic love as worldless is that it obfuscates the world: in addition to love's institutional condition of possibility it also obscures the potential opposition and conflict within the love relationship.[13] This latter point has been elaborated by Beauvoir, who states that women are incapable of uttering "we" because of the affective ties to their oppressor (Beauvoir 2011b, 9). The unease that is palpable in discussions of Arendt's love affair with Heidegger and their postwar reconciliation reads mostly as the suspicion that she was duped and that her affection hindered an astute assessment of his politics and their unequal social and political status before and during the war (Wolin 2015; Ettinger 1997). Even if that analysis has some explanatory force, it does not do justice to Arendt's substantial criticism of his politics and his philosophy. Furthermore, by superimposing the binary of oppressed and oppressor, it runs the risk of leveling out the many ways in which Arendt negotiates their postwar relationship.[14]

There is, however, another sense in which love's worldlessness is problematic. Importantly, love is not only a force that passively reconfigures our intersubjective relationships; it also provides a site for doing things. As we have seen, Arendt omits the quotidian from her account of love, and yet, it is exactly everyday activities in which the world reasserts itself in the love relationship. This applies not so much to the drudgery of household chores (much lamented by Beauvoir as by Arendt), but primarily to professional and political activities shared by the lovers. Reading her correspondence with Heidegger, one is struck by how much they discuss publications, lectures, and other work-related tasks (again, mostly his rather than hers). The world is very much brought back into their relationship by their almost businesslike discussion of forthcoming projects. The erasure of worldliness, as I argue in the next chapter, has to do with Arendt's very specific reworking of *Mitsein*, which can be contrasted with that of Beauvoir.

Before turning to their respective appropriation of Heidegger's concept of being-with, let me summarize the preceding reconstruction of romantic love as the limit and negation of politics and action. At the core of her analysis lies a refusal to resolve the tension between the selective, exclusive, and passive principle of love on one hand, and the egalitarian, open-ended, and active principle of action. At times, she manages to render this tension productive, for instance when she invokes love in her discussion of forgiveness. Action, because it sets in motion a potentially endless chain of events, is in need of an activity that arrests this chain; furthermore, insofar as agents disclose themselves through actions that they cannot control themselves, action also requires an activity that severs the tie of an agent to an action they did not intend. Forgiveness is the speech act that effectuates this dual break. In doing so, it cannot rely on any maxim such as proportionality or usefulness but introduces a heterogenous principle into the public sphere, namely the intimately personal bond of love that defies public justification.[15] The tension between love and politics remains but is rendered productive insofar as love provides the contingent ground for acts of forgiveness, which are crucial to the maintenance of the collective, public web of relationships. More often than not, however, love's anti-political impulse does not fulfill such a restorative function. In these cases, what remains are two opposing forms of self-disclosure and the impossibility to synthesize these two.

MITSEIN IN ARENDT AND BEAUVOIR

To understand Arendt's disagreement with Beauvoir on the worldliness of love, we can contrast their respective appropriations of Heidegger's concept of *Mitsein*. The term appears in the first part of *Being and Time* to argue how Dasein always already finds itself in the world and with others. This thrownness is glossed over in modern philosophy due to the pervasive Cartesianism that locks the mind in a solipsistic skepticism and in everyday life because we become engrossed in a thoughtless relating to each other and the world.

Two points are particularly important about Heidegger's analysis of *Mitsein*. Firstly, it starts from the question who Dasein is—a question that he answers by stating that we ourselves are Dasein, but adding that we cannot uncritically assume that the "I" is given, for instance in introspection. In line with the assumption that what is nearest is also the most removed (Heidegger 2010, 15), we should not assume that we know what the "I" entails or that it is a given. Instead, we have to look for it in what is strangest and most removed from what we consider it to be. The self emerges by a continuity over time as well as the difference from others: "the who is what maintains itself as an identity throughout changes in behavior and experiences, and in this way relates itself to this multiplicity [of others]" (Heidegger 2010, 112). This notion of the self is thus not pre-given but marked by what is different from us: from who we are at a given moment and whom we might become, and from others, whom we resemble insofar as they are also Dasein. Very generally, questions of individual identity succeed that of the collective of which we are always already a part.

Secondly, the analysis of *Mitsein* emerges out of that of Being-in-the-World. More specifically, when we find ourselves in a world furnished with useful objects, the presence of others is already implied in that world. "The others who are 'encountered' in the context of useful things in the surrounding world at hand are not somehow added on in thought to an initially merely objectively present thing, but these 'things' are encountered from within the world in which they are at hand for others" (Heidegger 2010, 115). Our engagement with the world is practical (and specifically *instrumental* or productive) and presupposes others who are similarly engaged with the world. More correctly: those others are Dasein like me in the sense that we participate in similar activities that are concerned with the world (Heidegger 2010, 117).

To be with others thus indicates the collective and practical dimension of Dasein out of which questions of selfhood can arise.[16] These questions are foreclosed, however, when Dasein slips into a mode of everydayness in which concrete others, who are encountered in the practical concern with the world, are replaced with the "they" or "das Man" (Heidegger 2010, 123). Citing typical phenomena of mass society such as using public transport, reading the newspapers, and enjoying (to use Theodor Adorno's terms) the culture industry, Heidegger suggests that in these instances we no longer grasp ourselves in our authentic unicity but let ourselves merge into a diffuse sum of others. The criticism of the public space that is implied in Heidegger's analysis of *das Man* resonated with the young Arendt and Beauvoir. The latter occasionally deploys the term, for instance in January 1940 to describe a friend who "doesn't in the least live *her* situation in the world" (Beauvoir 1992, 260). Beauvoir's early prewar and wartime existentialism criticizes how in bourgeoise society, people identify themselves with their social function and take over the judgments and values that have been posited by others—as Heidegger (2010, 123) writes disapprovingly, "[w]e enjoy ourselves and have fun the way *they* enjoy themselves. We read, see and judge literature and art the way *they* see and judge." Arendt describes how her adolescence and student years were marked by a similar sentiment, namely a profound disdain for the public sphere, which "obscures everything" (Heidegger 2010, 124; Arendt 1968b, ix). Both in their own ways subscribed to Heidegger's rejection of the public sphere in favor of an aestheticization of the inner life.

Against this common historical background of the interwar period, we can understand better their eventual qualification of Heidegger's analysis. This appropriation is most critical in Arendt, who (1994c, 187, n.2) distanced herself in the mid-forties from "the last Romantic." Her notion of praxis reads as a long retort to Heidegger, rehabilitating the public space as a place for disclosure, truth and individual unicity. To be more precise, Arendt agrees with Heidegger that in times when public speech deteriorates to mindless clichés and "mere talk," it loses its truth-disclosing potential; yet, contrary to Heidegger, she argues that truth and uniqueness arise from within public speech (Arendt 2013, 180; Villa 1995, 215). Only in the company of others, who are speaking and acting from their own position, do the world and the events spoken about disclose themselves; similarly, only when speaking and acting in the presence of others, do agents reveal who they are. Even if Arendt partially subscribes to Heidegger's criticism of *das Man*, she also considers it typical of the philosophers' spite for publicity.

This brings us to her appropriation of *Mitsein*. The term as such is lacking from Arendt's writing, but if we follow Jacques Taminiaux's (1997) suggestion that her work from the fifties is an implicit response to Heidegger, we can see how it informs her analysis of plurality. Let me stress two points. Firstly, she criticizes philosophy for substituting work for action, that is, the instrumental, productive attitude is superimposed on the performative and noninstrumental mode of engagement. Whereas *action* is unpredictable, collective, and affirmative, *work* is predictable, solitary, and negating. Philosophers typically deride action and try to control politics—the realm par excellence of action—by imposing on it the closed, means-end reasoning of work (Arendt 2013, chap. 31). Heidegger is no exception to this tradition, as evinced in his support for the totalitarian utopianism of Nazism and also in the productive logic that pervades his early work, including his notion of *Mitsein*. Very concretely, his suggestion that we encounter the other primarily in an instrumental concern with useful objects, is for Arendt indicative of work. As a consequence, the encounter is not with a truly unique other but with someone who has a similar disposition to the world as I do. The activity in which we do encounter the other as a truly unique individual, according to Arendt, is action. So, secondly, Arendt extends Heidegger's concept of *Mitsein*. Being-with-others is not restricted to the presence of others who are indirectly experienced in my instrumental interaction with the world, but is more directly experienced when engaging with others and the world in a noninstrumental, performative manner—that is, when acting and speaking. Indeed, individual uniqueness is premised on this action in the presence of others. Brilliantly taking up Heidegger's claim that who "I" am, must be sought in what is not "I," Arendt argues that "the 'who,' which appears so clearly and unmistakably to others, remains hidden from the person himself" (Arendt 2013, 179).

So far, we have seen how Arendt appropriated Heidegger's notion of *Mitsein* to develop her concept of praxis and prove the importance of the public space. I would also argue that her reworked notion of *Mitsein*—which I use interchangeably with "plurality"—informs her conception of romantic love. That might seem counterintuitive, given Arendt's claim that plurality is the condition of action, and action is the opposite of romantic love. Yet, such a territorial reading forecloses the radical phenomenological nature of Arendt's project, namely to rethink all phenomena as constituted by (or at the very least corresponding to) a mode of being-with (Markell 2011). What matters is that both action and love are modes of being-with that disclose people in their uniqueness—a unicity that appears to (an) other(s). Crucially, and in clear distinction from Heidegger, *Mitsein* is not restricted to the productive logic that negates what exists but manifests more clearly in an open-ended affirmation of who and what exists in their singularity. The excision of any notion of instrumentality from the self-disclosure that is typical for both love and action also means that love is emptied of any connotation of a shared, future-oriented project. It is exactly this dimension that is crucial to Beauvoir's appropriation of *Mitsein* and her notion of romantic love.

Like Arendt, Beauvoir retains her critique of social conformity. While Arendt relates her criticism to the truth-disclosing potential of speech and action, Beauvoir links it to the status of values. Hence, we can hear the echo of Heidegger's *das Man* when she disapprovingly writes about women who "adopt without discussion the opinions and values recognized by their husband or their lover" (Beauvoir 2011c, 40; Bauer 2001). Very generally, Heidegger's analysis is incorporated into her social critique of oppression. Beauvoir deploys the term *Mitsein* at various key moments in the first volume of *The Second Sex*. In fact, she politicizes the concept to stress how equality comes about through shared, teleological activities, picking up the productive dimension that was dismissed by Arendt. She uses the concept in two ways. In the first, and wider sense, she deploys *Mitsein* to refer to humanity as a collective that engages in a self-transcending and world-building activity. Importantly, she uses the term normatively, arguing that women have hitherto been barred from this activity and hence excluded from humanity.[17] So, for instance, by "readily agree[ing] to exalt the woman as Other in order to make her alterity absolute and irreducible, [various civilizations including our own have] refuse[d] her access to the human *Mitsein*" (Beauvoir 2011b, 80, n.3; page 86). This exclusion has psychological-subjective implications, in the sense that women are denied full subjectivity and develop a range of coping mechanisms that are often detrimental and inauthentic; it also has political-cultural implications insofar as women live surrounded by institutions and cultural artifacts that exacerbate their alienation and oppression.[18] Women's liberation and the challenges that entails are described by Beauvoir as "the difficulties women are up against just when, trying to escape the sphere they have been assigned until now, they seek to be part of the human *Mitsein*" (Beauvoir 2011b, 17). Women's struggle for independence issues from an unfulfilled desire (to articulate it in a more Hegelian interpretation) for goal-oriented action and to shape the world they live in. In this sense, its impulse is very well formulated by Frantz Fanon: "I wanted quite simply to be a man among men. I would have liked to enter our world young and sleek, a world we could build together" (Fanon 2008, 92).

When Beauvoir is using the term *Mitsein*, she does so very much in a "horizontal" manner, referring to the collective practices in which we resemble other people (Loidolt 2017, 161). These practices show how *Dasein* projects itself into the future and makes itself into something different from what it is at present. However, because of her anthropological approach she does not quite provide a hermeneutics in the way that Heidegger and Arendt do: the latter two sketch the historical changes in the self-constituting activities we engage in, while Beauvoir grounds self-transcendence in an a-historical notion of subjectivity.[19] This notion is informed by her reading of Hegel's master-slave dialectic. Beauvoir was highly aware of the tension between Hegel and Heidegger. This pertains to their conflicting notions of history (Beauvoir 2009, 319, 320; Heidegger 2010, 82) but for the current discussion I divorce the issue of historicity from that of intersubjectivity, on which the two authors also differed.[20] Reflecting on the origins of women's oppression as rooted in a process of othering, Beauvoir writes:

> These phenomena [of othering] could not be understood if human reality [réalité humaine, or Dasein] were solely a *Mitsein* based on solidarity and friendship. On the contrary, they become clear if, following Hegel, a fundamental hostility to any other consciousness is found in consciousness itself; the subject posits itself only in opposition; it asserts itself as the essential and sets up the other as inessential, as the object. (Beauvoir 2011b, 7)

In other words, by means of Hegel's master-slave dialectic Beauvoir inserts a "vertical" dimension into *Mitsein,* namely one that asserts the selfhood that appears against the background of a collective engagement with the world. This individuality emerges from within a relationship that is antagonistic and pertains to consciousnesses. The struggle for recognition implies the objectification of the other, and women's oppression and complicity is the result of a long historical process in which intersubjective recognition has been consistently denied to them. Two points are important about Beauvoir's appropriation of the master-slave dialectic for her discussion of romantic love. Firstly, romantic love is the privileged site for the drama of the struggle for recognition. Without explicitly giving reasons, Beauvoir mainly thematizes the intersubjective conflict by elaborating on love relationships. Tellingly, she takes the epigraph for her first novel *She Came to Stay*—the dramatized, autobiographical story of a love triangle going awry—from the sections on the master-slave dialectic in the *Phenomenology of Spirit* (Beauvoir 2009, 270). Her second novel, *The Blood of Others*, revolves around an unrequited love that she also thematizes in Hegelian terms as a "*struggle*" and as a "subject-object relationship" (Beauvoir 2009, 321, 322). Furthermore, she deploys the master-slave dialectic to indicate not only the conflictual dimension of affection, but also the possibility to overcome hostility. Beauvoir holds that the two opposing consciousnesses can surmount the impulse to objectify the other. This reconciliation entails a mutual recognition that also informs Beauvoir's positive ideal of romantic love. Secondly, she increasingly links the failure of recognition and the objectification of the other to social oppression. The change is already visible in the transition from her first to the second novel in 1941: the first focuses on the struggle for recognition between three lovers and locates the enmity very much in a desire to "*suppress* the other's consciousness [which] is a bit puerile"; the second pictures an unrequited love that considers the social dimension (Beauvoir 2009, 323). In *The Second Sex* (1949) she refines the thesis that patriarchy fixes women in the subordinate position of the other, and thus bars the chances of reconciliation and of attaining full, reciprocal recognition. As Beauvoir continues to privilege romantic love as the site for intersubjective conflict and starts to perceive this hostility increasingly as the effect of social oppression, it is not surprising that *The Second Sex* emphatically argues that patriarchy undermines truly reciprocal love relationships.

To return to the discussion of *Mitsein*: Beauvoir contrasts it to the Hegelian opposition between consciousnesses.[21] She writes for instance about "the human reality that is at once *Mitsein* and separation" (Beauvoir 2011b, 57). This brings me to the second, narrower sense in which she uses the term, namely to refer to the couple as "an original *Mitsein*" (Beauvoir 2011b, 47; 9). The couple is part of the wider collective and precedes (logically and historically) the conflict between consciousnesses that Beauvoir articulates in Hegelian terms and that originates in patriarchy. In the original couple, men and women work together for a shared goal. At times, she seems to suggest that this goal consists in the mere survival of the species, highlighting the mutual dependency of men and women for sexual reproduction. Yet Heidegger distinguishes the human species from Dasein (to which being-with belongs): the former moves within biology and provides a positivist definition of what a human being is, while the latter defies the closure of the sciences and is marked by being nothing but what it makes itself into[22]—a distinction that she is aware of (Beauvoir 2009, 319). Hence, her comments on the couple as the original *Mitsein* must point to something different from mere biological survival. Rather, she underscores the possibility for men and women to embark on a shared project, one through which they can shape their future together. This relationship is, as we have seen, one of friendship and solidarity, two terms that indicate a shared orientation to the world. In clear distinction from Arendt, Beauvoir defines the *Mitsein* of the couple by worldliness.

Of the two authors, Arendt more thoroughly reworks the notion of *Mitsein*, distinguishing various forms (action, love, friendship) and expanding it into a condition for phenomena and modes of self-disclosure. Yet, from a Beauvoirian perspective, the Arendtian critique that an instrumental comportment bars the encounter with the unique other, forecloses the possibility that the lovers relate to each other primarily through the projects they collectively pursue.

BEAUVOIR ON AMBIGUITY

Could we turn the tables on Beauvoir, and ask from an Arendtian perspective if she fails to thematize the encounter with the other? More specifically, Arendt's account of love underlines how facticity can be celebrated and affirmed, hinting in its own way at the other's uniqueness. The question thus arises if Beauvoir's account of love can accommodate this dimension of love—a question particularly important because it includes the erotic (which remains very underdeveloped in Arendt's reflections). By means of conclusion, I want to argue that she can. Love consists, she argues, both in the pursuit of common goals in a world shared with many others, as well as the sensuous encounter with the singular other (Beauvoir 2011a, 78). Indeed, while the former is a form of friendship that is presupposed in love, the latter sets love apart from other relationships.

Beauvoir primarily develops this point as a feminist rejoinder to those who object that women's emancipation will spell the end of romantic love and replace it with camaraderie. For instance, in the short essay "It's about Time Women Put a New Face on Love" (1950), she suggests that reciprocity between the lovers entails that "the two share the same aims in life or can reconcile them" (Beauvoir 2011a, 78). The Hegelian language should not confuse us that what is at stake here for Beauvoir is a being-with marked by worldliness. Put more precisely, the ideal of comradeship that she outlines here recuperates the original *Mitsein* by overcoming the patriarchal conflation of love with female submission and deconstructing oppressive representations of women. In addition to friendship—and here she addresses the anti-feminist fears of the demise of romance—truly reciprocal love also affirms the other person in their facticity, that is, the concrete, given, and often corporeal determinations of their existence.

> It is this love that is the most complete relationship possible with another person: to see him both in his impersonal activity and in his irreplaceable reality; as builder and as object; as all that transcends himself and as finite creature. (Beauvoir 2011a, 78)

Love is the most complete relationship because it affirms the other and oneself in our *ambiguity*. This key notion is deployed by Beauvoir to describe human existence as both corporeal, given, and finite, as well as conscious, in a constant process of becoming, and open-ended. Typically, she uses the term to describe how human existence is both immanent and transcendent, and how we are at once object and subject. These binaries are crucial in her critique of patriarchy, as men have monopolized the second term of each of these pairs and women have been systematically reduced to the first. Although this asymmetry was caused by the power wielded by men over women, the denial of one's own and others' ambiguity has been detrimental to both men and women. The reduction of the feminine to an object corresponded to the very few opportunities women are provided with to realize themselves in a process of becoming—opportunities that are determined by gender roles (such as motherhood) or material needs (such as renumerated labor for women who have to be financially independent). The masculine arrogation of subjectivity results, Beauvoir argues, in the denial of corporeality: disavowing that he is marked by his body, he alienates this part of his existence and projects it onto women.

Importantly, the ideal love that Beauvoir describes remedies this affliction. It brings about a relationship in which both women and men relate to each other as free subjects with their own projects to pursue, as well as finite objects, shaped by their specific corporeality. This ideal love thus restores the ambiguity that defines human existence. It also includes but is not exhausted by the mode of relating that Arendt names love, namely the concrete, sensuous presence of the other that points to their uniqueness.

> In order to believe in the importance of the world and his own place in it, each must find himself in his work and in his individuality, as a minute particle of humanity and as an irreplaceable being. And it is love given and love received that will be the most powerful aid in bringing about this paradoxical synthesis. (Beauvoir 2011a, 77)

Love forges a bond because of the future the lovers seek to create together, but also because of what each one happens to be in their singularity. To the extent that love asserts the two opposing dimensions of human existence at the same time, it is marked by a tension that is never quite resolved. The tension that Beauvoir locates at the core of her anthropology and turns into the main tenet of her ethics, is situated by Arendt in the incommensurability between the private and public space, between the different modes of plurality that are linked to institutions and other historical conditions. As a consequence, Beauvoir ascribes love a clear role in political and social emancipation, namely to integrate each one into the totality of humanity while maintaining their individuality, that Arendt would not be willing to grant it.

BIBLIOGRAPHY

Arendt, Hannah. 1966. *The Origins of Totalitarianism*. 3rd edition with added prefaces. New York: Harcourt Brace and Jovanovich.
———. 1968a. "Karl Jaspers: A Laudatio." In *Men in Dark Times*, translated by Clara Winston and Richard Winston, 71–80. San Diego: Harcourt Brace and Jovanovich.
———. 1968b. *Men in Dark Times*. San Diego: Harcourt Brace and Jovanovich.
———. 1968c. "On Humanity in Dark Times: Thoughts about Lessing." In *Men in Dark Times*, translated by Clara Winston and Richard Winston, 3–31. San Diego: Harcourt Brace and Jovanovich.
———. 1974. *Rahel Varnhagen: The Life of a Jewess*. Translated by Richard Winston and Clara Winston. Revised edition. San Diego: Harcourt Brace Jovanovich.
———. 1978. *The Life of the Mind*. San Diego: Harcourt Brace Jovanovich.
———. 1984. *On Revolution*. London: Penguin Books.
———. 1990. "Philosophy and Politics," *Social Research* 57, no. 1: 73–103.
———. 1994a. "Concern with Politics in Recent European Philosophical Thought." In *Essays in Understanding, 1930–1954: Formation, Exile, and Totalitarianism*, edited by Jerome Kohn, 428–47. New York: Schocken Books.
———. 1994b. "French Existentialism." In *Essays in Understanding, 1930–1954: Formation, Exile, and Totalitarianism*, edited by Jerome Kohn, 188–93. New York: Schocken Books.
———. 1994c. "What Is Existential Philosophy?" In *Essays in Understanding, 1930–1954: Formation, Exile, and Totalitarianism*, translated by Rita Kimber and Robert Kimber, 163–87. New York: Schocken Books.
———. 1996. *Love and Saint Augustine*. Chicago: University of Chicago Press.
———. 2002. *Vita Activa, Oder Vom Tätigen Leben*. München: Piper.
———. 2003a. *Denktagebuch*. Edited by Ursula Ludz. 2 vols. München: Piper.
———. 2003b. "Reflections on Little Rock." In *Responsibility and Judgment*, edited by Jerome Kohn, 193–213. New York: Schocken Books.
———. 2005. *The Promise of Politics*. New York: Schocken Books.
———. 2006. "Tradition and the Modern Age." In *Between Past and Future: Eighth Exercises in Political Thought*, edited by Jerome Kohn, 17–40. London: Penguin.
———. 2013. *The Human Condition*. 2nd ed. Chicago: University of Chicago Press.
Arendt, Hannah, and Martin Heidegger. 2004. *Letters, 1925–1975*. Edited by Ursula Ludz. Translated by Andrew Shields. New York: Harcourt Brace and Jovanovich.
Arendt, Hannah, and Karl Jaspers. 1993. *Correspondence 1926–1969*. Edited by Lotte Köhler and Hans Saner. Translated by Rita Kimber and Robert Kimber. San Diego: Harcourt Brace.
Arendt, Hannah, and Mary McCarthy. 1995. *Between Friends: The Correspondence of Hannah Arendt and Mary McCarthy, 1949–1975*. Edited by Carol Brightman. New York: Harcourt Brace and Jovanovich.

Bartky, Sandra Lee. 1975. "Toward a Phenomenology of Feminist Consciousness." *Social Theory and Practice* 3, no. 4: 425–39.
Bauer, Nancy. 2001. "Being-with as Being-against: Heidegger Meets Hegel in The Second Sex." *Continental Philosophy Review* 34, no. 2: 129–49. https://doi.org/10.1023/A:1017968905153.
Beauvoir, Simone de. 1968. *Force of Circumstance*. Translated by Richard Howard. London: Penguin Books.
———. 1977. *All Said and Done*. Translated by Patrick O'Brian. London: Penguin.
———. 1992. *Letters to Sartre*. Edited by Sylvie Le Bon de Beauvoir. Translated by Quintin Hoare. London: Vintage Books.
———. 1999. *America Day by Day*. Translated by Carol Cosman. Oakland, CA: University of California Press.
———. 2009. *Wartime Diary*. Edited by Margaret A. Simons and Sylvie Le Bon de Beauvoir. Translated by Anne Deing Cordero. The Beauvoir Series. Urbana/Chicago/Springfield: University of Illinois Press.
———. 2011a. "It's about Time Women Put a New Face on Love." In *Feminist Writings*, edited by Margaret A. Simons and Marybeth Timmermann, 76–80. The Beauvoir Series. Urbana: University of Illinois Press.
———. 2011b. *The Second Sex*. Translated by Constance Borde and Sheila Malovany-Chevalier. New York: Vintage Books.
———. 2011c. *The Ethics of Ambiguity*. Translated by Bernard Frechtman. New York: Open Road Media.
Borren, Marieke. 2013. "'A Sense of the World': Hannah Arendt's Hermeneutic Phenomenology of Common Sense." *International Journal of Philosophical Studies* 21, no. 2: 225–55. https://doi.org/10.1080/09672559.2012.743156.
Brander, Stefanie. 1990. "Philosophinnen Im Gespräch. Hannah Arendt, Simone de Beauvoir - Eine Fiktive Begegnung." *Die Philosophin*, no. 1 (March): 57–73.
Canovan, Margaret. 1992. *Hannah Arendt: A Reinterpretation of Her Political Thought*. Cambridge: Cambridge University Press.
Dietz, Mary. 1995. "Feminist Receptions of Hannah Arendt." In *Feminist Interpretations of Hannah Arendt*, edited by Bonnie Honig, 17–50. Philadelphia PA: Pennsylvania State university press.
Ettinger, Elzbieta. 1997. *Hannah Arendt/Martin Heidegger*. New Haven: Yale University Press.
Fanon, Frantz. 2008. *Black Skin, White Masks*. Translated by Richard Philcox. New York: Grove Press.
Foucault, Michel. 2012. *The Use of Pleasure*. Translated by Robert Hurley. Vol. 2. 4 vols. *The History of Sexuality*. London: Penguin Books.
Gothlin, Eva. 2003. "Reading Simone de Beauvoir with Martin Heidegger." In *The Cambridge Companion to Simone de Beauvoir*, edited by Claudia Card, 45–65. Cambridge: Cambridge University Press.
Heidegger, Martin. 2010. *Being and Time*. New York: SUNY Press.
hooks, bell. 2018. *All About Love: New Visions*. New York: HarperCollins.
Loidolt, Sophie. 2017. *Phenomenology of Plurality: Hannah Arendt on Political Intersubjectivity*. New York: Routledge.

Markell, Patchen. 2011. "Arendt's Work: On the Architecture of The Human Condition." *College Literature* 38, no. 1: 15–44.
Salamon, Gayle. 2018. "What's Critical about Critical Phenomenology?" *Puncta. Journal of Critical Phenomenology* 1, no. 1: 8–17.
Schoonheim, Liesbeth. 2018. "Among Lovers: Love and Personhood in Hannah Arendt." *Arendt Studies* no. 2 (August): 99–124. https://doi.org/10.5840/arendtstudies20187514.
Taminiaux, Jacques. 1997. *The Thracian Maid and the Professional Thinker: Arendt and Heidegger*. Translated by Michael Gendre. New York: SUNY Press.
Tömmel, Tatjana Noemi. 2013. *Wille Und Passion: Der Liebesbegriff Bei Heidegger Und Arendt*. Berlin: Suhrkamp.
———. 2017. "Vita Passiva: Love in Arendt's Denktagebuch." In *Artifacts of Thinking: Reading Hannah Arendt's Denktagebuch*, edited by Roger Berkowitz and Ian Storey, 106–23. New York: Fordham University Press.
Vasterling, Veronica. 2011 "Political Hermeneutics: Hannah Arendt's Contribution to Hermeneutic Philosophy." In: *Gadamer's Hermeneutics and the Art of Conversation*, edited by A. Wiercinski, 571–82. Berlin: LIT Verlag.
Villa, Dana. 1995. *Arendt and Heidegger: The Fate of the Political*. Princeton: Princeton University Press.
Weiss, Gail, Gayle Salamon, and Ann V. Murphy. 2019. *50 Concepts for a Critical Phenomenology*. Chicago: Northwestern University Press.
Wolin, Richard. 2015. *Heidegger's Children: Hannah Arendt, Karl Löwith, Hans Jonas, and Herbert Marcuse*. 2nd edition, with A new preface by the author. Princeton: Princeton University Press.
Young, Iris Marion. 2011. *Justice and the Politics of Difference*. Princeton: Princeton University Press.

NOTES

1. Research for this essay was funded by FWO Research Foundation—Flanders (grant nr. 63366).

2. Arendt extensively contributed to the popularity of existentialism in North America. See Arendt 1994c; 1994b; 1994a.

3. This is particularly clear in Arendt's critique of Beauvoir's wartime autobiography. Arendt and McCarthy 1995, 172, 176; On the prewar complacency of the French intelligentsia, see Arendt 1994b, 188–89. See also Brander (1990, 59–60) for their postwar meeting in New York.

4. Little has been published on romantic love in Arendt, except Tömmel (2013; 2017).

5. In this sense, their work resembles Young's, when she writes that "[m]ethodological and epistemological issues do arise in the course of this study, but I always treat them as interruptions of the substantive normative and social issues at hand" (Young 2011, 8).

6. In fact, questions of love bookend Arendt's oeuvre: her dissertation dealt with Augustine's concept of love (Arendt 1996), her Habilitation with Rahel Varnhagen, including Varnhagen's marriage and love affair (Arendt 1974); and she dedicated again attention to love in the second volume of *Life of the Mind* (Arendt 1978).

7. "This means, however, that the sharp eye of love blocks out all the aspects and qualities to which we owe our position and standing in the world, that it sees what is otherwise only seen with, in a purity detached from all worldly relationships." All translations mine.

8. "Love burns, pierces like lightning the in-between, i.e. the world-space between people."

9. "Love without children or without a new world is always destructive (anti-political!); but precisely then it brings forth what is actually human in purity."

10. For a more contemporary take on this issue, see hooks (2018).

11. But see Foucault (2012, 143–51, esp. pp. 149–50).

12. For Beauvoir's contending view, see America Day by Day (1999, 241).

13. This problem does not emerge in the context of friendship; quite the opposite, friendship insofar it consists in a dialogue about the world, also states explicitly the different and conflicting identities imposed on the friends (Arendt 1968c, 23).

14. I do not mean to suggest that Beauvoir's use of the term oppression does so: indeed, the second half of *The Second Sex* reads as a long meditation on the many ways in which women subvert, resist, and enact the gendered norms imposed on them.

15. Paradoxically, this personal bond can be generalized to what Arendt calls 'respect': like love, respect concerns the person regardless of their actions. It is unclear how the self-disclosure of love is extended to respect. Rather, I believe her reference to respect is connected to another 'train of thought' (Canovan 1992) connected to her observation that the late-modern bureaucratic state fails to consider its subjects as persons and is hence incapable of making exceptions in the enforcement of law.

16. Loidolt, citing Bedorf (2011) refers to these two dimensions as vertical and horizontal approaches to *Mitsein* (Loidolt 2017, 161).

17. My reading here disagrees with Nancy Bauer's assertion that "in none of these places [Beauvoir's appeals to *Mitsein* in *The Second Sex*] does she suggest that Mitsein has some obviously positive or normative value" because I disagree with her juxtaposition of a normative and an ontological claim (2001, 141). Exactly insofar we are ontologically thrown into our relations with others, do we have a normative duty to establish the conditions under which this Mitsein can actualize itself.

18. These issues have been more extensively discussed after Beauvoir and often in dialogue with other phenomenologies of oppression such as Fanon's, for instance by Bartky (1975, chaps. 3, 4); Young (2011, chap. 2); Weiss, Salamon, and Murphy (2019).

19. Beauvoir (1968, 202) eventually criticized *The Second Sex* for her idealist, ahistorical notion of the self.

20. Beauvoir's Marxism marks also a divergence with Arendt (2006).

21. Beauvoir's attempt to incorporate the two authors was common endeavour in French mid-century philosophy. See for instance Gothlin (2003, 58).

22. Thanks to Simon Truwant for pointing out this distinction. See Heidegger (2010, para. 10).

Chapter Six

Arendt and Hans Jonas
Acting and Thinking after Heidegger

Eric Stéphane Pommier

It is customary to underline the friendship that united Hannah Arendt and Hans Jonas while also recognizing the relative heterogeneity of their respective works. On one hand, we find a leading political philosophy without any real interest in morality or ontology. On the other hand, an ethics of responsibility devoid of any authentically political reflection and founded upon a philosophy of biology presenting itself as an ontology of life. Nonetheless, this divergence of viewpoints does not prevent us from identifying a field of common preoccupations between the two friends, and even a certain identity of approach, and establishing conditions for a properly philosophical dialogue between them. However, for this identification, we must turn to their common master, Martin Heidegger, because it is only by showing how they assume his legacy that these conditions can be revealed.

Heidegger claims, in *Sein und Zeit*, to renew the question of being which the tradition had repressed (Heidegger 1977, 1–6). To this end, he expounds a hermeneutical phenomenology of human existence as a point of departure, an existential analysis of *Dasein*. As only *Dasein* can make being a question, it is indeed this question that one needs to describe and interpret to clear a path toward being. That is not to suggest that Heidegger is interested in humanity. One must distinguish the concept of humanity from *Dasein*, which is nothing other than the one who asks the question of being. Ontology, rather than anthropology, therefore remains the fundamental orientation. The latter is too dependent on a determined conception of beings, whereas it is necessary to be interested in the being of beings. That is, Heidegger is not so much interested in what there is, as in the fact that there is being. However, we also know how this first statement of Heidegger's thought will not satisfy him. Indeed, this position still remains too dependent upon a transcendental and subjectivizing point of view. *Dasein* should not be so much a point of departure as a point of arrival. One must think Being as directly as possible, for its own sake but also because it is the only way to understand the meaning of *Dasein*. For Heidegger, this turn (*Kehre*) to thinking Being does not constitute an additional degree of distancing with regard to humanism, as if humanity had to be forgotten in favor of Being; on the contrary it is a way of redefining humanity in the light of the question of Being.

This questioning with a profoundly Heideggerian outlook, which we will have the opportunity to return to, does not seem to be foreign to the philosophical decisions made by Arendt and Jonas when elaborating their own anthropology. One could say that both of them inherit from Heidegger a conception of humanity that escapes an essentialist conception of metaphysics. Human beings cannot define themselves independently of their existence or action, since it is by acting that they give meaning to existence. In this respect, they are *Dasein*. The most essential action is giving meaning, and perhaps even preserving the source of meaning that they are. To act is to resist the essentialization of human life. This view is what we will establish in the first section of our reflection. For all that, this action—and in this Arendt and Jonas distinguish themselves from Heidegger—cannot be found in a solitary conception of existence resolved to assume its own possibilities by accepting its finitude in the light of mortality. Quite the contrary: to assume the human condition means to recognize a responsibility concerning humanity to come and to life, and to recognize the plural element in which we are immersed and that forces us to overcome contradictions that could be fatal to the realization of our being. It is this plurality that we will have to specify in the second section of the chapter. It will then be possible, in the third section, to present the elements of a dialogue between Arendt and Jonas concerning the elaboration of a non-metaphysical humanism. However, we will not be able to ignore how the critical position adopted by Jonas and Arendt could lead them to fall back into a subjectivizing and anthropocentric conception of humanity. That position will be elaborated in the final section of the chapter. From this point of view, only the exercise of thought, set up as a fundamental action, would then be able to "attune us to" Being in order to hope to be able to overcome its covering by beings, including by this being that is the human. Or, here again, it is by positioning ourselves critically in relation to the *Kehre*, and thus also in relation to the Heideggerian use of thought, that it seems possible to indicate the coordinates of a dialogue between Arendt and Jonas, thus completing the acquired vision of humanity, since we act through the elucidation of what it means for us to think. Articulating acting and thinking after Heidegger, with Arendt and Jonas, in order to know what it means to be human is the object of this chapter.

DECENTERING THE SUBJECT WITH HEIDEGGER

By reformulating the question of being, Heidegger is immediately led (which is to say from section 4 of *Sein und Zeit*) to the issue of the subject capable of formulating this question. This subject cannot have the structure of a determined being because it only understands itself in relation to being and its being. It does not have a predetermined essence since it consists above all in the fact of existing and, in this sense, its "essence [. . .] resides in its existence" (Heidegger 1977, 56). However, it does not exist as a thing of the world where meaning is always already defined and which, in fact, simply is. The whole point of the existential analytic and the essential task of *Sein und Zeit* is to reveal the temporal structure of *Dasein* insofar as it is ordered by the relation to the fact of dying. Indeed, contrary to trivial being, *Dasein* projects itself ahead of itself, cares for itself, and is a being made of possibilities. It is turned toward the future and, when it is lucid—or rather authentic—it assumes the necessity of having to die by showing resolve to choose those possibilities thanks to which it can affirm *who* it is. Understanding the possibilities that are offered to it, and between which it chooses, is equally an understanding of oneself, a way of choosing oneself. This is why being, or existing, for a *Dasein*, means above all having to be oneself. Certainly, this ambition, or this destination, can be denied. *Dasein* can flee itself, sink into inauthenticity, ignore that it has to be itself and find refuge in the anonymity of the *They* (*Das Man*) (Heidegger 1977, 222–39). Idle talk, equivocation, and feverish curiosity allow it to escape the anxiety of being a self by giving in to the temptation to be no matter who. Thus Heidegger goes against a certain traditional way of conceiving the human as a duality of a body and a soul. One has to break with any essentialist definition of humanity and recognize that we are what we make of ourselves. The structure of being is deeply historical. One cannot assign the human being a meaning that is external or preliminary to the project of being that we have assigned to ourselves.

It was necessary to have this brief reminder to take measure of what Arendt and Jonas inherit from Heidegger. Naturally, the exact nature of this legacy will have to be further specified; both inherit a conception of humanity whose essence cannot be fixed in advance and whose meaning proceeds from a fundamentally historical existence. No ideology, no metaphysics can therefore say what humanity is and only our existence can teach us what we are or will be, it being nonetheless understood that this teaching can never be definitive, there being no essential humanity. Thus, when Jonas elaborates an ethics of responsibility with regard to future generations, it is a question of preserving their right to enjoy a free projection for them, identical to that enjoyed by present generations. Humanity must conserve that space of indeterminacy in which its freedom consists. That space also enables humanity to choose possibilities of existence within the widest range that it is allowed to hope for. In this sense, to be human means to recognize oneself as responsible for the possible-being of humanity, to guarantee that it can always be the place of indeterminacy instead of having to be unilaterally configured under the yoke of a technology which reifies it (for example, genetic engineering), or because of consequences that an environmental devastation would bring. In effect, mere "mechanical" survival, and not the exercise of freedom, would then be the law that guides humanity. It is indeed the existence of humanity as humanity that is to be preserved according to Jonas. For him, to exist means being able to project oneself by giving meaning to one's existence without this meaning being a priori knowable (Jonas 2001, 185–87). That humanity can conserve its vocation in historicity is the deep concern that animates Jonas's ethics of responsibility and that he seems (to us) to owe to Heidegger (Pommier 2017, 583–93). If there is a Jonasian humanism, it can no longer be a narrowly metaphysical humanism, ontic as Heidegger would say, or essentialist. It must be rooted in being. Moreover, in the same way that the second Heidegger—the Heidegger after the *Kehre*—sees in technology the existential and inevitable threat weighing on the being of humanity (at least in a first approximation because we will have to qualify the nature of this rapprochement in the last section of this chapter), we could say that the technical hypertrophy of our civilization is, for Jonas, the danger which weighs on future humanity, and on present humanity insofar as it projects itself toward the future. Ethics will therefore have the task of controlling what is likely to control us, to return to us the power that technology could make us lose. Acting ethically constitutes the remedy to the unilaterality of technological action and permits us to guarantee our free power-to-be at a moment in our history where technology, because of its excess, no longer seems able to embody, without shadow, this power-to-be (Jonas 1979, 31–38).

However, it seems to us that Arendt equally draws on lessons from the Heideggerian conception of "humanism." Indeed, her aim in *The Human Condition* (2018 [1958]) is not to bring a supposed essence of humanity to light, but rather to show the historical forms under which it has developed and is developing as humanity. The triptych of labor, work, and action is presented as a historical inquiry into the concrete conditions of human existence and the meaning that emerges from these activities. Humanity is not knowable by virtue of a definition given in advance. It unfolds in the course of a historical process within which humanity constitutes the forms that allow it to come to itself. For all that, it is indeed in the last form of activity mentioned, action, that humanity finds its full accomplishment, and this category recalls, according to an analogy that it will be necessary to strongly qualify the Heideggerian notion of existence. Effectively action, which accompanies speech according to Arendt, allows the individual to affirm oneself and come to oneself, to exist in one's own right. Just as *Dasein* has the vocation to be itself, to affirm its singularity, the Arendtian subject must give birth to its own ipseity by acting and by declaring what it does. Its destiny is not played out in advance and every human being must fulfill their vocation as a personality. It is a universal law of humanity that everyone has to be a singular subject. Labor, which ensures the generic satisfaction of biological needs; and work, which establishes a world of artifacts where each one, as a user or an artisan, is interchangeable, do not allow one to satisfy this vocation to be oneself. Only action can fulfill this wish and, in this sense, it is the true condition of history. Arendt contests the value of grand philosophies of history which interpret it with respect to an end, to a predefined telos (Arendt 2018 [1958], 185). It is not the place of a hidden reason, it is not led by an "invisible hand," by a moral finality or a subterranean economic-dialectical process. (Arendt 2018 [1958], 185–86) There is history and contingency only because human beings act, want to be themselves, exist in their own right. The meaning of humanity is not fixed in advance by a metaphysics, a narrow conception of what humanity is or should be. This meaning is drawn according to the actions of human beings and their deployment (Arendt 2018 [1958], 184). Here again, therefore, the imprint of Heidegger seems visible. Arendt, like Jonas, joins him in dismissing the idea of an essence of humanity in which one could enclose it. On the contrary, it is a question of preserving the humanity of human beings by recognizing the profoundly open character of their destination, by preserving their profound indeterminacy against all that which could compromise the opening of this future.

AGAINST THE "ONTOLOGICAL HUMANISM" OF HEIDEGGER

Nevertheless, we must admit that this analogy would not be exact if we were to stick only to what brings the two students closer to the master while ignoring what distances them from him. This critical moment is indeed necessary if we want to establish the conditions for an authentic philosophical discussion between Jonas and Arendt. Let us therefore begin by recalling that, if it is true that the latter inherits a certain conception of the human as a place of indeterminacy from Heidegger, of openness to a space for its own meaning, we must however recall that her representation of action could just as well be presented as a radical critique of Heidegger's conception of existence. We must remember that the authentic framework for self-realization for Arendt is plurality. One cannot act outside of what is the proper milieu of the political subject, as she conceives it. The birth of the self in action, in accordance with the subject's vocation to natality (by virtue of which it is capable of initiative and of starting something really new), cannot be solitary. It supposes the collaboration of and confrontation with other subjects aspiring to singularity and to the construction of a world within which they can appear as being themselves. Here the world is not a neutral or homogeneous form but the link, the in-between of the subjects, thanks to which everyone can exist as a self while being part of the "same" world, the common world.

These first indications already suffice to mark the whole distance that separates Heidegger from Arendt. For the first, the existent comes to itself because it can extract itself from the homogeneity of public space. It can be itself only on the condition of getting rid—as much as it is in its power and even in its "ownmost" power—of the presence, in it, of the *They*. The Heideggerian alternative clearly opposes an inauthentic *Dasein*, submerged in the anonymous and public sphere of the *They*, and a *Dasein* that recovers itself, confronts its finitude but on the condition of being alone. Certainly, the Heidegger of *Sein und Zeit* in no way rules out the possibility of an authentic relationship with others. Each one can always relate to the other according to the modality of a quest where each one seeks to be themself and can integrate, into their own project, the care to aid the other to equally be themself (Heidegger 1977, 163).

However, this existential collaboration is in no way a necessary condition for achieving selfhood. The profound solitude of *Dasein* remains its truth (Heidegger 1977, 369). This is because no one can die in another's place. Only confrontation with our death allows us to open ourselves to our ownmost possibilities, to our possibilities as possibilities. Indeed, death opens the possibility of nothing and, in doing so, shows that the possible does not have the structure of a predefined plan, of a predetermined option already existing according to the proper mode of ideality and from which only concrete existence would be missing. Because death is a nothing of being and yet we have a relation to it, we discover the non-ontic structure of this relation, that is, the possible as existential. Nothing could be more opposed to the conception that Arendt makes of subjectivity. Humanity is not primarily made to die. We are first of all the one who is born and who, all our life, have a vocation to be born and thus to take initiatives in order to make our self appear (Arendt 2018 [1958], 176–78). This necessity of existence is concretized under the form of an action which takes place within the framework of a plurality which is also the place for the expression of opinions. These cannot therefore be dismissed on the grounds of their inappropriateness. On the contrary, they are the milieu within which the subject can exercise its judicial activity, take a position and say *who* it is. One cannot therefore be oneself by deserting the plural framework and withdrawing into the lived consideration of one's mortality as one can for Heidegger. Such an approach is, on the contrary, the surest way to renounce being able to be oneself and, in a certain manner, to remain dependent on the multitude because of one's incapacity to develop one's judicative activity in contact with plurality.

One could interpret Heidegger's engagement with Nazi barbarism as a loss of judgment leading him to adopt the fashionable viewpoint of the masses (Taminiaux 1992, 64). Such an interpretation puts us on a path to an Arendtian reading of what inauthenticity might consist of. Here the flight from oneself is no longer an anguishing flight in front of death because it puts us in the presence of our ownmost power-to-be. It is flight in front of the necessity to act. To be human, in its most proper sense, does not therefore consist in assuming one's mortality but in assuming natality. It is to decide to act rather than to exist. One could indeed say that there is a temptation not to act because action generates a form of anxiety that can lead to renouncing being oneself. This is because action is, in essence, ambivalent. On one hand, it is indisputably the condition of the advent of oneself. While in labor the subject only maintains itself in life like any representative of the human species; and in work, which ones makes or uses, one remains an interchangeable agent within the artificial world—it is action that permits one to assert who one is by building relations and by developing a personal history (Arendt 2018 [1958], 236). On the other hand, no one knows how the action one began will evolve. The unpredictability of its future can alter its meaning, the irrevocability of what has been realized can be transformed into a weight in the process of subjectivization. The aspiration to the free realization of oneself can thus be transformed into inflexible necessity and disfiguration of oneself. The burden to be assumed here is not therefore that of mortal existence but rather that of plural action which confronts the aporias of action, its dialogical condition and the experience of conflict. To assume humanity is not to assume one's mortality but to assume plurality.

Arendt retains from Heidegger the idea that the autonomy of the subject is not that of a substance folded onto itself. It has a relational dimension. The subject is in relation to itself, always already at a distance from itself and it must conquer itself in front of and within the world. However, relational autonomy in Arendt's sense immediately implies others without whom it is absolutely impossible to be me (Arendt 2018 [1958], 234). Action thus proves disappointing only for the one who conserves an ideal of autonomy closed in on itself and who does not accept the ambiguities inherent in action. From this point of view, Heideggerian *Dasein* conserves something of the model of substance, with which it pretends to break, because it does not accord any place to plurality.

Now this gesture of decentering of the subject, which breaks with any predetermined conception of humanity but also with its Heideggerian substitute which conceives the human as *Dasein* in search of itself through the confrontation with its mortality, finds an equivalent in Jonas. Let us indicate here at least two aspects under which our affirmation seems to make sense. In the first place, whereas Heidegger insisted forcefully on disassociating his conception of existence from the notion of life, Jonas shows how one would not be able to deliver the meaning of life without referring it to existence. Furthermore, Jonas shows how existence, which one would not think of as a vital inscription, would remain an abstract concept without any phenomenal basis. Contrary to Heidegger, Jonas does not understand life in the mode of determined being. On the contrary, it is a privileged access to the question of being (Jonas 2001, 19). The testimony that my (living) body gives me is precious in that it is a node of being, the intersection between the plane of matter and spirit. In it is articulated what tradition tends to separate (matter and spirit) or ignore (life, which is then reduced to one or the other of these substances). My body is not a block of inert matter because it is inhabited by a sensibility, which is to say a directionality that supposes a relationship to "oneself." It also gives a testimony against the thesis of the existence of a pure spiritual entity separated from matter. Indeed, all spiritual activity supposes a bodily inscription that puts it in a situation to manifest itself (Jonas 2001, 22). It is this privileged experience of my corporeality as being irreducible to the duality of mechanical body and spirit that invites me to interpret it in terms of existence, and that opens a window upon the being of life in general, upon the manner of being of other living beings, plants and animals. More precisely, by relying on the human and living testimony of my openness to the world that my body offers me the possibility of, Jonas proposes an existential interpretation of metabolism, a biological category which he frees from its materialist matrix. This consists of a ceaseless activity of renewal of its components thanks to its exchanges with the environment.

It is the experience of the body that I am which allows me to give the most authentic meaning to this metabolic activity (Jonas 2001, 79). It is in fact the principle of a meaningful opening to the outside that draws what interests the organism into the surrounding space. For this reason, it cannot remain enclosed within itself. However, it also manifests an opening to itself. The hetero-affection of the world is accompanied, for Jonas, by a self-affection. By distinguishing what is advantageous to it from what is harmful, the organism manifests a capacity of auto-apprehension which expresses the presence of an interiority. That is, organic life testifies to a capacity of choice, of freedom, which admits of degrees according to the living form under consideration. Suppose all life thus has a metabolic structure. In that case, the fact remains that humanity (with its capacity of imagination) manifests a greater freedom than animals (with their movement, perception and emotion), which themselves show a freedom higher than plants, which are not however devoid of any. Indeed, they too renew themselves in contact with the outside, are "sensitive" to it, and distinguish that which concerns it from that which is indifferent to it.

We have said that the point of departure for Jonas's existential interpretation of life is the experience that I make with *my* body. Irreducible to the duality of matter and spirit, it is rather a "self-transcendence." If one wants to give the full meaning to what I experience in the first person when I experience the life of my body as it interacts with the environment, I am indeed forced to recognize that each pole, matter or spirit, supposes the other. The insufficiency of "psycho-physical" conceptuality obliges Jonas to summon the category of existence, of openness to the world, in order to account for the experience of my corporeality. It is from this experience that he will draw conclusions about the meaning of life in general, insofar as it is the common principle of all living beings. We must therefore recognize that this point of departure is also a point of arrival. The experience of my body opens me to the (metabolic and existential) meaning of life in general, but this meaning allows me, in return, to specify the meaning of human life by questioning its specific type of opening to the world. The anthropological difference consists in a capacity to represent the world in the form of images and, more particularly, to give oneself a representation of oneself by questioning the meaning of one's existence and one's presence in the world (Jonas 2001, 185–86). Jonas seems to rejoin the Heideggerian conception of *Dasein* here, except that this *Dasein* ceases to be an abstract entity which, to be abstract, remains closed in on itself. On the contrary, this Jonasian *Dasein* is only the culminating point in a process of life which is its condition. In Jonas there is indeed a decentering of humanity with regard to being, as in Heidegger; but this decentering takes the concrete form of a decentering operated for the benefit of the being of life, life that is the true law of being, which encompasses the humanity from which life proceeds. If the humanity of human beings consists in a free and indeterminate existence, open to a sense of the possible, it is because the life from which it comes interprets itself according to the guiding thread of a freedom that develops with evolution.

It is time to add that Jonas also proposes an existential interpretation of evolution, which we cannot enter into here. Let us simply note that Darwinism inspires the philosopher to propose a non-"mechanistic" reading, which does not mean that he interprets it according to the category of metaphysical finality. He in fact considers that progress in freedom, in which life is its place, proceeds through an ever-riskier adventure with death (Jonas 2001, 106–7 and 276). The evolution of the forms of life is characterized by an existence that is always more precarious and always less assured. The animal must hunt to live, it may lack sustenance and, contrary to the plant, it does not find all that it needs on the spot. As for humanity, we do not possess the sure instinct of the animal to ensure our survival. We must go through representation, the elaboration of techniques to live. However, this increase in risk also means a greater freedom, a greater distance with respect to the outside world and oneself. Exposure to death is a guarantee of freedom. Such a reading of evolution, which could appear speculative, actually proceeds, in part, from a phenomenal trait observed on the ontogenic level by Jonas (Jonas 2001, 4–6 and 83). Metabolic existence is open to the world in order to renew itself, otherwise it would die. Life is inhabited by death and it is because life seeks to escape death that it exists and opens up possibilities. At the phylogenetic level, evolution is nothing other than the increase of the risk of mortality and freedom. The latter proceeds from the new forms of existence created by life to counter the increasing danger of death.

However, there is also a second sense in which Jonas criticizes the "ontological humanism" of Heidegger. He is not satisfied with showing in what sense it is necessary to "biologize" *Dasein* in order to deliver its true meaning; he also shows how the technological threat in the contemporary era acquires an unprecedented scope that obliges us to recognize ourselves as responsible not only for life but also for future generations. Contrary to Heidegger, the existent is therefore not primarily responsible for itself but for the preservation of life and the capacity of humanity to continue to project itself into the future. Without it being necessary to enter into the demonstration that allows the establishment of this new imperative of responsibility, it suffices to point out that technology has now reached such power that it can call the very presence of life and humanity on earth into question. In Jonas's work, there is therefore a decentering of humanity with regard to itself as a present reality. Indeed, Jonasian humanism is not anthropocentrism in the narrow sense, on one hand and above all because its object is life, and on the other hand because the humanity that it wants to preserve is not a given reality nor even a clearly assignable essence but rather a capacity for projection, a source of indeterminacy. The ethical self thus opens up to a non-egoistic dimension of itself which pushes it to take a superior but concrete ideal into consideration: the humanity which will come and the life that is.

ACTING AS A HUMAN BEING ACCORDING TO ARENDT AND JONAS

Without needing to say more about this last aspect, we can now take the measure of what brings Arendt and Jonas closer together, but also what distances them. Both break with a metaphysical vision of humanism and seem, in this respect, to be close to Heidegger. They owe nothing to a traditional anthropocentrism that would make humanity the center of all value. On the contrary, it is necessary to decenter humanity from itself in order to understand true meaning. However, this decentering cannot be done for the benefit of pure being. This abstract entity cannot have any meaning for philosophers attached to describing phenomena that give themselves in experience. For Arendt, it is the world of human affairs, it is the fabric of relations such as actions and speech acts that can constitute this world that matters and permits everyone to hope to be themselves. The most concrete phenomenon is not naked being but the relation, the in-between of human beings that permits them to be who they are.

For Jonas, humanity can only understand itself and even its own worth by acknowledging its biological origin. We can only understand the meaning of our existence by recognizing a responsibility toward future generations. On one hand and with Heidegger this community of inspiration lies in the fact of not granting to humanity a definitive assignable meaning, without, on the other hand and this time against Heidegger, referring it to being, gives way, as we have started to indicate, to profound divergences between the two students of Heidegger. Indeed, whereas Arendt conceives action and political existence apart from life (labor), and even, in a certain way, against it, Jonas understands the meaning of human subjectivity only from the ground of life. For the latter, the subject can make its existence a question because it comes from life, therefore from its evolution, which itself must be interpreted according to the guiding thread of freedom. For Arendt, the subject can only hope to reach ipseity on the condition of not sticking to the animal activity of restoring its metabolism.

From this crucial difference between Arendt and Jonas we can note further divergence in their respective thoughts on the *nature* of the threat posed by technology, even if they both see a possible threat in it. While for Arendt technology has been put into the service of labor, leading to the "socialization of humanity" and locking human existence in a cycle of production and consumption in an automation which imitates the vital "mechanism" (Arendt 2018 [1958], 145–53), Jonas considers technology as that which increasingly distances us from life as such (Jonas 1987, 48). Hence, there is a need for an imperative capable of preserving life against technological hypertrophy. It is undoubtedly also the importance given to the body that leads Jonas to take the threat weighing on the carnal nature of our terrestrial inscription very seriously, a threat that can just as well take the form of a direct technological modification to our body (Jonas 1979, 47–53) as of an indirect modification through the process of a large-scale ecological devastation (Jonas 1979, 247–48). It is probably because the body is not the condition of my openness to the world in Arendt that this threat seems less present in her thought. Both of them certainly make future generations an object of consideration; however, for her and unlike Jonas, it is less biotechnology or ecological disaster which represents a danger for these generations than the abdication of politics in the form of totalitarianism or consumer society.

This first mention of notable differences between the two authors nevertheless permits us to see in what sense they could happily complement each other to formulate a new humanist proposal. Indeed, the dualism of existence and life that we witness in Arendt does not allow us to understand their articulation on one hand, and the origin of this aspiration to be oneself on the part of the political subject on the other hand. How can we make sense of the dynamics of subjectivation if the political subject appears *ex abrupto* in rupture with a life from which the subject nevertheless comes? In contrast, Jonas gives us keys to understand this continuity of existence and life. He also allows us to think of an authentic care for our natural condition and earthly inscription that seem inseparable from our humanity. For all that, a mystery that has been insufficiently raised by commentators remains in the Jonas of *The Imperative of Responsibility* (1984). Here is indeed a work written to formulate and found an ethical imperative allowing the preservation of life and future generations. Here is also a principle that Jonas explicitly says must be addressed to public power and that must be usable in the political field. However, when it comes to evaluating the political regimes most likely to embody said principle, none of them are up to the task in Jonas's eyes (Jonas 1979, 256–390; Pommier 2013, 157–69). Should we then conclude that the Jonasian ethic is utopian and abandon it; or, on the contrary, should we conclude that no politics, not even the democratic regime, is worthy of the ethic, which must therefore impose its own law, including against democracy? This question, which is not trivial, highlights a blind spot in Jonas's thought.

Contrary to Arendt's thought, Jonas does not put plurality at the heart of his philosophy. He does not conceive the ethical (or political) subject as profoundly relational. This shortcoming most probably stems from his way of representing the living (metabolic) subject as polarized by death. This decision, marked by individualism, makes it difficult to understand how subjects can develop a common world among themselves through actions and speech acts, where a sense of responsibility for life and future generations prevails. Perhaps it is the Arendtian conception of politics that could help Jonas give meaning to a true politics of responsibility and thus overcome a crucial blind spot in his philosophy.

THE TRUE MEANING OF THOUGHT

One might however wonder whether both Arendt and Jonas do not remain prisoners of a certain (political or ethical) activism which is not, all in all, up to the times in which we are living. Should we not recognize, with the second

Heidegger, that our epoch is that of Technology, the ultimate expression of the history of metaphysics, which imposes itself everywhere, including in the field of ethics and politics; and that to claim to act against it, to produce effects, to want to change the course of the world, is still to be duped by this regime of thought? Would it not be better to take note of its predominance, not pretend to do something but on the contrary limit oneself to meditating on its meaning and try to attune oneself to the Being of forgetfulness from which Technology proceeds? Thus, it would be a matter of thinking rather than acting or, more precisely, of resignifying the notion of action. As Heidegger mentions at the beginning of his *Letter on Humanism*, acting would no longer mean producing effects (Heidegger 1976, 313) and would no longer be opposed to passivity (Heidegger 2002, 41–42). True action would be thought in that it would allow *Dasein* to be reconnected to its origin, Being, and thus give true hope to overcome, when the time comes . . . , the epoch of Technology. That would be the true way to "detranscendentalize" the subject, to free it from the influence metaphysics has had on its representation, and thus to understand it according to its ownmost meaning.

Here is a decision to which both Arendt and Jonas seem to be strongly opposed. Far from being naïve in refusing to make the *Kehre* Heidegger does, one should recognize their great lucidity in their decision not to make such a leap in the direction of Being by means of thought. Indeed, one could say that Arendt, unlike Heidegger, considers a recognition of the conflict between thought and action as essential (Taminiaux 1992, 155–75). Whereas Heidegger seems to want to abolish this conflict by reforming the concept of action, which he reduces to thought, Arendt reminds us that one is necessarily opposed to the other. Action is situated and therefore necessarily gives space to opposing viewpoints, because its natural environment is plurality. On one hand, it is action and speech that make the subject visible. Thought, on the other hand, overlooks any situation, and belongs to the invisible. In this sense, it serves no purpose, and does not, at least not immediately, illuminate action. Through action I belong to the world; through thought I withdraw myself from the world. There is necessarily a mismatch and even a conflict between the two. Therefore, it is inaccurate to make people believe that thought can be true action unless one wants to lose the specificity of action and abolish plurality. Jonas does not forgo pointing out, perhaps more explicitly, the practical consequences of a thought of Being (Jonas 2001, 258). The extremely vague character of this meditation leaves the question regarding the worldly manifestation of this abstraction open, thereby opening up the possibility of its concrete incarnation in the form of a brutal force. Being must be able to reveal itself to thought; however, no criterion, no other norm than "the sheer force of being that issues the call" (Jonas 2001, 247) allows us to identify when this imposition takes place. This lack of a criterion or norm is what permits Jonas to suggest that Hitler could be seen as the manifestation of such an event of Being, of a call to a change of epoch that forcefully reconfigures the regime of meaning. Jonas then reminds us of an excerpt from Heidegger's rectory speech: "Not doctrines and 'ideas' be the rules of your being. The Führer himself and alone is the present and future German reality and its law. Learn even deeper to know: that from now on each and every thing demands decision, and every action, responsibility. Heil Hitler"" (Jonas 2001, 247) But for Jonas, this conception of thought is not only dangerous on the ethical level but also the theological. The thought of Being absorbs (ethical) action and the theological regime of thought. The thought of Being is highly speculative and at bottom aims at a transcendent "reality," but it nevertheless takes on the trappings of immanence. Moreover, by thinking all that is it wants to encompass and annex theology by forbidding it to think God as pure transcendence, as Otherness. God would only be one being among others. According to Jonas, the thought of Being must on the contrary preserve its autonomy by claiming its own form of discourse with regard to this transcendence, instead of finding tools of thought in Heidegger that leads discourse to immanentize the divine.

These critiques of the Heideggerian conception and use of thought do not mean that he should be discredited in favor of ethical and political action. Simply, in Arendt and Jonas thought fulfills another function in line with the expectations we have already raised. Let us indicate here only that which serves our purpose. For Arendt, thinking is a spontaneous activity that responds to a need of the mind and does not fulfill an assignable finality (Arendt 1978, 72). Certainly, it enriches judgment (which is a by-product of it) and this latter illuminates action. However, one does not think with a view to action. Thought has no direct effect on action except when the simple fact of thinking and thus of establishing a dialogue between the soul with itself constitutes by itself alone an act of political resistance, as is the case in the totalitarian periods of history. One could say that for Jonas, thought plays a quite different role. He seems to come closer to Heidegger when he asserts, in the last sections of *The Imperative of Responsibility*, that the theoretical critique of utopia made in the book is already an "act in the ethics of responsibility" (Jonas 1979, 390) insofar as it allows for the rectification of will and thought. There would thus be an act of thought. Naturally, the type of thought in question here is in no way that of abstract being but on the contrary that of a critique of the abstract anthropology underlying the utopian and technological projects of transformation of humanity and nature, to which Jonas opposes his own anthropology. The fact remains here that acting would not only be being responsible for nature and future generations, working in the direction of their preservation, but would also be thinking humanity according to what we are against our false representations. This is moreover an argument that he highlights directly against Arendt.

In a text in which he pays homage to Arendt, Jonas reminds us that, in the eyes of his friend, thought has a free character and is not linked to action. However, he points out that the communication of thought can be considered as an action according to her (Jonas 1977, 42). To communicate one's thought is indeed to act in the world. One could nevertheless wonder whether this appreciation by Jonas gives us the opportunity to once again emphasize the blind spot of his philosophy we have already mentioned, namely his ignorance of the specificity of political action insofar as it brings a plurality into play and defies, by essence, any theoretical illumination that would make it lose its specificity. Indeed, action is not a manufacturing technique, it does not presuppose any preliminary theoretical knowledge, any *eidos*. On the contrary, it introduces contingency into the world. From this point of view, one could say that Jonasian action sins in its theorizing tendency, as in Heidegger, that fails to think the concrete (political) conditions of incarnation for an ethics of responsibility. Thus, one could believe that the critique of utopia carried out in *The Imperative of Responsibility* and the promotion of an alternative anthropology that accompanies it is not only *an* act of ethics but *the whole* of Jonas's ethics.

That is, his ethics would remain profoundly abstract, that the authentic meaning of ethics would be, here and in its core, speculative. In other words, true action would be concentrated in the act of thinking! However, such an assertion would not be exact since Jonas preserves the autonomy of thought without any ambiguity. Moreover, he distinguishes it not only from action but also from phenomenology. Whereas the latter consists in a description of concrete phenomena as they give themselves to us, thought on the contrary has a clearly speculative dimension. Thought gives meaning—which is not to know—to that which escapes experience (Jonas 1994, 7–8). It goes beyond the limits of available knowledge, is a hypothesis in charge of answering the ultimate questions of existence: the origin of life, the ultimate end of existence, the meaning of the presence of evil in the world, especially after Auschwitz. Through these preoccupations, Jonas will indulge in speculations of a metaphysical and theological nature, even forging the myth of a weak and powerless God to whose aid we must come. In this effort of thought, there will be, contrary to the suspicion he entertained with regard to Heidegger, no concern to annex theology to philosophy but simply a contribution to the effort to think Transcendence in such a way as to illuminate the meaning of our presence in the world without however abolishing the mystery of one or the other.

It is not for lack of profoundness that Jonas and Arendt choose not to turn to the thought of Being. Rather, it is by virtue of a concrete vow to devote themselves to the preservation of the world as it is given to us, the world of human affairs for Arendt, the world of life for Jonas. Of course, the way in which they represent the nature of this preservation is not the same: political for Arendt, ethical for Jonas. Such a difference in appreciation is not simply an opportunity to emphasize what is lacking in one by taking what is found in the other as a norm. On the contrary, it is an opportunity to highlight a complementarity. The Arendtian conception of action must be able to offer the means to think the politics missing from *The Imperative of Responsibility*. The ethics of responsibility and its bio-ontological background should allow us to "ecologize" and even "vitalize" Arendt's political conception. However, this interest in action nonetheless does not account for the whole of humanity. There is no humanity without the activity of thinking. However, it is probably by having correctly posed and circumscribed the field of action, unlike Heidegger, that it is possible to pose the question of thought. This latter does not get lost in speculation about Being, empty of meaning and methodologically uncertain. It can nourish action either because it inspires practical judgment in Arendt or contributes to elaborating an ethics in Jonas. Above all though it responds to a need of the spirit, a need to give meaning that can concern all things (with Arendt) or can (with Jonas) concentrate on the highest questions of existence (the origin, the end, the presence of evil). However, in both cases thought cannot substitute itself for action nor pretend to do so, except in a marginal or exceptional way on one hand; and although it must always keep a link to a phenomenal basis, it cannot ignore its speculative and, we might say, hypothetical character on the other hand. It is under these conditions that the meaning of the human, as it thinks and acts, will undoubtedly be able to gain in clarity.

Translated from French by Daniel O'Shiel.

BIBLIOGRAPHY

Arendt, Hannah. 2018 [1958] *The Human Condition*. 2nd ed. Chicago: University of Chicago Press.
Arendt, Hannah. 1978. *The Life of the Mind*. New York: A Harvest Book, Harcourt Brace & Company.
Heidegger, Martin. 1977. *Sein und Zeit*. Frankfurt am Main: Vittorio Klostermann.
Heidegger, Martin. 1976. *Wegmarken*. Frankfurt am Main: Vittorio Klostermann.
Heidegger, Martin. 2002. *Aus der Erfahrung des Denkens*. Frankfurt am Main: Vittorio Klostermann.

Jonas, Hans. 1977. "Acting, Knowing, Thinking: Gleanings from Hannah Arendt's Philosophical Work," *Social Research*, Spring, 44, no. 1: 25–43.

Jonas, Hans. 1979. *Das Prinzip Verantwortung. Versuch einer Ethik für die technologische Zivilisation.* Frankfurt am Main: Suhrkamp.

Jonas, Hans. 1984. *The Imperative of Responsibility: In Search of An Ethics for the Technological Age*, Chicago: University of Chicago Press.

Jonas, Hans. 1987. *Technik, Medizin und Ethik. Praxis des Prinzips Verantwortung.* Frankfurt am Main: Suhrkamp.

Jonas, Hans. 1994. *Philosophische Untersuchungen und metaphysische Vermutungen.* Frankfurt am Main: Suhrkamp.

Jonas, Hans. 2001. *The Phenomenon of Life: Toward a Philosophical Biology.* Evanston, IL, Northwestern University Press.

Pommier, Eric. 2013. *Jonas.* Paris: Les Belles Lettres.

Pommier, Eric. 2017. "La posibilidad de la historia en la época de la responsabilidad. Vida, historia y Ética en Hans Jonas," *Anuario Filosófico* 50, no. 3: https://doi.org/10.15581/009.50.3.575-600.

Taminiaux, Jacques. 1992. *La fille de Thrace et le penseur professionnel. Arendt et Heidegger*, Paris: Payot.

Chapter Seven

Hannah Arendt's Influence on Eastern European Dissidence

The Example of Poland

Katarzyna Stokłosa

Hannah Arendt is known in Eastern and Central Eastern Europe mostly for her writing on the Nazi dictatorship. Nevertheless, she also analyzed the communist dictatorship and the revolutionary changes in the former Eastern Bloc, specifically investigating the developments in Hungary during 1956. As the Hungarian revolution had a great impact on other revolutions in Eastern Europe, Arendt became well-known throughout the whole of the Eastern bloc. Her philosophy was important for the first democratic changes and the transformation period of many totalitarian/authoritarian countries. With her theory of totalitarianism, Arendt influenced dissident intellectuals in Hungary, Poland, and Czechoslovakia. For instance, in Czechoslovakia, Arendt had a great influence on the philosophy professor Jan Patočka and the dramatist and dissident Václav Havel; in Hungary Arendt was an influential source for novelist and essayist György Konrád, and in Poland, the essayist and publicist Adam Michnik found her thinking important.

The influence of Arendt was not necessarily a one-way street, as political thinkers engaged with her ideas critically. For instance, Stefan Auer is of the opinion that Arendt's evaluation of the Hungarian revolution came three decades too early. The events in Hungary were not as nonviolent as she initially thought (Auer 2020, 85–86). From Arendt's perspective, the revolutions in 1956 in Hungary, 1968 in Czechoslovakia, and 1980/81 in Poland showed the weakness of real socialism (Auer 2020, 87). However, what Arendt underestimated was the ability of the totalitarian regimes to develop conditions in which physical violence did not have to be present in order to sustain the regime (Auer 2020, 87). Hence it is timely to consider Arendt's reception in the Eastern Bloc, not as a clichéd hagiography, but in its motion over the course of turbulent decades. This chapter focuses on Arendt's reception in Poland to begin such an exploration.

In doing so, this chapter analyzes Arendt's influence and effect on Polish scholarly and political life before and after the collapse of the communist bloc. The discussion mainly focuses on Poland, as it is representative of the countries of the former communist bloc, in which revolutionary movements contributed to the transformation process and later, system change. The question explored is how the work and the personification of Arendt have been presented, received and used in Poland before and after the transformation process. That is, how can the fascination for Arendt in Poland be explained? This chapter considers and evaluates sources of Polish and international scholars who deal with Arendt's texts in relation to the communist system in Poland and the changes in that scholarship after the collapse of the socialist government.

HANNAH ARENDT AND THE COMMUNIST BLOC

The Polish political scientist Piotr Buras states that the permanent presence of Arendt in "today's marketplace of ideas and world-views" is presently a fact, yet representatives of the Polish anti-communist opposition were captivated earlier by Arendt's republicanism and criticism of totalitarianism (Buras 2003, 10). There was a fascination with Arendt within postcommunist countries, especially in Poland, that proved very strong. Polish historian Wojciech Duda discovered that in the seventies and eighties, Arendt's ideas were debated in Polish intellectual and political oppositional circles, and additionally, her works were discussed in the intellectual circles of the opposition movement Solidarność (Solidarity). This movement, founded on September 17, 1980, was the main opposition in communist Poland. Its leader was the electrician Lech Wałęsa, later president in democratic Poland (1990–1995). Solidarność brought not only the end of communism and the beginning of the transformation process in Poland but also had an influence on political changes in the whole Eastern bloc and furthermore on the Soviet Union's collapse. (Besier/Stokłosa 2013, 431–32).

Arendt's analysis of the Hungarian revolution in 1956 was an inspiration for Polish intellectuals inside the movement as well (Duda/Śpiewak 2002, 40). Her interpretation assisted in understanding what had happened in their own country. She was quoted in oppositional writings, such as *ResPublica*, *Arka*, and *Przegląd Polityczny*. Despite censorship problems, the Cracow publishing house Znak published *Eichmann in Jerusalem* in 1988, and

Warsaw underground publishers released *The Life of the Mind: Thinking* (Aletheia, 1988) and *The Origins of Totalitarianism* (NOWA, 1989). Arendt was perceived as an intellectual inspiration for the opposition movements (Duda/Śpiewak 2002, 34). At the famous Polish universities of Warsaw, Cracow, and Danzig, illegal seminars and debates took place in which Arendt's theories and thoughts were analyzed. After 1976, several hundred documents, testimonials, and analyses of the totalitarian system were published in the independent press. Concurrently, the first works of George Orwell, Arendt, Karl Mannheim, Hans Kelsen, Isaiah Berlin, Friedrich von Hayek, Zbigniew Brzeziński, Richard Conquest, Raymond Aron, and Nicola Chiaromonte appeared (Śpiewak 2003, 25).

Through the historian and anti-communist activist Jerzy Jedlicki's private seminars between 1976 and 1980, his students became acquainted with Arendt's literature. Jedlicki organized the seminars in secret at home. The goal was to teach his students about Western liberal thought. (Stokłosa 2008, 232). The Polish sociologist and historian Paweł Śpiewak, who was expelled from the university because he did not want to conform with the demands of the communist system, had his first experience with Arendt's works in these seminars. In 2002 he reported on this experience in the following manner: "We read Hannah Arendt for the first time and we didn't really realize what we were reading. We read her *The Origins of Totalitarianism* without knowledge that its author had died only some months before. I also remember that her way of thinking seemed to be a bit strange to us." The Polish scholar was fascinated by Arendt's thesis about the importance of participation in public debates. Without the possibility of participating in political debates, politics will change into ideology, and the possibility of debating and arguing will disappear. Śpiewak found this way of thinking new and fascinating at the same time (Duda/Śpiewak 2002, 38).

In communist Poland, Arendt was an intellectual inspiration to the oppositional movement and its thought. In the 1980s, the Poles showed great bravery in resisting communist ideology and the institutions that served it by accepting the repression this resistance instigated. Polish critical intellectuals profited from the ideas of Western European thinkers and Polish exiles and immigrants, such as Arendt, Zbigniew Brzezinski, Isaiah Berlin, Zygmunt Bauman, and Alain Besançon (Legutko 2003, 262).

PERCEPTIONS OF HANNAH ARENDT AFTER 1989

After the various political changes in early 1989—the so-called "round-table," the free elections of June 1989 and the beginning of the transformation period at the beginning of the 1990s—Arendt's works were no longer forbidden and concealed. (Duda/Śpiewak 2002, 34). The uncensored version of *The Origins of Totalitarianism* had already been published in 1989 and republished in 1993, in a free Poland. In Duda's opinion, on one hand, it was too late to make the book well-known in Poland. On other hand, he thought that even if the book had been published earlier, it would not have provoked debate because the intellectual atmosphere in communist Poland in the 1980s in Poland did not allow such a discussion. There was simply no intellectual freedom. (Duda/Śpiewak 2002, 38).

At the end of the 1980s and the beginning of the 1990s, the translations of the following works by Arendt were published: *The Life of the Mind* (1989), *On Revolution* (1991), *Between Past and Future: Eight Exercises in Political Thought* (1994), *On Violence,* (1998) and *The Human Condition* (2000). In 1990, Nina Gładziuk published an analysis of the thoughts of Hannah Arendt (Gładziuk 1991). Paweł Śpiewak observed that after 1989, the difference between Western and Polish thinking quickly disappeared. In his opinion Polish thinkers adopted Western thinking very quickly and integrated very many ideas of Western thinkers in their works (Śpiewak 2003, 25).

One important work concerned with Arendt's thought is a book by the philosopher Włodzimierz Heller, *Hannah Arendt: Źródła pluralizmu politycznego*, in which he attempts to describe the problems of political pluralism as a property of the political sphere. In search of sources for the pluralist perception of politics, he refers to Arendt's concept of the human condition and the "political being," as well as two activities, the power of judgment and the power of political action, which according to Arendt, determine what is political (Heller 2000, 14). Włodzimierz Heller observed that since the mid-1980s, Arendt's thoughts have served as a cure for proceedings in the political sphere. In his opinion, Arendt helped Poland to overcome its totalitarian past and make progress regarding democratization. She shows the patterns of civil society, such as freedom and democracy (Heller 2000, 13–14). For Arendt, it was important first to understand the political sphere, then make one's own judgment, and finally act. Heller concludes by describing images of the Polish political sphere at the end of the 1990s, which reflect the topicality and vitality of the Arendt project. Here, he makes a link to Arendt's idea about the importance of nongovernmental organizations for civic freedom. As the first proof of the effectiveness of Arendt's thought in Poland, he lists the establishment of a great number of nongovernmental organizations. The incorporation of several citizen groups into the framework of nongovernmental organizations was characteristic of the first years of democratic Poland after the 1989 regime change. Foundations, unions, political organizations, and informal groups form the third sector of the democratic system after national and local government. They are the "expression of civil freedom and express civil needs and emotions" (Heller 2000, 170–71).

Polish correspondents became involved with the *Hannah Arendt Newsletter*, an international discussion and information forum established in the mid-1990s by scholars influenced by Arendt's ideas (Leszczyńska 2002, 214). The fact that Polish thinkers actively participated in Western European debates confirms Paweł Śpiewak's thesis about the slow harmonization between Western and Polish thinking after 1989. Number 55 of *Przegląd Polityczny* from 2002 has the title "Powrót Hanny Arendt" (The Return of Hannah Arendt). In this political and cultural magazine, Polish and international scholars and writers contributed articles on Hannah Arendt's philosophy. It was the first broad presentation in Poland of Arendt's scholarly and private life (Buras, 2003, 11). Undoubtedly, the impact of the Solidarność movement was important for disseminating knowledge about Arendt in certain Polish intellectual circles, as Śpiewak shows. The sociologist and historian uses Arendt for the explanation of the totalitarian system because, in his view, it is necessary to use much broader language than that of political science or sociology to explain the phenomenon, which is precisely what Arendt had done (Śpiewak 2006, 200).

In the anthology *Totalitaryzm a zachodnia tradycja* (*Totalitarianism and the Western Tradition*), which was published in 2006, contributors from the fields of history, philosophy, sociology, and politics repeatedly return to Arendt in their analysis of totalitarianism, mostly when they analyze the communist system. The sociologist Zdzisław Krasnodębski reminded readers that the term "totalitarianism" could not be found in Polish dictionaries during the cold war period. After 1989, the concept of totalitarianism replaced the theory of fascism and started to become very popular in left-wing political circles. The term started to be used in everyday language as well as in scholarly milieux. Krasnodębski underlines that Arendt's model of totalitarianism can be used better in relation to communism than fascism or national socialism because the last two were more pluralistic and anarchistic than the meaning of "totalitarianism" (Krasnodębski, 2006, 93).

Miłowit Kuniński, in his contribution, presents the most important points of Arendt's totalitarian theory, namely that the development of the capitalist economy goes hand in hand with the extension of the social sphere, which transforms the private sphere into the public sphere. The possibility of an open society, which actively cares about common welfare, is reduced. For individuals in the public sphere, economic goals become the most important, and agents act to achieve those goals instead of engaging in pluralistic action aimed at generating new political possibilities. Mass society without a traditional class structure grows increasingly isolated in the sphere of politics as well as increasingly lonely. Such societies become progressively more susceptible to totalitarian ideologies. Kuniński states that the nontotalitarian world for a very long period had problems understanding the mechanism of the communist version of a totalitarian world. For this reason, the transformation period in many postcommunist countries lasted for a long time and, in many cases, has not been successful (Kuniński 2006, 141–42).

Philosopher and historian Krzysztof Pomian emphasizes in his analysis of totalitarianism the significance of Arendt, first in 1950s in North American social sciences and later in Europe (Pomian 2006, 123). Polish American political scientist Zbigniew Brzeziński disagrees with Arendt regarding Soviet totalitarianism. In her work *The Origins of Totalitarianism*, Hannah Arendt has written that Soviet totalitarianism came into being under Stalin. In Brzeziński's opinion, Stalin and the Stalinist system would not have appeared without the prior existence of Lenin. Consistently, Stalin continued Lenin's politics and realized his totalitarian aspirations (Brzeziński, Kornat 2006, 139).

Polish scholars also referred to Arendt's work when analyzing the state of war, with martial law and a military junta, from December 13, 1981. In celebration of the twenty-fifth anniversary of the introduction of this martial state, Polish quarterly, *Przegląd Polityczny* (Political Review), surveyed well-known Polish historians, sociologists, philosophers, and political scientists as to whether Poland was a totalitarian state as of December 13, 1981. Daniel Grinberg, a historian, analyzed Poland under Edward Gierek and declared the following: "Against the background of a democratic, modern Western Europe, Gierek's Poland represents a relatively mild form of a state that is not entirely sovereign, ruled in an authoritarian manner, but, despite all that, still has many of the trappings of Democracy" (Grinberg 2006, 173). He asserted that Poland had little to do with the classical "totalitarian syndrome" and Arendt's analysis at that time, since elements of pluralism were present in almost all areas of life. The various connections between the communist Poland and the Western world in political and cultural spheres helped to win over the communism. In Grinberg's opinion, Poland was less communist than other Eastern bloc countries. (Grinberg 2006, 173).

Marek Kornat, also a historian, responds to the concept of totalitarianism. He asserts that not every authoritarian discrepancy in democracy can automatically be classified as totalitarianism. The author argues for Arendt's theory of totalitarianism as it was presented in *The Origins of Totalitarianism*. According to Arendt, the Third Reich only had a totalitarian character in the years from 1938 through 1945, and the Soviet Union possessed one during the Stalinist times from 1929 through 1956. Before 1938, there was a totalitarian movement and totalitarian leadership (Adolf Hitler), but still not a totalitarian state. Kornat emphasized this differentiation in Arendt's work. According to this idea, he asserts that there was a turning away from totalitarianism in the time between the end of Stalinism and the appearance of Solidarność, which was very meaningful to the People's Republic of Poland. This process put Polish society, not party reformers, in action. When Arendt wrote *The Origins of Totalitarianism*, she knew that her theories would have to be supplemented in view of the experiences of 1956. The most important was the famous "secret speech" that Nikita Khrushchev held after the official end of the meeting of the Twentieth Party Congress of the CPSU. In his speech, he announced that there would be a certain internal and external openness (Besier/Stokłosa 2013, 366).

In further paragraphs, Kornat discusses the question of what the state of war, introduced on December 13, 1981, means according to the perspective of engagement with totalitarianism. (Kornat 2006, 176–77). The historian came to the conclusion that if the characteristic of a totalitarian system is a totalitarian mass movement—as Arendt asserted—after the introduction of a state of war, Poland was not a totalitarian state anymore because no such mass movements were happening in Poland. This is the best proof of the thesis that Poland was already a post-totalitarian state at that time (Kornat 2006, 180). Post-totalitarian is a term that characterizes postcommunist societies. Eastern European countries in the "transition" period were called post-totalitarian countries (Besier/Stokłosa 2013, 567–70).

Ireneusz Krzemiński, a sociologist, Paweł Machcewicz, a historian, and Zdzisław Najder, a literature historian, also all refer to Arendt in their analyses of the state of war in Poland. Machcewicz emphasizes that the point of reference was, for Arendt, the Soviet Union and the Eastern bloc in its strongest period of dynamism and expansion. He underlines the fact that Arendt revised her thesis that totalitarianism eliminates the possibility of the development of inner opposition and that it cannot be eliminated through inner strength after the Hungarian Revolution of 1956 (Machcewicz 2006, 187). Krzemiński stresses the significance of a social movement for the term "totalitarianism" used by Arendt. This is the idea of a social movement in which one's own beliefs, interests, and actions meet. Such movement is not possible without a radical element, that is, an ideological imagination of an ideal or idealized order. For this reason, the Polish system, after the declaration of a state of war (martial law) on December 13, 1981, continued to be totalitarian (Krzemiński 2006, 181–84).

Zdzisław Najder, literary historian, critic, and political activist, is of the opinion that the Polish People's Republic was, until 1989, a totalitarian state. With this statement, he contradicts Arendt, who had underlined the significance of the system change after Stalin's death (Najder 2006, 191). In contrast, Polish historian Jerzy Holzer supports Arendt's theory by stating that Poland after 1956 was no longer a totalitarian state. He confirms this assumption when analyzing Poland after the declaration of a state of war in 1981 (Holzer 2006, 175).

Aleksander Smolar, publicist and political scientist, writes supporting Arendt's views at length in his contribution. He begins by discussing the concept of totalitarianism, stating that while this concept is presently of great importance in Poland and other Central-Eastern European countries, it has lost topicality in the West. Smolar refers to intensive discussions that took place among scientists and publicists in Western Europe throughout the fifties, where the totalitarian paradigm prevailed until the middle of the decade. Here, Smolar mentions the work of Carl J. Friedrich and Zbigniew K. Brzezinski, *Totalitarian Dictatorship and Autocracy*, as well as Arendt's *The Origins of Totalitarianism*. According to his contribution, Arendt's model of totalitarianism remains true, even to this day, due to her deep philosophical reflection and literary strength. The cooling of ideology, abolition of mass terror, and the stabilization of the ruling class led to totalitarianism's self-destruction. Arendt subsequently announced the end of communist totalitarianism in the 1960s, where these changes led to the collapse of totalitarianism as a system of government in the years 1989–1991. Smolar agrees with Arendt that totalitarianism would decline, along with the deep belief and conviction in the system and the terror that sustained it. After the totalitarian system had lost the revolutionary triad—movement, ideology, and terror—it had no chance of survival (Smolar 2006, 194–97).

Popular Polish historian of ideas Adrzej Walicki used Arendt's ideas to prove his thesis, which was that Poland was no longer a totalitarian state after 1956. According to Walicki, the first signs of a thaw had already appeared in Poland by 1954, and by 1956, Gomulka's Poland had lost its totalitarian characteristics altogether. Walicki responds first to the concept of totalitarianism. He declares that the concept of totalitarianism, used as a simple tool of the anti-communist right during the period of the Cold War, was mistakenly applied. There were definitely representatives of a leftist philosophy among the great thinkers who engaged in the fight against totalitarianism, including: radicals (George Orwell, Hannah Arendt), liberals (Karl Popper), or the ex-communist left (Arthur Koestler, Ignazio Silone, Stephen Spender, and Richard Wright). Walicki emphasized an essential characteristic of totalitarianism: the ability to rob people of not only outer but also inner freedom. With that loss, individuals further lose their deepest identity, the right to be themselves (Walicki 2006, 209–10). Here, Walicki makes a connection with Arendt's argument that "totalitarianism is never content to rule by external means (. . .) totalitarianism has discovered a means of dominating and terrorizing human beings from within" (Arendt 1976, 325). The model of totalitarianism described by Carl J. Friedrich and Zbigniew Brzezinski, according to Walicki, proved too static and ideological since they did not take into account the consequences of its unplanned evolution. This model did not clarify the process of changes that began in the USSR through Stalinization. Here, Walicki refers again to Arendt. In the preface to the second edition of *The Origins of Totalitarianism*, Arendt states that the Soviet Union began an authentic, although not clear-cut process, of destroying totalitarianism after Stalin's death and, therefore, one could no longer label the Soviet Union of the 1960s "totalitarian" in the narrowest meaning of the word (Arendt 1976: xxxv–xxxvii). In the end, Walicki emphasizes again that Poland was no longer totalitarian after 1956. The most important changes to the system were not the division of power and thus political democratization, but rather the limitation of the amount of power and thus liberalization. In place of a system of totalitarian control over all areas of life, political authoritarianism took over, which gave the individual in society considerable freedoms in the private sphere as well as in cultural and intellectual life. Walicki mentions the appearance of independent writing, cinema movies, poetry, pluralism in philosophy, and the great development of Polish sociology (Walicki 2006, 214–16.)

Arendt has been used in Poland again and again for critical analyses of the political system and institutions. Her work has been examined not only in relation to the communist period but also after the transition period, where doubt was expressed about whether democracy in Poland was stable enough to continue. Forty years after Arendt's death, *Przegląd Polityczny* was again dedicated to Arendt's work. In this period, Polish parliamentary elections took place in which the conservative Law and Justice party won convincingly. In connection with the analysis of the Polish political situation after these elections, Polish and international intellectuals in the magazine ask what will remain from Arendt's ideas. Very important for the Polish scene was the issue of social aspects in relation to freedom that Arendt dealt with. Under the difficult circumstances of the transformation period, many Poles doubted the importance of political freedom because they struggled with huge economic problems, with low incomes. German philosopher Rahel Jaeggi states that Arendt became, in Central-Eastern Europe, a symbol or even an icon of freedom and a new beginning. However, as soon as the heroic fight for freedom was replaced by the not-so-heroic fight in the job market, the fascination for Arendt decreased. So "What do we need Hannah Arendt for?" asks Jaeggi. The philosopher underlines that Arendt should not be characterized as an elite thinker because that would exclude the social aspects that Arendt dealt with. The concept of politics as an instrument for world formation can lead to new considerations of social issues (Jaeggi 2015, 187). The philosopher Ágnes Heller agrees with Arendt regarding the thesis that in larger societies, all public considerations of issues regarding freedom were replaced with discussions of social issues. However, Heller thinks that Arendt was not right in her assertion that free people cannot deal with social issues. In opposition to Arendt,

Heller thinks that not only scholars should solve social problems but that this is a task that matters to all participants of society. Although politicians are not always responsible for finding concrete solutions to certain problems, they should discuss openly issues that are important for citizens. Revolutions usually promise more than they can fulfill (Heller 2015, 182). The English political theorist Margaret Canovan emphasizes that Arendt's political thinking developed under the influence of concrete events after which ideas appeared (Canovan 2015, 140). That move from event to idea was precisely the aspect that many Polish intellectuals found fascinating about Arendt.

Wojciech Duda and Paweł Śpiewak maintain that after the political system transformed, engagement with Arendt decreased. The events of 1989 meant that Arendt's works were no longer forbidden fruit and were not widely discussed. Śpiewak thinks that there are two reasons for this phenomenon. The first one is related to the defeat of politics in dialogue with others in Poland after 1989. For the sociologist, it means concretely "the defeat of thinking about politics" (Duda/Śpiewak 2002, 34). The second reason, in his opinion, is the fact that there is a lack of self-awareness. For Arendt, the reference point was the Holocaust and totalitarianism. In Poland, neither the war nor the communist time is such a reference point. For this reason, today there is no deeper reflection about totalitarianism that would be the continuation of Tischner's, Kołakowski's or Walicki's ideas. Śpiewak underlines that "We live separated from the past" (Duda/Śpiewak 2002, 35).

However, in Polish intellectual circles, the fascination for Arendt is still very much present. She is indelibly linked to freedom and the fight against communism and is often equated with a saint. I experienced this fascination personally during my work in the Hannah Arendt Institute for Research on Totalitarianism at the Technical University in Dresden from 2004 until 2010. Polish universities and scholarly institutions were looking for cooperation with the Hannah Arendt Institute because of Hannah Arendt's name. When asking for the possibility of cooperation they did not ask very many questions about the research topics. The Hannah Arendt name was enough and all that mattered. It shows how much power the name of Hannah Arendt has in Polish scholarly life. She is like a magnet, a significant myth.

FUTURE DIRECTIONS

Polish intellectuals very often ask whether there is a risk that the totalitarian past could come back. The already mentioned Piotr Buras analyzes the question of whether Eichmann could exist outside of the totalitarian world. To answer this question, he turns to Arendt's account. Buras states that for individuals to avoid becoming like Eichmann in certain aspects, individuals must be able to act in the public sphere, and furthermore, that political institutions respect and support the rules governing public action, as Arendt describes them. That is, it is vital to not limit people's freedoms, to make education better, and to strengthen civic consciousness. The "force to think" is, in Buras's opinion, the necessary prevention of Eichmann in society (Buras 2003, 18). By the idea of the "Eichmann in us," Buras means a lack of empathy and an inhuman way of thinking and acting. These inhuman feelings are present in all human beings and can be identified in recent Polish society, too. For instance, the relations in the Polish political sphere and Polish society regarding the refugee crisis in 2015 demonstrated that the great majority of Polish society was not prepared to show solidarity. Instead, Warsaw opposed the EU quota regulation and was not ready even to take a small percentage of the newcomers. Poland—as well as Hungary and the Czech Republic—demonstrated that values and norms are cultural habits with only superficial relevance. In appropriately perceived cases of emergency, human beings do reveal their true nature: at first, they think of themselves and their "tribe" in the categories of "We" and "the others" (Besier 2014, 73–127). Of course, the Holocaust is not an example of only keeping yourself and your family in mind. It is a singular and incomparable crime against humanity in history. This is what Hannah Arendt puts on record—in spite of her well-known thesis on the banality of evil.

Arendt is very often referred to in Polish analyses of freedom or the lack of it. She also appears more often than other philosophers in the analysis of Polish society. Her popularity is due to her methods of analyzing reality that many intellectuals have used for their interpretations. Polish philosopher Piotr Nowak explains this fascination with Arendt's analyses in Poland in the following way:

> Hannah Arendt's greatness is found in the fact that she does not decide on either of the two ways (the Roman way of thinking or the Greek). The bottom line is that she makes the decision to think somewhere in between the two varying cultures, in an area between past and future. (Nowak 2005, 244)

Hannah Arendt was used in Poland as both a philosopher and an icon of freedom. She was of great importance for the part of the Polish population that were struggling for freedom against the totalitarian communist system. But it would not correspond to reality if we say that in present Polish politics and society, everything is fine. There are still many problems regarding political freedom or equality issues. For this reason, this chapter has dealt with the significance of Hannah Arendt in the Polish past, present, and future. The question that is still open is how much Hannah Arendt we will need in the Polish public sphere in future.

Hannah Arendt will unquestionably remain important within Polish scholarship. Her work is present in both Polish philosophy and sociology, as well as many other disciplines. In many cases, Polish scholars agree with Arendt's theses, whereas in others, she is sometimes criticized. Nevertheless, this philosopher is very much present in the Polish scholarly life of modern times and will moreover not disappear from the discipline in the future.

BIBLIOGRAPHY

Arendt, Hannah. 1976. *The Origins of Totalitarianism*. New York: Harcourt Brace.

Auer, Stefan. 2020. "Arendt-Lektüre in Osteuropa. Zwischen existenzieller Philosophie und Politik." In *Hannah Arendt und das 20. Jahrhundert. Begleitband zur Ausstellung des Deutschen Historischen Museums (27.3.-18.10.2020)*, edited by Dorlis Blume, Monika Boll and Raphael Gross, 83–92. München: Piper.

Besier, Gerhard. 2014. *Neither Good nor Bad. Why Human Beings Behave How They Do*. Newcastle upon Tyne: Cambridge Scholars.

Besier, Gerhard, and Katarzyna Stokłosa. 2013. *European Dictatorships. A Comparative History of the Twentieth Century*. Newcastle upon Tyne: Cambridge Scholars Publishing.

Brzeziński, Zbigniew, and Marek Kornat. 2006. "Pięćdziesiąt lat później." *Przegląd Polityczny* no. 79/80: 138–41.

Buras, Piotr. 2003. "Powroty Hannah Arendt." In *Niemieckie lekcje historii. Szkice i portrety*, edited by Piotr Buras, 9–18. Szczecin: Polsko-Niemiecka Biblioteka Szczecińska.

Canovan, Margaret. 2015. "Filozofia a polityka. Reinterpretacja myśli politycznej Hannah Arendt." *Przegląd Polityczny*, 133/134: 126–40.

Duda, Wojciech, and Paweł Śpiewak. 2002. "Świat ten wart jest troski." *Przegląd Polityczny*. 55: 34–43.

Gładziuk, Nina. 1991. *Cóż po Grekach? Archetyp polis w twórczości Hannah Arendt*. Warszawa: Instytut Studiów Politycznych: Polska Akademia Nauk.

Grinberg, Daniel. 2006. "Czy Polska była 13 grudnia 1981 roku państwem totalitarnym." *Przegląd Polityczny* no. 79/80: 172–74.

Heller, Ágnes. 2015. "Lekcja Arendt. Rzecz o późnej nowoczesności." *Przegląd Polityczny*. 133/134: 176–82.

Heller, Włodzimierz. 2000. *Źródła pluralizmu politycznego*. Poznań: Uniwersytet im. Adama Mickiewicza.

Holzer, Jerzy. 2006. "Czy Polska była 13 grudnia 1981 roku państwem totalitarnym." *Przegląd Polityczny*. 79/80: 174–75.

Jaeggi, Rahel. 2015. "Co dalej z Hannah Arendt." *Przegląd Polityczny*. 133/134: 187–97.

Kornat, Marek. 2006. "Czy Polska była 13 grudnia 1981 roku państwem totalitarnym." *Przegląd Polityczny*. 79/80: 175–80.

Krasnodębski, Zdzisław. 2006. "Intelektualne źródła totalitaryzmu." In *Totalitaryzm a zachodnia tradycja* [Totalitarianism and the Western Tradition], edited by Miłowit Kuniński, 90–101. Kraków: Księgarnia Akademicka.
Krzemiński, Ireneusz. 2006. "Czy Polska była 13 grudnia 1981 roku państwem totalitarnym." *Przegląd Polityczny*. 79/80: 180–84.
Kuniński, Miłowit. 2006. "Totalitaryzm w ujęciu Hannah Arendt." [Totalitarianism in the understanding of Hannah Arendt]. In *Totalitaryzm a zachodnia tradycja* [Totalitarianism and the Western Tradition], edited by Miłowit Kuniński, 116–42. Kraków: Księgarnia Akademicka.
Legutko, Ryszard. 2003. "Die Intellektuellen und der Kommunismus." *Anti-Totalitarismus. Eine polnische Debatte*, edited by Paweł Śpiewak, 235–64. Frankfurt a. M: Suhrkamp.
Legutko, Ryszard. 2006. "Totalitaryzm i dusza ludzka." [Totalitarianism and the Human Soul]. *Totalitaryzm a zachodnia tradycja* [Totalitarianism and the Western Tradition], edited by Miłowit Kuniński, 46–56. Kraków: Księgarnia Akademicka.
Leszczyńska, Katarzyna. 2002. "Hannah Arendt Newsletter." *Przegląd Polityczny*. 55: 214–15.
Machcewicz, Paweł. 2006. "Czy Polska była 13 grudnia 1981 roku państwem totalitarnym." *Przegląd Polityczny*. 79/80: 186–89.
Najder, Zdzisław. 2006. "Czy Polska była 13 grudnia 1981 roku państwem totalitarnym." *Przegląd Polityczny*. 79/80: 190–91.
Nowak, Piotr. 2005. "Posłowie." In *Hannah Arendt. Polityka jako obietnica*, edited by Jerome Kohn, 226–44. Kraków: Prószyński i S-ka.
Pomian, Krzysztof. 2006. "Totalitaryzm." *Przegląd Polityczny*. 79/80: 123–27.
Smolar, Aleksander. 2006. "Czy Polska była 13 grudnia 1981 roku państwem totalitarnym." *Przegląd Polityczny* 79/80: 193–97.
Śpiewak, Paweł. 2003. "Polnische Erfahrungen mit dem Totalitarismus." *Anti-Totalitarismus. Eine polnische Debatte*, edited by Śpiewak, 15–67. Frankfurt a. M.: Suhrkamp.
Śpiewak, Paweł. 2006. "Czy Polska była 13 grudnia 1981 roku państwem totalitarnym." *Przegląd Polityczny*. 79/80: 200–1.
Stokłosa, Katarzyna. 2008. "The Reception of Hannah Arendt in Poland." In *Totalitarianism and Liberty. Hannah Arendt in the 21st Century*, edited by Gerhard Besier, Katarzyna Stokłosa and Andrew Wisely, 231–40. Kraków: Księgarnia Akademicka.
Walicki, Andrzej. 2006. "Czy Polska była 13 grudnia 1981 roku państwem totalitarnym." *Przegląd Polityczny*. 79/80: 209–18.

PART III

In Prospect

Chapter Eight

The Phenomenological Sense of Hannah Arendt

Plurality, Modernity, and Political Action

Laura McMahon

On April 5, 1977, about 120 activists with disabilities entered the San Francisco offices of the United States Department of Health, Education, and Welfare (HEW). The activists, organized by thirty-year-old Judith Heumann, President of the group Disabled in Action (DIA), were protesting the failure of Joseph A. Califano, Secretary of HEW under President Jimmy Carter, to concretize and sign into law Section 504 of the 1973 Rehabilitation Act. Using language drawn from Civil Rights legislation in the 1960s, Section 504 prohibited discrimination against people with disabilities on the part of any federally funded institution (*New York Times* 1977; Patterson 2012; Lebrecht and Newnham 2020). Heumann and the other activists wound up occupying the HEW building for twenty-five days, supported by daily meals supplied by the Black Panthers, large-scale demonstrations of support outside the building, and the skills and ingenuity of the occupiers against the interventions of the Federal Bureau of Investigations (FBI); for example, when the FBI cut off the HEW building's phone lines, Deaf individuals communicated with others outside of the building through the windows, using sign language (Lebrecht and Newnham 2020). On April 29, 1977, Califano signed Bill 504 into law, bringing the nearly monthlong sit-in to a victorious conclusion.

This chapter offers a phenomenological interpretation of the human significance of contemporary political actions such as the Bill 504 sit-in, through a close engagement with the philosophy of Hannah Arendt. Arendt was not a phenomenologist in any classical sense of the term, and her own attitude toward phenomenology was ambivalent: although she once called herself "a sort of phenomenologist," she also published essays highly critical of existential phenomenology (Young-Bruehl 1982, 405).[1] However, whatever she herself had to say about the matter, Arendt's work offers profound phenomenological insight into the human condition of being with others, the lived experience of the modern world, and the creative and tenuous nature of political action.[2] As this chapter demonstrates, central insights from the work of Edmund Husserl, Martin Heidegger, and Maurice Merleau-Ponty resonate throughout Arendt's writings (even, as is often the case, when they are not explicitly identified as such), and appreciating the philosophical contributions of the former group can enable a richer appreciation of the sense and significance of Arendt's philosophy. For her part, Arendt offers a phenomenological account of political existence unrivaled by any other phenomenological philosopher, and interpreting her work with a phenomenological eye can thus in turn shed new light on the specifically political significance of key ideas from the phenomenological tradition. Divided into three parts, this chapter offers a phenomenological interpretation of three important and interrelated themes that run through Arendt's body of work—themes that can also help us to understand both the political and the phenomenological import of grassroots collective action like the Bill 504 sit-in.

Section 1 discusses Arendt's deeply phenomenological understanding of *plurality*. Drawing on Arendt's discussion of the "public" in *The Human Condition* (1958), I argue that—in keeping with Husserl's concept of "transcendental intersubjectivity," Heidegger's understanding of "Being-with," and Merleau-Ponty's concept of "intercorporeality"—it is only the ontological condition of sharing a world with others that guarantees our lived experience of the world, and ourselves, as *real*. I also explore the truth of Arendt's (very phenomenological) thesis in *The Life of the Mind* (1971) that to *be* is always to *appear*, and that to experience the substance of one's own identity always requires experiencing oneself as visible to others.

Section 2 explores Arendt's argument that modernity tends to undermine the lived sense of the world as a site of shared appearance and shared reality, and hence as a site for individual distinction and collective belonging. Drawing on *The Human Condition*, *The Origins of Totalitarianism* (1951), and her 1954 essays "Understanding and Politics" and "On the Nature of Totalitarianism," I argue here that Arendt's diagnosis of the ills of modern life—a diagnosis that resonates with Husserl's, Merleau-Ponty's, and especially Heidegger's criticisms of modernity—constitutes a phenomenological criticism of the manner in which our social and political institutions can fail to live up to crucial features of our ontological condition as human individuals and communities.

Finally, section 3 demonstrates the importance of Arendt's proposed solutions to the ills of modern existence in her call to recover from the Ancient Greek *polis* a more profound sense of democracy than that at play in modern politics. Putting Arendt's concepts of *natality*, *action*, and *power* in *The Human Condition* and her essay "What is Freedom" (1968) into conversation with Merleau-Ponty's phenomenological concepts of *expression*, *institution*, and *dialogue*, I argue that the kind of community and collective action that we witness in movements such as that of the disability rights activists in the United States in the 1970s constitute a reanimation of the Greek sense of freedom as an inherently collective and political, rather than merely individual, matter, while at the same time remaining devoted to modern principles of equality, rights, and justice. Their political success requires a capacity for judgment and a political virtuosity in Arendt's specific, phenomenological sense of these terms: politics cannot dwell in the realm of abstract, universal values but must find creative and strategic ways to bring to life these values with the unique, plural, and fragile possibilities and demands of the shared present.

PLURALITY, REALITY, AND THE WORLD OF APPEARANCE

In her discussion of "the public realm" or "the common" in *The Human Condition*, Arendt draws an analogy between the shared world and a table at which we each have a seat:

> To live together in the world means essentially that a world of things is between those who have it in common, as a table is located between those who sit around it; the world, like every in-between, relates and separates men at the same time. (1958, 52)

Without an appreciation of work in the phenomenological tradition on the lived human experience of things, the world, and of other people, it is easy to miss the phenomenological weight of this analogy.

Phenomenology is the rigorous description of experience as it is actually lived. While describing their own experience might initially seem simple or obvious to novice students of phenomenology, it becomes evident quite quickly that such a task is no small feat. Phenomenological description reveals that in our everyday lives we are typically quite ignorant of the constitutive features of experience that enable it to take the meaningful forms that it does. Inquiring into what makes lived experiences meaningful thus renders strange—and by means of this wonder is able to grasp with newfound insight—our most familiar everyday experiences, while never ceasing to take its guide from and be beholden to these lived experiences themselves.[3]

Lived experience is not simply transparent to us, on account of a number of prejudices that, while arising from within lived experience, work to obscure their own origins in lived experience. One such prejudice concerns the nature of our experience of objects. Husserl argues that in the "natural attitude" of everyday experience, we take it for granted that there is a world of physical objects that exist independently of us (Husserl 1982, 51–57). On one hand, there is something basically right about this prejudice: our experience of things existing as real is an experience of their having no need of being perceived in order to exist. On the other hand, however, what this prejudice overlooks is that our experience of things in their own reality is, precisely, an *experience* of real things, and that this experience has terms and conditions of its own. When we attend, not naively to the *objects of our experience*, but phenomenologically to our *experience of objects*, these terms and conditions can begin to come to light. One thing we can notice straight off the bat is that the object does not give itself all at once in our perceptual experience, but rather from one "side" or in "profile" (Husserl 1999, 39–41; Husserl 2001, 39–46). However, I do not mistake the particular side or profile of the object available from my situated, and hence intrinsically limited, perspective to be the whole reality of the thing; rather, the object gives itself as unfolding beyond what I can currently see of it, of having further sides available to ongoing perceptual exploration. Merleau-Ponty gives a vivid description of this fundamental Husserlian observation:

> When I see the lamp on my table, I attribute to it not merely the qualities that are visible from my location, but also those that the fireplace, the walls, and the table can "see." The back of my lamp is merely the face that it "shows" the fireplace. Thus, I can see one object insofar as objects form a system or a world, and insofar as each of them arranges the others around itself like spectators of its hidden aspects and as the guarantee of their permanence. (2012, 71)

Far from being given all at once and independently, therefore, the object gives itself to experience always partially and always contextually. Things in their own, independent reality reveal themselves not as "seen from nowhere" or as "seen from everywhere"; rather, they reveal themselves to a perspective that is embodied and situated, *as* always offering more to see (Merleau-Ponty 2012, 71; Husserl 1999, 44–45; see also Mensch 2007, 36). Husserl's thesis concerning the "intentional" structure of consciousness speaks to this point: consciousness is always consciousness *of* some object or another, and objects can only show themselves *in* and *for* conscious experience (Husserl 1982, 73–75; Husserl 1999, 33). Rather than objects simply existing independently of consciousness, then, they appear meaningfully only in an ongoing "dialogue" between perceiving subject and appearing things; in Merleau-Ponty's formulation, they appear as an "in-itself-for-me," or, better, an "in-itself-for-us" (2012, 74, 336; see also Bredlau 2018, 5–6).

To notice that things always appear within meaningful, embodied *contexts* is also to notice that experience always takes place not "inside" the isolate minds of subjects—another common prejudice of the natural attitude—but rather in the "world" (Heidegger 1962, 91–106). The world is not a collection or totality of things but, rather, the inescapable horizon of significance in which things meaningfully appear for us, and in which our lives unfold in meaningful ways (2012, 345). Importantly, the world is a specifically human phenomenon: it is a way of taking up and giving meaningful shape to nature—which, to use Aristotle's definition, has its own principles of motion and rest indifferent to human existence—in a historically and a culturally meaningful manner.[4] As Arendt says, a world comes into being through the "fabrication of human hands" over multiple generations, and is the meaningful, conditioning context for the "affairs which go on among those who inhabit the man-made world together" (1958, 52, 9).[5] Through their shared perceptions, activities, and (as we shall see further below) speaking over time, human beings collectively create a meaningful world in which to live together; this world of things, in turn, provides the meaningful context for any possible individual or collective human experience.

Other people are implicitly involved, then, in our most basic experiences of the shared human world. As Arendt continually stresses, we do not begin as isolated subjects, but rather plurality is fundamental to the human condition. This is so even when no one else is physically present on the scene. Things—tables, lamps, fireplaces—give themselves as having been made by, and as available to the perception and use of, others like myself (Husserl 1999, 92–99; Heidegger 1962, 153–63; Merleau-Ponty 2012, 361–83). Furthermore, others are implicitly involved in each of our senses of ourselves *as* real and effective perceivers, actors, and speakers inhabiting a world with others. In her phenomenological studies of the experience of prisoners held in solitary confinement, Lisa Guenther argues that we rely on the complementary perspectives of other selves in order to confirm our most basic sense of reality of self and world—a sense of reality that becomes undermined when a person is deprived for extended periods of the company of others. Guenther writes:

> The other confirms, contests, enriches, and challenges my experience and interpretation of things. . . . When we isolate a prisoner in solitary confinement, we deprive him of this network of perceptual and existential orientation. He still might have an experience of this table bolted in place in his cell, and he still

might have the memory of what tables mean for other people. But the lived experience of these objects as both for-me and for-another is, by and large, denied to him. The "there" that would otherwise anchor his experience of the world from "here" has been pulled up, casting him adrift without a clear view of the horizon. (2014; see also Husserl 1999, 116–17)

Indeed, prisoners who have been held in solitary confinement report beginning to lose their perceptual grip on reality, with objects coming to appear unreal, and on themselves as an integrated personality (Guenther 2011, 258–59). Our experience, and our identities as experiencers, therefore, never simply take place "in" our own minds and are never simply our own. In what Husserl calls "transcendental intersubjectivity," Heidegger calls "Being-with," and Merleau-Ponty calls "intercorporeality," others' situated, embodied perspectives "gear into" and form a "system" with our own, such that the integrity of each of our first-personal experiences is conditioned, accomplished, and supported (or undermined) by this shared system (Husserl 1970, 184–86; Heidegger 1962, 153–63; Merleau-Ponty 1968, 141; Merleau-Ponty 2012, 367).

With these phenomenological accounts of our experience of things, world, and other people in mind, we can appreciate the significance of Arendt's analogy between living together in a world and sitting together around a table, with which we began this section. Living with others—the "sharing of words and deeds"—requires an objective, built common space in which we can dwell together, just as friendships need living rooms, classrooms, restaurants, parks, and so on in order to have a worldly place to exist and to flourish (Arendt 1958, 197). Such spaces are only maintained through the ongoing perception, use, and care of plural subjects; absent this, they become merely the ruins of former worlds.[6] At the same time, it is only among our companions around the (metaphorical) table that each of us can properly be ourselves *as* the individuals that we are; in Arendt's terms, it is only within a shared space of appearance that we can appear to others—and, as we saw in Guenther's analysis of solitary confinement, appear to ourselves—in our own uniqueness. The common world relates us to others and, precisely by way of this relation, allows us to become and to shine as distinct, irreplaceable selves—in Arendt's words again, "the world, like every in-between, relates and separates men at the same time" (1958, 52).

Thanks to its ability to simultaneously relate and separate us from our fellows, human plurality within a common world has "the twofold character of equality and distinctness" (Arendt 1958, 175). "Equality" here does not name a natural sameness with which we are each born simply by virtue of being members of the human species, and by sharing in some essential "human nature," as if we were instances of a type ("whats") rather than unique, lived perspectives on the world ("whos") (Arendt 1958, 10). As Arendt argues, equality does not make human beings interchangeable as members of the same species, but is rather that which enables them, qua lived human experiences, to "understand each other and those who came before them," and to "foresee the needs of those who will come after them" (1958, 175).[7] Our lived experience of equality with other human beings thus points toward, rather than away from, our lived experience of our own and others' distinctness *as* distinct, experiencing "whos."[8] Equality allows us to understand and sympathize with one another, while still each occupying our own perspective. As Arendt argues, in the "meeting ground" of the common world "[b]eing seen and heard by others derive their significance from the fact that everybody sees and hears from a different position" (1958, 57). And as James Mensch argues, in the public world our perspectives always overlap, but never entirely (2007, 36). From where we each stand, we are each capable of seeing, speaking, and acting in unique and unprecedented ways, and of having our unique visions, words, and actions appear to and be recognized by others from where *they* stand.

We shall discuss this human capacity for the initiation of the new—the "natality" that goes hand-in-hand with our "plurality"—in section 3. For now, it is worthwhile to bring out the ontological weight of Arendt's phenomenological attention to the shared human world as simultaneously the site of the intersubjective and intercorporeal disclosure of reality and the site for the disclosure of the "who." A temptation within the modern natural attitude is to dismiss the phenomenological attention to the manners in which things are given in experience—the phenomena or appearances—as merely psychological, subjective, or epiphenomenal. As Arendt argues in *The Life of the Mind*, this temptation is due to the emphasis in much of modern science and philosophy on a radical distinction between appearance and being. Modern natural and social sciences, for example, often seek reality not in the diversity of appearances in the natural world or in the richness and diversity of human personality and relationships, but in underlying, hidden "causes" of which the prosaic appearances of the world are merely "effects" (1971, 25). For example, certain strains of modern psychology would attempt to reduce all of the subtle and diverse expressions of human love to an underlying sexual urge (1971, 23). There are two major problems with such a metaphysical prejudice that seeks to reduce effect to cause, mere appearance to true being.

The first problem concerns the ontological status of human experience. The world of appearances is our native habitat. Although we can withdraw from this world in private thought, we are not "godlike creatures" who can gaze at the world from some space outside it; rather, we can only see, hear, and touch the world because we are ourselves visible, audible, and tangible parts *of* the world (Arendt 1971, 22, 20, 50; see also Merleau-Ponty 1968,

137, 142). Although we can direct our attentions and investigations to realities that do not appear but are at play within appearances, no one—including the scientist or the philosopher—can in the end *live* among causes (Arendt 1971, 26). We can only approach the invisible through the visible, the hidden through the manifest. Appearances do not *divorce* us from reality, but are our ineluctable and indispensable *initiation* into the real. Of course, error and deception are possible in the world of appearances, but it is not by stepping outside of appearances that these errors can be dispelled, but on the contrary only through further and more adequate experiences (Husserl 2001, 69–72; Merleau-Ponty 1968, 8). Others, as we have seen, are crucial here. As Arendt writes, "[o]nly where things can be seen by many in a variety of aspects without changing their identity, so that those who are gathered around them know they see sameness in utter diversity, can worldly reality truly and reliably appear" (1958, 57; see also 1973, 475–76 and 2005, 169).

The second problem with the metaphysical prejudice for being over appearance concerns the ontological status of appearances themselves. Drawing on Aristotle's philosophy of perception alongside more recent work in biology, Arendt argues that at play in the vast diversity of appearances is an "urge to self-display" (1971, 29). Far from being merely epiphenomenal, the appearance of things is expressive of the very reality of natural, animal, and human life. Arendt draws an analogy between the metaphysical preference for cause over effect to locating the "true" reality of an animal in its inner organs rather than in its outer display of specific and individual diversity and difference. Whereas "[t]he outside shapes are infinitely varied and highly differentiated; among the higher animals we can usually tell one individual from another ... not even the various animal species, let alone the individuals, are easy to tell from each other by the mere inspection of their intestines" (1971, 28–29). It is on the surface, visible to others in the shared world, that individuality can be recognized; inside, shielded from the light of day, we all appear more or less the same. As Arendt sums up the issue, "If this inside were to appear, we would all look alike" (1971, 28–29).

Reality is not indifferent to human experience; as Arendt writes, "whatever can see wants to be seen, whatever can hear calls out to be heard, whatever can touch presents itself to be touched" (1971, 29). From the other side, the human perception of reality is not merely a private, solitary affair, but a tenuous capacity that needs others in the context of a shared world in order to be enacted, and is for this same reason vulnerable to neglect and exploitation. In section 2, let us explore this latter point in the context of Arendt's criticism of modern political life, before turning in section 3 to a discussion of what it can mean to politically live up to our ontological reality as appearing beings in a world of appearances.

MODERNITY AND THE DESTRUCTION OF THE COMMON WORLD

The modern prejudice for being over appearance, cause over effect, is not only a theoretical issue, but has pervasive political ramifications. Arendt argues that modern political existence is characterized by a strong tendency to undermine the common world in which individuals can experience themselves both as participating in a shared reality with others, and as distinguishing themselves as unique "whos"—a strong tendency to undermine the very realm, as we shall see, in which a properly political life is possible. As Seyla Benhabib argues, while what Arendt calls "the space of appearance" and "the common world" should be understood as phenomenological dimensions of the human condition "under whatever sociohistorical conditions, in whatever epoch," the existence of a common world qua public realm of politics is "more fragile and more closely linked to sociohistorical conditions" (2003, 128). In other words, sociohistorical conditions can do justice to and support, or betray and undermine, our ontological reality as human selves among others identified and elaborated in the phenomenological description of lived experience, and modern society can be criticized on the grounds that it tends to prevent individuals from living a genuinely political life with others.

As we have already begun to see, much of what is at stake in the phenomenological criticism of modernity can be seen in the orientation of modern experimental science in contrast to the orientation of Aristotelian science. In Arendt's words, while ancient science was "content to observe, to register, and [to] contemplate whatever nature was willing to yield in her own appearance," modern science began "to prescribe conditions and to provoke natural processes" (1958, 231). Ancient science attended to natural forms within their living contexts so as to understand the natural world as it shows itself, on its own terms. Modern science, by contrast, came to view nature as matter that, within the isolated and controlled conditions of the laboratory, could be manipulated and compelled to serve human purposes, apparently without end. As Francis Bacon wrote in 1620, "the secrets of nature reveal themselves better through harassments applied by the arts than when they go on in their own way" and "it is very much to be expected that many exceedingly useful things are still hidden in the bosom of nature which have no kinship or analogy with things already discovered, which lie altogether outside of the paths of the imagination," such that, thanks to the discoveries of the sciences, "man is a god to man" (2000, 81, 86, 100; see also Merchant 2013). However, as phenomenology's (including Arendt's) criticisms of modernity point out, the hubristic modern notion that nature can be made a slave to human purposes and unlimited human progress is matched with an ironic—and tragic—subservience of human beings to scientific and technological innovations. These scientific and technological innovations take on a pervasive and irresistible life of their own, which, in cases such as atomic devastation and climate change, have the power not to serve but on the contrary to devastate human life along with the natural world.[9] The orientation and advances of modern science represent at once human emancipation—the democratic power of shaping the world through reason and art celebrated by the Enlightenment—and the degradation of the very conditions of human flourishing.[10]

This critical, ambivalent attitude toward modern science and modernity more generally can be found in each of Husserl, Merleau-Ponty, and Heidegger. Husserl's 1936 *The Crisis of the European Sciences and Transcendental Phenomenology* argues that on one hand, the modern sciences in many ways embody a powerful promise of human rationality: a power, from within one's sociohistorical situation, to discover and orient oneself toward universal truths that transcend any given sociohistorical situation (1970, 11–14, 269–99). On the other hand, however, the modern sciences have lost their vital connection to their roots in human (inter)subjective constitution, in the "lifeworld" in which they were born as meaningful projects to begin with (Husserl 1970, 5–7, 103–32; see also Loidolt 2018, 80). Merleau-Ponty's sustained criticisms of the rationalist and empiricist schools of modern philosophy in his 1945 *Phenomenology of Perception* speak to the rationalist tendencies of modern thought to envision the self as a thinking, disembodied mind radically separate from the world of nature, and to the empiricist tendencies to envision the world of nature (including the human body) as a complex system of mechanistic, calculable cause and effect. These rationalist and empiricist prejudices ignore the phenomenon of lived experience as simultaneously in and of the world, and ignore the phenomenon of things (including animal and human life) as figures that appear within meaningful contexts with an indeterminate and open-ended integrity of their own (Merleau-Ponty 2012, 3–65; see also Merleau-Ponty 1963, 3–128). Finally, Heidegger's 1954 "The Question Concerning Technology" argues that, while we might think of modern technology as a human activity that applies modern physics to nature for the sake of bringing about specific human ends, modern technology is in truth an entire metaphysical worldview that *precedes* modern physics insofar as it "enframes" nature as "standing reserve," or as so much indifferent material for human use (1993b, 312, 318–20, 322–26, 328). Furthermore, although as modern human beings we fancy ourselves "lord of the earth," we in fact ourselves become part of the standing reserve (as indicated by the phrase "human resources") (Heidegger 1993b, 332, 323).

Resonances of all of these phenomenological critiques of modernity, but especially Heidegger's, can be found throughout Arendt's account of the modern age. Arendt's particular interest is in the implications of the instrumentalist and technocratic worldview for modern political life, which, Arendt argues, can be broadly characterized by its tendency to treat human beings as "material" for larger political ends. Arendt writes:

> Recent political history is full of examples indicating that the term "human material" is no harmless metaphor, and the same is true for a whole host of modern scientific experiments in social engineering, biochemistry, brain surgery, etc., all of which tend to treat and change human material like other matter. This mechanistic approach is typical of the modern age . . . The only possible achievement . . . is to kill man, not indeed necessarily as a living organism, but *qua* man. (1958, 188n15)

The tendency of modern politics to treat human beings as "human material like other matter" and in the process to "kill man . . . *qua* man" can be seen, on the more benign end of the spectrum, in liberal, capitalist, democratic societies and, at the other extreme, in the totalitarian experiments of the twentieth century.

There is a paradox at the heart of liberal, capitalist, democratic modern societies that parallels the ambivalence at the heart of modern science. On the one hand, the expressed values of such societies—and of an international politics created in their image—celebrate the equal rights and dignity of each and every individual, simply by virtue of being born human. As the French Revolution's 1789 Declaration of the Rights of Man and Citizen states, "[m]en are born and remain free and equal in rights," and "[t]he aim of all political association is the preservation of the natural and imprescriptible rights of man" (2008, Articles 1 and 2). On the other hand, however, these societies at the same time recognize the subordination of individuals to the state; in the words of the Declaration of the Rights of Man and Citizen again, "[s]ocial distinctions may be founded only upon the general good" and "[n]o body nor individual may exercise any authority which does not proceed directly from the nation" (2008, Articles 1 and 3).[11] Out of this tension arises what Arendt calls "the rise of the social" in *The Human Condition*: the equal rights of individuals become the sameness and interchangeability of all human beings, while "society . . . demands that its members act as though they were members of one enormous family" (1958, 39).[12] From the perspective of such an "enormous family," modern politics becomes a giant and elaborate economic "housekeeping," an administration *of* by-and-large passive citizens rather than a rule *by* active (and unpredictably act*ing*) citizens sharing in a common world.

Key to Arendt's understanding of the social is its distortion of the relationship between the private and the public spheres of human life. In section 1, we discussed Arendt's phenomenological argument that it is in the context of a common world that we can both experience ourselves as participating in shared reality, and feel ourselves properly to exist as singular "whos." The realm of the private is a comparatively priva*tive* domain (1958, 38). While each of us fundamentally need a domain of privacy and intimacy in which our basic needs can be met, and in which we can withdraw and be hidden from the light of the public, Arendt is adamant that it is not in the space of the private that we feel ourselves to share in, and to properly count within, a common reality (1958, 38). This argument should not be interpreted as a denigration of the domain of the private; indeed, Arendt argues that certain deeply important human experiences, such as love and goodness, can only really take place within the domain of our private lives with intimate others (1958, 51–52, 76). Rather, we should interpret Arendt's argument as pointing to the insufficiency of the private realm to do justice to the full parameters of human existence. As phenomenological accounts of the experience of home elaborate, there is a basically ambivalent character to the home, in that (when all goes well) it serves to both protect us from, and initiate and support our endeavors within, the larger outside world (Jacobson 2010; Russon 2017, 61–65). If to be confined to the sphere of the home and domestic relationships is commonly experienced as isolating—as we see, for example, in the young adult's desire to leave the parental home and to make her own way in the larger world, or in the common malaise of the "housewife" in a world in which public opportunities for women are severely curtailed—then this is because there are distinctly human experiences that are only possible in the public world of equal citizens, where one's identity can be seen within the context of, and one's worth measured according to the standards of, the larger cultural and historical world (Russon 2017, 66–67). Arendt argues that from the perspective of this larger cultural and historical world, what goes on in private is relatively uninteresting, since it does not serve to distinguish us but rather renders us (more or less) the same as others; much like the internal organs of animals, what goes on in private does not reveal but rather conceals who we are as distinct individuals. As Marieke Borren writes, "[h]uman dignity . . . does not refer to some natural quality, but only flourishes under conditions of plurality and publicity: in public visibility and natural invisibility" (2008, 219). It is the contributions we make to the public world—for example, our distinctive intellectual, artistic, entrepreneurial, or political projects—that enable us to be seen and remembered as unique selves by a human community beyond the fulfillment of our natural needs and the bounds of our most intimate circles.

One of the chief problems with the modern phenomenon of "the social," in Arendt's view, is that it transforms and distorts the distinction between the private and the public, the inside and the outside. First, modern society erodes the lived experience of the common world as a shared human space in which one's own identity can be seen and recognized. Continuing with her metaphor of the table, Arendt writes:

> What makes mass society so difficult to bear is not the number of people involved . . . but the fact that the world between them has lost its power to gather them together, to relate and to separate them. The weirdness of this situation resembles a spiritualistic séance where a number of people gathered around a table might suddenly, through some magic trick, see the table vanish from their midst, so that two people sitting opposite each other were no longer separated but also would be entirely unrelated to each other by anything tangible. (1958, 53)

Modern society isolates and atomizes individuals, such that they can exist *alongside* each other but not properly *with* each other, much like box apartments in a high-rise building or cubicles in an office building (Arendt 1994c, 357; see also Foucault 1977, 195–228). Modern politics then becomes not about the actions and self-expressions of distinct "whos," but rather about the management of the basic needs of a population of interchangeable "whats."[13] In its concern with the economic management of life—a domain that Arendt argues properly belongs to the private household—modern society displays the inner organs of life, so to speak, on the outside.[14] The properly private and the properly public are thus inverted in modern life: the outside world demands that we conform to the "leveling demands of the social," such that "distinction and difference . . . become private matters of the individual" (1958, 41; see also Heidegger 1962, 163–68, 210–24 and Weber 1946, 224–28). We become anonymous in public, and distinctly ourselves only within the intimate parameters of private life.[15]

We can see the leveling demands of the social at play in two distinctly modern practices: that of social sciences such as economics and that of the political institution of bureaucracy. The social sciences study human behavior from the outside, and are interested in statistical averages among large populations and over significant periods of time, rather than on the rare deeds of individuals or the anomalous events of history (Arendt 1958, 42; see also Foucault 1977, 224–28). In studying what is normal rather than what is rare, average behavior rather than the actions of distinct individuals, the statistical sciences lose sight of "meaning in politics or significance in history" (Arendt 1958, 42–43). While, as Arendt writes, "[t]he justification of statistics is that deeds and events are rare occurrences in everyday life and in history," bureaucracy can be seen as the attempt to actively *prevent* deeds and events—genuine human action—from taking place in the political management of human affairs (1958, 42). Bureaucracy—the "rule by no one" that constitutes "the most social form of government"—is designed to take the personality out of political leadership, replacing persons with offices, idiosyncrasy with uniformity, and judgment with rules and procedures (Arendt 1958, 40; Weber 1946, 198–204, 214–16, 219–21; see also Foucault 1977, 218–24). Bureaucracy in modern democratic societies embodies the equality qua interchangeability and the democratic fairness emblematic of modern science and politics, but it is at the same time—as no doubt personal experience as well as the novels of Franz Kafka will attest—a deeply dehumanizing method of administration.

Bureaucracy may be inherently dehumanizing, but it need not be democratic. In his 1921 essay "Bureaucracy," Max Weber points out the political neutrality of the bureaucratic form of government: its consequences "depend . . . upon the direction which the powers using the apparatus give to it" (1946, 230). Indeed, as Arendt's analysis of the trial of Adolf Eichmann (1964) demonstrates, bureaucracies can be turned to genocidal ends like the mass deportation and internment of Jews, queer people, people with disabilities, and other targeted minorities, all while depending on the unquestioning cooperation of career-oriented bureaucrats simply "following orders." More generally, the same social forces that Arendt and earlier phenomenologists diagnose as at play in modern science and modern democratic societies are deployed in extreme forms in the totalitarian regimes of the twentieth century (Villa 1999, 188–89). Modern science's abstraction from lived experience and the world of common sense can be transformed into totalitarian ideologies that can take hold only when they operate independently from the lived experience that would challenge them, and according to a strict "logicality" that—in contrast to the honest search for understanding and truth in the company of others both equal to and distinct from oneself—can operate best and most consistently in the privacy of one's own mind or in the isolation of the laboratory (Arendt 1973, 470–72, 477; 1994b, 318; 1994c, 355). Modern science's search for underlying causes—for the true "being" beneath "appearances"—can be seen reflected in the totalitarian regime's ironclad faith in so-called objective laws of Nature or History, which are seen to move with a force of their own that sweeps the entire human species along with them, and which serve to justify the elimination of all elements superfluous, or in opposition to, their suprahuman movement (Arendt 1973, 465; 1994c, 341; see also Fromm 1969, 224–25, 233–35). Modern democracy's tension between universal human rights and national sovereignty, and its ultimate subordination of the former to the latter, can be subverted so as to further justify the elimination of enemy elements or those disloyal to the regime. Finally, the atomization and isolation of individuals in modern capitalist society provide fertile ground for the growth of a totalitarian regime whose very principle is the freezing of the inherent dynamism of human existence, so as to allow for the "fabrication of mankind" according to their ideological image (Arendt 1973, 465; 1994c, 356–57; see also Fromm 1969, 183–204).

Despite totalitarianism's resonances with the ambivalent values and practices of modern science and politics, Arendt is clear that the events of the Scientific Revolution, the Enlightenment, and the democratic political revolutions of the Eighteenth Century did not *cause* Nazism or Stalinism (1964b, 26–27).[16] If the events of totalitarianism lead us to tell a destructive and dehumanizing story of the modern tradition, then different kinds of political events can allow different possibilities of the modern tradition, and of our historical heritage more generally, to come to light, and different stories to be told (Benhabib 1990, 187–88). Arendt observes a further ambivalence in modernity: its rupture with the traditional authorities of the past in favor of independent scientific thinking and democratic rule can give way to terror, but also to new ways of living more humanly together (1964c, 91, 141). In the third and final section of this chapter, we will examine the emancipatory possibilities of Arendt's own creative reappropriations of both premodern understandings of political life and some of the best principles of modern revolutionary politics—creative reappropriations that point us in the direction not of atomization, isolation, and domination, but of collective action, political self-expression, and the human capacity to begin anew.

EXPRESSION, COLLECTIVE POWER, AND POLITICAL ACTION

If modern society tends to suppress the human condition of plurality and the common space of appearances, it also tends, concomitantly, to suppress the human condition of natality and the human power of action. *Natality* is Arendt's name for the condition of being, in Anne O'Byrne's words, "born new into an old world" (2010). As Arendt writes, the birth of each new human being "is not the beginning of something but of somebody, who is a beginner himself" (1958, 177). Our birthright as human beings is our capacity to initiate new processes and new realities in the shared world of appearances; in other words, our birthright is the capacity for *action*. In contrast to the repetitive sustenance of life through the activity of labor, and in contrast to the manufacturing of artifacts through work, human action has the twofold character of simultaneously effecting material changes in collective reality, and disclosing the actor as the unique, distinctive individual that she is; as contemporary phenomenologist John Russon writes, action is "an event of the world" that is at the same time "an event of me" (Arendt 1958, 175–81; Russon 2017, 36; see also McMahon 2018, 63–71). As we have begun to see, any "event of me" requires a space of appearance and the support and recognition of others, and action—our experience of our own freedom to shape our world and express who we are—will hence prove to be a necessarily collective, and a deeply political, phenomenon. Let us look more closely at the phenomenological nature of action, with help from Merleau-Ponty's concept of expression—and his closely related concepts of dialogue and institution—before turning to Arendt's argument for the inherently political nature of human freedom and an analysis of the disability rights movement in the United States in the 1970s as an example of collective action that recovers a richer sense of politics than that of modern bureaucratic administration.

In his phenomenological account of expression, Merleau-Ponty criticizes tendencies in modern psychology and philosophy to regard speech as either an anonymous process of a behaving organism (as we see in empiricist theories), or as the vocalization of fully formed meanings on the part of a self-possessed, thinking mind (as we see in rationalist theories) (2012, 179–80, 187). In contrast to such theories, a phenomenological account of expression as it in fact takes place in lived experience points us to the manner in which our richest experiences of expression are the efforts we make to give voice to meanings for which there are not already ready-made terms. Of course, we can and often do speak in manners that traffic in everyday, familiar meanings that do not properly speaking *say* anything new or surprising; we speak for merely utilitarian purposes, or in clichés and platitudes, so as to "get the job done" without seriously engaging ourselves in the meaning of what we are saying (Merleau-Ponty 2012, 200–3; see also Arendt 1958, 179). However, in what Merleau-Ponty calls "authentic" or "originary" expression, we experience ourselves as responsible for the birth of new meanings in the shared world—meanings that are very real, and thus not simply arbitrarily invented by us, but that require our active participation if they are to be born and to take hold in the shared world (2012, 200–3). Merleau-Ponty's description in his essay "Cézanne's Doubt" of the painter Paul Cézanne in the act of creation captures both the inspired, and the deeply vulnerable, experience of originary expression:

> [H]e speaks as the first man spoke and paints as if no one had ever painted before. What he expresses cannot, therefore, be the translation of a clearly defined thought, since such clear thoughts are those which have already been uttered by ourselves or by others. "Conception" cannot precede "execution." There is nothing but a vague fever before the act of artistic expression, and only the work itself, completed and understood, is proof that there was *something* rather than *nothing* to be said. (1964, 19)

In successful originary expression, a novel meaning is not so much compelled or controlled by us as it comes into the shared world *through* us. As the "doubt" in the title of Merleau-Ponty's essay indicates—and as anyone who has struggled existentially with creative or intellectual work will surely recognize—successful expression is in no way guaranteed. Rather, it must *take hold* in a common world in a manner that is meaningful for (contemporary or future) others; as Merleau-Ponty puts it, "[a] piece of music or a painting . . . creates its own public—so long as it truly *says* something—which is to say, by secreting its own signification" (2012, 185). It is only in finding a place in the common world that this signification becomes *real*, and only among others that the artist can properly experience it as her *own*. As Rainer Maria Rilke advises the young poet, "read the lines as though they were someone else's, and you will feel deep within you how much they are your own" (1934, 40; see also McMahon 2017, 329).

Expression does not simply issue from a self-possessed, sovereign subject, but from the "in-between" (in Arendt's words) that enables individuals to be(come) themselves and to give voice to what is most their "own." Merleau-Ponty's phenomenological account of *dialogue* helps us to see concretely how this is so. He writes:

> In the experience of dialogue, a common ground is constituted between me and another; my thought and his form a single fabric, my words and those of my interlocutor are called forth by the state of the discussion and are inserted into a shared operation of which neither of us is the creator . . . our perspectives slip into each other, we coexist through a single world. I am freed from myself in the present dialogue, even though the other's thoughts are certainly his own, since I do not form them, I nonetheless grasp them as soon as they are born or I even anticipate them. And even the objection raised by my interlocutor draws from me thoughts I did not know I possessed such that if I lend him my thoughts, he makes me think in return. (2012, 370–71)

Speaking with another enables each of us to realize—in the double sense of to *bring about* and to *make real*—our "own" thoughts and ideas, and, with these, our very identity over time (Maclaren 2008, 81). Russon speaks to the political significance of this phenomenology of dialogue by contrasting the institution of voting with that of collective decision making. As with political bureaucracy, voting requires that each voter come to the polling booth with a decision already made, and thus "puts pressure upon each of us to function as a discrete individual, rather than as a member of a collectivity: it pressures us, that is, to house our decision-making process within the limits of our own, isolated perspective" (2020, 161). Collective decision-making, by contrast, demands that we "put our otherwise inchoate thoughts into determinate form" in the context of collective conversation (not unlike Cézanne giving concrete shape to his "vague fever" in the act of painting) (Russon 2020, 158). Akin to what Arendt calls (following Immanuel Kant) "enlarged mentality," this process compels us to take responsibility for our own views in a manner that can be evaded in the privacy of our own isolated perspectives, in a manner that can enable others' views to be shaped and transformed by our perspective on the matter at hand and, in turn, that can cause us to clarify, modify, or perhaps abandon our view in light of the critical perspectives of others (Arendt 1971, 94–96; Russon 2020, 158–60).

When they take hold in the shared world through public recognition and collective dialogue, individual and collective human (self-)expressions take on a historically significant life of their own. Merleau-Ponty's phenomenological conception of *institution* captures the manner in which expressive actions open up new spaces of meaning for the future, exceeding the intentions of the actors that initiated them. Merleau-Ponty writes:

> [W]hat we understand by the concept of institution are those events in experience which endow it with durable dimensions, in relation to which a whole series of other experiences will acquire meaning, will form an intelligible series or a history—or again those events which sediment in me a meaning, not just as survivals or residues, but as the invitation to a sequel, the necessity of a future. (1970, 108–9)

Unprecedented expressions and actions serve as a hinge between past and future. Drawing upon the resources of the past so as to sketch out the beginnings of a new future, they change the landscape of what can be seen, said, and done in the shared space of appearances. In the same stroke, such events transform our understanding of the historical past; as Arendt writes, the historical event "illuminate[s] its own past," such that "the chaotic maze of past happenings emerge as a story which can be told" (1994b, 319; see also McMahon 2019, 72–79).

Merleau-Ponty's accounts of expression, dialogue, and institution shed light on the lived experience of human freedom, and help us to grasp the phenomenological weight of Arendt's argument in her essay "What is Freedom?" that human freedom—intimately connected to the human condition of natality and the capacity for action—is inseparable from the collective space of appearances and inseparable from political life. Arendt distinguishes between conceptions of freedom as the liberty of the individual subject—conceptions that we can see at play in philosophies of the freedom of the will; in negative conceptions of freedom as freedom *from* external constraint; and in associations of freedom with sovereignty—and her own, richer understanding of freedom as the capacity to act within the plural space of appearances. Arendt writes:

> Without a guaranteed public realm, freedom lacks the worldly space to make its appearance. To be sure it may still dwell in men's hearts as desire or will or hope or yearning; but the human heart . . . is a very dark place, and whatever goes on in its obscurity can hardly be called a demonstrable fact. Freedom as a demonstrable fact and politics coincide and are related to each other like two sides of the same matter. (1968d, 147)

In terms of the relationship between being and appearing discussed in section 1, freedom should be understood not as some occult property of the human mind or will ("being"), but in terms of the concrete capacities for individual action and (self-)expression opened up by the public world ("appearance"). Freedom is thus inherently political when politics is understood not in terms of the bureaucratic management of interchangeable "whats," governed by the laws of statistics, but in terms of the human capacity for action, (self-)expression, and the historical institution of new kinds of understanding and alternative ways of living together.

The ancient Greek *polis*, which celebrated not individual liberty but collective self-rule, offers an antidote to impoverished modern conceptions of both freedom and politics (Russon 2017, 102). In contrast to the emphasis of modern statistical science on the ordinary and the predictable, Arendt argues that the *polis*'s "foremost aim was to make the extraordinary an ordinary occurrence in everyday life" (Arendt 1958, 197). Ancient Greek city-states opened a common space in which citizens could distinguish themselves through brave deeds or persuasive speeches not only among their contemporaries, but for posterity, through the telling of stories (Arendt 1958, 197). At the same time, the political space of the *polis* was only enacted and maintained thanks to the active participation of its citizens; as Pericles says in his Funeral Oration, "I have sung the praises of our city; but it was the courage and gallantry of these men, and of people like them, which made her splendid" (Thucydides 1972, 148). It is in this sense that we should see the *polis* not primarily as a physical place but as a properly human space; as Arendt argues, the *polis* "is the organization of people as it arises out of acting and speaking together, and its true space lies between people living together for this purpose, no matter where they happen to be" (1958, 198). In contrast to the modern politics of administration—the "rule of no one"—the *polis* is the space of politics in Arendt's far richer understanding of the term—the collective rule of acting "whos."[17]

Arendt's celebration of ancient Greek politics should not be understood as a nostalgic celebration of an aristocratic past, in which, as Arendt is at pains to point out, the majority had to labor and work so that a select group of citizens had the opportunity to distinguish themselves in great words and deeds. Rather, we should interpret her analysis of the Greek *polis* in terms of its phenomenological significance for the lived experience of the modern present. As Sophie Loidolt argues, Arendt's analysis of the Greek *polis* does not present a claim to historical accuracy regarding Greek experience so much as a demand that we "delve into what the tradition has to offer . . . to recover something that we would not be able to see with the eyes of our *zeitgeist* only" (2018, 80–81). The concrete demands, possibilities, and values of the political present are not the same concrete demands, possibilities, and values of the ancient Greek world. The principles of universal human rights developed by the political revolutions and the philosophical thought of the eighteenth century, ambivalent as their historical trajectory has been, are felt as moral and political imperatives on the part of modern political actors concerned with human freedom, equality, and dignity, not just for the few, but for all. The challenge is to discover how an active political commitment to such ideals can work not to isolate and atomize modern subjects, but on the contrary to mobilize communities that can create concrete, effective spaces for the collective realization of these ideals, and thus to experientially enact the twofold nature of plurality as equality and distinction. It is in answer to this challenge that the disability rights movement in the 1970s has important lessons to offer.

The 1977 occupation of the San Francisco HEW offices on the part of some 120 activists with disabilities, with which we opened this chapter, did not arise out of nowhere. On the contrary: many of the leaders and the activists involved had known each other for many years, and had extensive experience in engaging in collective decision-making together. As explored in the 2020 documentary *Crip Camp*, an important setting of many of the activists' involvement with one another was Camp Jened, a summer camp for disabled youth in the Catskill mountains of New York, opened in 1952 by Leona Burger and Nora Rubenstein, two women working in the field of special education (Patterson 2012, 481; Lebrecht and Newnham 2020). Many of the adolescents and young adults who attended Camp Jened as campers and counselors went on to become prominent members of a generation of disability activists in the 1970s. These activists gave enormous credit to Jened as affording them a sense of self-esteem and inclusion that was by and large denied them in their everyday lives at a time when the institutionalization of children with disabilities was common, when public schools and places of employment were in large part closed to individuals with disabilities, and where public buildings, sidewalks, and transportation were generally inaccessible. In Arendt's language, Camp Jened enabled individuals with a range of disabilities to experience themselves as *visible*, and as members of a community occupying a common space together. In the words of Judy Heumann, President of Disabled in Action (DIA) and leader of the Bill-504 sit-in and a Camp Jened camper and counselor, "I don't think I felt really shame about my disability. What I felt more was exclusion. For me, the camp experience really was empowering, because we helped empower each other that the status quo was not what it needed to be" (Lebrecht and Newnham 2020). From the relative obscurity of life in their private homes, young individuals with disabilities found themselves in a public place where everyone had a space to speak and be heard, no matter their particular challenges: individuals with advanced cerebral palsy, for example, would be patiently listened to without discrimination on account of the slowness or laboriousness of their speech. Rather than being seen—and perhaps in important respects seeing themselves—as identified with their disability, and hence as a "what," at Camp Jened individuals with disabilities were able to appear as unique "whos."

As well as visibility, Camp Jened provided a space for the dialogical cultivation of what Arendt calls "power." Arendt writes:

> Power is what keeps the public realm, the potential space of acting and speaking men, in existence . . . While strength is the natural quality of an individual seen in isolation, power springs up between men when they act together and vanishes the moment they disperse. Because of this peculiarity . . . power is to an astonishing degree independent of material factors, either numbers or means . . . Popular revolt against materially strong rulers . . . may engender an almost irresistible power. (1958, 200)

Camp Jened was the fertile ground of many important relationships in these young people's lives: friendships and romances were forged in a world that largely dismissed and desexualized individuals with disabilities, and social and political allegiances were formed that would bear fruit for decades—indeed for generations—to come. The development of techniques of dialogue and collective decision-making opened a "potential space of acting and speaking" that, while established at a physical location in the Catskills, did not remain tied to any given place but rather expanded among disability rights activists across the United States. For example, activists who had attended Camp Jened helped to found the Center for Independent Living in Berkeley, California in the 1970s, which provided material and social supports for adults with a range of disabilities to live on their own and to lead rich and active lives. It was the creation and maintenance of such human spaces—and not merely the abstract freedom and equality of the individual—that nurtured the collective power of the growing disability rights movement, a collective power that, through political actions such as the Bill 504 sit-in, proved victorious over the bureaucratic indifference of the immeasurably materially stronger US government.

In her essay "Introduction *Into* Politics," Arendt distinguishes four elements of political action (2005, 194–95). First, political action pursues a concrete *end*. The end of the Bill 504 sit-in, for example, was to see an important bill of the 1973 Rehabilitation Act signed into law and enforced. But ends, which political action either achieves or fails to achieve, are comparatively small and always relative to the larger goals of the action—Arendt's second element of political action. Arendt writes: "the goals of politics are never anything more than the guidelines and directives by which we orient ourselves and which, as such, are never cast in stone, but whose concrete realizations are constantly changing because we are dealing with other people who also have goals" (2005, 195). The goals of the disability rights movement were multiple: for example, the end of educational and employment discrimination and the accessibility of public spaces. But these goals by necessity did not have the same concreteness or the same criterion of success or failure as the more specific ends of the movement, for what accessibility and educational and employment accommodation look like is not set in stone, but depends upon the particular needs of the individuals involved and the particular circumstances of the institutions in question. Arendt's third element of political action is the meaning that reveals itself in the performance of the action itself (2005, 195). As in a painting, drama, or musical performance, the meaning is not located outside of the action but is performatively brought to life within it (Arendt 1958, 196; Arendt 1968d, 151; Merleau-Ponty 2012, 152–53; see also Villa 1996, 46–48). In the visibility, relationships, and experience of empowerment that they forge, spaces like Camp Jened and direct actions like the Bill-504 occupation do not simply aim at some desirable future state of affairs with only an extrinsic relationship to the activities of the present, but performatively *enact* the very kind of common world they are trying to create.[18] As disability activist Jim Lebrecht put it, "there was this whole movement brewing, where this group of radical disabled people were making this new world for themselves" (Lebrecht and Newnham 2020).

Arendt's fourth and final element of action—and the one most important for helping us to see how the ancient Greek model of the *polis* can be creatively wedded to specifically modern values—is what she calls the "principle of action" (2005, 195). Different principles have animated action in different historical ages: while the desire for fame and immortality might have animated heroic action in the Greek *polis*, grassroots politics aimed at social justice in the United States in the 1970s was animated by an urgent commitment to rights and freedoms for all people, regardless of sex, race, or ability. It is not only self-interested ends and goals that serve as the raison d'être for political action; groups can act (as well) *for the sake of* principles such as universal human rights. Arendt writes: "The extraordinary significance of these principles is not only that they first move human beings to act but that they are also the source of constant nourishment for their actions"

(2005, 195). These values do not exist in some "metaphysical heaven," as Merleau-Ponty says, apart from the embodied world of appearance; rather, they can be concretely realized only in and through political actions that work to expressively institute and maintain them in the shared historical world (Merleau-Ponty 2012, 17; see also McMahon 2019, 78–79). Indeed, in the absence of their concrete expression in the specific historical circumstances in which they matter to people, these principles are, at best, mere platitudes or clichés—Merleau-Ponty's inauthentic speech. At worst, as we saw in Arendt's analysis of totalitarianism in section 2, principles divorced from collective action—values separated from facts and experience—can take on inhuman, ideological lives of their own. Action that is not only principled but effective requires, in Arendt's words, a capacity for judgment, which is to say the collective reckoning with the particularities of circumstances, the diverse abilities and capacities for specific individuals, and the concrete possibilities for change—and the concrete possibilities for future generations and a future public—that emerge in the dynamic spaces of meaning opened between people speaking and acting together. As with Cézanne standing before his canvas, results are not guaranteed, for no rulebook or blueprint exists ahead of time in collective political existence. Such is the price—and the priceless benefit—of freedom enacted in a shared world with others; as Arendt says, "if men wish to be free, it is precisely sovereignty they must renounce" (1968d, 163).

CONCLUSION

In this chapter, I have argued that the full significance of Arendt's ontological understanding of the human significance of the common world, of her criticism of the failure of modern society to live up to this ontological significance, and of her explorations of the nature of human freedom and action, is best grasped when we engage with her work phenomenologically, that is, with a careful eye to the parameters and requirements of human experience fully lived. The disability rights community developed in the 1970s in the United States provides a powerful example of what is required to politically live up to the human condition of plurality and natality, as well as an indication of what is at stake when we fail to do so. We can only be fully ourselves—and can only be concretely free to act and to give shape to the world on our own terms—when we belong to a community that recognizes and values what makes us distinct, and when we collectively care for this community as a space for living and acting together. There is more at stake in the modern undermining of the common world than the psychological experience of loneliness; the very fabric of our shared human reality—the space in which human beings in their diverse perspectives can appear and have a place, or on the contrary can remain in obscurity—is in question.

BIBLIOGRAPHY

Arendt, Hannah. 1958. *The Human Condition*. Chicago: The University of Chicago Press.
Arendt, Hannah. 1964 [1963]. *Eichmann in Jerusalem: A Report on the Banality of Evil*. New York: Penguin Books.
Arendt, Hannah. 1968a. "Preface: The Gap Between Past and Future." In *Between Past and Future: Eight Exercises in Political Thought*, 3–15. New York: Penguin Books.
Arendt, Hannah. 1968b. "Tradition and the Modern Age." In *Between Past and Future: Eight Exercises in Political Thought*, 17–40. New York: Penguin Books.
Arendt, Hannah. 1968c. "What is Authority?" In *Between Past and Future: Eight Exercises in Political Thought*, 91–141. New York: Penguin Books.
Arendt, Hannah. 1968d. "What is Freedom?" In *Between Past and Future: Eight Exercises in Political Thought*, 142–69. New York: Penguin Books.
Arendt, Hannah. 1971. *The Life of the Mind*, Volume One. New York: Harcourt.
Arendt, Hannah. 1973 [1948]. *The Origins of Totalitarianism*. New York: Harcourt.
Arendt, Hannah. 1994a [1948]. "What is Existential Philosophy?" In *Essays in Understanding, 1930–1954: Formation, Exile, and Totalitarianism*, 163–87. New York: Schocken Books.
Arendt, Hannah. 1994b [1954]. "Understanding and Politics (The Difficulties of Understanding)." In *Essays in Understanding, 1930–1954: Formation, Exile, and Totalitarianism*, 307–27. New York: Schocken Books.
Arendt, Hannah. 1994c [1954]. "On the Nature of Totalitarianism: An Essay in Understanding." In *Essays in Understanding, 1930–1954: Formation, Exile, and Totalitarianism*, 328–60. New York: Schocken Books.
Arendt, Hannah. 1994d [1954]. "Concern With Politics in Recent European Thought." In *Essays in Understanding, 1930–1954: Formation, Exile, and Totalitarianism*, 428–77. New York: Schocken Books.
Arendt, Hannah. 2005 [1956–1959]. "Introduction Into Politics." In *The Promise of Politics*, 93–200. New York: Schocken Books.
Aristotle. 1947. *Introduction to Aristotle*. Edited by Richard McKeon. New York: The Modern Library.
Bacon, Francis. 2000 [1620]. *The New Organon*. New York: Cambridge University Press.
Benhabib, Seyla. 1990. "Hannah Arendt and the Redemptive Power of Narrative." *Social Research* 57, no. 1: 167–96.
Benhabib, Seyla. 2003 [1995]. *The Reluctant Modernism of Hannah Arendt*. Lanham, MD: Rowman & Littlefield.
Borren, Marieke. 2008. "Arendt's Politics of In/Visibility: On Stateless Refugees and Undocumented Aliens." *Ethical Perspectives*. 15, no. 2: 213–37.

Borren, Marieke. 2013. "'A Sense of the World': Hannah Arendt's Hermeneutic Phenomenology of Common Sense." *International Journal of Philosophical Studies* 21, no. 2: 225–55.

Bredlau, Susan. 2018. *The Other in Perception: A Phenomenological Account of Our Experience of Other Persons*. Albany: State University of New York Press.

Diprose, Rosalyn and Ewa Plonowska Ziarek. 2018. *Arendt, Natality, and Biopolitics: Toward Democratic Plurality and Reproductive Justice*. Edinburgh: Edinburgh University Press.

Foucault, Michel. 1977. *Discipline and Punish: The Birth of the Prison*. Translated by Alan Sheridan. New York: Vintage Books.

Fromm, Erich. 1969 [1941]. *Escape From Freedom*. New York: Henry Holt and Company.

Guenther, Lisa. 2011. "Subjects Without a World? A Husserlian Analysis of Solitary Confinement." *Human Studies* 34: 257–76.

Guenther, Lisa. 2014. "The Concrete Abyss." *Aeon*, April 16. https://aeon.co/essays/why-solitary-confinement-degrades-us-all. Accessed July 23, 2021.

Heidegger, Martin. 1962 [1927]. *Being and Time*. Translated by John Macquarrie and Edward Robinson. New York: Harper Perennial.

Heidegger, Martin. 1993a [1935–36]. "The Origin of the Work of Art." In *Basic Writings*, edited by David Farrell Krell, 143–203. New York: HarperCollins.

Heidegger, Martin. 1993b [1954]. "The Question Concerning Technology." In *Basic Writings*, edited by David Farrell Krell, 307–42. New York: HarperCollins.

Husserl, Edmund. 1970 [1936]. *Crisis of the European Sciences and Transcendental Phenomenology*. Translated by David Carr. Evanston: Northwestern University Press.

Husserl, Edmund. 1982 [1913]. *Ideas Pertaining to a Pure Phenomenology and to Phenomenological Philosophy*, First Book. Translated by F. Kersten. Boston: Martinus Nijhoff Publishers.

Husserl, Edmund. 1999 [1931]. *Cartesian Meditations*. Translated by Dorian Cairns. Dordrecht: Kluwer Academic Publishers.

Husserl, Edmund. 2001. *Analyses Concerning Passive and Active Synthesis: Lectures on Transcendental Logic*. Translated by Anthony J. Steinbock. Dordrecht: Kluwer Academic Publishers.

Jacobson, Kirsten. 2010. "The Experience of Home and the Space of Citizenship." *The Southern Journal of Philosophy* 48, no. 3: 219–45.

Jacobson, Kirsten. 2011. "Embodied Domestics, Embodied Politics: Women, Home, and Agoraphobia." *Human Studies* 34: 1–21.

Lebrecht, James and Nicole Newnham (dirs.). 2020. *Crip Camp: A Disability Revolution*. Good Gravy Films/Higher Ground Productions.

Loidolt, Sophie. 2018. *Phenomenology of Plurality: Hannah Arendt on Political Intersubjectivity*. New York: Routledge.

Maclaren, Kym. 2008. "Embodied Perceptions of Others as a Condition of Selfhood? Empirical and Phenomenological Considerations." *Journal of Consciousness Studies* 15, no. 1: 63–93.

Marx, Karl. 1994 [1844]. "Alienated Labor." In *Selected Writings*, 58–68. Edited by Lawrence H. Simon. Indianapolis: Hackett Publishing Company.

McMahon, Laura. 2017. "Phenomenology as First-Order Perception: Speech, Vision, and Reflection in Merleau-Ponty." In *Perception and Its Developments in Merleau-Ponty's Phenomenology*. Edited by Kirsten Jacobson and John Russon, 308–37. Toronto: University of Toronto Press.

McMahon, Laura. 2019. "Freedom as (Self-)Expression: Natality and the Temporality of Action in Merleau-Ponty and Arendt." *The Southern Journal of Philosophy* 57, no. 1: 56–79.

Mensch, James. 2007. "Public Space." Continental Philosophy Review 40: 31–47.

Merchant, Carolyn. 2013. "Francis Bacon and the 'Vexations of Art': Experimentation as Intervention." *British Journal for the History of Science* 46, no. 4: 551–99.

Merleau-Ponty, Maurice. 1963 [1942]. *The Structure of Behavior*. Translated by Alden L. Fisher. Pittsburgh: Duquesne University Press.

Merleau-Ponty. 1964. "Cézanne's Doubt." In *Sense and Non-Sense*. Translated by Hubert L. Dreyfus and Patricia Allen Dreyfus. Evanston: Northwestern University Press.

Merleau-Ponty, Maurice. 1968 [1964]. *The Visible and the Invisible*. Translated by Alphonso Lingis. Evanston: Northwestern University Press.

Merleau-Ponty, Maurice. 1969 [1947]. *Humanism and Terror: An Essay on the Communist Problem*. Translated by John O'Neill. Boston: Beacon Press.

Merleau-Ponty, Maurice. 2012 [1945]. *Phenomenology of Perception*. Translated by Donald A. Landes. New York: Routledge.

National Assembly of France. 2008 [1789]. *The Declaration of the Rights of Man and Citizen. The Avalon Project: Documents in History, Law and Diplomacy*. Yale Law School: Lillian Goldman Law Library. https://avalon.law.yale.edu/18th_century/rightsof.asp. Accessed July 23, 2021.

New York Times. 1977. "Disabled in San Francisco Vow to Continue Sit-In." April 17. https://www.nytimes.com/1977/04/17/archives/disabled-in-san-francisco-vow-to-continue-sitin.html. Accessed July 16, 2021.

National Assembly of France. 2008 [1789]. *The Declaration of the Rights of Man and Citizen. The Avalon Project: Documents in History, Law and Diplomacy*. Yale Law School: Lillian Goldman Law Library. https://avalon.law.yale.edu/18th_century/rightsof.asp. Accessed July 23, 2021.

Patterson, Lindsey. 2012. "Points of Access: Rehabilitation Centers, Summer Camps, and Student Life in the Making of Disability Activism, 1960–1973." *Journal of Social History* 46, no. 2: 473–99.

Rilke, Rainer Maria. 1934 [1929]. *Letters to a Young Poet*. Translated by M. D. Herter Norton. New York: W. W. Norton.

Russon, John. 2017. *Sites of Exposure: Art, Politics, and the Nature of Experience*. Albany: State University of New York Press.

Russon, John. 2020. *Adult Life: Aging, Responsibility, and the Pursuit of Happiness*. Albany: State University of New York Press.

Salamon, Gayle. 2018. "What's Critical About Critical Phenomenology?" *Puncta: Journal of Critical Phenomenology* 1: 8–17.

Thucydides. 1972. *History of the Peloponnesian War*. Translated by Rex Warner. New York: Penguin Books.
Vasterling, Veronica. 2015. "The Hermeneutic Phenomenological Approach to Plurality: Arendt, Habermas, and Gadamer." In *Phenomenological Perspectives on Plurality*. Edited by Gert-Jan van der Heiden, 158–74. Boston: Brill.
Vasterling, Veronica. 2012. "Hannah Arendt." In *The Routledge Companion to Phenomenology*. Edited by Sebastian Luft and Søren Overgaard, 82–91. New York: Routledge.
Villa, Dana R. 1996. *Arendt and Heidegger: The Fate of the Political*. Princeton: Princeton University Press.
Villa, Dana R. 1999. "Totalitarianism, Modernity, Tradition." In *Politics, Philosophy, Terror: Essays on the Thought of Hannah Arendt*, 180–203. Princeton: Princeton University Press.
Weber, Max. 1946 [1921]. "Bureaucracy." In *From Max Weber: Essays in Sociology*. Translated and edited by H. H. Gerth and C. Wright Mills, 196–244. New York: Oxford University Press.
Young-Bruehl, Elisabeth. 1982. *Hannah Arendt: For Love of the World*. New Haven: Yale University Press.

NOTES

1. In her 1948 essay "What is Existential Philosophy?" for example, Arendt advances highly critical interpretations of the phenomenological work of, among other figures, Edmund Husserl and Martin Heidegger (1994a, 164–67, 176–82). I agree with Sophie Loidolt that these are quite poor scholarly interpretations of phenomenology in general and Husserl and Heidegger in particular; their interest lies rather in what they reveal about what was on how Arendt was working to situate her own philosophical project (2018, 20). I also agree with Loidolt that we should interpret Arendt's critical relationship to existential phenomenology not as an outright rejection of the latter but as part of her *"continuous transformation of Existenz philosophy toward a political phenomenology"* (2018, 20).

2. For helpful recent scholarship that interprets Arendt as a phenomenologist of political life, see Loidolt (2018), Vasterling (2012, 2015), and Borren (2008, 2013).

3. On philosophy and political thought's beginning in, and ultimate accountability to, lived experience, see Arendt in the Preface to *Between Past and Future*: "my assumption is that thought itself arises out of incidents of living experience and must remain bound to them as the only guideposts by which to take its bearings" (1968a, 14).

On phenomenology as the "making strange" or "wondrous" our everyday lived experience, see Merleau-Ponty (2012, lxxvii), Salamon (2018, 10–11), and McMahon (2017, 325). See also Arendt's discussion of wonder as the beginning of all philosophy (Arendt 1994d, 445).

4. See Aristotle's distinction between the natural and the artificial in *Physics* II.1, his definition of the human being as the animal with *logos* in *Nicomachean Ethics*

I.7, and his argument that the *polis* is the proper environment for the human being in *Politics* I.2. (1947, 116–19, 316–19, 554–57). See also Heidegger's distinction between "earth" and "world" (1993a, 165–82).

5. For phenomenological accounts of Arendt's understanding of human beings as "worldly" and "conditioned," see Vasterling (2015, 163) and Borren (2013, 235–37).

6. As Veronica Vasterling writes, "[i]lluminating the same worldly theater from many different, and often conflicting, viewpoints, plurality turns the ephemeral and fragile web of human relations and affairs into a perceptibly existing and, in this sense, shared and shareable world. (2012, 85).

7. As Marieke Borren puts Arendt's point, "[w]hereas natural sameness homogenizes us; political equality, on the contrary, heterogenizes" (2013, 231). We shall explore the nature of political equality in section 3.

8. Importantly, distinctness can no more than equality be adequately grasped "from the outside." As Sophie Loidolt argues,

[O]nly a phenomenological analysis can bring out that plurality is not a plurality of properties (a "what") but a plurality of first-person perspectives (a "who") actualizing their potential of becoming visible subjects in interaction. Plurality is thus only superficially understood when conceived of as a simple preference for political pluralism, especially when differences are taken to be properties belonging to readymade individuals (2018, 10).

9. On the manner in which hubris and determinism go hand-in-hand in modernity, see Villa (1999, 184–85).

10. For an account of the ambivalence of modern science, and parallel ambivalences in modern capitalism, democracy, and human rights, from a phenomenological perspective, see Russon (2017, 88–100).

11. For further discussion of the tension between "man" and "citizen" in the title of this document, see Arendt (1973, 290–302).11. For further discussion of the tension between "man" and "citizen" in the title of this document, see Arendt (1973, 290–302).

12. There is some ambiguity concerning how to understand "the social" in Arendt's philosophy: should it be understood as naming specific domains or contents of modern political life, or should it be understood as a certain manner of regarding or treating political phenomena? I agree with Benhabib that the social is best understood as an "attitudinal orientation"—and one rooted in the modern tendencies toward hubris, mechanization, and instrumentalization—despite Arendt's own lack of clarity across her writings about how best to understand the social (Benhabib 2003, 139–41).

13. For an analysis of "biopolitics" in Arendt's philosophy, see Diprose and Ziarek (2018).

14. I am grateful to Shannon Hoff for this helpful observation.

15. Compare to Karl Marx on the worker under alienated labor: "He is at home when he is not working and when he is working he is not at home . . . The result, therefore, is that man (the worker) feels that he is acting freely in his animal functions—eating, drinking, and procreating, or at most in his shelter or finery—while in

his human functions he feels only like an animal. The animalistic becomes the human and the human becomes the animalistic" (1994, 62). See also Villa: "To lose the world is to become a member of the animal species" (1999, 202).

16. Indeed, as Dana R. Villa points out, such a grand narrative of a historical cause and effect to which we are all subject would more resemble totalitarian logic than serve to criticize it (1999, 181).

17. I am grateful to David Ciavatta for drawing my attention to this contrast between the political "who" and the political "no one."

18. On the political significance of plurality as not a natural given of the human species but as a lived experience that must be politically *enacted*, see Loidolt (2018, 109–24).

Chapter Nine

Arendt's Phenomenologically Informed Political Thinking

A Proto-Normative Account of Human Worldliness

Marieke Borren

Hannah Arendt had strong reservations about discourses of human dignity and the institutions designed to protect or foster it. In *The Origins of Totalitarianism*, she established the human rights regimes' conceptual and practical (political and legal) perplexities by demonstrating that they failed to protect stateless people. She frequently characterized human rights defenders as "hopelessly idealistic" at best or hypocritical at worst (1982, 44, 54; 1963a, 116; 1973, 269, 279). In the same vein, in her report about the trial of Eichmann, she expressed doubts about the possibility of establishing an international tribunal for the prosecution of crimes against humanity. She was unsentimentally committed to take the world as it happens to be at any given moment, rather than as an "imaginary world 'as it ought to be' or as it once upon a time had been" (1968, 19). In spite of her concern about the political catastrophes of the twentieth century—large-scale denationalizations, expulsions, and genocides—she dismissed remedial or redemptive ideals of cosmopolitanism and "brotherhood" as unfaithful to the world and qualified them as "sentimental utopianism" (1968, 5; cf. 2005, 93). More generally, she did not see any place for morality in the political domain, at least not in any conventional sense of the concept of morality. And her work is far removed from ideal theory and normative theory.

Many readers have found, and continue to find, Arendt's "realism" and her non- or a-normative—some even say: anti-normative—stance disturbing. It has led to charges of irresponsible aestheticism, decisionism, and anti-foundationalism.[1] Other, much more sympathetic readers of Arendt in deliberative democratic theory do not underwrite this type of criticism, but still regret the alleged normative deficit in her work. Seyla Benhabib points at the "normative melancholia" that runs through Arendt's work: "Although [Arendt's] conception of politics and of the political is quite inconceivable, unintelligible even, without a strongly grounded normative position in universal human rights, equality, and respect, one does not find her engaging in any such exercises of normative justification in her writings" (Benhabib 2000, 80). Others, on the contrary, especially within agonistic pluralism, see the alleged lack of normativity in Arendt's work as inspiring a *political* or *politicizing* approach to human rights issues, criminalization of crimes against humanity and conceptions of human dignity; as opposed to moral, and/or foundationalist (especially naturalist) approaches.[2] This type of reading seems indeed much closer to the spirit of Arendt's work than recent attempts to construe it as an ethically informed theory of the political, involving, for instance, a positive "right to have rights," the principle of "natality" (Birmingham 2006) or of "cohabitation" (Butler 2013) as ethical demands.

What all of the readings—the aestheticist, the deliberative-democratic, the agonistic and the ethical—share, however, is a disregard for the particular type of normativity that Arendt's phenomenological inspiration brings to her work. I will argue that her work, indeed, is averse to normative theory, yet it *does* feature an account of human dignity that is informed by a "proto-normative" commitment—to the *world*. Acknowledging the phenomenological spirit of Arendt's work is crucial for understanding this commitment.

To be sure, Arendt is an implicit, unorthodox, yet consistent and original phenomenologist. Her work is only recently gaining recognition as a belonging to the phenomenological tradition, more particularly its hermeneutic, existential (*Existenz*) and/or enactive families.[3] The reception of her work has mainly taken place in political theory, probably as a result of the Anglo-American predominance in Arendt scholarship. However, being immersed in the emerging phenomenological movement in German academia in the first half of the twentieth century at a formative age, her philosophical habitus is deeply shaped by phenomenological concerns and approaches. Since it does not fit into the phenomenological orthodoxy (that is, Edmund Husserl) and because Arendt keeps her method largely implicit, it took some decades after her death for the phenomenological inspiration to be appreciated (Birmingham 2006; Mensch 2009; Vasterling 2011; Borren 2013; Topolski 2015; Loidolt 2018).

Two key interconnected phenomenological features that Arendt brings to political philosophy are a particular "realism," a philosophical habitus of "unpremeditated, attentive facing up to, and resisting of, reality—whatever it may be" (1973, viii) which is also reflected in a keen attentiveness to distinctions, the paradoxes and perplexities typical of the human condition once we take seriously its plural appearance in the world. Being faithful to appearances and then describing them as accurately as possible implies that one should bracket especially theoretical preconceived ideas, or "pre-understandings" (*Vorverständnisse*). Defending an *epoché* of sorts, she wished to examine human affairs without theoretical or metaphysical prejudice, third-person perspective, or as she put it in an interview, her aim was "to look at politics [. . .] with eyes unclouded by philosophy" (1994, 2), Examples of such theoretical prejudices include the Being-Appearance dichotomy which she calls a "metaphysical fallacy" (1978, 23–26). but also the foundational naturalist pre-understandings that underpin the human rights discourse. Her work is committed to understanding rather than causally explaining political phenomena and to being faithful to reality, that is: phenomenal reality, reality as it appears in the world and so is visible and common to all people and hence intersubjectively validated. As she put it, "Being and Appearing coincide" (1978, 19).

Second, phenomenology informs her distinctive style or "method." Arendt held an unconventional conception of political philosophy, as much distinct from empirical political science as from political theory, that I would call "political thinking." Arendtian political thinking is committed to careful and open-ended descriptive analysis of first-person lived experiences of the plural world of human affairs, consistent with her conception of the thinking process (1978). This commitment to reality and to political thinking made Arendt not just, obviously, aversive to any type of wishful thinking, and to romantic or radical utopianism. She also stayed clear from normative political theory, such as ideal theory and normative value theory—then as much as now the mainstream of political theory.

Typical for Arendt's phenomenology is her world-centered ontology, partly following from, partly translating into, incisive analyses of concrete, empirical (that is, "ontic") political phenomena and historical events, such as the production of mass statelessness in interwar Europe and the Holocaust. Indeed, one of the claims defended in this contribution is that the ontological and the ontic in Arendt's work cannot be separated. Arendt's ontological account of what makes us human (that is, human conditionality, or the human conditions[4]), is informed by her historical accounts of violations of human dignity and vice versa. Like the chicken or the egg dilemma, the question of which one is prior to the other is undecidable.[5] Arendt's analysis of particular instances of violations of human dignity, such as the predicament of statelessness or crimes against humanity, make sense in light of her ontology of the human condition, as well as the other way around. I will discuss Arendt's first published work, *The Origins of Totalitarianism* (1951), alongside *The Human*

Condition (1958), *Eichmann in Jerusalem* (1963), and *The Life of the Mind* (unfinished as a project and posthumously published), with the first and the third being primarily historical studies and the second and the latter more strictly philosophical works that feature her phenomenological ontology.

I will demonstrate how for Arendt the *world*, not primarily humankind, or even human beings (in the plural), is at stake when human dignity comes under pressure. Worldliness provides a political and surprisingly nonhuman notion of human dignity underpinning human rights and the criminalization of crimes against humanity. The argument proceeds as follows. In section 1, I reconstruct Arendt's world-centered ontology through an extensive exploration of the multiple dimensions of her conception of "world" and worldliness. Radicalizing the general ontological claim made by phenomenologists of human "being in the world," Arendt demonstrates the mutual conditionality of humans (the "human condition") and the world (worldliness).

Section 2, concerning Arendt's "ontic" accounts of human rights and of crimes against humanity, pushes the argument from the plane of human condition(ality) to human dignity. I take a close look at those segments of Arendt's work in which she engages most directly with the historical trajectories and challenges of the human rights regime and of the criminalization of crimes against humanity in international law: on one hand the predicament of mass statelessness that emerged in interwar Europe and beyond, and on the other the Holocaust. In both cases, human dignity is related to placedness in the world and sharing the world with others.

Finally, in section 3, I return to the current academic debate on the lack of normativity in Arendt's political philosophy. Based on her world-centered ontology and rethinking of the principle of human dignity in worldly terms, I argue that even if Arendtian realist political thinking takes a non-normative stance, and refrains from putting forward ethical demands, it is not normatively empty. It features a "proto-normative" notion of human dignity that is best described as "care for the world" (*amor mundi*). It is a fair indication of the comprehensiveness of Arendt's acknowledgement of the ontological dignity—perhaps even primacy—of the *world* that plural human beings inhabit together. As she writes:

> [A]ny response that places man in the center of our current worries and suggests that he must be changed before any relief is to be found is profoundly unpolitical. For at the center of politics lies concern for the world, not for man [. . .] If we want to change an institution, an organization, some public body existing within the world, we can only revise its constitution, its laws, its statutes, and hope that all the rest will take care of itself. (2005, 105–6)

ARENDT'S WORLD-CENTERED ONTOLOGY OF HUMAN CONDITIONALITY

A key assumption of phenomenology is that there is no separation between self, others and the world: they are fundamentally related (Zahavi 2005, 2011; Heinämaa 2003). Starting with Martin Heidegger's groundbreaking work *Being and Time* (1927), phenomenologists, however different in various respects, posit that the self (also called the subject or Dasein) is always "in the world"—that is, embedded in a historical, cultural and social world comprised of other people and things. We will see how Arendt radicalizes this notion into human being *of* the world.

Put in the most general sense, the world for Arendt is the typically *human* world, the *Umwelt* in which human existence takes place, our common habitat or house (1958, 134).[5] Arendt regards the world as dwelling place for human beings on earth and, as such, both content and context of human existence. Conversely, what makes humans human is that they are worldly beings. Human beings are worldly creatures not only because they need the artificial habitat of a world to survive but also because the world enables them to lead a meaningful life. To contribute in word and deed to the world is what makes life meaningful and truly human in Arendt's view.

Arendt's phenomenological ontology—her answer to the question: what makes humans human? Or: what does it mean to be human?—is captured in her analysis of human conditionality and the human conditions in *The Human Condition* and *The Life of the Mind*. Arendt challenges metaphysical and scientific definitions of human nature, that is: of an essence that is supposed to be universally shared by all human beings (1958, 10, 193).

However, for Arendt, what makes humans human cannot be described by answering the question "What is Man?," because, like Heidegger, she held that human existence and coexistence cannot be interrogated in the manner of an object (1958, 10–11). Metaphysical and scientific definitions of human nature are reductionist because they generalize the differentiated complexity of human existence to a single feature or a few traits. Although true and sensible, these answers will never be sufficient because they do not, and never can, do justice to human plurality. Human nature is a generic abstraction that cannot account for the distinguishing feature of human beings, that is plurality. Not "Man," in the singular, but "men," in the plural, that is, in all their diversity, inhabit the world.

Human plurality is, for Arendt, the "paradoxical plurality of similar but unique beings" (1958, 176). Plurality is paradoxical because, on one hand, human beings are similar as members of the same species, Homo sapiens, but on the other hand, they individuate into distinctive beings *by appearing in the world shared with others* through speech and action and being seen by others. This paradox of similarity and difference recurs in Arendt's distinctions between "who" and "what" we are on one hand and between ζωή and βίος on the other. Human beings are not just a "what," describing collective identity, but also a "who," individual (unique) identity that is enacted in their dealings and interactions with the world and others. Likewise, human life is not only ζωή (zoe), a natural or biological life, but also βίος (bios), a meaningful life in the world that can only be described in a story, a biography.

Instead of asking "what" a human being is, that is, the misguided question of human nature, Arendt asks how different human activities each in their own way contribute to the establishment of a shared human world and what the conditions are for these contributions. She focuses upon the way in which human experience and existence is shaped in relation to a number of conditions (in the plural). Human conditions, somewhat similar to Heidegger's "existentialia," are features of the common human situation. Together they constitute the coordinates within which human existence and coexistence unfold. They combine naturally given circumstances ("life itself" and the earth) with conditions human beings create themselves in a bidirectional mode: they shape human existence and are shaped by it in return.

In other words, humans and the world are mutually conditional. Because of their conditioned existence, the relation between human beings and their environment is circular, but not in the sense of a vicious circle. Additionally, unlike the idea of human nature, a condition may or may not be realized, depending on other conditions and circumstances. And unlike an essential characteristic, a condition is not a causal mechanism. Conditionality is as much opposed to absolute or one-way *external* determination as it is to *self*-determination. Conditions are both constants of human experience and existence and historically variable in their particular constellations and combinations: "in different historical periods, the terms are differently connected, and the concepts men have of the terms vary with the different connections" (Young-Bruehl, 1982, 319–20).

We are situated in the world, which means that we are both shaping and shaped by the world, which is public, visible, and common to all. Arendt shares Heidegger's phenomenological understanding of Dasein as "being-in-the-world," but she puts an emphasis on human plurality, the fact that we appear to many different others. Arendt's account of the human conditionality radicalizes and exteriorizes the phenomenological first-person perspective, which Loidolt captures in the idea of "being-*of*-the-world" (Loidolt 2018, 63–64).

Arendt's use of "world" encompasses two broad and intimately related dimensions: the world of "things" and the discursive (or symbolic) world of meanings (1958, 52). Both dimensions of the world refer to *practices*—of respectively world-building and world-disclosing—as well as to their *results*—respectively human-made things (including material artifacts and institutions) and shared meanings and stories.[7] It is perhaps surprising to learn that someone who is primarily seen as a philosopher of *action* relates the world first of all to *work*, the human activity of making or producing things. The world first of all consists of human-made things (1958, 52, cf. 1961, 209). While producing, we are more or less in control, but as soon as the fabrication process achieves its end and the product is finished, things start to feed back into the realm of human beings who produced them and start to serve as a human condition in turn. Artifacts are of course made by human beings, but they gain a certain autonomy vis-à-vis their makers (and user) and human beings in general. As soon as they present themselves to us, artifacts are no longer completely human and acquire an "objective quality" (1958, 89). The thing world is thus both made and given. This process of reification is a feature of human conditionality: whatever we make starts to condition human existence and coexistence—for better or worse (1958, 95). The things human beings make may boomerang back on them, as in the case of climate change as a consequence of technological advancement and market-driven economic development using fossil fuel, making things by excavating resources (or the development of weapons of mass destruction). The emphasis in *The Human Condition* is on things' constructive contribution to human existence and coexistence. They provide for the relative durability and stability that we need, given the continuous threat of unlivable impermanence and transience from two sides, the human condition of life itself and of plurality, respectively. On one hand, as beings that are embodied and embedded in nature, we, as *animal laborans*, are subject to endless, repetitive and perpetual change: the relentless struggle for life and self-preservation (1958, 96–97). On the other hand, indeterminacy, unpredictability and irreversibility are inherent in human existence, for as "acting" beings (that is, citizens), we live our lives among many others. Public things provide the relative stability that is needed in light of the fragility that is typical of human life and coexistence. Most of all, public things create a space in between people, an *inter-esse*, and hence facilitate and maintain plurality (1958, 52).

So the world includes the practices of world-building by human beings in their capacity as producers (*homo faber*) and their results, the artifact. However, it also consists of the meanings that are generated by human beings in their capacity as citizens, that is, as acting and speaking beings who are both equal to, and different from, their fellow-citizens. Human "words and deeds" encompass interactions and relationships between people, and the exchanged interpretations of events, things, states of affairs. These typically take the form of narratives, opinions, judgments (including prejudices) and the debates and fights ensuing from them (1958, 183). The world in this sense is also an archive of events, as far as they are recorded in history.

Arendt uses a variety of concepts to describe the discursive dimension of the world, each emphasizing different although related aspects, of which I will briefly mention four. First, the discursive world is a *"space of appearances"* (1958, 199): a public space to show oneself in deed and words to one's fellow-citizens—to be seen and heard by them, and vice versa, and in the process achieve equality and distinctness. The *"res publica"* serves to displace the political from a relation between "subjects" (citizens, the people or the *demos*) to their shared relation to "objects": public things (1958, 56; cf. Honig 2017). The "web of relations" stresses the network character of the human world, the fact that it strictly comes about between a plurality of acting and speaking people (1958, 183, 88). In addition, it is meant to underline its relative vulnerability if compared to the material world. It is telling that Arendt uses the image of the web, instead of a close-knit fabric. It is a strictly *political* community. The political significance of keeping a distance is also key to a final image, the "in between" (*inter-esse*) (1958, 7–8; 1963b, 86). The world as the whole of shared meanings and human-made things lies *outside of* human beings. It constitutes a third between self and others that binds them into a community, whether or not by contestation of this third. Except for intimate conversations, people usually talk or fight *about* some worldly reality. The world of (public) things offers an "objective frame of reference to test our impressions against reality" (Canovan 1985, 619). Testing one's impressions against reality does not necessarily lead to agreement and consensus about these issues with others. As Bonnie Honig writes: "Without things to fight about—public parks, climate change, kinship structures—democracies cannot exist. That is, democracy postulates not only a *demos* (or many *demoi*) but also a (or many) *res publica(e)*; democracy needs not just democratic subjects but also democratic objects" (Honig 2014, 211).

Like the "thing" dimension of the world, the discursive dimension is practice-based or performative. The practice that corresponds to this dimension of the world could be called *world disclosing*. Heidegger demonstrates that phenomena appear against a background of concealment, by carrying some things into the light from darkness, which fits in with the figure/background image in Husserl's and Maurice Merleau-Ponty's phenomenological accounts of the structure of perception. In sharp contrast to Heidegger, Arendt points at the indispensability of narrating, interpreting, judging, and sharing and discussing our opinions and evaluations *with others*. By "talking about" (1958, 183) things and events, we make them meaningful or disclose their meanings. What disclosure boils down to can be clarified by using the analogy of unlocking an archive. A collection of files first needs to be processed actively in order to become available to its users (such as historians), by way of a database or catalog. Also, when nobody ever consults this database, it becomes a dead archive.

Both world disclosing and world building allow for developing a personal identity. In stabilizing the world, the things we make simultaneously stabilize who *we* are, our personal identities as relative permanence through time, by providing a point of reference which remains constant through time and which is shared with other people. Likewise, in the process of world disclosure, those who act and speak also disclose or reveal *themselves*. The "disclosure of the agent in speech and action" is not the intended purpose of action and speech (in that sense it is a kind of epiphenomenon of action, but it should not be confused with a facade). Only by acting in the world do people individuate, according to Arendt (1958, 97, 175; 1994, 23).

The world-centered ontology of *The Human Condition* is developed further in *The Life of the Mind* Volume I, in Arendt's insistence on the coincidence of Being and Appearance—that is, appearance to many others—which translates in the ontological dignity (perhaps even primacy) of the world (1971, 19). Here, Arendt leaves behind the juxtaposition, implicit in *The Human Condition*, of world and earth. In the time span separating the publication of *The Human Condition* (1958) and the preparatory work for *The Life of the Mind Volume I* in the early 1970s, she apparently broadened her conception of world to include the earth. Plurality is now defined as the "law of the *earth*" (1971, 19; emphasis added). This extension may explain why Arendt used the concepts of "world" and "earth" interchangeably after *The Human Condition*.[8]

In conclusion, Arendt's phenomenology of the human conditions foregrounds the mutual conditionality of human subjectivity and the common world of things and meanings. Her dismantling of definitions of an innate human essence in favor of being-of-the-world does not merely reflect an abstract intra-philosophical position, but is developed in relation to a particular historical context: the large-scale violations of human dignity in the twentieth century, especially the totalitarian experience and mass displacements and denationalizations. Her respective ontological and ontic accounts mutually inform each other, as I will demonstrate in the next section.

HISTORICAL FORMATIONS: HUMAN DIGNITY AS WORLDLINESS

The twentieth-century political reality Arendt was confronted with emerged from historical formations and developments, most notably, what we would call today the globalizing force of European imperialism, the consolidation of a globe-encompassing territorial nation-state system and the globalization of armed conflict, migration (including forced migration and displacement), and the reach of weapons of mass destruction (1958a, 1–6). Today, we could add climate change, and viruses such as corona that lead to epidemics literally affecting all (*pan*) nations or people (*demos*). These developments have increasingly integrated mankind, Arendt observed—and not, for that matter, in some rosy cosmopolitan sense, a "beautiful dream of unity" (1951, 434), or no more than as a Kantian regulative ideal (1973, 298), but in the factual historical sense that we are all in the same boat, bound by "negative solidarity" (1968, 83). This "inescapable fact" (1973, 298), "this situation," namely "the emergence of mankind as one political entity" (1949, 36; 1951, 436) for Arendt clearly confronts us with new burdens and responsibilities that call for a "political principle, [. . .] a new law on earth" (1973, ix). Just as much as the extreme infringements on human dignity the world had witnessed in the preceding decades are expressive of the political integration of "mankind," are those institutions designed to redress them. World War II accelerated the institutionalizations of human rights and of international criminal justice. The United Nations (UN) was established in 1945. In 1948, one day apart, it adopted the Genocide Convention and proclaimed the Universal Declaration of Human Rights (UDHR, 1948), article 15 of which formulates the "right to nationality"), and in 1951 it adopted the Refugee Convention.[9] A series of high-profile Holocaust trials and tribunals took place, first and foremost the Nuremberg trials by the International Military Tribunal (1945–1946) and including the first mass-media trial, of Nazi official Adolf Eichmann, by the Jerusalem District Court (1963a). Together, these institutions brought about a number of groundbreaking legal innovations such as the invocation of universal jurisdiction and the codification of genocide and crimes against humanity, and paved the way for the establishment of a number of ad hoc international criminal tribunals in the 1990s (starting with the tribunal on the Yugoslav wars and the Rwandan genocide) and of the permanent International Criminal Court (2002).

Below, I will discuss two cases, taken from Arendt's historical work, that result from the political integration and in which human dignity is explicitly at stake, namely statelessness and the Holocaust. I will juxtapose two sections, the first about the stateless' loss of the "right to have rights," the second Arendt's "death sentence" (Butler 2011) of Eichmann. Even though these sections are both much commented on in their own right, they are rarely read in conjunction, whence it has so far gone unnoticed that both explicitly tie human dignity to worldliness, that is, to sharing the world, and being placed in it.

Arendt is usually cited as one of first philosophers to attend to the concept of crimes against humanity, and her work remains a key point of reference for political and legal philosophers reflecting on crimes against humanity, in particular the epilogue to *Eichmann in Jerusalem*.[10] Even if she has become known as a fierce critic of both the Nuremberg and Eichmann trials, Arendt unequivocally applauded the judicial innovation enacted in the Nuremberg trials: the introduction of crimes against humanity as a category in positive law. In 1949 (and again in 1963), Arendt writes that she believes that "the new concept of 'crimes against humanity,'" as mentioned in the London Charter (the legal foundation of the trials) and in the opening addresses of respectively the American and the French chief prosecutors at the Nuremberg trial, is "the first and most important notion of international law" (1949, 36).[11]

The famous (or infamous) closing lines of the epilogue of *Eichmann in Jerusalem*, in which Arendt addresses Eichmann directly (her "death sentence") contains important clues to her notion of the "humanity" (or human dignity) which is violated in the case of crimes against humanity, in terms of the human *world* that people inhabit: "[Y]ou supported and carried out *a policy of not wanting to share the earth* with the Jewish people and the people of a number of other nations—as though you and your superiors had any right to determine who should and who should not inhabit the world" (1963a, 279; italics mine).

The reference to the condition of sharing the earth or the world is a recurrent one in *Eichmann in Jerusalem*. Earlier in the epilogue, she had argued that "the new crime" (that is, crimes against humanity), appeared "when the Nazi regime declared that the German people not only were unwilling to have any Jews in Germany but wished to make the entire Jewish people disappear from the face of the earth" (1963a, 268–69) with the Holocaust being characterized as "an enterprise whose open purpose was to eliminate forever certain 'races' from the face of the earth" (1963a, 277). In previous chapters, she qualifies crimes against humanity as "the end of the world": "What for Hitler [. . .] was among the war's main objectives, with its implementation given top priority, regardless of economic and military considerations, and what for Eichmann was a job, with its daily routine, its ups and downs, was for the Jews quite literally the end of the world" (1963a, 153–54).

It seems no coincidence that Arendt uses the formulation of "sharing the earth" in her verdict on Eichmann. Several interpreters have suggested that this formulation resonates with the Kantian notion of the "common possession of the earth," whether or not unwittingly.[12] In the "Third definitive article for a perpetual peace" of *Perpetual Peace* (1795), Kant addresses the conditions of "universal hospitality" and asserts the moral foundation of the right to hospitality (*Besuchrecht*) in men's "common possession of the face of the earth."[13] Since the earth is a globe, Kant argues, humans "cannot infinitely disperse and hence must finally tolerate the presence of each other." As a consequence, "no one originally has any greater right than anyone else to occupy any particular portion of the earth." In the lectures on Kant that Arendt delivered from 1964, she argued that she considered *Perpetual Peace* to contain some of the few shreds of a genuinely *political* philosophy that was never finished in Kant's work, in addition to his *Critique of Judgement* (1790): "[C]oncern with the world which is the task of political philosophy for which man is primarily a worldly being can be found in traces everywhere in Kant's writings about history and even in his moral philosophy." She mentions the right of hospitality as an example of that genuine political philosophy: "Hence violation in one place is felt throughout the world [. . .]. Here, Kant raises his question not from the side of men, but of the earth which is held in common by men (plural), concerned with the many" (1964, 032259).

Even if Arendt, like Kant, appreciates the enormous political significance of the fact that human beings share the world, it did not lead her to embrace his moral theory of cosmopolitanism. She was suspicious of the normative consequences Kant drew from this fact in his formulation of the regulative ideal of a *weltbürgerliche Gesellschaft*, because she held that this ideal was based on the conceptual pre-understanding of nature as a guarantee, that only much later, in the first half of the twentieth century, turned out to be highly exclusive.

It is the common situation of individual human beings and of particular groups that they are one among many inhabiting the common world. Crimes against humanity could be seen as attempts to destroy key world disclosing and world building capacities. They especially affect the human capacity to contribute meaningfully to the world, to bring about new state of affairs and to be a "cobuilder of a common world" (1973, 458), but also of our common sense, or "sense of reality" which is intersubjectively validated. Moreover, it jeopardizes various dimensions of the plural world that humans share, such as the fragile texture ("web") of human relationships. The fundamental and long-term scattering of communities is a well-documented phenomenon in historiography, as well as victims' and survivors' (and perpetrators') testimonials and documentary and narrative nonfiction about the aftermath of historical injustice, genocide, and crimes against humanity.

Also, crimes against humanity constitute an attack on shared public things that provide for relative stability (and hence on the res publica and the in-between), from the material infrastructure, cultural artifacts, and common land to legal personhood, legal institutions, and the political community "whose law is violated." Legal justice requires the restoration of this "order of mankind," not of the victims (1963a, 261). Here Arendt cites Telford Taylor, the former assistant of Justice Jackson in Nuremberg, who attended the Eichmann trial: "the essence of law is that a crime is not committed only against the victim, but primarily against the community whose law is violated" (1963a, 261). Taylor emphatically argued that attacks on a particular group, such as Jews, are not just a crime against the direct "objects," the victims, but equally against those who do not belong to that group. For that reason, he considered "Crimes against the Jewish People" an absurd charge. He draws a parallel here with what we today call hate crimes, against black people in the American Southern states and in South Africa: "true justice declares that such an act is as much a crime against whites as blacks" (Taylor 1961, 22; cf. idem, 1962). For Arendt, crimes against humanity consist not in crimes against individual human beings, nor against groups *as* groups, or of some inalienable human dignity, but, more pertinently, against something that does not coincide with human beings but is outside of them, namely the common, plural world.

Despite the obvious differences, Arendt points out important similarities between the Holocaust as a crime against humanity on one hand and the rightlessness of stateless refugees on other hand. Discussing the predicament that stateless refugees find themselves in, such as masses of Europeans in the interwar period and Palestinians after 1948, Arendt argues that their loss of human rights is most accurately captured in the idea of their loss of a *place in the world*, a legal and political community which, in her own words, "makes opinions significant and actions effective," or in other words, "a community willing and able to guarantee any rights whatsoever." As she writes: "Man, it turns out, can lose all so-called Rights of Man without losing his essential quality as man, his human dignity. Only *the loss of a polity* itself expels him from humanity" (1973, 296–97).[14]

The key to rightlessness as a result of displacement and denationalization in modernity, Arendt argued, is the deprivation of one's membership in a legal-political community and the concomitant reduction of humans to natural beings, mere members of the species Homo sapiens. The real problem of stateless people is that they do not belong to any political community whatsoever and are, exactly, "only human," deprived of the worldly space in which actions are performed and seen, opinions articulated and heard. Under conditions of a globalized nation-state system, the human rights as formulated in the 1948 UN human rights declaration are in fact civil rights, so the stateless had lost their human rights *because* they had lost their civil rights/ citizenship through sovereign expulsion. By losing one's *political* rights (that is, citizenship status, nationality), refugees turn out to become *completely* rightless, which indicates that so-called "natural" rights (which are supposed to be given at birth and to be inalienable) are worthless unless backed up by political rights.[15] What ultimately determines the regrettable fate of the stateless individual is not so much that he or she has lost civil rights and therefore human rights, but the only human right deserving of that name though it "was never even mentioned among the human rights," namely the "right to have rights" (1973, 297).

Crimes against humanity and human rights were indeed intimately related for Arendt. In an essay written in the midst of the drafting process of the UDHR, "'The Rights of Man,' What are They?," Arendt identified expulsion under conditions of the nation-state which causes refugees to become stateless as "the one crime against humanity." It is a violation of the "one human right," the right "never to be excluded from the rights granted by his own community," that is, never to be stripped of one's citizenship (1949, 36–37), in other words: the right to have rights. This situation was repeated some decennia later at the gates of Auschwitz where Jews were carefully deprived of their legal personality (1973, 447; 1955, section 12).

World destruction is the shared feature of the rightlessness that comes with denationalization and expulsion and with crimes against humanity. Both constitute an attack on human dignity by robbing people of their "placedness in the world" and the condition of sharing the earth, their worldly coexistence. Against foundationalist (especially naturalist) accounts of human dignity, Arendt alerts us to its worldliness: "[R]espect for human dignity implies the recognition of my fellow-men or our fellow-nations as subjects, as builders of worlds or cobuilders of a common world" (1973, 458).

Indeed, what was most urgent was the work of world-building. The events of mass statelessness and the Holocaust had in Arendt's eyes made abundantly clear that new institutions, laws, and constitutions were needed to protect human dignity, that is, to prevent offenses against the world and to warrant the right to have rights. However, the international legal order and the human rights regime that emerged after World War II were based on old conceptual pre-understandings about human dignity and understandings of international law still predicated on international agreements between sovereign nation-states. The UN in Arendt's view no less than its predecessor, the League of Nations, expressed human rights in "terms of the 18th century," especially the naturalist—hence: unworldly—principles of inalienable rights and innate human dignity, expressed in the French Declaration of 1789, which are derived from a long tradition of natural law theory.

As regards crimes against humanity: she regretted that the Holocaust trials in Nuremberg and Jerusalem had failed because the courts, the judges and the foundational legal documents (the London Charter in the case of Nuremberg, the Nazi and Nazi Collaborators [Punishment] Act in the case of Jerusalem) clung to an understanding of international law still based on sovereign nation-states. She denounced the tendency of both courts of adjudicating the Holocaust—in her view a new and unprecedented crime—by old legal categories (1963a, 269). More concretely, she regretted the reluctance on the part of the Nuremberg and Jerusalem prosecutors and judges to apply the novel category of crimes against humanity in their charges and sentences. Instead, the Nazi officials who stood trial were predominantly charged for war crimes (Nuremberg) or crimes against the Jewish people (Jerusalem).[16]

CARE FOR THE WORLD AS PROTO-NORMATIVE COMMITMENT

In the preceding sections, I have made the case that for Arendt, what makes humans human is the world of things and meanings *outside* of and *between* them. Likewise, her accounts of statelessness and the Holocaust suggest a nonhuman, that is, worldly, notion of human dignity: placedness in the world and sharing the world with plural others. Returning to the scholarly debates on the alleged lack of normativity in Arendt's work, I would now argue that it indeed does not provide (derive or justify) an independent, external (a- or non-political) normative foundation for good or just (not even better or more just) political orders, in the form of substantive principles or procedures for decision making or moral argumentation, deliberation and justification, unlike the mainstream of contemporary political theory, be it in its liberal political theoretical or deliberative democratic varieties, which is still largely indebted to Kantian moral theory. However, it is not normatively empty, but informed by a "proto-normative" commitment—to the material and discursive world. It explores that which precedes normative and moral justification, decision making, argumentation, and deliberation: the *meaning* of human dignity, and why people, as soon as they start acting and speaking in public, *care at all*.[17]

Sharing the world with plural others, or, in Butler's words, "cohabitation with others we never choose" (Butler 2013, 152), is a feature of human conditionality (cf. idem, 166). However, I argue that it is not a norm—"a norm [. . .] of how the state might be formed in ways that would reverse statelessness and accommodate the heterogeneity of its populations" (idem, 152)—or "a fundamental task of Jewish ethics" (idem, 153). Rather, it is what allows for moral or normative argumentation and for justification of norms and ethical tasks in the first place.

Here I follow Sophie Loidolt who has recently argued, from a phenomenological perspective, that Arendtian plurality (more precisely: "actualized plurality") "confronts us with intrinsic ethical demands [. . .] [which] are 'proto-normative' in the sense that they constitute the field of meaning where [. . .] normative questions gain relevance: Freedom, trust, and sociability as an end in itself, for example, must be experienced (and described in their experiential features) first before they can be made relevant for moral arguments" (Loidolt 2018, 234). However, I believe Loidolt is not radical enough in drawing the consequences from Arendt's ontology of "being-of-the-world." Even if Loidolt stresses—contra deconstructions of the subject in postfoundationalism—that self, other, and world are intertwined, so that the one cannot even exist in isolation from the others, the focus in her account is somewhat out of balance: the self, even if it is pluralized, receives a disproportionate amount of attention, at the expense of the world.

The proto-normative commitment that Arendt's work features could be described as "care for the world."[18] Starting with Heidegger, phenomenologists consider "caring about" as a fundamental structure of human existence. "Care" (*Sorge*) refers to our daily practical and embodied involvement with the world that precedes and is the basis of reflective processes and rational deliberation, including moral and political deliberation. Since their own being is at issue, human beings fundamentally care about existence. Since this self is considered as always in the world—that is, embedded in a historical, cultural and social world comprised of other people and things—caring about ourselves as a principle entails caring about others and about the world. While Heidegger focuses on care for the self, and Levinas on care for the Other, Arendt's phenomenology resolutely "takes sides for the world's sake" (1968, 7–8). This is an exercise in "turning the tables." Musing on totalitarianism, she wrote: "What is lost is not merely this weightless race of men but the world that was supposed to house them" (1968, 219).[19] For "the world and the people who inhabit it are not the same. The world lies between people, and this in-between—much more than (as is often thought) men or even man—is today the object of the greatest concern and the most obvious upheaval in almost all the countries of the globe" (1968, 4).

What Arendt wrote in her notes for a 1964 lecture on Kant's *Critique of Judgment*—"the only one of Kant's writings where his point of departure is the World and the senses and capabilities which made men (in the plural) fit to be inhabitants of it"—could be said to apply to her own brand of what I have called, "political thinking" as well: "This is perhaps not yet political philosophy, but it certainly is its condition *sine qua non*" (1964, 032259). Arendt's work is "not yet" political philosophy, if the latter is taken to be concerned with determining what people *should* do and how they should act, for instance, according to which principles. Rather, she brings to light what makes people start to act and speak in public in the first place, namely that they care about the world to which they always already belong. Political thinking implies delving into the structures of caring that precede normative questions and enable moral and political deliberation.

Care has the structure of a response to an appeal that is made on us, that is, of "response-ability." It is *worldly problems* that solicit, call forth and enable us to act and speak politically. Arendt gives the example of taking the initiative to act: "When I make [the] decision [to appear to others], I am not merely reacting to whatever qualities may be given me; I am making an act of deliberate choice among the various potentialities of conduct which the world has presented me" (1971, 37).[20]

Arendt's proto-normative commitment helps clarify her slightly grumpy rejoinder when a discussant at a roundtable discussion in 1972 requested her political instructions ("I wonder, as someone who is or feels himself to be a political actor, how would you instruct me? Or wouldn't you instruct me at all?"): "I wouldn't instruct you, and I think this would be presumptuous of me. I think that you should be instructed when you sit together with your peers around a table and exchange opinions . . . And I think that every other road of the theoretician who tells his students what to think and how to act is . . . my God! These are adults! We are not in the nursery! Real political action comes out as a group act. And you join that group or you don't" (1979, 310).

The normative political question of how to act is not a theoretical issue (which could in principle be determined by a single solitary and disengaged individual from a third-person perspective), but a practical one (intrinsic to praxis), that is, enacted by a plurality of actors themselves the moment they start to act together.[21] Arendt's work does not provide (even pursue) normative foundations for human dignity, not because she suffered from "normative melancholia," but because she held a phenomenologically informed conception of what "political thinking" is for. This conception may, on the other hand, be compatible with non-foundational, politicizing interpretations of her work on human rights, the right to have rights and crimes against humanity, but for reasons usually not fully acknowledged. Arendtian non-foundationalism is only derivative of a proto-normative commitment—to the world. As a political thinker, inspired by phenomenology, Arendt was interested above all in exploring why those who venture to act and speak in public care in the first place.

BIBLIOGRAPHY

Arendt, Hannah. 1949. "'The Rights of Man': What Are They?" *Modern Review* 3: 24–37.

———. 1951. *The Origins of Totalitarianism*. (1st edition) New York: Harcourt.

———. 1955. lecture "Statelessness," University of California, Berkeley Course "History of political theory," The Hannah Arendt papers at the Library of Congress, Washington: http://memory.loc.gov/cgi-bin/query/P?mharendt:2:./temp/~ammem_HvZ8: [last consulted: August 9, 2021].

———. 1958. *The Human Condition*. Chicago: University of Chicago Press.

———. 1961. *Between Past and Future. Eight Exercises in Political Thought*. New York: Penguin.

———. 1963a. *Eichmann in Jerusalem. A Report on the Banality of Evil*. New York: Viking Press.

———. 1963b. *On Revolution*. New York: Viking Press.

———. 1964. Lecture "Kant's Political Philosophy," University of Chicago, Fall 1964, 1970, Hannah Arendt Papers, Library of Congress: http://memory.loc.gov/cgi-bin/query/P?mharendt:1:./temp/~ammem_s3qa:: [last consulted: August 9, 2021].

———. 1968. *Men in Dark Times*. New York: Harcourt.

———. 1971. *The Life of the Mind I* (Thinking). New York: Harcourt.

———. 1973. *The Origins of Totalitarianism*. New edition with added prefaces (5th edition). New York: Harcourt.

———. 1978. *The Life of the Mind II* (Willing). New York: Harcourt.

———. 1979. "On Hannah Arendt." In *Hannah Arendt. The Recovery of the Public World*, edited by M. Hill, 301–39. New York: St. Martin's Press.

———. 1982. *Lectures on Kant's Political Philosophy*, edited by Ronald Beiner, Chicago: Chicago University Press.

———. 1994. *Essays in Understanding, 1930–1954*, edited by Jerome Kohn. New York: Schocken.

———. 2005. *The Promise of Politics*, edited by Jerome Kohn. New York: Schocken.

Azouleh, Ariella, and Bonnie. 2016. "Between Nuremberg and Jerusalem: Hannah Arendt's *Tikkun Olam*." *Differences* 27, no. 1: 48–93.

Benhabib, Seyla. 2000. "Arendt's *Eichmann in Jerusalem*." In *The Cambridge Companion to Hannah Arendt*, edited by Dana Villa, 65–85. Cambridge: Cambridge University Press.

———. 2006. "The Philosophical Foundation of Cosmopolitan Norms." In *Another Cosmopolitanism*, edited by Seyla Benhabib and Robert Post, 13–44. Oxford: Oxford University Press.

Birmingham, Peg. 2006. *Hannah Arendt and Human Rights: The Predicament of Common Responsibility*. Bloomington: Indiana University Press.

Borren, Marieke. 2013. "'A Sense of the World': Hannah Arendt's Hermeneutic Phenomenology of Common Sense." *International Journal of Philosophical Studies* 21, no. 1: 225–55.

———. 2014. "The Human Condition of Being Undeportable and the Abyss of the 'Right to Have Rights.'" *Open. Cahier on Art and the Public Domain*, 2014: onlineopen.org/essays/the-human-condition-of-being-undeportable.

Butler, Judith. 2011. "Hannah Arendt's Death Sentences." *Comparative Literature Studies* 48, no. 3: 280–95.

———. 2013. *Parting Ways: Jewishness and the Critique of Zionism*. New York: Columbia University Press.

Cane, Lucy. 2015. "Hannah Arendt on the Principles of Political Action." *European Journal of Political Theory* 14, no.1: 55–75.

Canovan, Margaret. 1985. "Politics as Culture: Hannah Arendt and the Public Realm," *History of Political Thought* 6, no. 3: 617–42.

———. 1992. *Hannah Arendt: A Reinterpretation of Her Political Thought*. Cambridge: Cambridge University Press.

Chacón, Rodrigo. 2013. "Arendt's *Denktagebuch, 1950–1973*: An Unwritten Ethics for the Human Condition?" *History of European Ideas* 39, no. 4: 561–82.

Fine, Robert. 2000. "Crimes Against Humanity: Hannah Arendt and the Nuremberg Debates." *European Journal of Social Theory* 3, no. 3: 293–311.

Gündoğdu, Ayten. 2015. *Rightlessness in an Age of Rights: Hannah Arendt and the Contemporary Struggles of Migrants*. Oxford: Oxford University Press.

Hayden, Patrick. 2009. *Political Evil in a Global Age: Hannah Arendt and International Theory*. London: Routledge.

Heinämaa, Sara. 2003. *Toward a Phenomenology of Sexual Difference. Husserl, Merleau-Ponty, Beauvoir*. Lanham, MD: Rowman & Littlefield.

Honig, Bonnie. 2006. "Another Cosmopolitanism? Law and Politics in the New Europe." In *Another Cosmopolitanism,* edited by Seyla Benhabib and Robert Post, 102–27. Oxford: Oxford University Press.

———. 2014. "What is Agonism For? Reply to Finlayson, Woodford, and Stears." *Contemporary Political Theory* 13, no. 2: 208–17.

———. 2017. *Public Things: Democracy in Disrepair*. New York: Fordham University Press.

King, Richard H. and Dan Stone eds. 2007. *Hannah Arendt and the Uses of History: Imperialism, Nation, Race, and Genocide*. Oxford: Berghahn Books.

Kistner, Ulrike. 2008. "Lineages of Racism in Genocidal Contexts. Lessons from Hannah Arendt in Contemporary African Genocide Scholarship." *Development Dialogue*, 50: 155–71.

Loidolt, Sophie. 2018. *Phenomenology of Plurality: Hannah Arendt on Political Intersubjectivity*. London: Routledge.

Luban, David. 2004. "A Theory of Crimes against Humanity," *The Yale Journal of International Law* 29, no.1: 85–167.

———. 2011. "Hannah Arendt as a Theorist of International Criminal Law." *International Criminal Law Review* 11, no. 3: 621–41

Macready, John. 2018. *Hannah Arendt and the Fragility of Human Dignity*. Lanham: Lexington Books.

Markell, Patchen. 2011. "Arendt's Work: On the Architecture of *The Human Condition*," *College Literature* 38, no.1: 15–44.

Maxwell, Lida. 2012. "Toward an Agonistic Understanding of Law: Law and Politics in Hannah Arendt's *Eichmann in Jerusalem*." *Contemporary Political Theory* 11, no.1: 88–108.

May, Larry. 2006. "Symposium on *Crimes Against Humanity. A Normative Account*." *Ethics & International Affairs* 20, no. 3: 349–52.

McLeod, Christopher. 2010. "Towards a Philosophical Account of Crimes Against Humanity." *European Journal of International Law* 21, no. 2: 281–302.

Mensch, James. 2009. *Embodiments: From the Body to the Body Politic*. Evanston, Il.: Northwestern University Press.

Moses, A. Dirk. 2010. "Hannah Arendt, Imperialism, and the Holocaust." In *German Colonialism: Race, the Holocaust, and Postwar Germany*, edited by Volker Langbehn and Mohammad Salama, 72–92. New York: Columbia University Press.

Myers, Ella. 2013. *Worldly Ethics: Democratic Politics and Care for the World*. Durham, NC: Duke University Press.

Näsström, Sofia. 2014. 'The Right to Have Rights: Democratic, Not Political,' *Political Theory* 42, no. 5: 543–68.

Oliver, Kelly. 2015. *Earth and World: Philosophy After the Apollo Missions*. New York: Columbia University Press.

Stone, Dan. 2011. "Defending the Plural: Hannah Arendt and Genocide Studies." *New Formations*, 71: 46–57.

Taminiaux, Jacques. 1997. *The Thracian Maid and the Professional Thinker: Arendt and Heidegger*, Albany: SUNY Press.

Taylor, Telford. 1961. "Large Questions in the Eichmann Case," *New York Times Magazine*, January 22: 21–25.

———. 1962. "The Faces of Justice in Jerusalem." *The Spectator*, January 5: 21.

Topolski, Anya. 2015. *Arendt, Levinas, and a Politics of Relationality*. London: Rowman & Littlefield.

Universal Declaration of Human Rights. 1948. United Nations General Assembly.

Vasterling, Veronica. 2011. "Hannah Arendt," In *Routledge Companion to Phenomenology*, edited by Sebastian Luft and Søren Overgaard, 82–91. London and New York: Routledge.

Vernon, Richard. 2002. "What Is Crime against Humanity?" *The Journal of Political Philosophy* 10, no. 3: 231–49.

Villa, Dana. 1996. *Arendt and Heidegger: The Fate of the Political*, Princeton: Princeton University Press.

Vollrath, Ernst. 1977. "Arendt and the Method of Political Thinking." *Social Research* 44, no.1: 160–82.

———. 1979. "Politik und Metaphysik. Zum politischen Denken Hannah Arendts." In *Hannah Arendt: Materialien zu ihrem Werk*, edited by Adelbert Reif, 19–57. Wien: Europaverlag.

Young-Bruehl, Elisabeth. 1982. *Hannah Arendt. For Love of the World*. New Haven: Yale University Press.

Zahavi, Dan. 2005. *Subjectivity and Selfhood: Investigating the First-Person Perspective*. Cambridge, MA: MIT.

———. 2011. "Intersubjectivity." In *Routledge Companion to Phenomenology*, edited by Sebastian Luft and Søren Overgaard, 180–89. London: Routledge.

Zerilli, Linda. 2005. *Feminism and the Abyss of Freedom*. Chicago: University of Chicago Press.

Zimmerer, Jürgen. 2004. "Colonialism and the Holocaust. Towards an Archaeology of Genocide." In *Genocide and Settler Society: Frontier Violence and Stolen Indigenous Children in Australian History*, edited by A. Dirk Moses, 49–76. New York: Berghahn Books.

NOTES

1. For example, Martin Jay, Luc Ferry, Alain Renault, and, especially, Richard Wolin (Villa 1996, 115–16). Some commentators on the other hand praise Arendt for her "cosmopolitan realism" or her "critical," "rugged," or "worldly" cosmopolitanism (Fine 2000), "shorn of historical and moral idealism" (Hayden 2009, 9).

2. For political or politicizing readings of Arendt's account of human rights and/or "the right to have rights," see: Nässtrom 2014; Gündoğdu 2015; Cane 2015; and Honig 2006. For political or politicizing readings of Arendt's account of crimes against humanity, see Maxwell 2012; Honig 2006, Azoulay & Honig 2016; Gündoğdu 2015. For a political reading of the principle of human dignity in general, see Macready 2018.

3. Early exceptions are Ernst Vollrath 1977, 1979, and Jacques Taminiaux 1997.

4. Even if Arendt's most well-known book is called *The Human Condition*, the very notion of "the human condition" (in the singular) is somewhat misleading, for it is often used in a sense that is actually the opposite from the historical and contextual meaning with which Arendt invests it, namely human *nature*. In her own German translation of *The Human Condition* (published in 1960 under a title which no longer makes mention of the "human condition," *Vita Activa*), she uses the term *Bedingtheit* for "condition." *Bedingtheit*, though, is in fact more accurately translated as "conditionality" or, to use a neologism, "conditionedness." On this, also see Chacón 2013; Macready 2018; Loidolt 2018. Therefore, in this article I will use "human conditionality" and the "human conditions" (in the plural) rather than the "human condition."

5. Here my account differs from Sophie Loidolt (2018), whose central claim is that Arendt's conceptual work and method are less idiosyncratic and eclectic than is usually assumed, as phenomenology provides the systematic grounding underlying her method and the key notions that inform her work. One of her aims is to provide a corrective to exclusively empirical-political (or "ontic") readings of Arendt's work. Adamant to stress the philosophical (ontological) rather than "merely" political (ontic) meaning of Arendt's work, Loidolt sometimes overstates her point with the risk of dehistoricizing it, which in my view is a missed opportunity to explore a truly original feature of Arendt's phenomenology, namely how concrete political (ontic) events and a radical phenomenological ontology *work together* in it.

6. Even if the world is the human habitat or house, it is not a place of comfort: it requires our constant attention in order to keep it a place fit for human coexistence, as the examples of the Holocaust and statelessness in section 2 show. One has to actively involve oneself to be able to appreciate the world as a meaningful context.

7. The distinction between things and discourse might suggest that first there is a pre-political "object" to which subsequently meaning is attributed, with only the discursive world being truly political. However, worldly things and discourse are closely related for Arendt. For most of the time, it is exactly things that are the point of reference (topic) and/or the stage and context of discourse (1958, 204). Arendt was well aware that undisclosed objects lack any meaning for us. The world in Arendt's sense does not consist in "objects," as the word is used in the natural sciences, that is as meaningless ('dead') matter, but more accurately in "things" that are meaningful

for us, that is, useful (or useless), beautiful (or ugly), and so on. Second, things and discourse refer to one and the same world, *our* human world, like nature and world also refer to the same planet, *our* planet, namely earth. Finally, especially in her later writings on the revolutionary and the republican tradition, the distinction between things and discourse becomes even less clear-cut. For example, in her essay "What is Freedom?" (1961) Arendt calls the phenomenon that in her view rightfully qualifies as freedom a "worldly, tangible reality": it "develops fully only when action has created its own worldly space where it can come out of hiding, as it were, and make its appearance" (1961, 169).

8. *Eichmann in Jerusalem* and *The Life of the Mind* are closely related works in Arendt's oeuvre. In the introduction to *The Life of the Mind* Volume I, she explains that the lessons she learned from *Eichmann in Jerusalem* prompted her to start on the *Life of the Mind* project.

9. Article 15 reads: "1. Everyone has the right to a nationality. 2. No one shall be arbitrarily deprived of his nationality nor denied the right to change his nationality."

10. Most prominently Luban 2004, 2011; Vernon 2002; McLeod 2010; Fine 2000; and May 2006, 373. Also see historians in the field of Genocide Studies (Stone 2011; King & Stone 2007, Moses 2010; Zimmerer 2004; and Kistner 2008). Also see Oliver 2015.

11. Arendt was deeply impressed by the opening address of the American chief prosecutor, Robert H. Jackson, on the second day of the Nuremberg trial, November 21, 1945, as the first judge ever to use this expression (1949, 36). A few months later, the French prosecutor, Francois de Menthon, spoke of a *"crime contre la condition humaine"* (January 17, 1946). In 1963 she wrote that to her these were words of "great clarity" (1963a, 268, 257).

12. This has been suggested by several interpreters, such as Luban 2011; Vernon 2002.

13. The common possession of the earth's surface later became a pivotal aspect of Kant's Doctrine of Right, particularly pertaining to property law, in *The Metaphysics of Morals* (1797).

14. The precarious legal, political, and human status of today's refugees and undocumented immigrants further illustrates this argument. Practices of detention, deportation, and encampment may dehumanize refugees, because they deprive them of a place in the world (Gündoğdu 2015).

15. For a more detailed reconstruction of this argument, see Borren 2014.

16. Arendt held, on the contrary, that the Holocaust had nothing to do with World War II—a war between sovereign nations—so the charge of war crimes was sadly beside the point. And her misgivings about Eichmann's prosecution on account of Crimes against the Jewish People concerns the implied failure to acknowledge the radical novelty of the crime. Second, she held that Eichmann should have stood trial at an international tribunal. She was alarmed by what she considered had become a "show trial" that was instrumentalized for ulterior particularistic political ends: to provide a justification for the foundation and existence of the state of Israel (1963a, 4, 176, 254). Hence the reluctance to prosecute perpetrators of the Holocaust for crimes against humanity, instead of crimes against the Jewish people.

17. What is said about action in respect of the actor arguably applies to judging in respect to the spectator as well.

18. Democratic theorist Ella Myers has put Arendtian care for the world as "home" and "in-between" convincingly within the recent literature on democratic *ethos* (2013). Although Myers does not engage with phenomenology, she arrives at a number of similar features, such as the appeal-and-response structure of care.

19. Here Arendt is commenting upon Bertolt Brecht's life and poems, but this remark fits her own views as well.

20. For a similar argument, see Zerilli 2005, 11–13, 17.

21. See n. 17 above.

Chapter Ten

Denaturalizing Hannah Arendt and Claudia Jones

Statelessness, Citizenship, and Racialization

Andrew Schaap

Claudia Jones (1915–1964) and Hannah Arendt (1906–1975) were both illegalized by states seeking to shape populations through citizenship legislation and immigration control. The political thinking of each was informed by their respective experience of state violence and their belonging to a diaspora. Arendt fled Nazi Germany for France in 1933, following her arrest and detention for several days by police in Berlin. Having lived in Paris throughout the 1930s, she spent several weeks in Gurs internment camp for "enemy aliens" in May 1940 before finding refuge in New York with her husband and mother the following year. Jones immigrated to Harlem from Trinidad as a child in 1924 to join her parents as a part of the interwar wave of Caribbean emigration. She was harassed by police for many years due to her anti-racist organizing through the Communist Youth League. In 1953, Jones was convicted of seeking to overthrow the US government by force or violence under the 1940 Alien Registration (Smith) Act. She served a year in prison before her deportation to the United Kingdom as a foreign criminal. Despite struggling with poor health and poverty, she became politically active in the growing Caribbean community in London.

While born hemispheres apart (in Trinidad and Germany), both women lived in New York from the time that Arendt arrived as a refugee in 1941 until Jones was deported in 1955. While the trajectories of their lives converged in remarkable ways, their political thinking diverged fundamentally in several respects. Despite her admiration for Marx and the revolutionary workers' councils, Arendt viewed the Soviet Union as a totalitarian state. She believed that capitalism and socialism both created the conditions for totalitarianism to emerge since they privileged life itself as the highest good, reducing politics to collective housekeeping and spreading loneliness among their populations. In contrast, Jones was a committed member of the American Communist Party, who pioneered intersectional analysis, centering the super-exploitation of black, working women as the basis of an emancipatory politics. Jones viewed the existence of the USSR as essential to the emancipation of colonized peoples and women as part of a broader anti-capitalist struggle.

Despite the centrality of the lives and writings of both women to some of the most significant events of the twentieth century, the different reception of each in the history of thought is striking. While Arendt is now canonized as a preeminent political thinker, the significance of Jones's activism and political thought has only recently begun to receive sustained scholarly attention (for example, Boyce-Jones 2008; Burden-Stelly 2019; Chevannes 2020; Dunstan and Owens 2021; Henry 2021). In this chapter, I situate Arendt's reflections on citizenship and statelessness in relation to the intellectual biography of Jones and the contexts in which she worked and wrote: the Harlem Renaissance, the Red Scare and the Notting Hill riots in Britain. I explore how the development of citizenship rights in the twentieth century was intertwined with race and colonialism in ways that Arendt neglected. In particular, the experiences and political thinking of Claudia Jones draw attention to how immigration control is not simply an instrument of exclusion but has been integral to the racial ordering of societies such as the United States and the UK.

"OUR" AWARENESS OF THE "RIGHT TO HAVE RIGHTS."

Hannah Arendt arrived in New York in 1941 as a German-Jewish refugee. In a 1964 interview for German television, Arendt describes the burning of the Reichstag and the illegal arrests that followed in 1933 (when she was twenty-seven years old) as a politicizing moment, which made clear to her that she could not remain a bystander. Arendt decided to emigrate since she "did not intend to run around Germany as a second-class citizen" (Arendt 1994, 5). However, before doing so, she was arrested and detained in Berlin for eight days. Arendt had been collating anti-Semitic statements by Nazi officials from the Prussian State Library on behalf of a Zionist organization. Upon her release, Arendt illegally crossed the border into France (see Young-Bruehl 1982, 105–10). While living in Paris throughout the 1930s, Arendt worked for a Zionist organization, assisting in the resettlement of

Jewish children in Palestine. In May 1940, she was detained by the French government as an "enemy alien" for several weeks in Gurs internment camp. However, she was able to escape in the confusion of the German invasion (see Bernstein 2005). In an unusually personal reflection published two years after her arrival in New York, Arendt (2007, 265) observed that the world had witnessed the creation of a "new kind of human beings—the kind which can be put in concentration camps by their foes and in internment camps by their friends" (see Young-Bruehl 2004, 150–58).

Arendt's reflections on the plight of stateless people continue to resonate in our contemporary political conjuncture as "we" (in the Global North) are confronted by the spectacle of migrants exposed to violence by nominally democratic states: as illegalized people are detained, denationalized, deported and made destitute in "our name." Arendt thought stateless people were the "most symptomatic group in contemporary politics" because they embodied the crisis of the nation-state system insofar as they were "forced to exist outside all legal structures" (Arendt 1949, 24). This condition of rightlessness was brought about by the twofold loss of home and government protection. Their plight was unprecedented since this was "a problem not of space but of political organization": the division of the globe into nation-states meant that stateless people had nowhere else to go when persecuted by their government; for these people, the camp became "a substitute for a non-existent homeland" (Arendt 1949, 26). Moreover, the sheer scale of the number of people who were denationalized and displaced, not due to their beliefs, opinions or actions, but because they were "born into the wrong kind of race or . . . class" meant that they could not be accommodated as refugees within the states to which they fled (Arendt 1949, 26). Arendt thus observed at the time of the United Nations' Declaration of Human Rights that "we only became aware of the existence of a right to have rights . . . when there suddenly emerged millions of people who had lost and could not regain these rights because of the new global situation" (1949, 24). This disaster, she argued, was not due to any regression of civilized standards. On the contrary, it came about "because there was no longer any 'uncivilized' spot on earth to which stateless people could go" (Arendt 1949, 30). It was only in this context of a "completely organized humanity" that loss of membership in a political community could coincide with expulsion from humanity (Arendt 1949, 30).

In her characterization of a dawning awareness of the precarity of citizenship among the predominantly white, settled populations of Europe and North America whom she addresses, Arendt neglects a longer process through which hundreds of thousands of people of color outside of Europe became aware of the right to have rights. This awareness among colonized people was produced, as Lara Putnam recounts, "not by expulsion from [their] homelands, but by migrating within or beyond empire and discovering that their governing state was not prepared to enforce the rights that they had been promised and that Britain's white subjects enjoyed" (2014, 188). Indeed, the experience of anti-Black racism by British West Indians living outside the British Empire in the interwar period made them politically conscious of the significance of citizen status and its relation to racial hierarchies. While white "Englishmen" were welcomed in countries surrounding the Caribbean (such as Panama, Cuba, Venezuela, Costa Rica, and the United States), Black Caribbean British subjects found themselves vilified in these places to which they were forced to migrate, having their "visas denied, bribes demanded, employment barred and family cut off" (Putnam 2014, 170). As states enacted race-based bans on entry and employment, British Consuls raised no objection to the treatment of Black Britons abroad.

Members of the Caribbean diaspora thus grappled with the fundamental tension between citizenship as a *civic standing* (developed through participation in politics), on one hand, and citizenship as a state-conferred *legal status* (which could be arbitrarily withdrawn), on the other hand. As Putnam puts it, "nonwhite imperial subjects found themselves outside the borders, literal and figurative, in an era of expanding rights" (2014, 185). Despite the fact that the status of British citizen was not established until 1948, colonized people from the British West Indies invoked and demanded their rights to political participation, freedom of movement and employment as self-proclaimed British citizens throughout the interwar period. Indeed, despite their presumptive exclusion from citizenship by the white British governing class, most English-speaking Caribbean people "never doubted that citizenship was theirs" (Putnam 2014, 172).

Claudia Jones was part of this interwar Caribbean diaspora. Born in Trinidad, she immigrated to New York in 1924 to join her parents at the age of nine, just months before the 1924 Johnson-Reed act effectively barred further Caribbean migration to the United States (Boyce-Davies 2008, 198–201). As Jones herself recounts, in a letter written a few days before her deportation in 1955, her middle-class parents had immigrated to the United States in 1922 following the collapse of the world cocoa trade, which had impoverished the British West Indies. While they migrated to the United States in search of a better life, Jones says her family "suffered not only the impoverished lot of working-class native families" but also the "special scourge and indignity stemming from Jim Crow national oppression" (Jones 2011, 11). Jones's mother was only thirty-seven when she died suddenly (of spinal meningitis) while at work in a garment shop in 1933: the year that Claudia turned eighteen and completed high school. Jones reflected that the harsh working conditions and difficult circumstances of being an immigrant that her mother contended with surely 'contributed to her early death' (Jones in Boyce Davies 2011, 11).

Growing up during the Harlem Renaissance and completing high school in the midst of the Great Depression, Jones experienced both the poverty of urban black America and the displacement of being an immigrant (Boyce-Davies 2008, 159). Outrage within the Black community in Harlem over the "Scottsboro Boys frame up" in the early 1930s was a politicizing event, which led Jones to join the Communist Party. The Scottsboro Boys were nine black teenagers (aged 12–19) accused of raping two white women in Alabama in 1931. Eight of the boys were convicted and sentenced to death through hastily held trials at which they were poorly represented before all-white juries. Jones says that she "spent a lot of time coming from work listening . . . to the street corner meeting of the various political parties and movements in Harlem" and was "impressed by the Communist speakers" who drew parallels between the struggle for racial justice in America and that of the "Ethiopians against fascism and Mussolini's invasion" (Jones 2011, 13–14).

In her 1949 essay, "An End to the Neglect of the Problems of Negro Women" (published the same year as Arendt's essay on the Rights of Man), Jones posits the situation of Black women as symptomatic of rising fascism: "nothing so exposes the drive to fascization in the nation," she insists, "as the callous attitude which the bourgeoisie displays and cultivates toward Negro women" (2011, 75). The growing militancy of Black women is essential for the liberation of African Americans and the anti-fascist movement due to their super-exploitation: their triple oppression due to class, race and gender (see Weigand 2001, 103–8). "As mother, as Negro, and as worker," she argues, "the Negro woman fights against the wiping out of the Negro family, against the Jim Crow ghetto existence which destroys the health, morale, and the very life of millions of her sisters, brothers and children" (Jones 2011, 74).

She highlights how the super exploitation of Black women is related to being forced into menial and underpaid employment in domestic and personal service. This is reinforced by the 'white chauvinist stereotype' perpetuated by the media according to which "the Negro woman is not pictured as breadwinner, mother and protector of the family, but as a traditional 'mammy' who puts the care of children and families of others above her own" (Jones 2011, 74). While Jones attributes the super-exploitation of Black women to the white bourgeoisie, she describes how white chauvinism is expressed and reproduced in "progressive circles" through what we would today name as micro-aggressions. For instance, she refers to encounters in which a white woman expresses "paternalistic surprise when it is learned that Negroes are professional people" or inquires "whether 'someone in the family' would like to take a job as a domestic worker" in their home (Jones in Boyce-Jones 2011, 81). She insists that the responsibility for overcoming white chauvinism rests "squarely on the shoulders of white men and women." Anticipating what is now commonly described as an intersectional approach to political struggle, she argues that the inclusion of Black working women is essential to the development of a "heightened political consciousness" among all people in the struggle against fascism and imperialism (Jones 2011, 83, 75).

Jones's insistence that the *super-exploitation* of Black women is indicative of rising fascism parallels Arendt's claim that the *superfluity* experienced by stateless people is symptomatic of the emergence of totalitarian government. According to Arendt, the plight, of stateless people, "is not that they are not equal before the law, but that no law exists for them, not that they are oppressed but that *nobody even wants to oppress them*" [emphasis added] (1949, 28–29). In this context, indeed, Arendt explicitly contrasts the situation of the stateless person with that of the slave, who, although dominated, still had a subordinate place in society since they served an economic function (see Røstball 2014; Schaap 2020). In contrast, she suggests, the stateless person was deemed to be of no use to society at all and, once deprived of citizenship status, could be exposed to extreme state violence, which was exemplified, above all, in the Nazi death camps. Arendt views stateless people as the most symptomatic group in contemporary politics because they indicate this ever-present temptation to resort to totalitarian solutions when confronted with the problem of "excess" populations. However, the production of such populations was, she believed, a consequence of elevating life itself to the highest good in politics within both capitalist and socialist societies (Arendt 1972, 213–214; see Beiner 1990). If the function of the state was reduced to the satisfaction of the needs of its population, then the implication of this was that the lives of some subaltern populations might be seen as unnecessary (or even a threat) to the health of the population as whole. It was in this context that she viewed the recuperation of a "right to have rights," that is, a right not just to citizenship as legal status but as the right to appear as political beings as an antidote to the threat of totalitarianism.

Arendt's account of the production of superfluous human beings (exemplified in the figure of the stateless person) and their exposure to state violence (exemplified by the camp) continues to inform contemporary thinking about citizenship and immigration today (for example, see Borren 2008; Krause 2008; Gündoğdu 2015; Arnold 2018). However, the limitations of her thought for understanding anti-Black racism are also widely acknowledged (for example, see Norton 1995; Bernasconi 1996; Allen 2004; Gines 2014). In particular, Arendt's distinction between the social and the political not only differentiates her political thinking from a Marxian perspective but limits her capacity to adequately address race politics (Chevannes 2020). Reconsidering Arendt's reflections on citizenship and statelessness in relation to the intellectual biography of Jones therefore affords insights into how citizenship, racialization and immigration control may be mutually constitutive in particular historical circumstances. This becomes particularly clear when we consider Arendt's and Jones's different experiences and perspectives in the context of the anti-communist fervor of postwar America.

ANTI-COMMUNISM, FASCISM AND ANTI-BLACK RACISM

While Arendt admired the political freedom that citizens enjoyed in America, she viewed the emergence of anti-communist hysteria of the late 1940s and 1950s with trepidation. Once the principle of equality before the law is no longer observed, Arendt pointed out in *The Origins of Totalitarianism*, the nation-state loses its legitimacy: as "arbitrary rule by police decree" is extended over illegalized populations, states are increasingly tempted to "deprive all citizens of legal status and rule them with an omnipotent police" (Arendt 2004, 368). While denaturalization had previously been a weapon of totalitarian states, however, it was increasingly employed by democratic states, such as the United States, which was "seriously considering depriving native Americans who are Communists of their citizenship" (Arendt 2004, 356). The "sinister aspect of these measures," Arendt remarked, was that they were "being considered in all innocence" (2004, 256). For one only had to reflect on the care that the Nazis took to ensure that all those Jewish people who they "deported" were first stripped of their citizenship to recognize how statelessness exposes populations to extreme state violence.

Jones could speak directly to the experience of state violence in the United States. The US government's order to deport Jones on December 5, 1955, followed over a decade of surveillance and harassment by the police and FBI agents empowered by the 1940 Alien Registration (Smith) Act and the 1950 Internal Security (McCarran) Act (Charisse Burden-Stelly 2019, 46). In a letter to the *Daily Worker* in 1950, Jones reflected on the lack of due process through which she and sixteen other Communist Party members (a "virtual United Nations") were detained on Ellis Island:

> Many of us have had no hearings or legal examinations of any kind. We have never been confronted with any evidence, or made familiar with any crime, alleged or charged against us . . . We are threatened by the government with becoming the first inmates of America's concentration camps, the direct victims of the mad drive of the ruling circles to fascism at home and atomic war abroad. (Jones cited in Boyce 2008, 154–55)

Under the Immigration and Nationality (McCarran-Walter) Act 1952, foreign-born citizens could be denaturalized, and noncitizens could be arrested, indefinitely detained, and deported if suspected of criminal activity (which included "practicing the ideas of communism"). Following her prison sentence, rather than being deported to Trinidad, which she had known only as a child and where the colonial government was reluctant to receive her, Jones flew to London (since she was a citizen of the United Kingdom and Colonies under the British Nationality Act 1948). In a 1956 interview in London, Jones was clear that she had been deported because she was "a Negro woman Communist of West Indian descent" who had been a thorn in the side of the US government for her anti-racist political activism and support for the rights of women and all workers (2011, 16). She recognized herself as a victim of McCarthyite hysteria, "which penalizes anyone who holds ideas contrary to the official pro-war, pro-reactionary, pro-fascist line of the white ruling class of that country" (Jones 2011, 16).

Arendt became a US citizen in 1951, soon after Joseph McCarthy had commenced his anti-communist purge through the work of the House Committee of Un-American Activities (King 2015, 98). As Lara Putnam points out, Arendt "began building a respected career as an anti-communist public intellectual" within the same political milieu that had such devastating consequences for Jones (2014, 186). Yet Arendt's attitude to Marxism and communism were more complex that Putnam's observation implies. She believed that the radical movement of the early twentieth century was derailed by its identification with the Russian Revolution and subsequent subordination to Soviet-led communism (Arendt 1994, 219). She characterized the form of government that emerged in the Soviet Union as totalitarian since it (like the Nazi regime) was animated by the principle of terror, which found its institutional expression in the concentration camp (Young Bruehl 2004, 206). Moreover, *The Human Condition*, was first envisaged in a research proposal to examine the totalitarian elements in Marxism (see Canovan 1994, ch. 3).

If Arendt rejected what Jones (2011, 137) refers to as socialism's "scientific understanding of society," she nonetheless held Marx and many Marxist intellectuals, such as Rosa Luxemburg and Walter Benjamin, in high regard. In fact, Arendt's husband, Heinrich Blücher, was potentially deportable under the 1952 McCarran-Walter Act due to his former membership in the German Communist Party, which he had lied about when entering the United States in 1941 (King 2015, 99). At the age of nineteen, Blücher had returned to Berlin from the war to join one of the soldiers' councils that, together with the workers' councils, brought about the German Republic in 1918. Blücher joined the Spartacists led by Karl Liebknecht and Rosa Luxemburg and participated in the unsuccessful strikes and battles of 1919 (Young-Bruehl 2004, 124–27). Arendt most likely had her husband in mind when, in 1953, she described former Communists as a group of politically motivated people in whose lives "Communism had played a decisive role" but had left when they sensed how "a revolutionary party" was developing into a "totalitarian movement" (1994, 391).[1]

While Arendt was clearly a critic of communism, she viewed McCarthyism as a greater threat to public freedom in postwar America. Indeed, she found the political atmosphere of the McCarthy era unbearable, describing it in a letter to Karl Jaspers in 1949 as "a physical nerve torture" (Arendt cited in Young-Bruehl 2004, 207). This atmosphere, she told Jaspers, "reminded her of the early days of National Socialism with its embrace of 'police methods' and encouragement of the 'expansion of lawlessness'" (King 2015, 99, citing Arendt). Contributing to this atmosphere were, what Arendt called "ex-Communists," exemplified by people like Whittaker Chambers: a journalist and former member of the American Communist Party who had been a Soviet spy before becoming a committed anti-communist.[2] Such ex-communists posed a threat to democracy in the United States, in Arendt's view, since they continued to "think of themselves as being the makers of history" rather than political actors (1994, 396). They retained a certain kind of totalitarian thinking since they sought to follow procedures through which to achieve an ultimate victory over communism rather than recognize the fragility of political action (its unpredictability and irreversibility) and its inherent frustrations (since political actors never quite know what they are doing). Arendt insisted that a free society had to defend itself against such "makers of history" since totalitarianism as a new form of government remained "a potentiality and ever-present danger" (Arendt 1994, 399).

However, Arendt's understanding of communism and anti-communism in the United States was as limited by her European perspective as it was informed by it. In a 1948 lecture, in which she considered the significance of anti-Stalinism in America and Europe, Arendt remarked that "although fascist groups in this country were never very strong, they existed nonetheless" (1994, 220).[3] Such a complacent observation would be difficult to accept within the Black community. Indeed, black left feminists organizing within the Communist Party "viewed white supremacy, the subjugation of black womanhood, lynching, and black poverty as forms of genocide" that were continuous with the history of slavery (McDuffie 2011, 162). Moreover, Jones recognized parallels between Italian fascism and white supremacy in the United States: while Black people suffered from Jim Crow in the South (including white nationalism, economic segregation and suppression of civil liberties), they were also subject to state and street violence in the North (including race riots, lynching and false imprisonment) (Burden-Stelly 2019, 48). Indeed, in 1951 the Civil Rights Congress petitioned the UN to protect the human rights of African Americans against the wave of white racial terror in the United States (McDuffie 2011, 176).

In her assessment of the fascist threat in the United States, Arendt overlooked the extent to which anti-communism was associated with anti-Black racism (Burden-Stelly 2019, 50–53). In his 1947 speech before the House Unamerican Activities Committee, for instance, FBI Director J. Edgar Hoover imbued anti-communism with anti-Blackness by describing it as a "malignant way of life" whose proponents needed to be quarantined from the American body politic, together with any "fellow travelers" (Burden-Stelly 2019, 54). In doing so, he explicitly linked advocacy of racial justice with communism and anti-Americanism. The link between anti-communism and anti-Blackness was further evident in the prosecution of Ben Davis, together with ten other CPUSA leaders in 1948 who were charged with "teaching and advocating the overthrow of the US government by force or violence" (Burden-Stelly 2019, 58). Davis was a lawyer and a member of the Communist Party, who had represented Harlem as a Councilor in New York City since 1943. When sentenced to five years in prison, he was expelled from the Council as required under state law. In a booklet published by the Communist Party in 1954, *Ben Davis: Fighter for Freedom*, Jones insists that McCarthyism is not only an attack on the "Negro Communist leadership in the United States" but an attack on any Black person advocating for racial equality, which unavoidably entails radicalism against the status quo (2011, 145). As Jones asked polemically, "can anyone support the great national liberation struggles of the peoples of Africa—without facing the accusation of being a 'Communist?'" (2011, 146). Davis himself concurred with Jones, insisting from prison that "it was the purpose of the court in giving me the maximum sentence to intimidate and terrorize all militant Negroes, to serve notice that a fight for free and equal citizenship would be met with severe reprisal" (cited in Burden-Stelly 2019, 59).

Jones described the 1940 Smith Act (Alien Registration Act) as a "fascism-breeding statute" since it constituted a form of thought control, which criminalized ideas by treating them as acts of force while specifically targeting Black radicals (2011, 134). The Act prohibited subversive activities, including the dissemination of any ideas that condone the forceful or violent overthrow or destruction of a US government (Burden-Stelly 2019, 57). Under the legislation, any person belonging to an organization that encouraged such ideas could be imprisoned, fined and/or deported (Boyce-Davies 2008, 149). As Jones pointed out, the threat that the Smith Act posed to the struggle for racial equality was that it "censors speech, thought, teaching and advocacy of social change" (2011, 135). This meant that "any Negro citizen or organization advocating" change to Jim Crow laws or practices could find themselves charged with intent to overthrow the US government by force or violence. In this way, the Act also criminalized freedom of association since membership in the CPUSA was accepted as sufficient evidence that a person might attempt to overthrow the government by force or violence in the future (Burden-Stelly 2019, 59). The 1950 McCarran (Internal Security) Act further intensified the state's surveillance, harassment, and criminalization of people of color by enabling immigration checks, deportation, and detention of those suspected of advocating revolutionary ideas.[4] The 1952 McCarran-Walter (Immigration and Nationality Act) consolidated the state's power to deport aliens who were members of or affiliated with the Communist Party while also introducing national quotas on the number of immigrants eligible to enter the United States from Asian and Caribbean countries. As Jones observed: "This law, which came into being as a result of the whole reactionary drive against progressive ideas in the United States, encourages immigration of fascist scum from Europe but restricts West Indian immigration, once in their thousands annually to the United States, to 100 persons per year, from all the Caribbean islands. This works special hardship among West Indians who have family ties and who are permanent residents and citizens of the USA" (2011, 17).

Moreover, while Arendt (1994, 324) chided American anti-Stalinists for their inability to recognize that communist parties in most parts of the world remained "mass movements or potential mass movements," she was herself ignorant of the role that the Communist Party in America had played in anti-racist organizing, especially within New York. As Jones wrote in 1946, the Communist Party had been at the "forefront of the struggle for equality of the Negro people" since it recognized the specificity of the "Negro question . . . as an issue whose solution requires *special* demands, in addition to the general demands of the American working class" (2011, 61, 62). Jones was part of a small but influential number of radical Black women who viewed the Communist Party as an effective vehicle through which to advance women's rights and black liberation due its organizational capacity and transnational links (McDuffie 2011, 2–3). As such, it provided an alternative site for organizing to church, women's clubs, and Black nationalist groups, within which she may have felt more bound by "middle class political agendas and cultural sensibilities" (McDuffie 2011, 7). At the same time, radical black feminists within the Communist Party maintained social and political links and solidarities with these other organizations (Jones 2011, 145–46). Due to their participation, by the late 1940s, the Communist Party was arguably the "foremost defender of African American women's rights and the chief advocate of their equality" (Weigand 2001, 99).

The McCarran Act and McCarran-Walter Act exemplify how Cold War anti-communism was racialized and racializing. It had a devastating impact on the lives of Black people in the United States, such as Jones, by producing them as precarious (non)citizens whose civic standing and legal status could be imperiled, stripped or denied to the extent that they participated in the struggle against anti-Black racism. While Arendt recognized the threat that McCarthyite anti-communism posed to the American republic in the postwar period, Jones's experiences and reflections highlight how repressive legislation that criminalizes people due to their political commitments can also function to mobilize and produce racism within a political community. Indeed, Jones's deportation highlights how criminal law and immigration control intersect in ways that disproportionately impact on people of color (see de Noronha 2020). The particular forms that anti-Black racism takes are historically specific and largely internal to the societies in which they are produced. As Jones was soon to experience, the homegrown British racism of the postwar era, which targeted Caribbean immigrants, was associated with the emergent crisis of the welfare state and predicated on a profound historical amnesia of Britain's colonial past (Hall 2017: 144).

THE WHITE MOB, THE CIVIL RIGHTS MOVEMENT, AND THE CARIBBEAN COMMUNITY IN BRITAIN

Due to the intensity of state repression, anti-racist campaigners who had been associated with the Communist Party in the United States found themselves isolated from the emergent civil rights movement. The huge personal costs suffered by radical black women due to anti-communist persecution was exemplified in the deportation of Jones (McDuffie 2011, 188). When she arrived in London in December 1955, Jones was seriously ill and socially isolated. She had no passport, only a temporary travel document, which was confiscated on her arrival. The stress of her persecution by police, imprisonment, and deportation had a terrible impact on Jones's health and well-being. Jones spent her first two months in the UK in hospital where she was diagnosed with arrested tuberculosis, heart disease, arteriosclerosis, and hypertension.[5] She struggled with poverty, relying on remittances from friends and family in the United States and a small income from her journalism (Sherwood 1999, 15, 39–42).

Jones's extensive experience of anti-racist organizing and senior leadership went unrecognized by the British Communist Party. As Marika Sherwood (1999, 76) observes, Jones "was sidelined by the CPBP and was never given a position in its leadership (or elsewhere in the Party) commensurate with her abilities, experience and status in the USA." She was given a job as a typist and subeditor in the New China News Agency on her release from the hospital but found herself in conflict with others in the office. She was rarely invited to write for the Party's publications and, when she did, her contribution was severely edited (Sherwood 1999, 76). There were no Black members in the Party's leadership; it had hardly engaged with anti-colonial struggles and had not addressed the forms of white chauvinism within its own ranks such as Jones had called out within the Communist Party in America. Moreover, as fellow Trinidadian and Communist Party member Trevor Carter recalled, "Claudia's arrival in this country coincided with rifts within the international communist movement" (cited in Sherwood 1999, 69). While Carter refers to Khrushchev's denunciation of Stalin, the discrediting of the British Communist Party following its support for the Soviet repression of the Hungarian Revolution in 1956 must also have had an impact.

Across the Atlantic, the Supreme Court had ruled against segregated schooling in *Brown v. Board of Education* in 1954. Ironically, the judgment only briefly made headlines since it was overshadowed by media interest in the final stages of McCarthyism. In the South, however, billboards emerged opposing the decision, which accused the Court of being anti-American and pro-communist (King 2015, 150). Yet, in September 1957, less than two years after Jones's deportation, the public controversy over the desegregation of Central High School in Little Rock, Arkansas, sustained international media attention. The photograph of Elizabeth Eckford being harassed by a white mob after being turned away from entering her school made politically visible the racialized public sphere that existed in the United States (Allen 2004, 5). The event forced a public reckoning with the racialized nature of citizenship in the United States and signaled the emergence of the nascent civil rights struggle. As Danielle Allen (2004, 5) observed, once the habits of citizenship (of white dominance and black acquiescence) that sustained the social order were made public, "citizens in the rest of the country had no choice but to reject or affirm it." In her controversial "Reflections on Little Rock," Arendt decried the "sorry fact . . . that the town's law-abiding citizens left the streets to the mob, that neither white nor black citizens felt it their duty to see the Negro children safely to school" (1959, 49).[6] She argued that the abolition of laws that criminalize mixed marriages ought to take priority over the desegregation of schools and found it objectionable that children were being required to fight adults' political battles.

In one of several controversial statements that expressed and reproduced the white chauvinism among progressives that Jones challenged, Arendt wrote: "the girl was asked to be a hero—something neither her absent father nor the equally absent representative of the NAACP felt called upon to be" (Arendt 1959, 50). This drew a sharp reaction from Ralph Ellison, who remarked in a 1965 interview that Arendt "has no conception of what goes on in the minds of Negro parents when they send their kids through those lines of hostile people" (cited in Young-Bruehl 2004, 316). He emphasized that this was a "rite of initiation" for African American people through which they must take their place in society by confronting the "terrors of social life" and "master the inner tensions created by [their] racial situation" by containing their fear and anger (Ellison cited in Young-Bruehl 2004, 316). Arendt later acknowledged in a personal letter to Ellison that she had not "grasped the element of stark violence, of elementary, bodily fear in the situation" and that she therefore had not understood the complexities of the situation (Arendt cited in Young-Bruehl 2004, 316).

Arendt's reflections were shaped by her personal experience, historical context, and political theory. The repugnance she expressed toward laws forbidding racial intermarriage in the South was likely informed her own marriage to a German gentile (King 2015, 175). Furthermore, her shock at seeing Elizabeth Eckford exposed and isolated before a white mob was likely shaped by her own experience at an "integrated" public school in Königsberg (see Gines 2014, 123; King 2015, 179). Her mother insisted that she must defend herself against anti-Semitic remarks from her classmates, but she should leave class immediately and return home if she, or any other student, was subjected to anti-Semitism by a teacher. As Arendt recalled in an interview for German television in 1964, "these were rules of conduct by which I retained my dignity, so to speak, and I was protected absolutely, at home" (Arendt 1994, 8).[7]

Moreover, Arendt's intervention relied on the threefold distinction between public, private and social, that was central to *The Human Condition*. Arendt wrote, "What equality is to the body politic, discrimination is to society" (1959, 51). While the artificial equality sustained by institutions is a condition of possibility for participation as citizen in the public realm, in Arendt's view, the freedom to discriminate about who one associates with is essential to society, the hybrid space between public and private. In her view, it is a political mistake to seek to abolish social discrimination through public means. Rather, the proper response is to confine discrimination to the social realm due to its potentially destructive impact on public life. The weakness in Arendt's argument was her characterization of schools as primarily social rather than political institutions. Consequently, she characterized the demand for integrated schooling as a form of social climbing rather than the exercise of a citizenship right.

Nonetheless, as Ainsley LeSure (2021) argues, Arendt's reflections on Little Rock indicate how struggles for integration and social equality may lead to intensified racism and the emergence of a mob mentality. In Arendt's view, the white mob that threatened Elizabeth Eckford was a symptom of antidemocratic formations that threaten the public sphere. She believed that the more equal people become in society, the more that differences will be resented, "the more conspicuous will those become who are visibly unlike the others" (Arendt 1959, 48). Arendt wrote that African Americans "are not the only 'visible minority,' but they are the most visible one." She continued: "In this respect, they somewhat resemble new immigrants who invariably constitute the most 'audible' of all minorities and therefore are always the most likely to arouse xenophobic sentiments. But while audibility is a temporary phenomenon, rarely persisting beyond one generation, the Negroes' visibility is unalterable and permanent" (Arendt 1959, 47). Arendt did not seem to consider that, due to the history of colonization, most immigrants, such as Claudia Jones, also happen to be people of color (El-Enany 2020). Nor did she seem to be aware of how racialization is itself a matter of political appearance since whether and how some people appear more or less visible depends on how public spaces are constituted (Allen 2004).

Arendt warned that "the achievement of social, economic and educational equality for the Negro may sharpen the color problem in this country instead of assuaging it" (Arendt 1959, 48). This foreboding was informed by Arendt's analysis of the history of Jewish emancipation in anti-Semitic Europe in the nineteenth century (LeSure 2021, 11–14). Arendt believed that Jewish emancipation failed because the extension of political equality to this racially different group was conditional on their social integration. In other words, rather than equality being a *political* presupposition of citizenship (a "working principle of a political organization in which otherwise unequal principle have equal rights"), equality is viewed as conditional on *social* integration (equality is mistaken as an "innate quality of every individual, who is 'normal' if he is like everybody else and 'abnormal' if he happens to be different") (Arendt 2004, 74). Consequently, what LeSure calls "racial common sense" was adapted and cultivated in everyday social interactions in a way that maintained the conditionality of citizenship for racialized people, despite the emancipation decrees in Europe. Arendt believed that anti-Black racism would similarly adapt to the Supreme Court ruling against segregated schooling, which did occur through phenomena such as school closures and white flight to suburbs. In this way, as LeSure argues, "equality lives a double life in an integrated racist polity" since it functions both as a principle that guides political organization within which all citizens are formally recognized as equal while also being "practiced as an entitlement or privilege one secures when held as normal by one's fellow citizens" (2021, 17).

Only a year after Little Rock, a white mob appeared in Britain, subjecting the Caribbean community to street violence in Notting Hill and Nottingham, which culminated in the white race riots of 1958 and the racist murder of Kelso Cochrane in Notting Hill in 1959. For Jones, the racist street violence in the UK, "nakedly revealed" the "canker of racialism" toward West Indians and "exposed the smugness" of those who denounced racism in Little Rock and South Africa but denied its existence in Britain (2011, 169). As Ivan Weekes, who had recently immigrated to the UK from Barbados, later reflected, the riots "shattered the whole concept of the "mother country.' Those of us who were on the front-line were in psychological no man's land, thinking 'What's next?'" (cited by Olden 2020). Like Claudia Jones, West Indians who immigrated to the UK in the postwar period were British citizens. They regarded themselves as British and typically identified with various aspects of British culture. Yet, upon relocating to the mother country, they "experienced their Britishness, in all its deep, affective forms, as something precarious: both as resource and liability. Located in British civilization, they found themselves simultaneously dislocated from its privileges" (Schwarz 2003: 267).

In this context, the *West Indian Gazette*, which Jones had cofounded earlier in that year, became an important focal point for a community that was reeling from the experience of racial terror. In 1964, in one of her last published articles, Jones described "The Caribbean Community in Britain" for a predominantly African American readership in the journal *Freedomways*. She pointed out that by the time of writing, there were more West Indians living in Britain than the United States. This change was the result of the coincidence of the 1952 McCarran-Walter Immigration Act in the United States with the 1948 British Nationality Act in the UK. Jones insisted that the former was designed to restrict entry of people of color to the United States by limiting immigration from the West Indian countries to one hundred persons per year. In contrast, the British legislation was intended to import cheap labor from the former colonies to support the postwar recovery. She noted that emigration from the West Indies in the twentieth century had been driven primarily by an "impoverished agricultural economy; in which under colonial-capitalist-imperialist relations, the wealth of these islands is dominated by the few, with the vast majority of the people living under unbearable conditions" (Jones 2011, 168). The failure of the West Indian Federation, which would have allowed freedom of movement between the islands, might have enabled more people to remain in the West Indies. However, people had effectively been "compelled to leave their homelands to survive" (Jones 2011, 168).

By integrating local issues with global events, the *West Indian Gazette* sought to develop a public voice for the Black community in Britain. Faced with a hostile white society, the *Gazette* affirmed the Black British experience by locating it within the black Atlantic world (Schwarz 2003, 271). Jones herself wrote that the *Gazette* "served as a catalyst, quickening the awareness, socially and politically, of West Indians, Afro-Asians and their friends" (2011, 179) She continued:

> Whether against numerous police frame-ups, to which West Indians and other colored migrants are frequently subject, to opposing discrimination and to advocating support for trade unionism and unity of colored and white workers, [the *Gazette* has] attempted to emulate the path of progressive "Negro" (Afro Asian, Latin American and Afro American) journals who uncompromisingly

and fearlessly fight against imperialist outrages and indignities to our peoples. (Jones 2011, 179)

As such, the *Gazette* gave expression to "a lived form of Britishness that was in the process of imploding," combining a creolization of British culture with an uncompromising anti-colonialism (Schwarz 2003, 279). By situating the experience of the Caribbean diaspora in London in relation to struggles for decolonization globally, the *Gazette* worked, as Bill Schwarz puts it, "to articulate the experience of being black. Or more precisely, made it possible to *be* black" (2003, 282). This was noticed by fascist groups in the UK, which sent racist letters, made threatening phone calls and ransacked the offices of the *Gazette* (Schwarz 2003, 283).

Jones and the *Gazette* were therefore at the forefront of the cultural and political assertion by the Caribbean community of its presence in Britain (Boyce-Davies 2008, 173). This position was akin to, what Arendt (1944) called, the attitude of the conscious pariah rather than the parvenu insofar as Jones, like other Caribbean immigrants, rejected the conditionality of equal citizenship upon assimilation to "white" British culture. Significantly, the *Gazette* supported the establishment of a Caribbean Carnival, which anteceded the Notting Hill Street carnival (see Younge 2002). The carnival was conceived as a direct response to the white riots of 1958 and a determination, as Jones put it, "that such happenings should not recur" (Jones 2011, 166). The carnival was both an expression of pride in being West Indian and intended as a cultural exchange and extension of friendship to white people in Britain. It is, Jones wrote, "as if the vividness of our national life was itself the spark urging translation to new surroundings, to convey and to transplant our folk origins to British soil." As Carol Boyce-Davies observes, carnivals "in the African diaspora tradition, demonstrate the joy that its people experience in 'taking space'" (2008, 167). In contrast to Arendt's insistence on a clear separation between the social and political, Jones viewed economics, politics and culture as mutually conditioning. She had to battle against others in the Communist Party and black community who scoffed at the idea of turning to carnival, dances, and beauty contests as part of political struggle (Boyce-Davies 2008, 175). Yet, such a strategy of creolization is precisely what LeSure identifies as integral to the transformation of "racial common sense" in her analysis of Arendt's reflections on Little Rock. For it challenges those habits of perception in daily interactions that reproduce the double life of equality in racialized polities.

In contrast to the progressive legislation associated with the extension of civil rights movement in the United States in the 1960s, a series of regressive legislative acts were passed in Britain following the 1948 British Nationality Act, which sought to limit immigration of people of color from (former) colonies (see El-Enany 2020, 73–132). When the Commonwealth Immigration Act was announced in 1961, Jones condemned it as racist and the *Gazette* campaigned against the legislation, in which she recognized parallels to the US legislation under which she had been persecuted and deported (Schwarz 2003, 284; Boyce-Davies 2008, 150). The Act established quotas and controls on Commonwealth immigration by establishing a voucher system that only allowed entry to those who had already secured employment. It also included deportation measures for migrants from Asia, Africa, and the Caribbean. Jones debunked a number of anti-immigration tropes in public discourse surrounding the Act.[8] Despite their significant contribution to rebuilding the economy in postwar Britain, as a national minority, Caribbean people found themselves excluded from skilled jobs, forced to pay higher than average rents and treated unequally in education. In this context, she referred to a profound historical amnesia among the British public regarding the colonial roots of racism in British colonialism: its origin in the racist propaganda that rationalized "the wholesale exploitation, extermination and looting of the islands by British imperialism" (2011, 173). She highlighted how British elites exploit "artificial divisions and antagonisms between British and colonial workers" to prevent social change (Jones 2011, 173).

Jones's experiences of illegalization in the United States had made her acutely aware of the conditionality of citizenship for Black people (Boyce-Davies 2008, 147). She criticized the 1962 Commonwealth Immigration Act for discriminating against colored Commonwealth citizens and establishing a "second-class citizenship status for West Indians and other Afro Asian peoples in Britain" precisely at the time "when apartheid and racialism is under attack throughout the world" (2011, 169, 174). She castigated the Labour government for allowing the Immigration Act to pass unopposed in exchange for some minor amendments, while also expressing Labour's support for "quotas" and "controls" on immigration.[9] Jones wrote:

> The Act sets up a voucher system allowing entry only to those who have a job to come to. Some of its sections carry deportation penalties for migrants from the West Indies, Asia and Africa, whom it especially circumscribes. Its passage was accompanied by the most foul racialist propaganda perpetuated against West Indians and other Afro-Asians by Tory and fascist elements. (Jones 2011, 171)

The Act had the desired effect, with over 80 percent of Indian and Pakistani applicants being refused entry in the year after the Act came into effect and the number of West Indians qualifying for immigration falling to just over 4,000 compared to over 60,000 at its peak in 1961 (Jones 2011, 171, 169).

While Jones would not live to see it, the 1961 Act was part of a series of anti-immigration legislation, which culminated in the British Nationality

Act 1981 and subsequent immigration Acts, which established the hostile environment that produced the Windrush scandal in 2018 (see Tyler 2010). The scandal concerned older Caribbean migrants who had moved to the UK in the postwar period being treated as illegal migrants and denied access to healthcare, welfare, and housing and, in some cases, detained and deported if they failed to prove their right to abode (see Gentleman 2020). The fears and concerns that Jones raised in opposing the 1962 Act, just two years before her death at the age of forty-nine, were, therefore, sadly vindicated. Arendt's fears about the relation between the struggle for social equality and the emergence of the white mob have perhaps also been borne out with resurgence of racist right-wing populism in the United States and the UK. Yet this only emphasizes the importance of the kinds of cultural strategies that Jones developed through the establishment of the Caribbean carnival, which seek to challenge and transform the racial common sense that elites on both sides of politics produce and mobilize through anti-immigration rhetoric and legislation. As Carol Boyce-Davies (2008, 162) observes, Jones's politics was radical because she was able to translate the lived experience of her deportation (which might have led to a "limbo-like existence of unbelonging") into one of exile (in which she cultivated an "international black subject identity" based on a sense of diasporic belonging).

CONCLUSION

Hannah Arendt famously analyzed the plight of the stateless person by comparing their situation to that of a criminal. In this context, Arendt (2004, 363–64) observes that the best way to judge if someone has been "forced outside the pale of the law" is to consider whether they would "benefit by committing a crime." The same person who could be detained indefinitely for their "mere presence in the world" may become "a respectable person" once arrested for a crime since they will be entitled to the due process of the law (Arendt 2004, 364; see Gündoğdu 2015, 96–98). While this observation provides some insights into the plight of the stateless person in interwar Europe, it does not speak to the experience of Jones who was deportable precisely because she was found guilty of a crime and was legally a citizen of the United Kingdom and Colonies—despite having lived in the United States since she was nine years old. As Ben Davis (cited in Sherwood 1999, 35) wrote to her in 1962:

> It seems to me that you are an American, not a "British citizen." This is where you spent your life and made your contributions to American democracy—and they were very important contributions. Only in the technical sense—frankly

not even that—are you a "British citizen." Then if you're an American, you should still be here.

The criminal charges brought against Jones in 1951 were made, as she later reflected, for "writing an article which described the forward movement of Negro and white women in opposition to the fascist bent world domination of US foreign policy" (Jones 2011, 14). Jones had applied for US citizenship twice (when she was twenty-three and, again, while married to a US citizen) but the process was delayed and eventually refused.

The distinction Arendt implicitly invokes between the criminal justice system and the immigration system is predicated on that between the welfare state and warfare state (Arnold 2018, 70). While criminal justice (and its instantiation in the prison) is supposed to reintegrate the rights-bearing delinquent citizen into the polity, immigration control (and its instantiation in the detention center) is supposed to exclude the "illegal migrant" from the polity. However, the boundaries between these two systems and accompanying logics of the welfare/warfare state are increasingly blurred. Moreover, the mutual relation between processes of illegalization and criminalization are intensely racialized and racializing. Jones's imprisonment and deportation prefigured contemporary strategies of illegalization and deportation in the United States (Boyce Davies 2008, 131). Deportation of Black Britons to the Caribbean as foreign criminals, many of whom have grown up here as children, has also only intensified in the twenty-first century (see de Noronha 2020).

Arendt's influential analysis of the plight of stateless people remains a touchstone for contemporary studies of citizenship and migration. However, the consideration of her life and work in relation to Jones highlights how any analysis of the politics of immigration must remain attentive to historical specificities of migration and citizenship legislation, their relation to colonialism and the ways in which they are implicated in the racial ordering of a particular society. As such, the right to have rights cannot simply refer to the legal status of citizenship alone since citizenship itself often functions as a regime through which racial inequality and colonial relations are maintained. Rather, the right to have rights should be understood precisely as a right of social and political appearance, such as the Caribbean carnival exemplifies, through which citizenship is enacted and racial common sense transformed.

BIBLIOGRAPHY

Allen, Danielle. 2004. *Talking to Strangers: Anxieties of Citizenship since Brown v Board of Education*. Chicago: Chicago University Press.

Arendt, Hannah. 1944. "The Jew as Pariah: A Hidden Tradition." *Jewish Social Studies*. 6, no. 2: 99–122.

Arendt, Hannah. 1949. "'The Rights of Man': What Are They?" *Modern Review*. 3, no. 1: 24–36.

Arendt, Hannah. 1959. "Reflections on Little Rock." *Dissent*. 6, no. 1: 45–56.

Arendt, Hannah. 2007. [1943] "We Refugees." In *The Jewish Writings*, edited by Jerome Kohn and Ron H. Feldman, 264–74. New York: Schocken Books.

Arendt, Hannah. 1994. [1964] "What Remains? The Language Remains." In *Essays in Understanding 1930–1954*, edited by Jerome Kohn. New York: Schocken Books.

Arendt, Hannah. 2004. *The Origins of Totalitarianism*, revised edition. New York: Schocken Books.

Arnold, Kathleen R. 2018. *Arendt, Agamben and the Issue of Hyper-Legality: In Between the Prisoner-Stateless Nexus*. New York & London: Routledge.

Beiner, Ronald S. 1990. "Hannah Arendt on Capitalism and Socialism." *Government and Opposition* 25, no. 3: 359–70.

Bernasconi, Robert. 1996. "The Double Face of the Political and the Social: Hannah Arendt and America's Racial Divisions." *Research in Phenomenology* 26: 3–24

Bernstein, Richard. 2005. "Hannah Arendt on the Stateless." *parallax* 11, no. 1: 46–60.

Borren, Marieke. 2008. "Towards an Arendtian Politics of In/Visibility: On Stateless Refugees and Undocumented Aliens." *Ethical Perspectives* 15, no. 2: 213–37.

Boyce-Davies, Carole. 2008. *Left of Karl Marx: The Political Life of Black Communist Claudia Jones*. Durham: Duke University Press.

Burden-Stelly, Charisse. 2019. "Claudia Jones, the Longue Durée of McCarthyism, and the Threat of US Fascism." *The Journal of Intersectionality* 3, no. 1: 46–66.

Canovan, Margaret. 1994. *Hannah Arendt: A Reinterpretation of her Political Thought*. Cambridge: Cambridge University Press.

Chambers, Whittaker, 1952. *Witnesss*. Washington: Regnery.

Chevannes, Derefe Kimarley. 2020. "The Laboring of Black Politics: Decolonial Meditations on Claudia Jones." *Political Research Quarterly*, https://doi.org/10.1177/1065912920979107.

de Noronha, Luke. 2020. *Deporting Black Britons: Portraits of Deportation to Jamaica*. Manchester: Manchester University Press.

Dunstan, Sarah, and Patricia Owens. 2021. "'Claudia Jones, International Thinker." *Modern Intellectual History*: 1–24, doi:10.1017/S1479244321000093.

El-Enany, Nadine. 2020. *Bordering Britain: Law, Race and Empire*. Manchester: Manchester University Press.

Gentleman, Amelia. 2020. *The Windrush Betrayal: Exposing the Hostile Environment*. London: Guardian Faber.

Gines, Kathryn T. 2014. *Hannah Arendt and the Negro Question*. Bloomington: Indiana University Press.

Gündoğdu, Ayten. 2015. *Rightlessness in an Age of Rights: Hannah Arendt and the Contemporary Struggles of Migrants*. New York & Oxford: Oxford University Press.

Hall, Stuart. 2017. [1978] "Racism and Reaction." In *The Great Moving Right Show and Other Essays: Selected Political Writings*, edited by Sally Davidson, David Featherstone, Michael Rustin, and Bill Schwarz, 142–57. Durham: Duke University Press.

Henry, Paget. 2021. "Claudia Jones, Political Economy and the Creolizing of Rosa Luxemburg." In *Creolizing Rosa Luxemburg*, edited by Jane Anna Gordon and Drucilla Cornell, 431–56. London: Rowman & Littlefield.

Hinds, Donald. 2000. "The West Indian Gazette." In *Claudia Jones: A Life in Exile*, edited by Marika Sherwood with Donald Hinds and Colin Prescod, 125–49. London: Lawrence & Wishart.

Jeffries, Stuart. 2014. "Britain's most racist election: The story of Smethwick, 50 years on." *The Guardian*, 15 October. https://www.theguardian.com/world/2014/oct/15/britains-most-racist-election-smethwick-50-years-on, last accessed: August 5, 2021.

Jones, Claudia. 2011. *Claudia Jones: Beyond Containment Autobiographical Reflections, Essays and Poems*, edited by Carole Boyce-Jones. Banbury: Ayebia Clarke Publishing.

King, Richard H. 2015. *Arendt and America*. Chicago: University of Chicago Press.

Krause Monika. 2008. "Undocumented Migrants: An Arendtian Perspective." *European Journal of Political Theory* 7, no. 3: 331–48.

LeSure, Ainsley. 2021. "The White Mob, (In) Equality Before the Law, and Racial Common Sense: A Critical Race Reading of the Negro Question in 'Reflections on Little Rock.'" *Political Theory* 49, no. 1: 3–27.

McDuffie, Erik S. 2011. *Sojourning for Freedom: Black Women, American Communism, and the Making of Black Left Feminism*. Durham: Duke University Press.

Olden, Mark. 2020. "White riot: The week Notting Hill exploded." *The Independent*, 4 June. https://www.independent.co.uk/news/uk/home-news/white-riot-week-notting-hill-exploded-912105.html, last accessed: August 4, 2021.

Putnam, Lara. 2014. "Citizenship from the Margins: Vernacular Theories of Rights and the State from the Interwar Caribbean." *Journal of British Studies* 53, no.1: 162–91.

Røstball, Christian. 2014. "Statelessness, Domination and Unfreedom: Arendt and Petit in Dialogue." In *To Be Unfree: Republicanism and Unfreedom in History, Literature, and Philosophy*, edited by Christian Dahl and Tue Andersen Nexö, 19–36. Bielefelt: Transcript Verlag.

Schaap, Andrew. 2020. "Inequality, Loneliness, and Political Appearance: Picturing Radical Democracy with Hannah Arendt and Jacques Rancière." *Political Theory* 49, no.1:28–53.

Schwarz, Bill. 2003. "Claudia Jones and the *West Indian Gazette*: Reflections on the Emergence of Post-colonial Britain." *Twentieth Century British History* 14, no. 3: 264–85.

Sherwood, Marika with Donald Hinds and Colin Prescod. 2000. *Claudia Jones: A Life in Exile*. London: Lawrence & Wishart.

Tyler, Imogen. 2010. "Designed to Fail: A Biopolitics of British Citizenship." *Citizenship Studies* 14, no.1: 61–74.
Weigand, Kate. 2001. *Red Feminism: American Communism and the Making of Women's Liberation*. Baltimore: Johns Hopkins University Press.
Young-Bruehl, Elisabeth. 2004. *Hannah Arendt: For Love of the World.* New Haven: Yale University Press, second edition.
Younge, Gary. 2002. "The Politics of Partying." *The Guardian*, 17 August. https://www.theguardian.com/culture/2002/aug/17/nottinghillcarnival2002.nottinghillcarnival Last accessed: August 4, 2021.

NOTES

1. Among the developments that led these former Communists to leave the party were the abolition of internal party democracy and the subordination of national parties to control from Moscow. This culminated in the Moscow trials in the mid-1930s through which Stalin purged the Party of any possible political opponents.

2. Chambers was a journalist who had been a member of the American Communist Party (and had written for the *Daily Worker* from 1927 to 1929) before serving as a Soviet spy in the 1930s. He left the Communist Party in 1938 following the Moscow Trials and began working for *Time* Magazine. He appeared before the House Un-American Activities in 1948 and published his autobiography, *Witness*, in 1952.

3. As Robert Bernasconi points out, this was a view that Arendt would reiterate in 1968 preface to *The Origins of Totalitarianism*: "It certainly would be a serious error to underestimate the role sheer racism has played and is still playing in the government of the Southern states, but it would be an even more serious fallacy to arrive at the retrospective conclusion that large areas of the United States have been under totalitarian rule for more than a century" (Arendt cited in Bernasconi 1996, 10). Why, her reader might wonder, would it be "a more serious fallacy" to overestimate rather than underestimate racial terror in the United States?

4. As Burden-Stelly outlines, the McCarran Act, "authorised the loss of American citizenship for naturalized citizens based solely on their political beliefs or activities; annual registration for non-citizens; arrests without a warrant and denial of bail for non-citizens; and the deportation of non-citizens, no matter how long they had resided in the country, for any political opinion deemed threatening to the government" (2019, 60).

5. Jones had contracted tuberculosis at the age of seventeen and spent a year recovering in a sanatorium in Harlem Hospital. She was in and out of hospital until her death by heart attack in 1964.

6. Arendt wrote about the event for *Commentary* whose readership was primarily liberal and Jewish. Yet the essay sparked a controversy even before its eventual publication in Dissent in 1959 (see Young-Bruehl 2004, 308–18; King 2015, 166–69).

7. Jones similarly recalled such experiences of attending her integrated school in Harlem in which she was "confronted by Jim Crow in the classrooms and the social life of the school" (2011, 12). White students who had borrowed notes from her

during the day would snub her in front of their peers after school, while teachers would ask if she or other African American students would be available to do domestic work for them.

8. In response to the claim that colored immigrants are "flooding Britain," she pointed out that people of color make up less than 1 percent of the population and that for every person entering Britain each year, three depart. In response to the claim that "immigrants take away houses and jobs" she attributes responsibility for the housing shortage and decline in industry to government policies. Moreover, she pointed out that West Indians are forced to pay high rents for dilapidated housing while many West Indians are employed in constructing new houses as well as making a significant contribution to the economy in health care, manufacturing, and transportation. And to the claim that migration from the West Indies creates an economic social burden, Jones pointed out that the Ministry of National Insurance had profited "from contributions of the surrendered cards of thousands of immigrants who returned home after a few years in Britain" (Jones 2011, 172).

9. Jones alluded to the reason for Labour's support for immigration control, given the election in Smethwick (near Birmingham) in 1964 in which conservative MP, Peter Griffiths had been elected using the campaign slogan that voting for Labour meant "having a nigger for a neighbour" (Jones 2011, 172). While there was an overall swing to Labour in the 1964 election, with Labour coming to power for the first time in 13 years, in Smethwick there was a 7.2 percent swing to the Tories with the sitting Labour MP, Patrick Gordon Walker, losing his seat (see Jeffries 2014).

Chapter Eleven

The Life of the Unruly in Ada Ushpiz's *Vita Activa: The Spirit of Hannah Arendt (2015)*

Joel Rosenberg

Israeli filmmaker Ada Ushpiz's 2015 film, *Vita Activa: The Spirit of Hannah Arendt*, captures well the polarities and aporia of Arendt's era. Through skillful editing of archival footage, photos, and documents, the film succeeds in re-creating the shape of Arendt's life, the textures of her personality, and the incisiveness of her intellect in assessing the modern era's most devastating and intractable problems. The film, like many other commentaries on Arendt's writing, places more emphasis on Arendt's 1963 book *Eichmann in Jerusalem: A Report on the Banality of Evil*, a purportedly journalistic coverage of the trial of Nazi bureaucrat/war criminal Adolf Eichmann, than on her masterwork, *The Origins of Totalitarianism*, first published in 1951 (Arendt, 1951, 1968).[1] It was most likely because of *Origins* that *The New Yorker* magazine gave her the assignment (requested by her) to write about the trial in the first place. Her Eichmann book is understandably a more mediagenic subject, but *Origins* must be preserved in our awareness as the latter's infrastructure. *Origins* chose, as its pivotal historical moment, not the era of World War II but that of the end of World War I, then known as "The Great War" of 1914–1918. It was then that modern warfare's widespread power of upheaval and devastation was first felt most acutely. The following description by Arendt is arguably the single most important paragraph of that book, and the chapter it introduced ("The Decline of the Nation-State and the End of the Rights of Man") was one of the most important thirty-five pages of political thought in the whole modern era.[2] It placed the Age of Revolution of 1776–1789 and onward, and the Era of Enlightenment from which it drew, into counterpoint with the hard realities that inaugurated the era of catastrophe of 1914–1945. Although a sentence or two of this passage is quoted near the beginning of Ushpiz's *Vita Activa*, it should be viewed here in fuller measure:

> It is almost impossible even now to describe what actually happened in Europe on August 4, 1914. The days before and the days after the first World War are separated not like the end of an old and beginning of a new period, but like the day before and day after an explosion. Yet this . . . is inaccurate because the quiet of sorrow which settles down after a catastrophe has never come to pass. The first explosion seems to have touched off a chain reaction in which we have been caught ever since and which nobody seems able to stop. The first World War exploded the European comity of nations beyond repair, which no other war has ever done. Inflation destroyed small property owners beyond hope for recovery . . . which no other monetary crisis has ever done. . . . Unemployment [which] . . . reached fabulous proportions was no longer restricted to the working class but seized whole nations. Civil wars . . . were not only bloodier and more cruel [but] followed by migrations of groups who . . . were welcomed nowhere, assimilated nowhere—homeless . . . stateless . . . rightless, the scum of the earth. Every event had the finality of a last judgment . . . passed neither by God nor by the devil, but . . . like the expression of some irredeemably stupid fatality. (Arendt 1951, 267)

This situation destroyed the already long-fragile right of asylum granted by sovereign states; rendered meaningless and unenforceable the Minorities Treaties of the peace agreements (aimed at protecting ethnic minorities in the affected countries); deprived the stateless even of a place to which to be deported; fostered the widespread use of internment camps; caused nations to rely increasingly on the role of police authorities, both at and within national borders, thus easing the creation of police states (with which democratic nations routinely cooperated during the Stalin and Hitler eras); and, above all, supplied a fertile ground for the xenophobic demagoguery, directed against peoples and social classes alike, that was essential to the rise of fascism, Nazism, Stalinism, and totalitarianism more generally.

In Ushpiz's film, Israeli historian Idith Zertal comments: "[Arendt] belonged to this generation that between two world wars loses its rights. This sense of being a refugee was a harsh existential experience, but it was also very valuable. And she maintained this condition, this mental awareness of being a refugee, her entire life. She believed that this perception, outside the home, outside the masses, outside the collective, provides a very distinctive observation point, and a unique one."

This statement is true enough, even if there were a significant number of writers, thinkers, and artists, Jewish and otherwise, who experienced similar displacements and dangers, leaving a magnificent legacy of that impact.

Some are drawn together in a collection of Arendt's essays titled *Men in Dark Times* (not all of them men)—to name a few, Rosa Luxembourg, Karl Jaspers, Hermann Broch, Walter Benjamin, Karen Blixen (Isak Dinesen), and Bertolt Brecht—a celebration of sui generis personalities who lived in antithesis to tyranny, often affirming the unruliness, individuality, and spontaneity that the totalitarian mind held categorically impermissible (1955).

YOUNG HANNAH AND HER ROOTS

Arendt was a child when the Great War began, and entering adolescence when it ended. The advance of Russian troops caused her family to flee from Königsberg, where they were then situated, to Berlin. By that time, Hannah had received nurturing encouragement of her intellectual development in her earliest years from her mother, Martha Arendt (née Cohn, 1874–1948). Through still photos and family home movies, Ushpiz's film presents some of the earliest recorded imagery of Hannah as tiny tot, toddler, and child. Her earliest childhood was in Linden, Prussia, now part of Hanover. But her family had been Jews of Russian origin living in Königsberg, East Prussia, the birthplace and lifelong home of Immanuel Kant.[3] Martha Arendt recorded in her diary that her daughter Johanna, at age four, was chatty, vivacious, and opinionated with a passion. Hannah had no artistic skills and she sang off-key, but she bore the traits of an intellectual. She loved letters and books.

Asked by a German interviewer in 1964 what growing up a Jew in Germany was like in the era of her childhood, Arendt observed that she did not learn from her family she was a Jew. She was not religious. Her father died when she was seven. (Hannah did not mourn him, but cried at the funeral because of the music.) And her mother was anti-religious. But her mother saw it unthinkable to deny that one was a Jew. Hannah's teachers did not attack her Jewishness, but often disparaged girls from the *Ostjuden*, the often orthodox Eastern European Jews, and her mother insisted that on such occasions Hannah should get up and leave the classroom. Martha Arendt would then write a registered letter of complaint to the school. "I was always protected," Hannah remembers, "absolutely protected at home."

Throughout the film, Hannah's voice is present in two different ways: as interview footage, in German or English, from the 1960s and 1970s, where we hear the hoarse and raspy, cigarette-smoker's voice of the actual Hannah Arendt; and as a smoother and more youthful voice of commentary, spoken by an actress, Alison Darcy, which we can call, for convenience, "the Arendtian voice." Voices of important men in her life are likewise spoken by actors: Hannah's teacher at the University of Marburg in 1925, the then-aspiring philosopher Martin Heidegger (Brett Donahue),with whom she had an affair; her eventual cherished mentor, philosopher Karl Jaspers (Ernest Hoffman), who guided her doctoral research in the late 1920s; and the love of her life, poet, philosopher, German communist, and political activist Heinrich Blücher (Max Walker), who eventually became her second husband.[4]

ARENDT AND HEIDEGGER / HANNAH AND MARTIN

It is perhaps inevitable that cinematic treatment of Arendt's life would highlight her much-vexed critique of Nazism by placing her in constellation with two men in particular who figured strongly in her preoccupations: Heidegger and Eichmann. Celebrated German filmmaker Margarethe von Trotta's 2012 fiction film *Hannah Arendt* spins much of its drama out of Arendt's relation to these otherwise dissimilar devotees of National Socialism. In my 2014 review-essay on that film, I drew chiefly on Arendt's controversial 1971 tribute to Heidegger in honor of his eightieth birthday, found in English in the *New York Review of Books*. There, Arendt provided a brilliant and intellectually generous assessment of the electrifying impact of Heidegger's thinking upon young philosophy students in the mid-1920s:

> The rumor about Heidegger [in university gossip] put it quite simply: Thinking has come to life again: the cultural treasures of the past, believed to be dead, are being made to speak, in the course of which it turns out that they propose things altogether different from the familiar, worn-out trivialities they had been presumed to say. There exists a teacher; perhaps one can learn to think . . . (Arendt 1971, 50–54)[5]

That this nineteen-year-old undergraduate's infatuation with her professor led pretty quickly to an affair is displayed prominently in Ushpiz's gleaning of letters from Heidegger to his attractive pupil, although we view only his perspective. These capture well Heidegger's faux-courtly, patriarchal, essentialist, and condescending attention—a sweet-talking preening he apparently distributed among other female students of his in that time: "Dear Miss Arendt," he writes initially, "Everything should be simple and clear and pure between us. Only then will we be worthy of being allowed to be together . . . I will never be able to call you mine. But from now on, you will belong in my life. You . . . have found your way to the innermost, purest, feminine essence. . . . I cannot . . . separate your loyal eyes and beautiful figure from your pure trust, the honor and goodness of your girlish essence."

Soon, he addresses his letters to "Dearest Hannah," and luxuriates in their nods and smiles in the classroom. When, on one occasion, his wife is not at home and he has the space for a rendezvous, he says "I live in joy for such moments," and tells her to arrive at 9:00 p.m. At base, he hungers for her admiration of his writing. When she writes him that he can have her, if he wishes, he exclaims, "What can I do in the face of such sighing and yet so resolute waiting?" The narcissism of such a declaration is astonishing.

The pattern was best summarized (circa 2015) by Prof. Heidegger's granddaughter, Gertrude Heidegger:

> His relations with women were . . . a means to an end. When he needed spiritual excitement, these women . . . academics, educated women, who revered him . . . gave him wings for his work. Hannah Arendt is surely, in a way, the originator of *Sein und Zeit* (Being and Time) . . . as were the other[s]. In terms of the age difference, and the class difference of teacher and student, it was not an equal love.

In von Trotta's *Hannah Arendt*, locating Arendt suspended, as it were, between Heidegger and Eichmann seemed a way of probing Nazism's relation to thought. Heidegger, for Arendt, represented a mode of thinking (*Denken*), whose radically probing power to demolish metaphysics in the Western philosophical tradition remained a model for her even in hindsight upon his embrace of National Socialism throughout the Hitler era—a turn that otherwise, unsurprisingly, effected a longtime rupture in their friendship. But what was the relation of Heidegger's *Denken* to the notoriously thoughtless Eichmann, the pivotally important Nazi bureaucrat whose inability to think facilitated mass deportation of Europe's Jewry to extermination? Arendt had spoken of Heidegger as decisively determining "the spiritual physiognomy of [the] century," but she never quite succeeded in establishing the link between the towering but crucially blind thinker and Eichmann, the thoughtless, cliché-nurtured minion of the totalitarian power she had otherwise so brilliantly anatomized in *Origins*.

DOCUMENTARY AND ITS DISCONTENTS

And so, I confess to finding some of the least convincing parts of Ushpiz's film to be the comments by Arendt's friends, colleagues, and disciples, whose insights are otherwise so often unimpeachable. This is, I think, largely because the heroes of the "dark times" whom Arendt celebrated for their incisive critique of a philosophical and intellectual tradition that had become, for them, inoperative, have come to comprise, along with Arendt herself, a tradition of its own. We cannot live without it, but it poses a certain embarrassment and challenge. In her exquisite essay on Walter Benjamin, Arendt quotes the challenge issued by Benjamin himself:

> Naturally, one must wish for the planet that one day it will experience a civilization that has abandoned blood and horror. . . . But it is terribly doubtful that we can bring such a present to its hundred—or four-hundred—millionth birthday party. And if we don't, the planet will finally punish us, its unthoughtful well-wishers, by presenting us with the Last Judgment. (Arendt 1955, 192)[6]

For Benjamin, this situation called forth a distinctive mode of writing that had long been a mainstay of his thought from his youth: quotational montage and aphoristic reflection.[7] Chief influences included Austrian-Jewish satirist Karl Kraus and especially the incomparable Bohemian Jew, Franz Kafka. His parables and aphorisms, as Arendt observed, "[did] not lie at the feet of doctrine . . . but unexpectedly raise[d] a heavy claw against it" (Arendt 1955, 196).[8] It was a mode admirably suited to a generation of Central European, German-speaking Jewish males, who, typically born into often affluent but always bourgeois families, and often supported financially by the household patriarch (not true of Kafka), had but two main modes of rebellion: Zionism and Socialism. A third option was irony, paradox, ellipsis. Far from being uttered in a defensive crouch, such expression grasped its subject firmly and intimately, often adorning it with a treasure from the depths, brought up with the calm self-confidence of a pearl diver. For Benjamin, it was partly embodied in the passion of the collector: "always anarchistic, destructive . . . its dialectic: to combine, with loyalty to . . . things sheltered in [one's] care, a stubborn, subversive protest against the typical, the classifiable" (Arendt 1955, 199; Cf. 193–206).

But while this mode seems admirably suited to the documentary-film genre, it is perforce compromised by an inevitable, if understandable, hagiographic passion. Even when talking heads are critical of Arendt (such as reservations expressed by novelist Aharon Appelfeld and historian Deborah Lipstadt, on which I shall comment elsewhere), they are adduced as such in implicit praise of Arendt's ability to cause a raised eyebrow. Still, they are not meant to settle between pro and con on Arendt, but to display the crosscurrents of social energies, both amid which she lived and worked, and to which her work gave rise. And this process enters—coaxially, as it were—into archival imagery from Europe in its era of catastrophe. Some of the film's most successful moments are found there, whose main components are several, not all of them consecutive: the rise of Hitler; totalitarian power in its heyday; 1930s Palestine; 1940s France; the death camps: imminent victims, emaciated survivors, piles of the dead; punishment of collaborators; victory parades in New York; the Nuremberg and Eichmann trials.

"A CRIME AGAINST HUMANITY, PERPETRATED UPON THE BODY OF THE JEWISH PEOPLE" (1963, 269)

And so, both films on Arendt, von Trotta's and Ushpiz's, establish a certain symmetry by locating Arendt's assessment of Nazism in the terrible, dark space that unites the Thinker and the Thoughtless. Both fiction-film and documentary have chosen to place her there, but it is *our* need to be addressed thus that requires our reflection. What we can at least say for sure is that Eichmann's voice comes across in both von Trotta's film and Ushpiz's very differently from the professionally acted voice given to Heidegger in both cases. Eichmann's is enclosed entirely within the actual black-and-white TV footage of his trial, and there he either speaks in answer to interrogators' questions or listens to a tape-recording of his own voice. He sits inside a bulletproof glass compartment and is ordered to stand for certain interrogations. His evasions and rationalizations are striking.

When the Judge asks him about his views on the Nazi aim to banish the Jews from Germany, he answers that in 1934 he never gave it much thought. When asked about a claim he had told his interrogators that he had never been an antisemite, he says this was so. And when the Judge comments that such a stance seems paradoxical for a conscious Nazi, Eichmann replies that, when serving as a clerk at Vacuum Oil, he was focused on his personal life and never gave attention to literature or intellectual matters. When asked if he would call himself an idealist at the time, he answers: "Yes, I understood nationalism, as it was preached back then, that as a nationalist I must fulfill my duty. Now, I know that any nationalism, in its exaggerated form, leads to selfishness, and from there it's a slippery slope to egoism and radicalism."

In Ushpiz's film, commentary is here given in the Arendtian voice, which observes that the longer one listened to him, the more obvious his inability to speak conveyed an inability to think—in particular, to think from the standpoint of somebody else. Just as a German society of eighty million people were shielded against reality and factuality, so were the same self-deception, lies and dumbness now engrained in Eichmann.

Here at last, perhaps, is the link between Thinker Heidegger and Thoughtless Eichmann—namely, how such self-anesthetization could enable a society of eighty million (and, by implication, *any* large society or nation, each with its acclaimed and supremely probing Thinkers) to be shielded "against [the] reality and factuality" aborning in their midst. But that same voice responded less to Eichmann, as such, and more to what Arendt famously considered to be the vacuousness of a show-trial, organized for state purposes.

Consider the voice of Eichmann's Israeli prosecutor Gideon Hausner. Hausner is shown in the trial's TV footage declaring the history of the Jewish people to be a continuous stretch of suffering and tears. He quotes Ezekiel 16:6, "In thy blood live," as a reality that confronted the Jewish nation at its earliest emergence on the stage of history. He calls to mind the plan of the Egyptian Pharaoh (Exodus 1:8–16) to cast newborn Israelite sons into the river Nile. He mentions that Haman gave orders to slay the Jews (Esther 3:8–14). And yet, he insists, never in the Jewish people's bloodstained course throughout history had anyone arisen who dealt such dreadful blows as Hitler's regime, as carried out by Eichmann.[9]

To such, the Arendtian voice (culled piecemeal from parts of *Eichmann in Jerusalem*) responds that "[i]t was bad history and cheap rhetoric." This was not a trial of an individual, nor even of history as such, but of anti-Semitism throughout history. In the eyes of the Jews, as cast by prosecutor Hausner, in which a third of world Jewry perished, the Nazi-instigated catastrophe appeared not as an unprecedented crime on a world scale by a totalitarian power. None of the actual horrors of Auschwitz were presented at the trial in a way that could yield clear understanding. Rather, the Nazi genocide was presented as "little more than the most horrible pogrom in history." What the courtroom missed was that the supreme crime they were adjudicating was "a crime against humanity, perpetrated upon the body of the Jewish people" (1963, 269). Only the choice of the victim, and not the nature of the crime, was derived from the long history of anti-Semitism. The crime was an attack on human diversity, without which the words "humanity" or "mankind" were meaningless.

We must keep in mind that Arendt was in Jerusalem not to assess Eichmann but to assess the trial. This was built into the assignment itself, and it shaped everything she saw, including how she eventually saw Eichmann. The famously contentious notion "banality of evil" seems primarily in reaction to what she considered the disingenuousness of the proceedings she was witnessing, and an effort to debunk the prosecution's characterizing Eichmann as a surreally evil monster, an archetypal Egyptian Pharaoh. Eichmann was evil enough, without such mythologizing as Hausner's—something Arendt did not perceive sufficiently in 1963, and it rendered her assessment of Eichmann profoundly wrong, even as she remained profoundly right about the system he served.

As Bettina Stangneth's 2013 book (German edition) about Eichmann made clear, Eichmann was no pencil-pushing clerk, as he tried to portray himself in his trial, but a "thinker" in a very deep, ideologically committed way—not a Heidegger, but his perfect complement: someone who thought from the standpoint of one carrying out the genocidal task (and pitying himself in the process for the horrors he had to witness, while proudly boasting to have been on the "front lines" of the war).[10] Ushpiz includes TV footage of the Jerusalem court listening to a recording of Eichmann wallowing in self-pity over his pangs of conscience, but the film does not contextualize it, leaving it disembodied and unexplained. In his postwar exile in Argentina, Eichmann hungrily read books about Nazi atrocities and believed himself to be gathering ammunition for a historical confrontation between Jews and Nazis that for him still lay in the future. Even Dutch SS journalist Willem Sassen, Eichmann's interlocutor and virtual amanuensis in Argentina, was somewhat taken aback by things he said, while remaining sympathetic. (Stangneth is ambiguous on this, because she also says Sassen regarded the crimes as "unforgiveable," but she may have meant that he saw clearly how others would see it.)[11]

Arguably, what incensed Arendt so keenly was how prosecutor Hausner's histrionics cut to the heart of her analysis of totalitarianism in *Origins*. Framing the trial in purely ethnocentric preoccupations was precisely to ignore the crime's systemic, universal, and unprecedented nature, something borne out (I would add) by the numerous genocides among other peoples in postwar times. But something is missing here, and I believe it is possible to say so less mythologically than prosecutor Hausner. If (as I, too, believe) the Nazi genocide of Jewry was a crime against humanity, it truncates the humanity of the Jews to dismiss or trivialize so casually both the Holocaust's subjective dimension as a site of trauma and scarring memory and its objective dimension as unprecedented in size and scope—if you will, as "the most horrible pogrom in history"—and, as such, it posed a crisis, not just for the Jews, but for humankind at large. I consider it both possible and necessary to retain such perspective coordinately with Arendt's otherwise admirable effort to read the situation cross-culturally and universally. But Arendt fell short here, and this must be noted. All this is quite apart from Arendt's complicated relation to Israel and Zionism, which will occupy us separately.

A PSYCHOSIS IN THE MAKING

Arendt's *Origins* distinguishes two main phases in the twentieth century totalitarian regimes: the movement in its rise; and its reign in power.[12] The former corresponds roughly to what Benjamin, in those years, was calling "fascism," perhaps resembling what was then mostly manifest as the Fascist regime of Mussolini's Italy. Elsewhere, Salazar's Portugal, and Franco's Spain, though resisting the term "fascist," were similarly authoritarian, militaristic, and serving a power elite.[13] But in Germany, it took on the malignant form of radical anti-Semitism, advanced most decisively by Hitler in his 1925 autobiographical manifesto *Mein Kampf*. Despite that work's extremism, Nazi Germany's "movement" phase was linked to the effort to defeat internal enemies and to gain legitimation and recognition, in the nontotalitarian world, of its sovereign power—something not yet fully realized even in the late 1930s, when Germany's rearming, its territorial claims, and preparations for war were still in progress. It was not until declaration of war in September 1939 that Hitler's unimpeded power was finally assured. It is at such a point that totalitarian reign gains a type of freedom that is downright psychotic. By this time, largely via the Nazis' Nuremberg Laws, Jews had been fully defined out of German society, something unprecedented in the postmedieval world (Tsarist Russia's "Pale of Settlement" notwithstanding). But intimations of the psychosis to follow were already inherent in that step.

Vita Activa sometimes represents the turning of eras by a conversation (in acted voices) between Hannah and her cherished mentor, Karl Jaspers. The one that introduces the beginning of the Nazi era consists of letters between them, whose ostensible subject is Max Weber but whose main preoccupation is the relation of Jews to German culture. Hannah questions Jaspers's finding in Weber a German essence identified with rationality and humanity, whereas she sees it rooted in passion. Jaspers questions Hannah's setting herself apart, as a Jew, from what is German, and suggests that counting herself in as German would effectively validate his effort to ascribe ethical content to Weber. Hannah says the very notion of "German character" is filled with misuse, and finds no trace of it in herself. This exchange and what follows are set against stock footage of Nazism on the rise. Muscular young men in military training and rowdy horseplay. A prosperous German family, their kinfolk smiling and waving, as one adult hoists a banner at their home, a shot whose last moment reveals it to display a swastika. An attractive young woman seated on concrete front steps chuckling as she gazes to her left at nothing in particular (46:25–28)—an inherently casual, nonpolitical moment we see thousands of times in our own lives, but which gains a retroactively sinister connotation when an open-convertible Mercedes speeds by with Hitler and his entourage, while citizens standing along the road give the "Heil Hitler" salute. It is the bourgeois normality of such moments that arrests us, and reflects back onto Hannah's exchange with Jaspers.

Asked by a TV interviewer (in 1960s or 1970s) what moment in particular drew her into political life, Arendt answered that it was February 27, 1933, the burning of the Reichstag and the illegal arrests that followed immediately upon it, whereby dissidents were taken to Gestapo cellars or concentration camps. Arendt considered this a terrible shock. No longer could she be a bystander.

Accompanying footage shows police of that year beating and arresting dissidents, and aerial views from a plane making its way through clouds. The film here gleans footage resembling or drawn from Leni Riefenstahl's controversial pseudo-documentary propaganda film *Triumph of the Will* (1934), depicting Hitler's arrival in Nuremberg for the 1934 Nazi Party

Congress. There are views of the urban landscape below; adoring masses, "Heil" salutes by thousands and tens of thousands; handsome, blond, muscular German youth in uniform; and Hermann Göring, on trial at Nuremberg in late 1945, recalling the 1933 "Freedom revolution," which he says relieved German poverty and unemployment, as "the most bloodless and disciplined in all history."

The film's collage interweaves Hitler addressing the Nuremberg rally, pronouncements by Heidegger as rector of Freiburg University in 1933, and latter-day Arendt reminiscing on her decision to leave Germany and the grotesqueness of fellow Jews of the time clinging to Hitler. Views from Alexanderplatz, Berlin, are shown, of Hitler Youth marching down the street, and spectators in line for an anti-Bolshevik exhibition.

One sequence (55:13–57:03) stands out vividly for its curious mixture of antisemitic pageantry and a surreal self-parody that hints of a nation becoming psychotic. Encompassing a shot of a Berlin park sign announcing "Juden sind hier unerwünscht" (Jews are unwanted here), the film displays in color a parade of floats from German towns, slowly making their way down a main street. One float displays papier-mâché Jews hanging by nooses from the blades of a windmill. A sign announces: "Jew, rat!" Another, "Fight against corruption!" Iconic teeth symbolizing gaping mouths adorn the corners of a float, as if portraying the rapaciousness of Jewish financiers. A person covered in a large, globular, bald head, mustached and goateed, with huge, fluttering eyelashes and long, phallic nose, arms unseen, walks at a float's rear—another Jewish plutocrat! Heard over this spectacle are words of Heidegger, crossing a lethal line. He is heard declaring enemies of the state an essential threat to the German people's existence. In grafting themselves to the "innermost root" of the people's existence, they harm the nation's instinct to react. It is thus necessary to find the enemy, or even create him, to surrender illusions about him, to be prepared to attack on a long-term basis, with the goal of "total extermination."[14]

These dire, Manichean pronouncements, horrific in themselves, acquire a strangely comic grotesqueness when a shot portrays two smiling women in archaically styled pink pinafores, with reddish hearts embroidered on their chests. Turning front-to-back, they reveal the same "frontal" costume with papier-mâché versions of their faces—thus gazing Janus-faced, in two directions. Simultaneously amusing and mocking their beholders, the women turn the business of murderous statecraft into a Kewpie-doll-like valentine, greeting a public made manageable and manipulable by the suspension of thought.

THE FELLING OF THE TREE—THE IDYLL, AND "INFERIOR" LIFE FORMS

A Nazi "educational" film from the 1930s opens with shots of a beautiful, mountainside forest, deer scampering through the underbrush. Soft, romantic choral music is accompanied by a mellow but majestically authoritative male voice: "Eternal forest, eternal nation. The tree lives like you and me. It strives for space like you and me. The nation stands like the tree, in eternity." This is accompanied by shots of a peaceful lake, rippling waters, and lily pads.

The Arendtian voice here comments on how, far from wielding power out of self-interest, totalitarianism is unabashedly prepared to sacrifice the interests of all to a supposed law of history or nature. The Darwinian concept of survival of the fittest can be historical as much as natural law, and thus suited to an ideology of racism. If properly carried out, it aims to produce a new breed of human being.

The idyllic woodland imagery gives way to a forest tree being felled and landing with a thud. A harsh, metallic, male voice proclaims: "We humans have transgressed the law of natural selection in the past decades. Not only have we supported inferior life forms, we have encouraged their propagation. The offspring of these sick people looked like this . . ." The camera now shows homely, sickly, presumably Jewish faces, in hospitals and asylums. Men with oversized, elfin ears. A mentally disturbed or retarded woman in deep-black hair with bangs. A writhing, limping boy with cerebral palsy.

The Arendtian voice comments on how, in eliminating the "objective" enemy of history or nature, class, or race, the Nazi regime renders senseless any notions of guilt or innocence. The guilty are those who obstruct the course of nature or history—inferior races, dying classes, the socially decadent. The verdict: extermination. This turn in authoritarian statecraft is made possible, or even obligatory, by a core principle of totalitarian rule that we should now consider.

PERPETUAL MOTION—WHEN POWER IS UNIMPEDED

It should be noted that while the films on Arendt focus entirely on her relation to the Holocaust, especially in her Eichmann book, part of the accomplishment of *Origins* was Arendt's largely speculative effort to analyze Nazi Germany and Stalinist USSR as parallel and comparable phenomena. The heart of her argument is more or less the following:

> The form of government the [Nazi and Bolshevik] movements developed is best characterized by Trotsky's slogan of "permanent revolution" . . . which would

spread from one country to another. . . . In the Soviet Union, revolutions, in the form of general purges, became a permanent institution of the Stalin regime after 1934. . . . In Nazi Germany, a similar tendency toward permanent revolution was clearly discernible. . . . Here . . . we find the notion of racial selection thus requiring a constant radicalization of the standards by which the selection, i. e., the extermination of the unfit, is carried out. . . . *[B]oth Hitler and Stalin held out promises of stability in order to hide their intention of creating a state of permanent instability.* [My italics.] . . . The totalitarian ruler must, at any price, prevent normalization from reaching the point where a new way of life could develop—one which might, after a time, lose its bastard qualities and take its place among the widely differing and profoundly contrasting ways of life of the nations of the earth. (Arendt 1951, 389–91)

In this connection, Arendt describes how the promotion of high state officials was often a prelude to their downfall. This situation went hand in hand with a systematic effort to maintain two states simultaneously: the ostensible state displayed to the world as "Germany" or "USSR," and a shadow-state of secret police and inner circle of the supreme Leader, where the real power lay. In Germany, the script often ran thus:

[I]t is not hard to understand today why at the outbreak of the war people like Alfred Rosenberg or Hans Frank were removed to state positions and thus eliminated from the real center of power, namely the Fuehrer's inner circle. The important thing is that they not only did not know the reasons for these moves, but presumably did not even suspect that such apparently exalted positions as Governor General of Poland or Reichsminister for all Eastern territories did not signify the climax but the end of their National Socialist careers. (1951, 404; Cf. 1951, 396–97)

Such realities went hand in hand with Nazi Germany's general indifference to legal foundations (it never bothered, for example, to abolish the Weimar-era constitution), civilian economic necessities, and even the war effort itself (1951, 411–15). Liquidation of the Jews, the "objective" enemy, took precedence over military aims (a policy to which the military vigorously objected, a discontent eventually leading to the failed assassination plot against Hitler). This priority was not merely the expression of racial hatred (though it was surely that, too) but was rooted in the dynamic of totalitarian ideology itself, whose fulfillment lay, in a sense, in an inherently ever-unreachable goal. Movement took precedence over realization, since realization would put an end to the system's ceaselessly unquenchable compulsion to organize and reorganize. Both Hitler and Stalin, accordingly, were wholly unconcerned with succession to their rule (1951, 408–9). The core principles Arendt summarized as follows:

The trouble with totalitarian regimes is not that they play power politics in an especially ruthless way, but that behind their politics is hidden an entirely new and unprecedented concept of power, just as behind their *Realpolitik* lies an entirely new and unprecedented concept of reality. Supreme disregard for immediate consequences rather than ruthlessness; rootlessness and neglect of national interests rather than nationalism; contempt for utilitarian motives rather than unconsidered pursuit of self-interest; "idealism," i.e., their unwavering faith in an ideological fictitious world rather than lust for power—these have all introduced into international politics a new and more disturbing factor than mere aggressiveness. (1951, 417–18)

In short, "The body politic of the country is shock-proof because of its shapelessness" (1951, 409). It is important to remember that when *Origins* was written, Stalin was still in power, and had recently instigated a new purge, this time against the Jews.

ARENDT AS REFUGEE, ZIONIST, AND POST-ZIONIST

In 1933, Arendt had fled Germany for Paris. France was then seesawing between progressive and reactionary constituencies, and would eventually become fertile ground for French fascism under Nazi occupation and the Vichy government of Pierre Laval. It was not an easy place for Jewish refugees in the 1930s, and the film shows a chanting right-wing crowd, in a torchlit, nighttime assembly around what appears to be a book-burning. Further footage shows Jewish refugees obtaining food and lodging at a community shelter. The Arendtian voice, based on her essay "We Refugees," declares the human being a social animal. For such an entity, life is not easy without social ties. Lacking courage to fight for change in our legal status, she observes, we change our identity. Not wanting to be refugees, we do not wish to be Jews as our primary mark of identity. Even though the majority are stateless in France of 1943, we do not call ourselves such. If patriotism were to be considered a matter of practice, we would be the most patriotic people in the whole world. When one loses one's place in the community, one's political status and legal persona, one loses the meaning of speech and all human connection. One is left with qualities that are normally relevant only in private life. In such naked existence, everything mysteriously given us by birth, such as the shape of our bodies and talents of our minds, is affirmed only by unpredictable advent of sympathy or friendship, or "by the great and incalculable grace of love."[15]

To this Idith Zertal comments on how, when Arendt was a refugee in Paris, banished from humanity and history, she met (in 1936) the love of her life, with whom she felt redeemed and given a sense of home. This was Heinrich Blücher, who became Hannah's second husband.

A non-Jew, Heinrich planned to attend a Zionist Congress in Palestine, but Hannah attended in his place. *Vita Activa* portrays her affectionate correspondence with Heinrich, as footage displays her train and boat journeys eastward along the Mediterranean. In Palestine, newsboys hawk *Ha'aretz*, *Davar*, and other Hebrew and German Zionist newspapers. One of Hannah's letters groups the Jewish Congress participants into "messiah trumpeters" and "rationalists"—herself belonging to the latter. Her keen skepticism is evident—one must recall here her anti-religious upbringing. She declares Palestine the center of Jewish national aspirations, not because Jews were descended from a people who lived there two thousand years earlier, but because for two millennia, "the craziest of people" took pleasure in preserving a past in which the ruins of Jerusalem were rooted in the heart of time. She signs her letter: "Think of me, and don't forget how to kiss. Hannah."

Idith Zertal, here as Israeli liberal and "New Historian," comments on Arendt's experience as refugee and pariah, which underlay her Zionism. Hannah, she says, was led to be a Zionist hero in the 1930s, but in the '40s she saw the movement taking a disturbing new direction—a constant, obstinate desire for national sovereignty. Hannah found problematic Palestinian Jewry's political display as a nation-state. She knew the slippery slope whereby a state dominated by nationalism ceases to be a nation of all its citizens, but rather one in which only the national majority rules.

Later in the film, Rabbi Abba Hillel Silver (unattributed), is shown in newsreel footage asserting the following—exhibiting, in the process, a disturbing blindness to the "other people" in the picture. He declares that the Christian world (!) owes the Jew expiation for centuries of injury, wrongdoing and humiliation, especially as dealt out in the Nazi era, namely, a free and democratic Jewish commonwealth in Eretz Yisrael, "even though it means little or nothing for other people."

The Arendtian voice (adapted from the 1944 Arendt essay "Zionism Reconsidered") is then heard commenting on how American Zionists unanimously adopted the demand for such a commonwealth as embracing the whole of Palestine—a major turning point for Zionism. Thus did the Revisionist (territorially maximalist) position, long repudiated within Zionism, eventually prove victorious (minus the additional Revisionist demand for what is today the country of Jordan). The Arabs, for their part, were never mentioned—given only the choice between second-class citizenship or voluntary emigration. This stance Arendt finds rooted in the misguided conviction that all gentiles are antisemitic, that everybody is against the Jews.[16]

As Arendt declares: "A home that my neighbor does not recognize is not a home. A Jewish national home that is not recognized and not respected by its neighboring people is not a home but an illusion, until it becomes a battlefield."

Footage follows of Palestinian refugees after Israel's 1967 war against the Arab league, here showing Arab children, a nursing mother, and, in separate shots, adult men being arrested.

The Arendtian voice comments on how a socialist, revolutionary Jewish movement started out with ideas so soaring it did not recognize either the realities of the Middle East or the overall wickedness of the world. But it ended up clearly supporting not just national but chauvinist claims. "Not against enemies of the Jewish people, but against its possible friends and present neighbors." Such a division between Jews and people it regards as enemies is not much different from other master-race theories.

Does this otherwise prescient perception of blindness to "possible friends and present neighbors" amount to a "master-race" theory? I am not so sure. Jews of that era, having witnessed the utter failure of even friendly governments to protect them, would reasonably conclude that only Jewish sovereignty could offer them a fighting chance. But the problem of Palestine was, on the other hand, already succinctly foreseen in *Origins*, where the relevant theme was the book's germinating principle—the plight of the stateless:

> After the [Second World] war, it turned out that the Jewish question, which was the only insoluble one, was indeed solved—namely by means of a colonized and then conquered territory—but this solved neither the problem of the minorities nor the stateless. On the contrary, like virtually all other events of our century, the solution of the Jewish question merely produced a new category of refugees, the Arabs, thereby increasing the number of stateless by another 700,000 to 800,000 people. And what happened in Palestine within the smallest territory, and in terms of hundreds of thousands, was then repeated in India on a large scale involving many millions. Since the Peace Treaties of 1919–20, the refugees have attached themselves like a curse to all the newly established states on earth, created in the image of the nation-state.[17]

This observation sets the Jews' creation of new stateless (which had resulted from their self-defense against what might have been a genocidal attack by a massive army of the Arab League) into the broader context of worldwide displacements in the creation of nation-states, as such.[18] In the same discussion, Arendt had perceived the world's absence (already dismayingly evident in 1918) of any supranational body with authority to guarantee a universally recognized standard of human rights, let alone the power to enforce it.[19] The problem persists unto today. The principle of totalitarianism whereby the outer shell of traditional-seeming national structures can conceal the most egregious violations of human freedom, dignity, and safety—often invisibly to the same nation's more privileged—is all too much with us, even at the heart of the world's most respected democracies.

THE TREE OF KNOWLEDGE—THE DEATH CAMPS

Arendt to a German TV interviewer:

> The decisive day was when we heard about Auschwitz. This was 1943, and at first, we didn't believe it. Then, six months later, we did. Because we had the proof. That was the real shock. That should never have happened. Something happened to which we can never reconcile ourselves. About everything else that happened to us [Jews and dissidents on the run], it was sometimes hard. We were very poor. We were hunted down, we had to flee. We had to spend our life lying. We had to find a way to survive. We were young. I even had a little fun with it—I can't say otherwise. But this was something very different.

It was this revelation, above all, that motivated Arendt to write *The Origins of Totalitarianism*. As Steven Aschheim writes:

> [It] satisfied an urgent need. Until then, and for at least a decade after that, there were virtually no attempts to forge the theoretical, historical, and conceptual tools necessary to illuminate the great cataclysms of the twentieth century. Indeed, to this day, historians find it difficult to integrate these events persuasively and coherently into the flow of this century's history. Arendt was seen to provide an account adequate to the enormity of the materials and problems at hand. To be sure, the term . . . "Holocaust" had not yet crystallized and does not appear in the book . . . Nevertheless, for contemporaries hungry for understanding, the work was regarded as revelatory because, as Alfred Kazin put it, it seemed to address itself "to the gas."[20]

As the Arendtian voice, puts it: in a world where a people are taught they are superfluous, and punishment has no relation to crime, where work is compelled without product, senselessness is a daily reality. Within a totalitarian ideology, nothing is more logical. When the inmate is viewed as vermin, it is appropriate for it to be killed by poison gas. If seen as degenerate, they cannot be permitted to contaminate the population. If their souls are slavelike, it is a waste of time trying to reeducate them.

Accompanying footage shows well-dressed Jews with yellow stars sewn on their garments being herded along an urban street with their hands up; then, processed by bureaucrats; and later, with thinner faces and less hopeful gaze, in an unspecified setting. Still later footage shows Jews behind barbed wire in what is presumably Auschwitz, or its like—some still clad in civilian garb, others in striped prison clothing, and, in one extraordinarily arresting shot, six naked, fearsomely emaciated men (the archetypal "Muselmann" prisoner) walking, with their backs to the camera, in a strangely slow, serene, and rhythmic pace. But how can this be? The Muselmann was the inmate most deteriorated, in whom the will to go on living had wholly disappeared.[21] But here, in their puzzling calm, they seem like masters of their fate. They walk away from us, as if deliberately receding from our memory. They dare us to go on living, in the face of what we see. But no. They surely were not masters of their fate. Their image is a portrait of the ravages of an evil system's perpetual motion. And while it is not the final image of the film, I wish to make it a signature to this essay. To them, and to the toil and travail of all the nameless dead, belongs the memorializing epitaph now found inscribed in glass that looks out onto the magnificent blue waters of the Mediterranean, in Dani Karavan's memorial to Walter Benjamin at Port Bou, Catalonia:

> It is harder to honor the memory of the nameless than that of the renowned . . .
> To the memory of the nameless is historical construction devoted. (Benjamin 2003, 406)[22]

SO MUCH TO SORT OUT

Any fifteen-minute segment of this film could yield a full essay about its interplay of theme and visual imagery, and whether the latter underscores or subverts the film's verbal content—a matter we spectators must often decide for ourselves. And it is impossible to do justice to the undecidables that this film, with justice, places in our laps. How *does* one decide if "the banality of evil" ascribed to Eichmann can be an adequate rubric for the larger nation that allowed the unspeakable to take place, or the larger world that had long postponed a reckoning with what was happening? Was it adequate to adduce internationally renowned novelist and Holocaust survivor Aharon Appelfeld (whose acclaimed 1980 novel *Badenheim 1939* had satirized the self-deception of Jews in an Austrian resort town being readied for Jewish deportation to concentration camps in Poland) and American historian Deborah Lipstadt (who, for her part, had commendably chronicled the failure of the US press to recognize and call attention to the Holocaust as it was happening) to fault Arendt for her naiveté and scorn?[23] How does one sort out the issue that aroused some of the bitterest condemnations of *Eichmann in Jerusalem* among Arendt's fellow Jews, survivors and historians alike: the role of the *Judenräte*, the Nazi-appointed Jewish councils and the Jewish-born ghetto police, many of them children, who helped ensure a logistically smooth transfer of stateless, rightless Jews to their eventual doom? How does one decide whether Zionism and the Jewish state it fostered—established in the absence of a mutually acceptable partition—amounted to a theory of a master race? (I myself believe otherwise, but I feel little certainty in my reservations.) Ushpiz's *Vita Activa* has assembled a meaningful array of talking heads, intersecting with striking archival footage, to weigh these imponderables and has woven these into a thoughtful narrative of Hannah Arendt's very consequential and accomplished life. Offering an anatomy of the era of catastrophe that spanned 1914–1945, it celebrates Arendt's relentless commitment to the unruly—to the power of untrammeled human thought as a force of resistance and critique. Although the film seems overly preoccupied with her relation to Heidegger and Eichmann, it places her voice outside of that stifling framework, and gazes into it. It meanwhile displays Hannah among the era's homeless and stateless—making her way by cunning and tenacity, by often random but crucial good luck, to a provisionally safer life. She, too, in the era's parlance, was scum of the earth. Unlike so many, she survived it. And despite her skepticism toward Jewish statehood, which she otherwise ambivalently supported, she never lost her involvement in Jewish life. Above all, she held to the concrete against totalitarian ideology's abstract idealism and the cliché-riddled dishonesty and self-deception of those who served it. Against world-cleansing efforts to simplify reality, Arendt spoke for human diversity, the beauty of random experience, and the unruliness of love. And she showed how textures of thought rooted in complexities of everyday life can yield understanding of crimes against humanity.

BIBLIOGRAPHY

Agamben, Giorgio, 1998. *Homo Sacer: Sovereign Power and Bare Life*. Stanford, CA: Stanford University Press.

Agamben, Giorgio 2002. *Remnants of Auschwitz: The Witness and the Archive*. New York: Zone Books.

Appelfeld, Aharon. 2009. *Badenheim, 1939*. Boston: David R. Godine.

Arendt, Hannah. 1968 [1951] *The Origins of Totalitarianism*. New York: A Harvest Book/Harcourt.

Arendt, Hannah 1955. *Men in Dark Times*. New York: Harcourt, Brace, and World.

Arendt, Hannah. 1963. *Eichmann in Jerusalem: A Report on the Banality of Evil*. New York: Viking Press.

Arendt, Hannah. 1971. "Martin Heidegger at Eighty," *The New York Review of Books*, October 21. https://www.nybooks.com/articles/1971/10/21/martin-heidegger-at-eighty/.

Arendt, Hannah. 1978. "We Refugees," in *The Jew as Pariah*, edited by Ron H. Feldman, 55–66. New York: Grove Press.

Arendt, Hannah, "Zionism Reconsidered," https://hannah-arendt-edition.net/vol_text. html?id=/3p_III-014-ZionismReconsidered.xml&lang=de accessed 06/01/21.
Aschheim, Steven, ed. 2001. *Arendt in Jerusalem*. Berkeley: University of California Press.
Benjamin, Walter. 1966. *Briefe II*, edited by Gershom Scholem and Theodor W. Adorno. Frankfurt am Main: Suhrkamp.
Benjamin, Walter. 2003. "On the Concept of History," in *Walter Benjamin: Selected Writings, Volume 4: 1938–40*, edited by Howard Eiland and Michael W. Jennings, 389–400. Cambridge, MA: The Belknap Press of Harvard University Press.
Benjamin, Walter. 2003. "Paralipomena to 'On the Concept of History,'" in *Walter Benjamin: Selected Writings*, Volume 4: 1938–1940, edited by Howard Eiland and Michael W. Jennings, 401–11. Cambridge, MA: The Belknap Press of Harvard University Press.
Benjamin, Walter. 1999. "Paris, Capital of the Nineteenth Century" (1935, 1939), in *The Arcades Project*, edited by Howard Eiland and Kevin McLaughlin, 3–13 and 14–26. Cambridge, MA: The Belknap Press of Harvard University Press.
Benjamin, Walter 1999. *Selected Writings Volume I: 1913–1926*, edited by Marcus Bullock and Michael W. Jennings. Cambridge, MA: The Belknap Press of Harvard University Press.
Benjamin, Walter. 1999. "Theories of German Fascism," in *Walter Benjamin: Selected Writings, Volume 2: 1927–1934*, edited by Michael W. Jennings, Howard Eiland and Gary Smith, 312–21. Cambridge, MA: The Belknap Press of Harvard University Press.
Burnet, John. 1930. *Early Greek Philosophy*. London: A. C. Black.
Farin, Ingo, and Jeff Malpas, ed. 2016. *Reading Heidegger's Black Notebooks, 1931–1941*. Cambridge, MA: MIT Press.
Faye, Emmanuel 2009. *Heidegger: The Introduction of Nazism into Philosophy in Light of the Unpublished Seminars of 1933–1935*. New Haven and London: Yale University Press.
Lilla, Mark. 2013 "Arendt and Eichmann: The New Truth," *The New York Review of Books* LX, 18 (Nov. 21): 35–45.
Lipstadt, Deborah E. 1986. *Beyond Belief: The American Press and the Coming of the Holocaust, 1933–1945*. New York: The Free Press.
Lipstadt, Deborah E. 2011. *The Eichmann Trial*. New York: Schocken Books.
Raz-Krakotzkin, Amnon 2001. "Binationalism and Jewish Identity: Hannah Arendt and the Question of Palestine," in *Arendt in Jerusalem*, edited by Steven E. Aschheim, 165–80. Berkeley: University of California Press.
Rosenberg, Joel. 2014. "Into the Woods: Eichmann, Heidegger, and Margarethe von Trotta's Hannah Arendt." *Jewish Film and New Media: An International Journal* 2 no. 2: 201–16.
Sofsky, Wolfgang 1999. *The Order of Terror: The Concentration Camp*. Princeton: Princeton University Press.
Stangneth, Bettina. 2014. *Eichmann before Jerusalem: The Unexamined Life of a Mass Murderer*. New York: Alfred A. Knopf.

Young-Bruehl, Elisabeth. 1982. *Hannah Arendt: For Love of the World*. New Haven and London: Yale University Press.

NOTES

1. Hannah Arendt, *The Origins of Totalitarianism* (New York: A Harvest Book / Harcourt, Inc, 1951, 1976). Henceforth "Arendt, *Origins*."
2. I would place into parallel with it Walter Benjamin's essay "Paris, Capital of the Nineteenth Century" (1935, 1939), in *The Arcades Project* (1999, 3–13 and 14–26). Both the essay (in two versions) and the longer work of which it is a part, Benjamin's mostly quotational montage, chronicled the forces of modernity, industrialist capitalism, the degradation of experience, and the political oppression and violence that these fostered.
3. I supplement the film's minimalist sketch with information from Elisabeth Young-Bruehl, *Hannah Arendt: For Love of the World* (1982), especially 5–41. Throughout the present essay, when dealing with Arendt's life as writer and public intellectual, I use her surname. When viewing her mostly private experience, I call her Hannah.
4. Hannah's first husband, Günther Stern, a friend from her youth, was a poet, essayist, philosopher, and aspiring academic, with whom she had been living during a period in life when she had numerous lovers. For further details about their relationship, see Young-Bruehl (1982, 77–81, 96–102, 134).
5. Hannah Arendt, "Martin Heidegger at Eighty," *New York Review of Books*, October 21, 1971, https://www.nybooks.com/articles/1971/10/21/martin-heidegger-at-eighty/. See my essay on the film (Rosenberg 2014, 201–16, especially 208–16). Cf. Young-Bruehl, *Hannah Arendt* (1982, 48–50).
6. Here quoting Benjamin, *Briefe II* (1966).
7. For the early years, see, for example, Benjamin (1996, 3–17, 48–49, 87–89, and especially 444–88).
8. Quoting from Benjamin's letters.
9. My translation's final words here differ from the film's somewhat misleading subtitle, which refers to Eichmann as the policy's "executive arm." The Hebrew word *bitsa'* ("carried out") is only a verb. The "executive arm" was the whole system, which included Eichmann as a fervently willing participant.
10. See Eichmann's disturbing conversations with Dutch Nazi sympathizer Willem Stassen, now found in English in Stangneth (2014, 234–310), in which Eichmann expressed regret and assumed responsibility for his *failure* to liquidate the whole of European Jewry. Cf. Lilla (2013, 35–45, especially 36).
11. Cf. Stangneth (2014, 280, 286), but contrast (2014, 291–92).
12. See, respectively, (1951, 341–88 and 389–459).
13. Cf. Benjamin (1951, 308–9. Cf. idem (1999, 312–21).
14. The film's quotation adapts from Heidegger's summer 1934 lecture on Heraclitus fragment #53, in Faye (2009, 168). Cf., more generally, Farin and Malpas (2016). Heraclitus fragment #53 reads: "War is the father of all and the king of all;

and some he has made gods and some men, some bond and some free." From Burnet (2014, 206) (there given as #44).

15. Cf. Arendt (1978, 55–66).

16. Cf. Arendt, "Zionism Reconsidered," https://hannah-arendt-edition.net/vol_text.html?id=/3p_III-014-ZionismReconsidered.xml&lang=de, accessed 06/01/21.

17. Arendt, "Zionism Reconsidered," 290.

18. The Arab League had in fact rejected the U.N.-approved partition plan, which the Jews supported, that would have established two co-equal states, Arab and Jewish, in Palestine. Cf., more generally, Raz-Krakotzkin (2001, 165–80).

19. See especially (1951, 289–302).

20. Steven E. Aschheim, Introduction to *Arendt in Jerusalem* (2001, 11–12).

21. Cf. Agamben (2002, 41–86); Agamben (1998); and Sofsky (1999, 25, 199–205).

22. See (2003, 401–11, and Benjamin's "On the Concept of History" (2003, 389–400).

23. See Appelfeld (2009). For Lipstadt's thoughtful critique of Arendt (part of whose strength is its willingness to acknowledge what was true or accurate in *Eichmann in Jerusalem*), see Lipstadt (2011, 148–87). Cf. Lipstadt (1986).

Index

action: *amor mundi* and political, 101; collective, 12, 151–53, 166–73; expression and, 166, 168–69; Heidegger, M., on, 129, 132; *The Human Condition* on, 43, 120–21; labor and, 120–21, 123, 127, 165; love and, 100–101, 103–4, 106–7; natality and, 165; political, elements of, 171–73; proto-normative commitment and political, 195–97; speech and, 43, 45–49, 120–21, 129; thought and, 10, 129–32; in Vita Activa, 46; work and, 106, 120–21, 123, 165, 187
aesthetics: Arendt, H., on, 7, 39–40, 42, 45, 48, 50–52; internal standard in, 51–52; Jaspers on, 42–43; Kant on, 7, 39–40, 42–43, 45, 48, 50–52
agonistic pluralism, 182
agonistic politics, 77–78, 90
Alien Registration Act (Smith Act) (US), 205, 214
Allen, Danielle, 217
ambiguity, 111
amor mundi, 8–9, 13, 16, 31; *Denktagebuch* on, 26, 78; political action and, 101; as proto-normative, 184; Véret-Gay and, 83, 85
anarchism. *See* Goldman, Emma

anti-Communism, US, 217, 227n2; Arendt, H., and, 211–16; Jones and, 205, 211–12, 214–16; racism and, 214–16
antisemitism, 219; Arendt, H., on, 70, 218, 243; Herder and, 59; Jewish question and, 58; Nazi, 236–37
appearance: being and, 157–59, 183; freedom and, 169; *The Life of the Mind* on, 152, 157; love and, 29–30, 34; phenomenology and, 182–83; space of, 188; world and, 156–59
Appelfeld, Aharon, 246
Arab League, 243–44, 250n18
Arabs, Palestinian. *See* Palestinians
Arendt, Hannah. *See specific topics*
Arendt, Martha, 231
Arendtian voice. *See Vita Activa* (film)
Aristotle, 155, 158–59, 177n4
Aron, Raymond, 97
art, politics and, 21, 35
Aschheim, Steven, 245
assimilation, 55, 74n3
Auer, Stefan, 135
Augustine, 4–5, 8–9, 25–26, 89
autonomy: of judgment, 47, 50–51; of subject, 123

Bacon, Francis, 159

251

Badenheim 1939 (Appelfeld), 246
Badiou, Alain, 88–90
Barnard, F. M., 74n6
Bauer, Nancy, 115n17
Beauvoir, Simone de: on ambiguity, 111; *The Blood of Others*, 108; on facticity, 100, 110; feminism of, 98, 103, 107–8, 110–11, 115n14; Heidegger, M., and, 97–98, 103, 105, 107–8; "It's About Time Women Put a New Face on Love," 110; on love, 10, 97–98, 100, 103, 108–12; on *Mitsein*, 9, 98, 103, 107–10, 115n17, 152; on politics, love and, 111–12; on romantic love, 10, 97–98, 103, 107–10; *The Second Sex*, 107, 109, 115n14, 115n17, 115n19; on self, 97, 108, 115n19; *She Came to Stay*, 108
being, appearance and, 157–59, 183
Being and Time (Heidegger, M.), 104, 117, 119, 122, 185, 233
being-with. *See Mitsein*
Beiser, Frederick, 60
Benhabib, Seyla, 13, 74n1, 159, 178n12, 182
Benjamin, Walter, 71, 237, 249n2; Arendt, H., influenced by, 23, 27, 234; memorial to, 246; *Origin of the German Trauerspiel*, 24; on storyteller, 23, 27
Berlin, Isaiah, 60
Bernasconi, Robert, 227n3
Between Past and Future (Arendt, H.), 177n3
Bill 504 sit-in, 151–52, 170–72
Birmingham, Peg, 12–13
Black Caribbeans: in Britain, 205, 208, 212, 216, 219–24, 228nn8–9; carnival of, 221, 223–24; citizenship and, 208, 221, 224; Jones and, 205, 208, 220–23, 228nn8–9; in US, 205, 208–9, 215, 219–20
Blacks, US: anti-Communism and, 214–16; citizenship of, 215, 217, 222; Communist Party and, 205, 213–16;

feminism and, 209–10, 213, 215; racism against, 208–10, 213–19, 224, 227n3, 227n7
Blixen, Karen (Isak Dinesen): Arendt, H., on, 23–24, 27–28; *A Midsummer Night's Dream* and, 27–28; Migel on, 27
The Blood of Others (Beauvoir), 108
The Bloomsbury Companion to Arendt (Gratton and Sari), 2
Blücher, Heinrich, 28, 101; as Communist, 212–13; *Vita Activa* film on, 232, 242
body, 124–25
Borren, Marieke, 162, 178n7
Boyce-Davies, Carol, 221, 223
Britain: Black Caribbeans in, 205, 208, 212, 216, 219–24, 228nn8–9; British Nationality Act, 1948, 220–21; British Nationality Act, 1981, 222; carnival, Caribbean, in, 221, 223–24; citizenship in, 208, 221, 224; colonialism of, 207, 216; Commonwealth Immigration Act, 221–22; Communist Party in, 216–17; Jones in, 205, 212, 216–17, 219–23; Labour in, 222, 228n9; racism in, 219–24, 228nn8–9; white race riots in, 219, 221; Windrush scandal, 222–23
British West Indies. *See* Black Caribbeans
Brzeziński, Zbigniew, 140, 142–43
Buras, Piotr, 136, 144–45
Burden-Stelly, Charisse, 227n4
bureaucracy, 163–64, 169
Butler, Judith, 195

Califano, Joseph A., 151
Camp Jened, 170–72
Camus, Albert, 97
Canovan, Margaret, 144
care, 203n18; Heidegger, M., on, 196; as proto-normative commitment, 195–97

Caribbeans. *See* Black Caribbeans
carnival, Caribbean, 221, 223–24
Carter, Jimmy, 151
Cartesianism, 98, 104
cause, effect and, 157, 160
Center for Independent Living, 171
Cézanne, Paul, 166–67, 173
"Cézanne's Doubt" (Merleau-Ponty), 166–67
Chambers, Whittaker, 213, 227n2
citizenship, 14–15; anti-Communism and, 215; Black, US, 215, 217, 222; Black Caribbeans and, 208, 221, 224; British, 208, 221, 223–24; as civic standing, 208, 215; colonialism and, 207–8; denaturalization, 211–12, 227n4; Jones and, 211–12, 215, 223–24; as legal status, 208, 215; statelessness and, 207, 224
civic standing, 208, 215
collective action: collective decision-making in, 167–68; disability rights movement, 12, 151–53, 166, 170–73; in *polis*, collective self-rule, 169–70
colonialism, 219; British, 207, 216; citizenship and, 207–8
Commonwealth Immigration Act (Britain), 221–22
common world. *See* world
Communism: anti-Communism, US, 205, 211–17, 227n2; Blücher and, 212–13; rifts in international, 217; totalitarianism and, 213
Communism, in Poland. *See* Poland
Communist bloc. *See* Eastern Europe
Communist Party, British, 216–17
Communist Party, German, 212
Communist Party, Moscow trials of, 227nn1–2
Communist Party, US (CPUSA): anti-racist organizing of, 205, 214–16; Black feminism in, 209–10, 213, 215; Chambers and, 213, 227n2; denaturalization and, 211–12; Jones and, 205–6, 209, 211–16

Communist Youth League, 205
consciousness, intentional structure of, 154–55
Considerant, Victor, 81, 84–85, 92n4
cosmopolitanism, 181, 192
CPUSA. *See* Communist Party, US
"Creating a Cultural Atmosphere" (Arendt, H.), 70–71
crimes against humanity: *Eichmann in Jerusalem* on, 191; Holocaust as, 191–94, 236–37; human rights and, 184, 190, 194; statelessness and, 184, 193–94
criminal justice system, immigration system and, 224
Crip Camp (documentary), 12, 170
"The Crisis in Culture" (Arendt, H.), 39–40, 48–49
The Crisis of the European Sciences and Transcendental Phenomenology (Husserl), 160
critical phenomenology, 99
Critique of Judgment (Kant): Arendt, H., on, 7, 39–47, 49–52, 192; Jaspers and, 7, 40–46, 52; political philosophy in, 7, 39, 41–47, 51–52, 192, 196; understanding and, 49, 51; worldliness and, 45, 51
Czechoslovakia, 135

Dasein, 121; action and, 129; Arendt, H., on, 186; Heidegger, M., on, 104–5, 109, 117–18, 122–23, 125–26, 129, 185–86; humanity and, 117–19, 123–24, 126; Jonas on, 125–26; *Kehre* and, 118; *Mitsein* and, 104–5, 108
Davis, Ben, 214, 223
debates, political, 137
Declaration of the Rights of Man and Citizen, French (1789), 161, 194
demos, 188
denaturalization, 211–12, 227n4
Denktagebuch (Arendt, H.), 2, 4; on *amor mundi*, 26, 78; on Kant, 7, 39,

42, 44, 50; on love, 9, 26, 77–79, 83, 90, 99
desegregation, US, 217–19, 221
DIA. *See* Disabled in Action
dialogue, 48, 155, 167–68, 171
Dinesen, Isak. *See* Blixen, Karen
disability rights movement, 12, 153, 166, 173; Bill 504 sit-in, 151–52, 170–72; Camp Jened, 170–72; power in, 171
Disabled in Action (DIA), 151, 170
disclosure, 188–89
discourse: political, truth and, 48; world, discursive dimension of, 186–88, 201n7
discrimination, 218
dissidents, Eastern European, 11, 135
doctoral dissertation, of Arendt, H. *See Love and Saint Augustine*
drama, 23–24
dreams, 66–70, 75n8
Duda, Wojciech, 136, 138, 144

earth, 189, 191–92, 202n13
Eastern Europe: Communist bloc, Arendt, H., and, 135–37; Czechoslovakia, 135; Hungarian Revolution, 1956, 11, 135–36, 141, 217; after 1989, Arendt, H., and, 135, 137–46; refugee crisis, European, in, 145; totalitarianism, Arendt, H., on, and, 11, 135, 139–45; totalitarianism in, 11, 139–43. *See also* Poland
Eichmann, Adolf, 233; Buras on, 144–45; *Hannah Arendt* on, 235; Stangneth on, 236–37, 249n10; trial of, 164, 181, 190, 192, 229, 235–37, 249n9; *Vita Activa* film on, 235–36, 247, 249n9
Eichmann in Jerusalem (Arendt, H.), 136–37, 164; on crimes against humanity, 191; criticism of, 62, 246; irony in, 62; *The Life of the Mind* and, 202n16; *The Origins of Totalitarianism* and, 229

Elienberger, Wolfram, 8
Ellison, Ralph, 217–18
emigration, of Arendt, H., 205–7
"An End to the Neglect of the Problems of Negro Women" (Jones), 209–10
Enfantin, 82–84
Enlightenment: Arendt, H., critiquing, 57–59, 64–65; Jews and, 57–59, 65; Kant and, 7; reason in, 58, 65; Romanticism and, 57
"The Enlightenment and the Jewish Question" (Arendt, H.), 55, 57, 65
epistolary narratives, 77–78, 80–81, 90
equality, 178n7; experience of, 156–57; modernity and, 161–62; racism and, 218–19; social and, 161
Eros, 78, 83, 99
Essays in Understanding (Arendt, H.), 5–6
ethics, 131–32
Europe, refugee crisis in, 145
evolution, 125–26
existentialism, 9, 97, 114n2
existential phenomenology, 152, 177n1, 182
experience: of equality, 156–57; Husserl on, 154; phenomenology on, 153–57, 177n3; in world, 155–56
expression: action and, 166, 168–69; Merleau-Ponty on, 166–68, 173

facticity, 100, 110
Fanon, Frantz, 107
fascism, 209–10, 213–15, 237
Faulkner, William, 5
February revolution, 1848 (France), 84–85
feminism, 10; of Beauvoir, 98, 103, 107–8, 110–11, 115n14; Black, 209–10, 213, 215; of Jones, 209–10, 215; of Véret-Gay, 82–85. *See also* gender
Fourier, Charles, 83–84, 92n4
Fourierism, 81–84, 92n4
fragment, in Romanticism, 8, 56, 61, 66–67, 71–72

France: Declaration of the Rights
  of Man and Citizen, 161, 194;
  February revolution, 1848, 84–85;
  French Revolution, 1789, 161; July
  Monarchy, 82, 92n6; Romantic
  socialist movements in, 81–82,
  84–85, 92n4
freedom, 168–69, 173
Friedrich, Carl J., 142–43
friendship, 30, 78, 108–10, 115n13
Frühromantik aesthetic, 56

gender, 3; Black women, Jones on,
  209–10; love and, 88; *Rahel
  Varnhagen* on, 64–65
genius, 7
Germany: Arendt, H., in, 218,
  231; Communist Party in, 212;
  Romanticism, early, in, 60–68, 75n9
Gładziuk, Nina, 138
Goldman, Emma, 9, 86–90
Gratton, Peter, 2
The Great Philosophers (Jaspers), 7,
  41–43, 45–46, 52
Greeks, ancient: Aristotle, 155, 158–59,
  177n4; *polis*, 21, 153, 169–70, 172,
  177n4; political discourse of, 48;
  private sphere and, 102
Grinberg, Daniel, 140
Die Grossen Philosophen (Jaspers). *See
  The Great Philosophers*
Guenther, Lisa, 155–56

Hamlet (Shakespeare), 24
Hannah Arendt (film), 15, 232–33, 235
Hannah Arendt and Human Rights
  (Birmingham), 12–13
Hannah Arendt Institute for Research on
  Totalitarianism, 144
Hausner, Gideon, 235–37
Health, Education, and Welfare, US
  Department of (HEW), 151, 170
Hegel, Georg Wilhelm Friedrich, 107–9
Heidegger, Gertrude, 233

Heidegger, Martin, 177n1; on action,
  129, 132; Beauvoir and, 97–98, 103,
  105, 107–8; *Being and Time*, 104,
  117, 119, 122, 185, 233; on care,
  196; Cartesianism critiqued by, 98,
  104; on *Dasein*, 104–5, 109, 117–18,
  122–23, 125–26, 129, 185–86; Hegel
  and, 108; on humanity, 117–21, 123–
  24, 126–27, 185–86; Jonas and, 10,
  117–21, 124, 126, 129–30; on *Kehre*,
  118, 120, 129; *Letter on Humanism*,
  129; on *das Man*, 105–7, 119, 122;
  on *Mitsein*, 9, 98, 103–7, 156; on
  modernity, 152, 160; Nazism and,
  123, 130, 233, 239; "The Question
  Concerning Technology," 160; on
  subject, 104–5, 119–23, 129, 185;
  on technology, 120, 128–29, 160;
  on thought, 130; *Vita Activa* film
  on, 232, 235, 239, 247; on world
  disclosure, 188
Heidegger, Martin, Arendt, H.,
  and: affair of, 28, 79, 101, 103,
  232–33; break of, 8–9, 28, 82, 105;
  correspondence of, 79, 82, 90, 103
Heller, Ágnes, 143–44
Heller, Włodzimierz, 138
Heraclitus, 249n14
Herder, Johann, 58–59, 74n6
Heumann, Judith, 12, 151, 170–71
HEW. *See* Health, Education, and
  Welfare, US Department of
Hill, Samantha Rose, 22, 83
Hitler, Adolf, 130, 140, 191,
  237–39, 241
Holocaust, 145, 184; as crime against
  humanity, 191–94, 236–37; human
  dignity and, 190–91, 193–95; *The
  Origins of Totalitarianism* and, 245;
  trials of, 190–91, 194–95, 202n16;
  Vita Activa film on, 229, 232–35,
  238–40, 245–46
Holzer, Jerzy, 141–42
Honig, Bonnie, 188
Hoover, J. Edgar, 214

hospitality, 191–92
human. *See* humanity
The Human Condition (Arendt, H.), 7, 13, 45, 212; on action, 43, 120–21; on humanity, 120, 185–87, 201n4; on love, 22, 25–26, 78, 89, 99–100; on poetry, 35; on public, 152–53, 187–88, 218; on social, 161, 218; on speech, 43, 120–21; on Vita Activa, 46; world-centered ontology of, 185–89
human dignity, 182; Holocaust and, 190–91, 193–95; proto-normative notion of, 13, 184; statelessness and, 181, 183–84, 190, 193–95; as worldliness, 184, 189–95
humanism, ontological, 126
humanity, 122, 132, 236; conditionality, conditions of, 183–86, 201n4; *Dasein* and, 117–19, 123–24, 126; *Eichmann in Jerusalem* on, 191; Heidegger, M., on, 117–21, 123–24, 126–27, 185–86; *The Human Condition* on, 120, 185–87, 201n4; Jonas on, 118–21, 124–28, 130–31; plurality and, 123, 185–86; in world-centered ontology, 183–87
humanity, crimes against. *See* crimes against humanity
human rights, 12–13; crimes against humanity and, 184, 190, 194; institutionalization of, 190, 193–94; *The Origins of Totalitarianism* on, 181; politicizing, 182, 193; statelessness and, 181, 193–94; UDHR, 190, 193–94, 202n9, 207
Hungarian Revolution (1956), 11, 135–36, 141, 217
Husserl, Edmund, 177n1, 182; *The Crisis of the European Sciences and Transcendental Phenomenology*, 160; on experience, 154; on modernity, 152, 160; on transcendental intersubjectivity, 152, 156

imagination, 6–7
immigrants: in Britain, 215, 220–23, 228nn8–9; criminal justice system, immigration system and, 224; Jones and, 208–9, 215, 219–22, 228nn7–8; in US, 208–9, 211–12, 215, 220, 222
Immigration and Nationality Act (McCarran-Walter Act) (US), 211–12, 215, 220
The Imperative of Responsibility (Jonas), 128, 130
institution, 168
institutionalization, of human rights, 190, 193–94
intentional structure, of consciousness, 154–55
intercorporeality, 152, 156
Internal Security Act (McCarran Act) (US), 211, 215, 227n4
internal standard, 51–52
International Military Tribunal, 190
intersubjectivity, transcendental, 152, 156
irony: in *Eichmann in Jerusalem*, 62; in *Rahel Varnhagen*, 63, 65; in Romanticism, 8, 61–63
Israel, 202n16, 243, 250n18
"It's About Time Women Put a New Face on Love" (Beauvoir), 110

Jaeggi, Rahel, 143
Jaspers, Karl, 4–5, 232; on aesthetics, 42–43; *The Great Philosophers*, 7, 41–43, 45–46, 52; on Kant, 7, 40–46, 52; *Vita Activa* film on, 238
Jedlicki, Jerzy, 137
Jews, 74n3, 193, 231, 234; antisemitism, 58–59, 70, 218–19, 236–37, 243; "Creating a Cultural Atmosphere" on, 70–71; emancipation of, in nineteenth century, 219; Enlightenment and, 57–59, 65; in Germany, Arendt, H., and, 218, 231; Jewish question, 57–59, 62–63, 74n6, 244; under Nazism, 191, 211,

236–39, 241; *Rahel Varnhagen* and, 55–56, 62–66, 69, 74n7; as refugees, 242–43; Romanticism and, 8, 55–56, 71; Zionism, 242–44, 246–47
Jim Crow, 208–9, 213, 227n7
Jonas, Hans: on Arendt, H., 131; on body, 124–25; on *Dasein*, 125–26; ethics of, 131–32; Heidegger, M., and, 10, 117–21, 124, 126, 129–30; on humanity, 118–21, 124–28, 130–31; *The Imperative of Responsibility*, 128, 130; on life, 124–28; on metabolism, 124–26, 128; on thought, 10, 130–31
Jones, Claudia: anti-Communism and, 205, 211–12, 214–16; anti-racist organizing of, 205, 215–16, 224; Arendt, H., compared with, 13–14, 205–6, 210–11, 221; Black Caribbeans and, 205, 208, 220–23, 228nn8–9; as Black immigrant, 208–9, 219–20; in Britain, 205, 212, 216–17, 219–23; citizenship and, 211–12, 215, 223–24; Communist Party, British, and, 216–17; Communist Party, US, and, 205–6, 209, 211–16; deportation, imprisonment of, 205, 211, 216, 223–24; "An End to the Neglect of the Problems of Negro Women," 209–10; feminism of, 209–10, 215; health of, 205, 216, 227n5; racism, US, and, 208–10, 213, 215–16, 227n7; on Soviet Union, 206
judgment: Arendt, H., on, 7, 45–51; autonomy of, 47, 50–51; Jaspers on, 7, 43; Kant on, 7, 39–47, 49–52; moral, 50; political, 7, 39–42, 44–46, 48–52, 54n1, 138; reflective, 7, 42–45, 50–52
July Monarchy (France), 82, 92n6

Kafka, Franz, 7, 234
Kant, Immanuel, 168, 190, 202n13, 231; aesthetics of, 7, 39–40, 42–43, 45, 48, 50–52; Arendt, H., on, 7, 39–47, 49–52, 67, 192, 196; *Critique of Judgment*, 7, 39–47, 49–52, 192, 196; *Denktagebuch* on, 7, 39, 42, 44, 50; on imagination, 6–7; Jaspers on, 7, 40–46, 52; Kafka and, 7; *Lectures on Kant's Political Philosophy* on, 39–40; *The Life of the Mind* on, 46; particularity and, 43–45, 51; *Perpetual Peace*, 191–92; on politics, 7, 39–47, 50–52, 191–92, 196; *Rahel Varnhagen* and, 67–69; Romanticism and, 60, 67–69, 71; on subjective universal validity, 46–47; on understanding, 49, 51; universality and, 43–47, 51; worldlessness and, 40, 42, 45; worldliness and, 45–46, 51
Kazin, Alfred, 2, 5, 245
Kehre (turn), 118, 120, 129
Khrushchev, Nikita, 141, 217
King, Richard, 22
King Lear (Shakespeare), 5–6
Kohn, Jerome, 71
Kornat, Marek, 140–41
Krasnodębski, Zdzisław, 139
Kristeva, Julia, 1, 4, 27, 83; on narratives, 79–80; on *Rahel Varnhagen*, 63, 74n1
Krzemiński, Ireneusz, 141
Kuniński, Miłowit, 139–40

labor: action and, 120–21, 123, 127, 165; Marx on alienated, 178n15; in *Vita Activa*, 46
Labour (British party), 222, 228n9
Lacoue-Labarthe, Philippe, 66–67, 71
Lebrecht, Jim, 172
Lectures on Kant's Political Philosophy (Arendt, H.), 39–40
legal status, citizenship as, 208, 214
Lenin, Vladimir, 140
Lessing, Gotthold, 9, 58–59
LeSure, Ainsley, 218–19, 221
Letter on Humanism (Heidegger, M.), 129

Levin, Rahel. *See* Varnhagen, Rahel
life, 124–28
The Life of the Mind (Arendt, H.), 27–28, 115n6, 137, 202n16; on appearance, 152, 157; on Kant, 46; world-centered ontology in, 185, 189
Lipstadt, Deborah, 246
literary references, 5–6, 22–23, 28–29
Little Rock, Arkansas, desegregation in, 217–18, 221
lived experience. *See* experience
Loidolt, Sophie, 170, 177n1, 178n8, 195–96, 201n5
love, 15, 91; action and, 100–101, 103–4, 106–7; *amor mundi*, 8–9, 13, 16, 26, 31, 78, 83, 85, 101, 184; appearance and, 29–30, 34; in Arendt, H., scholarship on, 25; Augustine on, 4, 8–9, 25–26, 89; Badiou on, 88–90; Beauvoir on, 10, 97–98, 100, 103, 108–12; *Denktagebuch* on, 9, 26, 77–79, 83, 90, 99; double configuration of, 79; epistolary narratives and, 90; as *Eros*, 78, 83, 99; friendship and, 30, 78, 110, 115n13; gender and, 88; Goldman and, 9, 88–90; *The Human Condition* on, 22, 25–26, 78, 89, 99–100; *Love and Saint Augustine* on, 25, 89, 115n6; *Men in Dark Times* on, 9, 27; in *A Midsummer Night's Dream*, 6, 23, 27–33; modalities of, Arendt, H., on, 78–79; natality and, 22, 25; plurality and, 78–79, 100, 102; politics, action, and, 100–101, 103–4; politics, relationality, and, 99; politics and, 25–26, 78–79, 82–83, 89–90, 98, 102, 111–12; private, public, and, 29–31, 78, 99, 102, 104, 111; *Rahel Varnhagen* on, 25, 115n6; respect and, 115n15; romantic, Arendt, H., on, 10, 30, 97–104, 106; romantic, Beauvoir on, 10, 97–98, 103, 107–10; in Shakespeare, 6, 22–23, 27–33; social, 82, 85; Véret-Gay and, 9, 82–83, 85; worldlessness of, 26, 30, 78–79, 101–3, 115n13, 115nn7–9
Love and Saint Augustine (Arendt, H.), 77; Augustine in, 4–5, 8–9, 25, 89; Heidegger, M., move from, in, 8; on love, 25, 89, 115n6
Luxemburg, Rosa, 212

MacArthur, Elizabeth, 81
das Man (they), 105–7, 119, 122
Markell, Patchen, 5
Marshall, David, 24, 40–41
Marx, Karl, 178n15
Marxism, 212
master-slave dialectic, 108
McCarran Act. *See* Internal Security Act
McCarran-Walter Act. *See* Immigration and Nationality Act
McCarthyism, 212–17
Mein Kampf (Hitler), 237
Mendelssohn, Moses, 58, 64
Men in Dark Times (Arendt, H.), 9, 27, 231
Mensch, James, 157
Merleau-Ponty, Maurice, 153–54, 172; "Cézanne's Doubt," 166–67; on dialogue, 155, 167–68; on expression, 166–68, 173; on institution, 168; on intercorporeality, 152, 156; on modernity, 152, 160; *Phenomenology of Perception*, 160
metabolism, 124–26, 128
method, phenomenology and, 183
Michnik, Adam, 11, 135
A Midsummer Night's Dream (Shakespeare), 24, 38nn9–10; Blixen and, 27–28; love in, 6, 23, 27–33; natality in, 34; private, public in, 31–35; "Pyramus and Thisbe" in, 33–35
Migel, Parmenia, 27
Millán-Zaibert, Elizabeth, 60–61, 66
Mitsein: Arendt, H., on, 9, 98, 103, 106–7, 109–10; Beauvoir on, 9, 98,

103, 107–10, 115n17, 152; *Dasein* and, 104–5, 108; Heidegger, M., on, 9, 98, 103–7, 156; plurality and, 106
modernity: Arendt, H., on, 152–53, 159–65; equality and, 161–62; Heidegger, M., on, 152, 160; Husserl on, 152, 160; Merleau-Ponty on, 152, 160; phenomenology on, 152, 159–60; private, public distorted in, 161–63; science in, 159–61, 164–65; social in, 161–63, 178n12; technology and, 159–60; totalitarianism and, 161, 164–65; world, common, undermined in, 159–65
moral judgment, 50
Moscow trials, 227nn1–2
Myers, Ella, 203n18

Najder, Zdzisław, 141
Nancy, Jean-Luc, 66–67, 71
narratives: epistolary, 77–78, 80–81, 90; Kristeva on, 79–80; in politics, 79–80, 90
natality, 23, 28; action and, 165; drama and, 24; love and, 22, 25; in *A Midsummer Night's Dream*, 34
Nazism, 135, 213; antisemitism in, 236–37; Arendt, H., fleeing, 205–6, 242; bureaucracy and, 164; Heidegger, M., and, 123, 130, 233, 239; Jews under, 191, 211, 236–39, 241; *The Origins of Totalitarianism* and, 240–41, 245; totalitarianism and, 140, 144–45, 164–65, 237–38, 240–41, 245; *Vita Activa* film on, 229, 232–35, 238–40, 245–46. *See also* Eichmann, Adolf; Holocaust
non-governmental organizations, 138–39
normativity: Arendt, H., adverse to, 11, 181–82, 184, 195; proto-normative commitment, of Arendt, H., 11, 13, 182, 184, 195–97
Novalis, 60, 67–68
Nowak, Piotr, 145

O'Byrne, Anne, 165
ontological humanism, 126
ontology, world-centered: disclosure in, 188–89; discursive dimension in, 186–88, 201n7; *The Human Condition* on, 185–89; humanity in, 183–87; *The Life of the Mind* on, 185, 189; plurality in, 185–86; politics in, 188; things in, 186–87, 201n7
Origin of the German Trauerspiel (Benjamin), 24
The Origins of Totalitarianism (Arendt, H.), 211, 227n3, 233, 237; criticism of, Arendt, H., responding to, 5–6; *Eichmann in Jerusalem* and, 229; Holocaust and, 245; on human rights, 181; Nazism and, 240–41, 245; in Poland, 11, 137–38, 140–43; Soviet Union and, 140–41, 143, 240–42; on statelessness, 244; on World War I, 229–30
Ovid, 23
Owenism, 82–84

Palestine, 71, 242–44, 250n18
Palestinians, 193, 243–44, 250n18
particularity, 43–45, 51
Passerin D'Entrèves, Maurizio, 49
performing arts, politics and, 21, 35
Pericles, 169
Perpetual Peace (Kant), 191–92
persona, 3
Pessoa, Fernando, 89
phenomenology, 131; appearance and, 182–83; of Arendt, H., 11–13, 106, 152, 177n1, 182–83, 201n5; critical, 99; on dialogue, 155, 167–68; existential, 152, 177n1, 182; experience in, 153–57, 177n3; on expression, 166–68, 173; human rights and, 13; Husserl, 152, 154, 156, 160, 177n1, 182; intercorporeality in, 152, 156; *The Life of the Mind* and, 152;

Merleau-Ponty, 152–56, 160, 166–68, 172–73; method and, 183; on modernity, 152, 159–60; plurality and, 12, 152–58, 178n6, 178n8; politics and, 11–13, 15–16, 177n1, 182–83, 201n5; proto-normative commitment and, 182; public and, 153, 157; transcendental intersubjectivity in, 152, 156; world in, 153, 155, 183, 185. *See also* Heidegger, Martin

Phenomenology of Perception (Merleau-Ponty), 160

Plummer, Keith, 80

pluralism: agonistic, 182; in judgment, 7; in literary references, 5–6; in Poland, Communist, 140; in politics, 138; *Rahel Varnhagen* and, 8

plurality, 52, 118, 131; humanity and, 123, 185–86; love and, 78–79, 100, 102; *Mitsein* and, 106; phenomenology and, 12, 152–58, 178n6, 178n8; proto-normative commitment in, 195; truth and, 48–49; in world-centered ontology, 185–86

poetry, 21–23, 35

Poland, 10; Arendt, H., and, after 1989, 135, 137–46; Arendt, H., and Communist, 135–37; non-governmental organizations in, 138–39; *The Origins of Totalitarianism* in, 11, 137–38, 140–43; pluralism in Communist, 140; politics, Arendt, H., on, and, 137–38; refugee crisis, European, in, 145; *Solidarność* in, 136, 139, 141; totalitarianism, Arendt, H., on, and, 11, 135, 139–45; totalitarianism in, 11, 139–42; war, state of, in, 140–42

polis, 21, 153, 169–70, 172, 177n4

political action: *amor mundi* and, 101; elements of, 171–73; proto-normative commitment and, 195–97

political rights, 102, 193

political speech, 43, 45–49

politics, 128, 132; agonistic, 77–78, 90; art and, 21, 35; Beauvoir on love and, 111–12; collective decision-making in, 167–68; common world, undermining of, and, 159; *Critique of Judgment* and, 7, 39, 41–47, 51–52, 192, 196; debates in, importance of, 137; disability rights movement, 12, 151–53, 166, 170–73; epistolary narratives and, 90; Greeks, ancient, political discourse of, 48; human rights, political approach to, 182, 193; internal standard in, 51–52; judgment in, 7, 39–42, 44–46, 48–52, 54n1, 138; Kant on, 7, 39–47, 50–52, 191–92, 196; love, action, and, 100–101, 103–4; love, relationality, and, 99; love and, 25–26, 78–79, 82–83, 89–90, 98, 102, 111–12; narratives in, 79–80, 90; normative position on, Arendt, H., lacking, 181–82; phenomenology and, 11–13, 15–16, 177n1, 182–83, 201n5; pluralism in, 138; Poland and Arendt, H., on, 137–38; *polis*, 21, 153, 169–70, 172, 177n4; truth and, 43, 47–50, 54n11; in Vita Activa, 46; in world-centered ontology, 188

Pomian, Krzysztof, 140

post-totalitarian state, 141

power, 171

private, public and, 218; love in, 29–31, 78, 99, 102, 104, 111; in *A Midsummer Night's Dream*, 31–35; in modernity, social distorting, 161–63. *See also* public

private sphere, 102

proto-normative commitment, 11; *amor mundi* as, 184; care for world as, 195–97; human dignity in, 13, 184; phenomenology and, 182; in plurality, 195; political action and, 195–97

public: *The Human Condition* on, 152–53, 187–88, 218; phenomenology and, 153, 157
Putnam, Lara, 207–8, 212
"Pyramus and Thisbe," 33–35

"The Question Concerning Technology" (Heidegger, M.), 160

race riots, British, 219, 221
racialization, 14–15, 219, 224
racism: anti-Communism and, 214–16; Arendt, H., and, 210, 213–15, 217–19, 227n3; in Britain, 219–24, 228nn8–9; equality and, 218–19; Jones and, 208–10, 213, 227n7; Jones organizing against, 205, 215–16, 224; in US, 208–10, 213–19, 224, 227n3, 227n7; white chauvinism, 209, 216–17
Rahel Varnhagen (Arendt, H.): on dreams, 66–70; as *Frühromantik* biography, 56; on gender, 64–65; introduction to, 2–3; irony in, 63, 65; Jewishness and, 55–56, 62–66, 69, 74n7; Kant and, 67–69; Kristeva on, 63, 74n1; on love, 25, 115n6; pluralism and, 8; Romanticism and, 4, 55–57, 62–63, 66–67, 70, 74n2. *See also* Varnhagen, Rahel
reason, 58, 65, 67
recognition, 108–9
"Reflections on Little Rock" (Arendt, H.), 217–18, 221, 227n6
reflective judgment. *See* judgment
Refugee Convention, UN, 190
refugees, 202n14, 207, 230; Arendt, H., as, 205–6, 242–43; European refugee crisis, 145; Jewish, 242–43; Palestinian, 193, 243–44; political rights and, 193; right, to have rights, and, 194
Rehabilitation Act, US, Section 504 of. *See* Bill 504 sit-in
Reitman, Ben, 86–90

relationality, 99
republicanism, 13–14
respect, 115n15
Responsibility and Judgment (Arendt, H.), 3
res publica, 188
right, to have rights, 182; citizenship and, 224; statelessness and, 13, 190, 193–94, 207, 210, 224
rights, political, 102, 193
"'The Rights of Man': What Are They?" (Arendt, H.), 194
Rilke, Rainer Maria, 167
Romanticism: early German, 60–68, 75n9; Enlightenment and, 57; fragment in, 8, 56, 61, 66–67, 71–72; irony in, 8, 61–63; Jews and, 8, 55–56, 71; Kant and, 60, 67–69, 71; *Rahel Varnhagen* and, 4, 55–57, 62–63, 66–67, 70, 74n2; Schlegel, F., 60–65, 75n9; socialist movements of, 81–85, 92n4
romantic love: Arendt, H., on, 10, 30, 97–104, 106; Beauvoir on, 10, 97–98, 103, 107–10
Russon, John, 165, 167

Saint-Simonianism, 82, 85
Sari, Yasemin, 2
Sassen, Willem, 237, 249n10
Schlegel, Dorothea, 64–65
Schlegel, Friedrich, 60–65, 75n9
Schleiermacher, Friedrich, 57, 60
Schmitt, Carl, 24
science: ancient and modern, 159; modern, 159–61, 164–65; totalitarianism and, 164–65
sciences, social, 163
Scott, Joanna, 77
Scottsboro Boys, 209
The Second Sex (Beauvoir), 107, 109, 115n14, 115n17, 115n19
Section 504. *See* Bill 504 sit-in
Sein und Zeit (Heidegger, M.). *See Being and Time*

self: Arendt, H., on, 121–23, 128; Beauvoir on, 97, 108, 115n19; Heidegger, M., on, 104–5, 119–23, 129, 185
self-rule, collective, 169–70
Shakespeare, William: Arendt, H., influenced by, 6, 22–24, 28; Blixen and, 27–28; *Hamlet*, 24; *King Lear*, 5–6; love in, 6, 22–23, 27–33; *A Midsummer Night's Dream*, 6, 23–24, 27–35, 38nn9–10; natality in, 34; Ovid and, 23; private, public in, 31–35; style and, 5–6; *The Tempest*, 23, 28
She Came to Stay (Beauvoir), 108
Sherwood, Marika, 216
Smith Act. *See* Alien Registration Act
Smolar, Aleksander, 142
social: equality and, 161; *The Human Condition* on, 161, 218; in modernity, 161–63, 178n12; private, public distorted by, 161–63
social love, 82, 85
social sciences, 163
socialist movements, Romantic, 81–85, 92n4
Solidarność (Solidarity), 136, 139, 141
solitary confinement, 155–56
"Some Questions of Moral Philosophy" (Arendt, H.), 5
sovereignty, 24
Soviet Union, 217; Jones on, 206; Moscow trials, 227nn1–2; *The Origins of Totalitarianism* and, 140–41, 143, 240–42; totalitarianism in, 140–41, 143, 206, 212, 240–42
space, of appearance, 188
Spartacists, 212
speech: action and, 43, 45–49, 120–21, 129; *The Human Condition* on, 43, 120–21; political, 43, 45–49. *See also* discourse
Śpiewak, Paweł, 137–39, 144
Stalinism, 217, 230; Moscow trials, 227nn1–2; *The Origins of Totalitarianism* and, 140–41, 143, 240–42; Poland and, 140–41, 143; in US, opposition to, 213, 215
Stangneth, Bettina, 236–37, 249n10
Stanley, Liz, 80–81
Stark, Judith, 77
statelessness: citizenship and, 207, 224; crimes against humanity and, 184, 193–94; human dignity and, 181, 183–84, 190, 193–95; human rights and, 181, 193–94; *The Origins of Totalitarianism* on, 244; racialization and, 14–15; right, to have rights, and, 13, 190, 193–94, 207, 210, 224; totalitarianism and, 210; world, place in, and, 193, 202n14; World War I and, 230
statistics, 163, 169
Stern, Günther, 249n4
storyteller, 23, 27–28
style: Romantic, 8; Shakespeare and, 5–6
subject: Arendt, H., on, 121–23, 128; autonomy of, 123; Heidegger, M., on, 104–5, 119–23, 129, 185. *See also* self; transcendental intersubjectivity
subjective universal validity, 46–47

Taminiaux, Jacques, 106
Taylor, Telford, 192–93
technology, 127; Heidegger, M., on, 120, 128–29, 160; modernity and, 159–60
The Tempest (Shakespeare), 23, 28
Tewarson, Heidi, 66
they (*das Man*), 105–7, 119, 122
things, world of, 186–87, 201n7
thought: action and, 10, 129–32; Heidegger, M., on, 130; Jonas on, 10, 130–31
Time of the Magicians (Elienberger), 8
Titania (Migel), 27
Tömmel, Tatjana Noemi, 26, 78–79, 82–83

totalitarianism, 178n16, 196, 244; Communism and, 213; modernity and, 161, 164–65; Nazism and, 140, 144–45, 164–65, 237–38, 240–41, 245; in Poland, 11, 139–43; Poland and Arendt, H., on, 11, 135, 139–45; post-totalitarian state, 141; science and, 164–65; Soviet, 140–41, 143, 206, 212, 240–42; statelessness and, 210; US and, 213, 227n3; World War I and, 230

Totalitaryzm a zachodnia tradycja (Totalitarianism and the Western Tradition) (Kuniński), 139

transcendental intersubjectivity, 152, 156

Trauerspiel, 24

Trinidad, 208

Trotta, Margarethe von. *See Hannah Arendt*

truth, 54n10; plurality and, 48–49; politics and, 43, 47–50, 54n11

"Truth and Politics" (Arendt, H.), 39–40, 47–48, 50, 54n10

turn (*Kehre*), 118, 120, 129

UDHR. *See* Universal Declaration of Human Rights

UK. *See* Britain

UN. *See* United Nations

understanding, 49, 51

United Kingdom. *See* Britain

United Nations (UN), 190, 193–94, 207, 213. *See also* Universal Declaration of Human Rights

United States (US): Alien Registration Act, 205, 214; anti-Communism in, 205, 211–17, 227n2; Black Caribbeans in, 205, 208–9, 215, 219–20; Blacks in, 208–10, 213–19, 222, 224, 227n3, 227n7; citizenship in, 215, 217, 222; Communist Party in, 205–6, 211–16, 227n2; desegregation in, 217–19, 221; disability rights movement in, 12, 151–53, 166, 170–73; fascism and, 209–10, 213–15; HEW, 151, 170; immigrants in, 208–9, 211–12, 215, 220, 222; Immigration and Nationality Act, 211–12, 215, 220; Internal Security Act, 211, 215, 227n4; racism in, 208–10, 213–19, 224, 227n3, 227n7; republicanism in, 13–14; totalitarianism and, 213, 227n3

Universal Declaration of Human Rights (UDHR), 190, 193–94, 202n9, 207

universality: Kant and, 43–47, 51; particularity and, 43–45, 51; subjective universal validity, 46–47

unworldliness, of love. *See* worldlessness

US. *See* United States

Ushpiz, Ada. *See Vita Activa* (film)

USSR. *See* Soviet Union

Varnhagen, Karl, 74n7

Varnhagen, Rahel, 56; Jewish identity of, 63–64, 74n7; letters of, 61, 66; Romanticism and, 60–61; salon of, 57, 60

Vasterling, Veronica, 178n6

Véret-Gay, Désirée: Considerant and, 81, 84–85; in February revolution, 1848, 84–85; feminism of, 82–85; Fourier and, 83–84; love and, 9, 82–83, 85

Villa, Dana, 48, 54n1, 178n16

Vita Activa, 46, 99

Vita Activa (Arendt, H.). *See The Human Condition*

Vita Activa (film), 15, 230; Arendtian voice in, 231, 235–36, 240, 242–44; on Blücher, 232, 242; on Eichmann, 235–36, 247, 249n9; on Heidegger, M., 232, 235, 239, 247; on Holocaust, 229, 232–35, 238–40, 245–46; on Jaspers, 238; on Zionism, 242–44

Vita Contemplativa, 46

Vogelin, Eric, 5

Wałęsa, Lech, 136
Walicki, Adrzej, 142–44
war, state of, in Poland, 140–42
Weber, Max, 164, 238
Weekes, Ivan, 219
Weissberg, Liliane, 2–3
"We Refugees" (Arendt, H.), 242
West Indian Gazette, 220–22
West Indians. *See* Black Caribbeans
"What is Existential Philosophy?" (Arendt, H.), 177n1
"What is Freedom?" (Arendt, H.), 168–69, 201n7
white chauvinism, 209, 216–17
Windrush scandal, 222–23
work: action and, 106, 120–21, 123, 165, 187; in Vita Activa, 46
world, 158n6, 201n6; appearance and, 156–59; care for, 195–97, 203n18; common, 153, 157, 173; common, modernity undermining, 159–65; disclosure of, 188–89; discursive dimension of, 186–88, 201n7; earth and, 189; experience in, 155–56; *The Human Condition* on, 46, 185–89; humanity and, 183–87; *The Life of the Mind* on, 185, 189; in phenomenology, 153, 155, 183, 185; politics and, 159, 188; proto-normative commitment and, 195–97; statelessness and place in, 193, 202n14; things in, 186–87, 201n7; world-centered ontology, 183–89, 201n7
worldlessness: Kant and, 40, 42, 45; of love, 26, 30, 78–79, 101–3, 115n13, 115nn7–9
worldliness, 13, 109; *The Human Condition* on, 46; human dignity as, 184, 189–95; Kant and, 45–46, 51
World War I, 229–31

Young, Iris Marion, 114n5
Young-Bruehl, Elisabeth, 1, 25

Zertal, Idith, 230, 242–43
Zionism, 242–44, 246–47
"Zionism Reconsidered" (Arendt, H.), 243

About the Contributors

Marieke Borren currently works as an assistant professor of philosophy at Open University Netherlands. Her research expertise lies at the intersection of continental political philosophy and phenomenology. She is particularly interested in critical feminist and postcolonial perspectives. She has widely published on Arendt's political phenomenology, among others in *Bloomsbury History: Theory and Method, Key Thinkers* (eds. M. Grever and S. Berger, coauthored with V. Vasterling, forthcoming), *Challenges of Plurality* (eds. M. Robaszkiewicz and T. Matzner), *Routledge Handbook of Phenomenology of Agency* (eds. C. Erhard and T. Keiling), *Netherlands Journal of Legal Philosophy*, *Contemporary Political Theory*, *International Journal of Philosophical Studies*, *Hypatia*, and *Ethical Perspectives*.

Daniel Brennan is lecturer in philosophy at Bond University. He teaches in ethics, and his research is in social and political philosophy, phenomenology, and the philosophy of sport. Daniel is the author of *The Political Thought of Václav Havel* (Brill), and *Surfing and the Philosophy of Sport* (Lexington).

Paul Dahlgren is professor and chair of English and modern languages at Georgia Southwestern State University. In addition to writing about Hannah Arendt and Shakespeare, his research focuses on histories and theories of rhetoric, critical theory, and pedagogical games.

Marguerite La Caze is associate professor of philosophy at the University of Queensland. She has published seven books, including *Ethical Restoration after Communal Violence: The Grieving and the Unrepentant* (2018), *Wonder and Generosity: Their Role in Ethics and Politics* (2013), and the edited collections *Phenomenology and Forgiveness* (2018) and *Contemporary Perspectives on Vladimir Jankélévitch* (2019) with Magdalena Zolkos, and *Truth in Visual Media* (2021) with Ted Nannicelli.

Kimberly Maslin is professor of politics at Hendrix College in Conway, Arkansas, where she teaches courses in political theory and American politics.

Her recent publications include *The Experiential Ontology of Hannah Arendt* with Lexington Press, and "The Paradox of Miss Marple: Agatha Christie's Epistemology" in *Clues: A Journal of Detection*. She is an avid knitter who also enjoys swing and ballroom dancing.

Laura McMahon is associate professor in the departments of History & Philosophy and Women's & Gender Studies at Eastern Michigan University, where she teaches courses in nineteenth- and twentieth-century continental philosophy, social and political philosophy, and feminist philosophy. Her research is devoted to the phenomenological interpretation of liberatory political transformation. Her work has appeared in *The Journal of Speculative Philosophy*, *Chiasmi International*, *The Southern Journal of Philosophy*, *Human Studies*, *Puncta,* and *Sartre Studies International*; in the edited volumes *Phenomenology and the Arts* (Lexington), *Perception and Its Development in Merleau-Ponty's Phenomenology* (University of Toronto Press), and *Transforming Politics with Merleau-Ponty: Thinking Beyond the State* (Rowman & Littlefield); and on the *Women in Philosophy* blog of the American Philosophical Association.

Eric Stéphane Pommier is director of research and associate professor at the Faculty of Philosophy of the *Pontificia Universidad Católica de Chile*. Among other publications, he is the author of *Ontologie de la vie et éthique de la responsabilité selon Hans Jonas* (Paris, Vrin, 2013), "The problem of history in Patočka on the basis of an appropriation of Arendt's anthropology" (*Philosophy Today* 64:1, 2020) and "Hans Jonas's Biological Philosophy: Metaphysics or Phenomenology?" (*International Philosophy Quarterly* 57:4, 2017). He is currently pursuing his research in three directions: environmental policy, the phenomenology of the sensible, the definition of a post-metaphysical, and post-Heideggerian humanism (Levinas, Jonas, Arendt, Patočka). Two books will be published soon: *La démocratie environnementale* (Paris, PUF, 2022) and *La condition sensible. Chair, événement, Eros* (Paris, Hermann, 2022).

Joel Rosenberg holds the Lee S. McCollester Chair in Biblical Literature at Tufts University and directs the Program in Judaic Studies. He is author of *King and Kin: Political Allegory in the Hebrew Bible* (1986) and has recently completed *Navigating Catastrophe: A Judeo-Cinematic Trajectory—Five Studies in Mass Media and Mass Destruction*. His essays in film studies, film history, and cultural studies have appeared in a variety of publications and anthologies, including *Prooftexts, Film and History, Jewish Film and New Media, Jewish Social Studies, The Modern Jewish Experience in World*

Cinema (2011), and *Memories and Monsters: Psychology, Trauma, and Narrative* (2018).

Andrew Schaap teaches politics at the University of Exeter's Cornwall campus in Penryn. His research interests include democratic theory, twentieth-century political thought, the politics of migration, transitional justice, Aboriginal politics and settler colonialism. He has published articles on Arendt in *Political Studies*, *Political Theory* and the *European Journal of Political Theory*. He co-edited a book on *Power, Judgment and Political Evil: In Conversation with Hannah Arendt* with Vrasidas Karalis and Danielle Celermajer and contributed to *The Bloomsbury Companion to Arendt*, ed. Peter Gratton & Yasemin Sari.

Liesbeth Schoonheim is a FWO Junior Post-Doctoral Fellow at the KU Leuven, Institute of Philosophy, and a Wissenschaftliche Mitarbeiterin in political theory at Humboldt-Universität zu Berlin. Her research interests lie at the intersection of political theory, feminism and social theory, and her work has appeared in *Foucault Studies, History of European Ideas, Philosophy Today* and *Arendt Studies*. She is currently a coeditor of a collection on the contemporary relevance of Beauvoir's political engagement with Marxist, anti-fascist, decolonial and feminist struggles.

Katarzyna Stokłosa is associate professor in the Department of Political Science and Public Management, Centre for Border Region Studies, at the University of Southern Denmark. She finished her PhD at the European University Viadrina in Frankfurt (Oder) and her habilitation thesis at the University of Potsdam. Stokłosa worked in the Hannah-Arendt-Institute for Research on Totalitarianism at the Technical University in Dresden. She has published various books and articles on European history, authoritarian, totalitarian systems and transformation processes. One of Stokłosa's research topics is the presence of Hannah Arendt in Eastern Europe. She edited (together with Gerhard Besier and Andrew Wisely) *Totalitarianism and Liberty. Hannah Arendt in the 21st Century*, Kraków, 2008.

Maria Tamboukou is professor of feminist studies at the University of East London and has held visiting research positions in a number of institutions in the UK and overseas. Her research activity develops in the areas of philosophies and epistemologies in the social sciences, feminist theories, narrative analytics and archival research. She is the author and editor of fourteen books and numerous journal articles. See the author's website for more details on research projects and publications: www.tamboukou.org, ORCID iD: https://orcid.org/0000-0002-6380-4415.

Matthew Wester received his PhD in philosophy in 2018 from Texas A&M University, where he wrote his dissertation on Hannah Arendt's theory of judgment and its relation to her analysis of Adolf Eichmann. His research is related to the history of German existential thought and social political philosophy. Presently, he is working on a detailed study of Karl Jaspers's influence on Hannah Arendt.

www.ingramcontent.com/pod-product-compliance
Lightning Source LLC
Chambersburg PA
CBHW021350300426
44114CB00012B/1158